JONATHAN CAPE
PAPERBACK
JCP 77

HENRY VIII

A. F. POLLARD

Henry VIII

With a new Introduction by
J. E. NEALE

JONATHAN CAPE
THIRTY BEDFORD SQUARE LONDON

FIRST PUBLISHED BY GOUPIL AND CO., JUNE 1902

PUBLISHED BY LONGMANS, MAY 1905

THIS PAPERBACK EDITION FIRST PUBLISHED 1970
INTRODUCTION © 1970 BY J. E. NEALE

JONATHAN CAPE LTD
30 BEDFORD SQUARE, LONDON WC1

SBN 224 61750 8

Printed in Great Britain by
Lowe & Brydone (Printers) Ltd, London
Bound by Richard Clay (The Chaucer Press) Ltd
Bungay Suffolk

PREFACE

IT is perhaps a matter rather for regret than for surprise that so few attempts have been made to describe, as a whole, the life and character of Henry VIII. No ruler has left a deeper impress on the history of his country, or done work which has been the subject of more keen and lasting contention. Courts of law are still debating the intention of statutes, the tenor of which he dictated ; and the moral, political, and religious, are as much in dispute as the legal, results of his reign. He is still the Great Erastian, the protagonist of laity against clergy. His policy is inextricably interwoven with the high and eternal dilemma of Church and State ; and it is well-nigh impossible for one who feels keenly on these questions to treat the reign of Henry VIII in a reasonably judicial spirit. No period illustrates more vividly the contradiction between morals and politics. In our desire to reprobate the immorality of Henry's methods, we are led to deny their success ; or, in our appreciation of the greatness of the ends he achieved, we seek to excuse the means he took to achieve them. As with his policy, so with his character. There was nothing commonplace about him ; his good and his bad qualities alike were exceptional. It is easy, by suppressing the one or the other, to paint him a hero or a villain. He lends himself readily to polemic ; but to depict his character in all its varied aspects, extenuating nothing nor setting down aught in malice, is a task of no little difficulty. It is two centuries and a half since Lord Herbert produced his *Life and Reign of Henry VIII*.[1] The late Mr. Brewer, in his prefaces to the first four volumes of the *Letters and Papers of the Reign of Henry VIII*, published under the direction of the Master of the Rolls, dealt adequately

[1] The edition cited in the text is that of 1672.

with the earlier portion of Henry's career. But Mr. Brewer died when his work reached the year 1530; his successor, Dr. James Gairdner, was directed to confine his prefaces to the later volumes within the narrowest possible limits; and students of history were deprived of the prospect of a satisfactory account of Henry's later years from a writer of unrivalled learning.

Henry's reign, from 1530 onwards, has been described by the late Mr. Froude in one of the most brilliant and fascinating masterpieces of historical literature, a work which still holds the field in popular, if not in scholarly, estimation. But Mr. Froude does not begin until Henry's reign was half over, until his character had been determined by influences and events which lie outside the scope of Mr. Froude's inquiry. Moreover, since Mr. Froude wrote, a flood of light has been thrown on the period by the publication of the above-mentioned *Letters and Papers;*[1] they already comprise a summary of between thirty and forty thousand documents in twenty thousand closely printed pages, and, when completed, will constitute the most magnificent body of materials for the history of any reign, ancient or modern, English or foreign. Simultaneously there have appeared a dozen volumes containing the State papers preserved at Simancas,[2] Vienna and Brussels and similar series comprising the correspondence relating to Venice,[3] Scotland[4]

[1] This series, unlike the *Calendars of State Papers*, includes documents not preserved at the Record Office; it is often inaccurately cited as *Calendar of State Papers*, but the word " Calendar " does not appear in the title and it includes much besides State papers; such a description also tends to confuse it with the eleven volumes of Henry VIII's State papers published *in extenso* in 1830-51. The series now extends to Dec., 1544, and is cited in the text as *L. and P.*

[2] Cited as *Sp. Cal.;* the volume completing Henry's reign was published in 1904.

[3] Cited as *Ven. Cal.;* this correspondence diminishes in importance as the reign proceeds, and also, after 1530, the documents are epitomised afresh in *L. and P.*

[4] Three series, *viz.,* that edited by Thorp (2 vols., 1858), a second edited by Bain (2 vols., 1898) and the *Hamilton Papers* (2 vols., 1800-92).

and Ireland;[1] while the despatches of French ambassadors
have been published under the auspices of the Ministry
for Foreign Affairs at Paris.[2] Still further information
has been provided by the labours of the Historical
Manuscripts Commission,[3] the Camden,[4] the Royal
Historical,[5] and other learned Societies.

These sources probably contain at least a million
definite facts relating to the reign of Henry VIII; and
it is obvious that the task of selection has become heavy
as well as invidious. Mr. Froude has expressed his
concurrence in the dictum that the facts of history are
like the letters of the alphabet; by selection and arrangement they can be made to spell anything, and nothing
can be arranged so easily as facts. *Experto crede.* Yet
selection is inevitable, and arrangement essential. The
historian has no option if he wishes to be intelligible.
He will naturally arrange his facts so that they spell what
he believes to be the truth; and he must of necessity
suppress those facts which he judges to be immaterial or
inconsistent with the scale on which he is writing. But
if the superabundance of facts compels both selection
and suppression, it counsels no less a restraint of judgment. A case in a court of law is not simplified by a
cloud of witnesses; and the new wealth of contemporary
evidence does not solve the problems of Henry's reign.
It elucidates some points hitherto obscure, but it raises
a host of others never before suggested. In ancient
history we often accept statements written hundreds of

[1] Vol. i. of the *Irish Calendar*, and also of the *Carew MSS.*; see also
the *Calendar of Fiants* published by the Deputy-Keeper of Records for
Ireland.

[2] *Correspondance de MM. Castillon et Marillac*, edited by Kaulek, and
of *Odet de Selve*, 1888.

[3] The most important of these is vol. i. of Lord Salisbury's MSS.;
other papers of Henry VIII's reign are scattered up and down the
Appendices to a score and more of reports.

[4] E.g. Wriothesley's *Chronicle*, *Chron. of Calais*, and *Greyfriars Chron.*

[5] E.g. Leadam, *Domesday of Inclosures*, and *Transactions, passim.*

years after the event, simply because we know no better ; in modern history we frequently have half a dozen witnesses giving inconsistent accounts of what they have seen with their own eyes. Dogmatism is merely the result of ignorance ; and no honest historian will pretend to have mastered all the facts, accurately weighed all the evidence, or pronounced a final judgment.

The present volume does not profess to do more than roughly sketch Henry VIII's more prominent character-istics, outline the chief features of his policy, and suggest some reasons for the measure of success he attained. Episodes such as the divorce of Catherine of Aragon, the dissolution of the monasteries, and the determination of the relations between Church and State, would severally demand for adequate treatment works of much greater bulk than the present. On the divorce valuable light has recently been thrown by Dr. Stephan Ehses in his *Römische Dokumente*.[1] The dissolution of the monasteries has been exhaustively treated from one point of view by Dr. Gasquet ;[2] but an adequate and impartial history of what is called the Reformation still remains to be written. Here it is possible to deal with these questions only in the briefest outline, and in so far as they were affected by Henry's personal action. For my facts I have relied entirely on contemporary records, and my deduc-tions from these facts are my own. I have depended as little as possible even on contemporary historians,[3] and scarcely at all on later writers.[4] I have, however, made

[1] Paderborn, 1893 ; cf. *Engl. Hist. Rev.* xix. 632-45.

[2] *Henry VIII and the English Monasteries*, 2 vols., 1888.

[3] Of these the most important are Polydore Vergil (Basel, 1534), Hall's *Chronicle* (1548) and Fabyan's *Chronicle* (edited by Ellis, 1811). Holinshed and Stow are not quite contemporary, but they occasionally add to earlier writers on apparently good authority.

[4] I have in this edition added references to those which seem most important ; for a collected bibliography see Dr. Gairdner in *Cambridge Modern History*, ii. 789-94. I have also for the purpose of this edition added references to the original sources—a task of some labour when nearly every fact is taken from a different document. The text has

frequent use of Dr. Gairdner's articles in the *Dictionary of National Biography*, particularly of that on Henry VIII, the best summary extant of his career ; and I owe not a little to Bishop Stubbs's two lectures on Henry VIII, which contain some fruitful suggestions as to his character.[1]

A. F. POLLARD

PUTNEY, 11*th January*, 1905

been revised, some errors removed, and notes added on special points, especially those on which fresh light has recently been thrown.

[1] In *Lectures on Mediæval and Modern History*, 1887.

A. F. POLLARD

CONTENTS

PLATES

The plates appear between pages 188-189 and 220-221

HENRY VIII, *attributed to Joos van Cleeve*

Painting on panel, 28¾ × 23 inches; recorded in the collection
of Charles I, who obtained it from the Earl of Arundel by
exchange; sold in the Commonwealth sale, but recovered at
the Restoration; now at Hampton Court. On the scroll
in his hand is written: *Marci 16 ite in mūdum universū et
predicate evangelium omni creature;* this is usually interpreted
as an allusion to Coverdale's English translation of the Bible
of 1536: in the same year also Henry set a fashion by ' causing
his head to be polled and his beard to be knotted and no more
shaven '. On this evidence the portrait is generally dated 1536,
but it may well be considerably earlier; compared with the
portraits by Holbein of only a year later, Henry here appears
disproportionately young, much closer to the handsome young
man of contemporary account.

(Reproduced by gracious permission of H.M. the Queen)

CATHERINE OF ARAGON, *attributed to Master Michiel*

Painting on panel, 11½ × 8 inches; formerly in the collection
of the Imperial family at Schloss Ambras, now in the Kunsthistorisches Museum, Vienna. The identification has only
recently been suggested, but is almost certainly right (the nimbus
round the head is a later addition); note the initial K repeated in her necklace. Painted about 1501.

(By permission of the Kunsthistorisches Museum.)

HENRY VIII, WITH HIS FATHER HENRY VII STANDING IN THE BACK-GROUND, *by Hans Holbein*

Drawing on paper, mounted on canvas, and pricked for transfer
for a mural painting; 105 × 55 inches (rather more than life-
size). In 1590 it was at Lumley Castle, but came later to the
collection of the Dukes of Devonshire at Chatsworth; now in the
possession of the National Portrait Gallery, London.

This is the left-hand part of the cartoon made by Holbein for the great wall-painting which he executed in the Privy Chamber at Whitehall Palace in 1537, and which was one of the sights of London until a fire destroyed it in 1698. A small copy of it by R. van Leemput is at Hampton Court. In the painting Henry's face seems to have been seen in full, not in profile; on the right hand side stood Jane Seymour, and behind her Elizabeth of York (the portraits of Henry VII and Elizabeth are of course not from the life, but posthumous memorials). The whole composition probably surrounded a fireplace.

(National Portrait Gallery, London)

ANNE BOLEYN, *by Hans Holbein*

Drawing, coloured chalks on pinkish paper, 9 × 8½ inches; in the collection of the Earl of Bradford. It bears an early inscription: *Anne Bulon, decollata fuit Londene*, 19 *May* 1536. As with most of Holbein's drawings, it has been retouched by a later hand. Believed to have been drawn soon after her coronation, 1533; no paintings by Holbein of this type are known.

(By permission of the Earl of Bradford.)

JANE SEYMOUR, *by Hans Holbein*

Painting on panel 25½ × 16 inches. Painted in 1536, and at one time probably in the collection of Thomas Howard, Earl of Arundel: now in the Kunsthistorisches Museum, Vienna. A drawing for this portrait by Holbein is at Windsor Castle.

(By permission of the Kunsthistorisches Museum.)

ANNE OF CLEVES, *by Hans Holbein*

Painting on vellum mounted on canvas, 26 × 19 inches. Formerly in the collection of Thomas Howard, Earl of Arundel, and of Louis XIV; now in the Louvre. It was painted in July-August, 1539, in Duren, at Henry's commission.

(Mansell Collection)

PLATES

HENRY VIII, PRINCE EDWARD, AND CATHERINE PARR (?), *by a follower of Hans Holbein*

This is a detail from the large painting on canvas (65 × 139 inches : the figures less than life-size), now at Hampton Court, once in Charles I.'s collection, sold by the Commonwealth, but recovered for the Royal collection after the Restoration. The whole picture includes Princess Mary, standing on the left, and Elizabeth on the right. If contemporary, as it seems to be, it must (from the ages of the children as shown) have been carried out at the close of Henry's life about 1546-47. The Queen represented is believed to be Catherine Parr, but it is just possible that this figure is a posthumous memorial to Edward's mother, Jane Seymour.

(Reproduced by gracious permission of H.M. the Queen)

The publishers are indebted to Mr. David Piper for his assistance in compiling these notes.

INTRODUCTION

PROFESSOR A. F. POLLARD, who died in 1948 at the age of 78, was by general consent the outstanding authority on Tudor history in his generation. He was also an academic statesman of exceptional vision and achievement. Fortune played a considerable part in his career. At a time when openings in academic work were exceedingly rare, he secured his first post as an assistant editor of the *Dictionary of National Biography*, and by the time the *Dictionary* was completed in 1901 had learnt his craft as a historian and written some 500 biographies for the *Dictionary*. He had also begun the production of independent works which marked him out as a young historian of exceptional promise.

Fortune played her part for a second time when in 1903 an opportune vacancy occurred in a professorship at University College, London. Superficially there was little attraction in the post. Indeed, the chairman of the appointments committee, faced with the dilemma of two candidates between whom they could not choose, remarked : 'Why not split the chair into two and take both? There is no stipend for either.' Pollard's emoluments to start with — derived from students' fees — were ludicrously inadequate, and there was nothing, either at the College or in the University, worthy to be called a school of history.

To a man of Pollard's ceaseless energy and drive the outlook was far from depressing. He proceeded at once to proclaim his purpose as the creation of a 'postgraduate school of Historical Research' in London, where a unique concentration of historical documents and the resources of a great capital offered unrivalled prospects. For twelve years he acted as Chairman of the University History Board, thus uniting his colleagues from other

Colleges in a common purpose. He secured the invaluable support and co-operation of the London County Council, and through the Historical Association, of which he was the virtual founder and for which he acquired and edited the journal *History*, he injected his ideas into the historical world at large. His concentration of purpose was remarkable. 'What a man does', he often said, 'depends upon what he can do without.'

As a statesman Pollard's success rested ultimately on his reputation as scholar and writer. During these years he published a number of notable books. His biography of *Henry VIII* made his name widely known and he will always be associated with this reign in particular. He also published books on *England under Protector Somerset* and *Thomas Cranmer* and the substantial volume on 1547–1603 in Longman's *Political History of England* – still perhaps the best single volume on this period. Later he revealed his growing interest in constitutional history with a volume on *The Evolution of Parliament* (1920) and added to his Henrician studies a striking biography on *Wolsey* (1929). Alongside these and other books he kept up a constant flow of high-quality occasional pieces in reviews and articles. He continued his research work until his death.

The outbreak of war in 1914 marked a third stage in Pollard's career. Temporarily it seemed a set-back, but in the end it brought him to his goal. The war stimulated the publicist in him. By various means he broadened his activities to become a national figure, ready to benefit from the notable expansion in historical studies that followed the war.

By then his great plan to establish an Institute of Historical Research in London had clarified itself, and within the limits of University College he had made preliminary moves to test some of its special features. Basically the Institute was to be a training centre for historical research, equipped with appropriate libraries where the techniques and practice of research could be taught. For mature scholars it was to be a centre where they could pursue their studies and meet their British and foreign colleagues for discussion. The idea was a novelty in British circles, and to some old-fashioned scholars, imbued with the traditions of individual craftsmanship, it was anathema.

In 1920 the time arrived to launch the scheme. Thanks largely to the generosity of a single, wealthy donor found by Pollard himself, the public appeal succeeded. But all Pollard's qualities and achievements — not excluding the good fortune that timed and shaped his career — had been needed to ensure success. A less forceful man, or one whose fame as scholar, writer and statesman did not extend into the wider world outside the University, would undoubtedly have failed; and then the development of historical studies in London and elsewhere might have proceeded along very different lines, and the shape of the University itself would have been different.

The Institute of Historical Research was formally opened in July 1921 with Pollard as its first Director and the first Anglo-American Conference as an initial activity. Over the years it has more than fulfilled all that Pollard expected of it and its oecumenical character has developed more rapidly than was foreseen. It is difficult nowadays, especially at the Institute's annual Anglo-American Historical Conference when several hundred scholars may attend, to imagine the isolation in which visiting American historians found themselves before 1914.

History is a more disciplined and scientific study today than it used to be. Its standards of scholarship owe an untold debt to A. F. Pollard — to his writings (not forgetting his trenchant reviews that exposed shoddy work), and above all to the exchange of method and ideas promoted in the postgraduate seminars and in discussions among established historians. Pollard conducted these activities in the seminar libraries, so that young and old might watch the historian at work with his sources as one might watch a scientist in his laboratory : a simile he often employed.

Pollard's writings alone place him among leading British historians. To write so much, of such quality, seems adequate for any lifetime. But to add to this the great labour involved in his organization of historical research is a feat beyond compare.

J. E. NEALE

CHAPTER I

THE EARLY TUDORS

In the whole range of English history there is no monarch whose character has been more variously depicted by contemporaries or more strenuously debated by posterity than the " majestic lord who broke the bonds of Rome ". To one historian an inhuman embodiment of cruelty and vice, to another a superhuman incarnation of courage, wisdom and strength of will, Henry VIII has, by an almost universal consent, been placed above or below the grade of humanity. So unique was his personality, so singular his achievements, that he appears in the light of a special dispensation sent like another Attila to be the scourge of mankind, or like a second Hercules to cleanse, or at least to demolish, Augean stables. The dictates of his will seemed as inexorable as the decrees of fate, and the history of his reign is strewn with records of the ruin of those who failed to placate his wrath. Of the six queens he married, two he divorced, and two he beheaded. Four English cardinals[1] lived in his reign ; one perished by the executioner's axe, one escaped it by absence, and a third by a timely but natural death. Of a similar number of dukes[2] half were condemned by attainder ; and the same method of speedy despatch accounted for six or seven earls and viscounts and for scores of lesser degree. He began his reign by executing the ministers of his father,[3] he continued it by sending his own to the scaffold. The Tower of London was both palace and prison, and statesmen passed swiftly from one to the other ; in silent obscurity alone lay salvation. Religion

---

[1] Bainbridge, Wolsey, Fisher, Pole. Bainbridge was a cardinal after Julius II's own heart, and he received the red hat for military services rendered to that warlike Pope (*Ven. Cal.* ii. 104).

[2] There were two Dukes of Norfolk, the second of whom was attainted, as was the Duke of Buckingham ; the fourth Duke was Henry's brother-in-law, Suffolk.   [3] Empson and Dudley.

and politics, rank and profession made little difference ;
priest and layman, cardinal-archbishop and "hammer of
the monks," men whom Henry had raised from the mire,
and peers, over whose heads they were placed, were
joined in a common fate. Wolsey and More, Cromwell
and Norfolk, trod the same dizzy path to the same fatal
end ; and the English people looked on powerless or un-
moved. They sent their burgesses and knights of the
shire to Westminster without let or hindrance, and Parliament met with a regularity that grew with the rigour of
Henry's rule ; but it seemed to assemble only to register
the royal edicts and clothe with a legal cloak the naked
violence of Henry's acts. It remembered its privileges
only to lay them at Henry's feet, it cancelled his debts, endowed his proclamations with the force of laws, and authorised him to repeal acts of attainder and dispose of his
crown at will. Secure of its support Henry turned and
rent the spiritual unity of Western Christendom, and
settled at a blow that perennial struggle between Church
and State, in which kings and emperors had bitten the
dust. With every epithet of contumely and scorn he
trampled under foot the jurisdiction of him who was
believed to hold the keys of heaven and hell. Borrowing
in practice the old maxim of Roman law, *cujus regio, ejus
religio*,[1] he placed himself in the seat of authority in
religion and presumed to define the faith of which Leo
had styled him defender. Others have made themselves
despots by their mastery of many legions, through the
agency of a secret police, or by means of an organised
bureaucracy. Yet Henry's standing army consisted of a
few gentlemen pensioners and yeomen of the guard ; he
had neither secret police nor organised bureaucracy. Even
then Englishmen boasted that they were not slaves like the
French,[2] and foreigners pointed a finger of scorn at their
turbulence. Had they not permanently or temporarily

[1] " Sua cuique civitati religio est, nostra nobis." Cicero, *Pro Flacco*,
28 ; cf. E. Bourre, *Des Inequalités de condition resultant de la religion
en droit Romain*, Paris, 1895.
[2] Cf. Bishop Scory to Edward VI in Strype, *Eccl. Mem.* II. ii. 482 ;
Fortescue, ed. Plummer, pp. 137-42.

deprived of power nearly half their kings who had reigned
since William the Conqueror ? Yet Henry VIII not only
left them their arms, but repeatedly urged them to keep
those arms ready for use.[1] He eschewed that air of mystery
with which tyrants have usually sought to impose on the
mind of the people. All his life he moved familiarly and
almost unguarded in the midst of his subjects, and he died
in his bed, full of years, with the spell of his power unbroken and the terror of his name unimpaired.

What manner of man was this, and wherein lay the
secret of his strength ? Is recourse necessary to a theory
of supernatural agency, or is there another and adequate
solution ? Was Henry's individual will of such miraculous force that he could ride roughshod in insolent pride
over public opinion at home and abroad ? Or did his
personal ends, dictated perhaps by selfish motives and
ignoble passions, so far coincide with the interests and
prejudices of the politically effective portion of his people,
that they were willing to condone a violence and tyranny,
the brunt of which fell after all on the few ? Such is the
riddle which propounds itself to every student of Tudor
history. It cannot be answered by pæans in honour of
Henry's intensity of will and force of character, nor by
invectives against his vices and lamentations over the
woes of his victims. The miraculous interpretation of
history is as obsolete as the catastrophic theory of
geology, and the explanation of Henry's career must be
sought not so much in the study of his character as in
the study of his environment, of the conditions which
made things possible to him that were not possible before
or since and are not likely to be so again.

It is a singular circumstance that the king who raised
the personal power of English monarchy to a height to
which it had never before attained, should have come of
humble race and belonged to an upstart dynasty. For
three centuries and a half before the battle of Bosworth
one family had occupied the English throne. Even the

[1] E g. *L. and P.* i. 679.

usurpers, Henry of Bolingbroke and Richard of York, were directly descended in unbroken male line from Henry II, and from 1154 to 1485 all the sovereigns of England were Plantagenets. But who were the Tudors? They were a Welsh family of modest means and doubtful antecedents.[1] They claimed, it is true, descent from Cadwallader, and their pedigree was as long and quite as veracious as most Welsh genealogies; but Henry VII's great-grandfather was steward or butler to the Bishop of Bangor. His son, Owen Tudor, came as a young man to seek his fortune at the Court of Henry V, and obtained a clerkship of the wardrobe to Henry's Queen, Catherine of France. So skilfully did he use or abuse this position of trust, that he won the heart of his mistress; and within a few years of Henry's death his widowed Queen and her clerk of the wardrobe were secretly, and possibly without legal sanction, living together as man and wife. The discovery of their relations resulted in Catherine's retirement to Bermondsey Abbey, and Owen's to Newgate prison. The Queen died in the following year, but Owen survived many romantic adventures. Twice he escaped from prison, twice he was recaptured. Once he took sanctuary in the precincts of Westminster Abbey, and various attempts to entrap him were made by enticing him to revels in a neighbouring tavern. Finally, on the outbreak of the Wars of the Roses, he espoused the Lancastrian cause, and was beheaded by order of Edward IV after the battle of Mortimer's Cross. Two sons Edmund and Jasper, were born of this singular match between Queen and clerk of her wardrobe. Both enjoyed the favour of their royal half-brother, Henry VI. Edmund, the elder, was first knighted and then created Earl of Richmond. In the Parliament of 1453, he was formally declared legitimate; he was enriched by the grant of broad estates and enrolled among the members of Henry's council. But the climax of his fortunes was reached when, in 1455, he married the Lady Margaret Beaufort. Owen Tudor had taken the first step which led to his family's greatness; Edmund took the second.

[1] *Archæologia Cambrensis*, 1st ser. iv. 267; 3rd ser. xv. 278, 379.

The blood-royal of France flowed in his veins, the blood-royal of England was to flow in his children's ; and the union between Edmund Tudor and Margaret Beaufort gave Henry VII such claim as he had by descent to the English throne.

The Beauforts were descended from Edward III, but a bar sinister marred their royal pedigree. John of Gaunt had three sons by Catherine Swynford before she became his wife. That marriage would, by canon law, have made legitimate the children, but the barons had, on a famous occasion, refused to assimilate in this respect the laws of England to the canons of the Church ; and it required a special Act of Parliament to confer on the Beauforts the status of legitimacy. When Henry IV confirmed this Act, he introduced a clause specifically barring their contingent claim to the English throne. This limitation could not legally abate the force of a statute ; but it sufficed to cast a doubt upon the Beaufort title, and has been considered a sufficient explanation of Henry VII's reluctance to base his claim upon hereditary right. However that may be, the Beauforts played no little part in the English history of the fifteenth century ; their influence was potent for peace or war in the councils of their royal half-brother, Henry IV, and of the later sovereigns of the House of Lancaster. One was Cardinal-Bishop of Winchester, another was Duke of Exeter, and a third was Earl of Somerset. Two of the sons of the Earl became Dukes of Somerset ; the younger fell at St. Albans, the earliest victim of the Wars of the Roses, which proved so fatal to his House ; and the male line of the Beauforts failed in the third generation. The sole heir to their claims was the daughter of the first Duke of Somerset, Margaret, now widow of Edmund Tudor ; for, after a year of wedded life, Edmund had died in November, 1456. Two months later his widow gave birth to a boy, the future Henry VII ; and, incredible as the fact may seem, the youthful mother was not quite fourteen years old. When fifteen more years had passed, the murder of Henry VI and his son left Margaret Beaufort and Henry Tudor in undisputed possession of the

Lancastrian title. A barren honour it seemed. Edward IV was firmly seated on the English throne. His right to it, by every test, was immeasurably superior to the Tudor claim, and Henry showed no inclination and possessed not the means to dispute it. The usurpation by Richard III, and the crimes which polluted his reign, put a different aspect on the situation, and set men seeking for an alternative to the blood-stained tyrant. The battle of Bosworth followed, and the last of the Plantagenets gave way to the first of the Tudors.

For the first time since the Norman Conquest a king of decisively British blood sat on the English throne. His lineage was, indeed, English in only a minor degree ; but England might seem to have lost at the battle of Hastings her right to native kings ; and Norman were succeeded by Angevin, Angevin by Welsh, Welsh by Scots, and Scots by Hanoverian sovereigns. The Tudors were probably more at home on the English throne than most of England's kings ; and their humble and British origin may have contributed to their unique capacity for understanding the needs, and expressing the mind, of the English nation. It was well for them that they established their throne in the hearts of their people, for no dynasty grasped the sceptre with less of hereditary right. Judged by that criterion, there were many claimants whose titles must have been preferred to Henry's. There were the daughters of Edward IV and the children of George, Duke of Clarence ; and their existence may account for Henry's neglect to press his hereditary claim. But there was a still better reason. Supposing the Lancastrian case to be valid and the Beauforts to be the true Lancastrian heirs, even so the rightful occupant of the throne was not Henry VII, but his mother, Margaret Beaufort. England had never recognised a Salic law at home ; on occasion she had disputed its validity abroad. But Henry VII was not disposed to let his mother rule ; she could not unite the Yorkist and Lancastrian claims by marriage, and, in addition to other disabilities, she had a second husband in Lord Stanley, who might demand the crown matrimonial.

So Henry VII's hereditary title was judiciously veiled in vague obscurity. Parliament wisely admitted the accomplished fact and recognised that the crown was vested in him, without rashly venturing upon the why or the wherefore. He had in truth been raised to the throne because men were weary of Richard. He was chosen to vindicate no theory of hereditary or other abstract right, but to govern with a firm hand, to establish peace within his gates and give prosperity to his people. That was the true Tudor title, and, as a rule, they remembered the fact ; they were *de facto* kings, and they left the *de jure* arguments to the Stuarts.

Peace, however, could not be obtained at once, nor the embers of thirty years' strife stamped out in a moment. For fifteen years open revolt and whispered sedition troubled the rest of the realm and threatened the stability of Henry's throne. Ireland remained a hot-bed of Yorkist sympathies, and Ireland was zealously aided by Edward IV's sister, Margaret of Burgundy ; she pursued, like a vendetta, the family quarrel with Henry VII, and earned the title of Henry's Juno by harassing him as vindictively as the Queen of Heaven vexed the pious Æneas. Other rulers, with no Yorkist bias, were slow to recognise the *parvenu* king and quick to profit by his difficulties. Pretenders to their rivals' thrones were useful pawns on the royal chess-board ; and though the princes of Europe had no reason to desire a Yorkist restoration, they thought that a little judicious backing of Yorkist claimants would be amply repaid by the restriction of Henry's energies to domestic affairs. Seven months after the battle of Bosworth there was a rising in the West under the Staffords, and in the North under Lovell ; and Henry himself was nearly captured while celebrating at York the feast of St. George. A year later a youth of obscure origin, Lambert Simnel,[1] claimed to be first the Duke of York and then the Earl of Warwick. The former was son, and the latter was nephew, of Edward IV. Lambert was crowned king at Dublin amid the acclamations of the Irish people. Not a voice was raised in

---

[1] See the present writer in *D.N.B.* lii. 261.

Henry's favour ; Kildare, the practical ruler of Ireland, earls and archbishops, bishops and barons, and great officers of State, from Lord Chancellor downwards, swore fealty to the reputed son of an Oxford tradesman. Ireland was only the volcano which gave vent to the subterranean flood ; treason in England and intrigue abroad were working in secret concert with open rebellion across St. George's Channel. The Queen Dowager was secluded in Bermondsey Abbey and deprived of her jointure lands. John de la Pole, who, as eldest son of Edward IV's sister, had been named his successor by Richard III, fled to Burgundy ; thence his aunt Margaret sent Martin Schwartz and two thousand mercenaries to co-operate with the Irish invasion. But at East Stoke, de la Pole and Lovell, Martin Schwartz and his merry men were slain ; and the most serious of the revolts against Henry ended in the consignment of Simnel to the royal scullery and of his tutor to the Tower.

Lambert, however, was barely initiated in his new duties when the son of a boatman of Tournay started on a similar errand with a less congenial end. An unwilling puppet at first, Perkin Warbeck was on a trading visit to Ireland, when the Irish, who saw a Yorkist prince in every likely face, insisted that Perkin was Earl of Warwick. This he denied on oath before the Mayor of Cork. Nothing deterred, they suggested that he was Richard III's bastard ; but the bastard was safe in Henry's keeping, and the imaginative Irish finally took refuge in the theory that Perkin was Duke of York. Lambert's old friends rallied round Perkin ; the re-animated Duke was promptly summoned to the Court of France and treated with princely honours. When Charles VIII had used him to beat down Henry's terms, Perkin found a home with Margaret, aunt to all the pretenders. As usual, there were traitors in high places in England. Sir William Stanley, whose brother had married Henry's mother, and to whom Henry himself owed his victory at Bosworth, was implicated. His sudden arrest disconcerted the plot, and when Perkin's fleet appeared off the coast of Kent, the rustics made short work of the few who were rash enough to land. Perkin sailed away to the Yorkist refuge in Ireland, but Kildare was no longer deputy. Waterford, to which he laid siege, was relieved, and the pretender sought in Scotland a third basis of operations. An abortive raid on the Borders and a high-born Scottish wife [1] were all that he obtained of James IV, and in 1497, after a second attempt in Ireland, he landed in Cornwall. The Cornishmen had just risen against Henry's extortions, marched on London and been defeated at Blackheath ; but Henry's lenience encouraged a fresh revolt, and three thousand men flocked to Perkin's standard. They failed to take Exeter ; Perkin was seized at Beaulieu and sent up to London to be paraded through the streets amid the jeers and taunts of the people. Two years later a foolish attempt at escape and a fresh persona-tion of the Earl of Warwick by one Ralf Wulford [2] led to the execution of all three, Perkin, Wulford, and the real Earl of Warwick, who had been a prisoner and probably the innocent centre of so many plots since the accession of Henry VII. Warwick's death may have been due to the instigation of Ferdinand and Isabella of Spain, who were negotiating for the marriage of Catherine of Aragon with Prince Arthur. They were naturally anxious for the security of the throne their daughter was to share with Henry's son ; and now their ambassador wrote triumphantly that there remained in England not a doubtful drop of royal blood. [3] There were no more pretenders, and for the rest of Henry's reign England enjoyed such peace as it had not known for nearly a century. The end which Henry had sought by fair means and foul was attained, and there was no practical alter-native to his children in the succession to the English throne.

But all his statecraft, his patience and labour would

[1] Perkin was the first of Lady Catherine Gordon's four husbands ; her second was James Strangways, gentleman-usher to Henry VIII, her third Sir Matthew Cradock (d. 1531), and her fourth Christopher Ashton, also gentleman-usher ; she died in 1537 and was buried in Fyfield Church (*L. and P.* ii. 3512).

[2] See the present writer in *Dict. Nat. Biog.* lxiii. 172.

[3] *Sp. Cal.* i. No. 249 ; see below, p. 143.

have been writ in water without children to succeed him
and carry on the work which he had begun ; and at times
it seemed probable that this necessary condition would
remain unfulfilled. For the Tudors were singularly luck-
less in the matter of children. They were scarcely a
sterile race, but their offspring had an unfortunate habit
of dying in childhood. It was the desire for a male heir
that involved Henry VIII in his breach with Rome, and
led Mary into a marriage which raised a revolt ; the last
of the Tudors perceived that heirs might be purchased at
too great a cost, and solved the difficulty by admitting its
insolubility. Henry VIII had six wives, but only three
children who survived infancy ; of these, Edward VI
withered away at the age of fifteen, and Mary died child-
less at forty-two. By his two [1] mistresses he seems to
have had only one son, who died at the age of eleven,
and as far as we know, he had not a single grandchild,
legitimate or other. His sisters were hardly more fortunate. Margaret's eldest son by James IV died a year
after his birth ; her eldest daughter died at birth ; her
second son lived only nine months ; her second daughter
died at birth ; her third son lived to be James V, but her
fourth found an early grave. Mary, the other sister of
Henry VIII, lost her only son in his teens. The appalling
death-rate among Tudor infants cannot be attributed
solely to medical ignorance, for Yorkist babies clung to
life with a tenacity which was quite as inconvenient as
the readiness with which Tudor infants relinquished it ;
and Richard III, Henry VII and Henry VIII all found
it necessary to accelerate, by artificial means, the exit
from the world of the superfluous children of other pretenders. This drastic process smoothed their path, but
could not completely solve the problem ; and the characteristic Tudor infirmity was already apparent in the reign
of Henry VII. He had three sons ; two predeceased
him, one at the age of fifteen years, the other at fifteen
months. Of his four daughters, two died in infancy, and
the youngest cost the mother her life.[2] The fruit of that

[1] There is no definite evidence that he had more.
[2] *Ven. Cal.* i. 833.

union between the Red Rose and the White, upon which so much store had been set,[1] seemed doomed to fail.

The hopes built upon it had largely contributed to the success of Henry's raid upon the English throne, and before he started on his quest he had solemnly promised to marry Elizabeth, eldest daughter of Edward IV, and heiress of the House of York. But he was resolute to avoid all appearance of ruling in her right ; his title had been recognised by Parliament, and he had been five months *de facto* king before he wedded his Yorkist wife (18th January, 1486). Eight months and two days later, the Queen gave birth, in the priory of St. Swithin's, at Winchester, to her first-born son. Four days later, on Sunday, 24th September, the child was christened in the minster of the old West Saxon capital, and given in baptism the name of Arthur, the old British king. It was neither Yorkist nor Lancastrian, it evoked no bitter memories of civil strife, and it recalled the fact that the Tudors claimed a pedigree and boasted a title to British sovereignty, beside the antiquity of which Yorkist pretensions were a mushroom growth. Duke of Cornwall from his birth, Prince Arthur was, when three years old, created Prince of Wales. Already negotiations had been begun for his marriage with Catherine, the daughter of Ferdinand of Aragon and Isabella of Castile. Both were cautious sovereigns, and many a rebellion had to be put down and many a pretender put away, before they would consent to entrust their daughter to the care of an English king. It was not till 2nd October, 1501, that Catherine landed at Plymouth. At her formal reception into England, and at her marriage, six weeks later, in St. Paul's, she was led by the hand of her little brother-in-law, Prince Henry, then ten years old.[2] Against the advice of his council, Henry VII sent the youthful bride and bridegroom to live as man and wife at Ludlow Castle, and there, five and a half months later, their married life came to a sudden end. Prince Arthur died on 2nd April, 1502, and was buried in princely state in Worcester Cathedral.

[1] Cf. Skelton, *Works*, ed. Dyce. vol. i. pp. ix-xi.
[2] *L. and P. Henry VII*, i. 413-15 ; *L. and P. Henry VIII*, iv. 5791.

CHAPTER II

PRINCE HENRY AND HIS ENVIRONMENT

The Prince, who now succeeded to the position of heir-apparent, was nearly five years younger than his brother. The third child and second son of his parents, he was born on 28th June, 1491, at Greenwich, a palace henceforth intimately associated with the history of Tudor sovereigns. The manor of Greenwich had belonged to the alien priory of Lewisham, and, on the dissolution of those houses, had passed into the hands of Henry IV. Then it was granted to Humphrey, Duke of Gloucester, who began to enclose the palace grounds; on his death it reverted to the Crown; and Edward IV, many of whose tastes and characteristics were inherited by his grandson, Henry VIII, took great delight in beautifying and extending the palace. He gave it to his Queen, Elizabeth, and in her possession it remained until her sympathy with Yorkist plots was punished by the forfeiture of her lands. Henry VII then bestowed it on his wife, the dowager's daughter, and thus it became the birthplace of her younger children. Here was the scene of many a joust and tournament, of many a masque and revel; here the young Henry, as soon as he came to the throne, was wedded to Catherine of Aragon; here Henry's sister was married to the Duke of Suffolk; and here were born all future Tudor sovereigns, Edward VI, Mary, and Elizabeth. At Greenwich, then, through the forfeit of his grandmother, Henry was born; he was baptised in the Church of the Observant Friars, an Order the object first of his special favour,[1] and then of an equally marked dislike; the ceremony was performed by Richard Fox,[2] then Bishop of Exeter, and afterwards one of the child's chief advisers. His nurse was named Ann Luke, and years afterwards, when Henry was King, he allowed her the annual pension of twenty pounds, equivalent to about

[1] L. and P. i. 4871.   [2] Fox's own statement, L. and P. iv. 5791.

three hundred in modern currency. The details of his early life are few and far between. Lord Herbert, who wrote his *Life and Reign* a century later, records that the young Prince was destined by his father for the see of Canterbury,[1] and provided with an education more suited to a clerical than to a lay career. The motive ascribed to Henry VII is typical of his character; it was more economical to provide for younger sons out of ecclesiastical, than royal, revenues. But the story is probably a mere inference from the excellence of the boy's education, and from his father's thrift. If the idea of an ecclesiastical career for young Henry was ever entertained, it was soon abandoned for secular preferment. On 5th April, 1492, before the child was ten months old, he was appointed to the ancient and important posts of Warden of the Cinque Ports and Constable of Dover Castle.[2] A little later he received the still more honourable office of Earl Marshal; the duties were performed by deputy, but a goodly portion of the fees was doubtless appropriated for the expenses of the boy's establishment, or found its way into the royal coffers. Further promotion awaited him at the mature age of three. On 12th September, 1494, he became Lord-Lieutenant of Ireland;[3] six weeks later he was created Duke of York, and dubbed, with the usual quaint and formal ceremonies,[4] a Knight of the Bath. In December, he was made Warden of the Scottish Marches, and he was invested with the Garter in the following May.[5]

The accumulation of these great offices of State, any one of which might have taxed the powers of a tried administrator, in the feeble hands of a child appears at first sight a trifle irrational; but there was always method in Henry's madness. In bestowing these administrative posts upon his children he was really concentrating them in his own person and bringing them directly under his own supervision. It was the policy whereby the early

[1] Herbert gives Paolo Sarpi as his authority.
[2] G. E. C [okayne], *Complete Peerage, s.v.* Cornwall.
[3] *L. and P. Henry VII*, Rolls Ser. ii. 374.
[4] *Ibid.* i. 388-404; *Paston Letters* iii. 384-85.
[5] *L. and P. Henry VII*, ii. 57.

Roman Emperors imposed upon Republican Rome the substance, without the form, of despotism. It limited the powers of mischief which Henry's nobles might otherwise have enjoyed, and provided incomes for his children without increasing taxation or diminishing the privy purse. The work of administration could be done at least as effectively, much more economically, and with far less danger to internal peace by deputies of lower rank than the dukes and earls and barons who had been wont to abuse these high positions for the furtherance of private ends, and often for the levying of private war. Nowhere were the advantages of Henry's policy more conspicuous than in his arrangements for the government of Ireland. Ever since Richard, Duke of York, and George, Duke of Clarence, had ruled as Irish viceroys, Ireland had been a Yorkist stronghold. There Simnel had been crowned king, and there peers and peasants had fought for Perkin Warbeck. Something must be done to heal the running sore. Possibly Henry thought that some of Ireland's loyalty might be diverted from Yorkist channels by the selection of a Tudor prince as its viceroy; but he put his trust in more solid measures. As deputy to his infant son he nominated one who, though but a knight, was perhaps the ablest man among his privy council. It was in this capacity that Sir Edward Poynings [1] crossed to Ireland about the close of 1494, and called the Parliament of Drogheda. Judged by the durability of its legislation, it was one of the most memorable of parliaments; and for nearly three hundred years Poynings' laws remained the foundation upon which rested the constitutional relations between the sister kingdoms. Even more lasting was the precedent set by Prince Henry's creation as Duke of York; from that day to this, from Henry VIII to the present Prince of Wales, the second son of the sovereign or of the heir-apparent has almost invariably been invested with that dukedom. [2] The original selection of the

[1] See the present writer in *D.N.B.* xlvi. 271.
[2] An exception was made in the case of the late Duke of Edinburgh. It was designed, if Henry VIII had a second son, to make him Duke of York (*L. and P.* vii. 1364).

title was due to substantial reasons. Henry's name was distinctively Lancastrian, his title was no less distinctively Yorkist ; it was adopted as a concession to Yorkist prejudice. It was a practical reminder of the fact which the Tudor laureate, Skelton, celebrated in song : " The rose both red and white, in one rose now doth grow ". It was also a tacit assertion of the death of the last Duke of York in the Tower and of the imposture of Perkin Warbeck, now pretending to the title.

But thoughts of the coercion of Ireland and conciliation of Yorkists were as yet far from the mind of the child round whose person these measures were made to centre. Precocious he must have been, if the phenomenal development of brow and the curiously mature expression attributed to him in his portrait [1] are any indication of his intellectual powers at the age at which he is represented. Without the childish lips and nose, the face might well be that of a man of fifty ; and with the addition of a beard, the portrait would be an unmistakable likeness of Henry himself in his later years. When the Prince was no more than a child, says Erasmus, he was set to study.[2] He had, we are told, a vivid and active mind, above measure able to execute whatever tasks he undertook ; and he never attempted anything in which he did not succeed.[3] The Tudors had no modern dread of educational over-pressure when applied to their children, and the young Henry was probably as forward a pupil as his son, Edward VI, his daughter, Elizabeth, or his grand-niece, Lady Jane Grey. But, fortunately for Henry, a physical exuberance corrected his mental precocity ; and, as he grew older, any excessive devotion to the Muses was checked by an unwearied pursuit of bodily culture. He was the first of English sovereigns to be educated under the new influence of the Renaissance. Scholars, divines and poets thronged the Court

[1] This is an anonymous portrait of Henry at the age of eighteen months or two years belonging to Sir Edmund and Lady Verney.

[2] Erasmus, *Epist.* p. 1182 ; *L. and P.* iv. 5412.

[3] This testimonial was written in 1528 before Henry VIII had given the most striking demonstration of its truth.

of Henry VII. Margaret Beaufort, who ruled in Henry's household, was a signal benefactor to the cause of English learning. Lady Margaret professors commemorate her name in both our ancient universities, and in their bidding prayers she is to this day remembered. Two colleges at Cambridge revere her as their foundress; Caxton, the greatest of English printers, owed much to her munificence, and she herself translated into English books from both Latin and French. Henry VII, though less accomplished than the later Tudors, evinced an intelligent interest in art and letters, and provided for his children efficient instructors; while his Queen, Elizabeth of York, is described by Erasmus as possessing the soundest judgment and as being remarkable for her prudence as well as for her piety. Bernard André,[1] historian and poet, who had been tutor to Prince Arthur, probably took no small part in the education of his younger brother; to him he dedicated, after Arthur's death, two of the annual summaries of events which he was in the habit of compiling. Giles D'Ewes,[2] apparently a Frenchman and the author of a notable French grammar, taught that language to Prince Henry, as many years later he did to his daughter, Queen Mary; probably either D'Ewes or André trained his handwriting, which is a curious compromise between the clear and bold Italian style, soon to be adopted by well-instructed Englishmen, and the old English hieroglyphics in which more humbly educated individuals, including Shakespeare, concealed the meaning of their words. But the most famous of Henry's teachers was the poet Skelton, the greatest name in English verse from Lydgate down to Surrey. Skelton was poet laureate to Henry VII's Court, and refers in his poems to his wearing of the white and green of Tudor liveries.[3] He celebrated in verse

[1] See *D.N.B.* i. 398. Erasmus, however, described André as being "of mean abilities" (*L. and P.* iv. 626).

[2] *D.N.B.* xiv. 449; cf. *L. and P.* i. 513. On Henry VIII's accession D'Ewes was appointed keeper of the King's library at Richmond with a salary of £10 per year.

[3] Skelton, *Works*, ed. Dyce, vol. i. p. xiii.; the white and green still survive as the colours of Jesus College, Oxford, founded by Queen Elizabeth.

Arthur's creation as Prince of Wales and Henry's as
Duke of York ;[1] and before the younger prince was nine
years old, this " incomparable light and ornament of
British Letters," as Erasmus styles him, was directing
Henry's studies. Skelton himself writes :—

> The honor of England I learned to spell,
> I gave him drink of the sugred well
> Of Helicon's waters crystalline,
> Acquainting him with the Muses nine.

The coarseness of Skelton's satires and his open dis-
regard of the clerical vows of chastity may justify some
doubt of the value of the poet's influence on Henry's
character ; but he so far observed the conventional duties
of his post as to dedicate to his royal pupil, in 1501, a
moral treatise in Latin of no particular worth.[2] More
deserving of Henry's study were two books inscribed to
him a little later by young Boerio, son of the King's
Genoese physician and a pupil of Erasmus, who, according
to his own account, suffered untold afflictions from the
father's temper. One was a translation of Isocrates' *De
Regno*, the other of Lucian's tract against believing
calumnies.[3] The latter was, to judge from the tale of
Henry's victims, a precept which he scarcely laid to heart
in youth. In other respects he was apt enough to learn.
He showed " remarkable docility for mathematics," became proficient in Latin, spoke French with ease, under-
stood Italian, and, later on, possibly from Catherine of
Aragon, acquired a knowledge of Spanish. In 1499
Erasmus himself, the greatest of the humanists, visited
his friend, Lord Mountjoy, near Greenwich, and made
young Henry's acquaintance. " I was staying," he
writes,[4] " at Lord Mountjoy's country house when
Thomas More came to see me, and took me out with
him for a walk as far as the next village, where all the
King's children, except Prince Arthur, who was then the
eldest son, were being educated. When we came into

---

[1] Skelton, *Works*, vol. i. p. xxi. ; a copy of the latter, which Dyce
could not find, is in *Brit. Mus. Addit. MS.* 26787.

[2] *Ibid.*   [3] *Ibid.* 19553.

[4] F. M. Nichols, *Epistles of Erasmus* i. 201.

the hall, the attendants not only of the palace, but also of Mountjoy's household, were all assembled. In the midst stood Prince Henry, now nine years old, and having already something of royalty in his demeanour in which there was a certain dignity combined with singular courtesy. On his right was Margaret, about eleven years of age, afterwards married to James, King of Scots ; and on his left played Mary, a child of four. Edmund was an infant in arms. More, with his companion Arnold, after paying his respects to the boy Henry, the same that is now King of England, presented him with some writing. For my part, not having expected anything of the sort, I had nothing to offer, but promised that, on another occasion, I would in some way declare my duty towards him. Meantime, I was angry with More for not having warned me, especially as the boy sent me a little note, while we were at dinner, to challenge something from my pen. I went home, and in the Muses' spite, from whom I had been so long divorced, finished the poem within three days." The poem,[1] in which Britain speaks her own praise and that of her princes, Henry VII and his children, was dedicated to the Duke of York and accompanied by a letter in which Erasmus commended Henry's devotion to learning. Seven years later Erasmus again wrote to Henry, now Prince of Wales, condoling with him upon the death of his brother-in-law, Philip of Burgundy, King of Castile. Henry replied in cordial manner, inviting the great scholar to continue the correspondence. The style of his letter so impressed Erasmus that he suspected, as he says,[2] " some help from others in the ideas and expressions. In a conversation I afterwards had with William, Lord Mountjoy, he tried by various arguments to dispel that suspicion, and when he found he could not do so he gave up the point and let it pass until he was sufficiently instructed in the case. On another occasion, when we were talking alone together, he brought out a number of the Prince's letters, some to other people and some to

---

[1] Printed in 1500 at the end of Erasmus's *Adagia*.
[2] F. M. Nichols pp. 423-24 ; *L. and P.* iv. 5412.

himself, and among them one which answered to mine : in these letters were manifest signs of comment, addition, suppression, correction and alteration—You might recognise the first drafting of a letter, and you might make out the second and third, and sometimes even the fourth correction ; but whatever was revised or added was in the same handwriting. I had then no further grounds for hesitation, and, overcome by the facts, I laid aside all suspicion." Neither, he adds, would his correspondent doubt Henry VIII's authorship of the book against Luther if he knew that king's " happy genius ". That famous book is sufficient proof that theological studies held no small place in Henry's education. They were cast in the traditional mould, for the Lancastrians were very orthodox, and the early Tudors followed in their steps. Margaret Beaufort left her husband to devote herself to good works and a semi-monastic life ; Henry VII converted a heretic at the stake and left him to burn ;[1] and the theological conservatism, which Henry VIII imbibed in youth, clung to him to the end of his days.

Nor were the arts neglected, and in his early years Henry acquired a passionate and lifelong devotion to music. Even as Duke of York he had a band of minstrels apart from those of the King and Prince Arthur ;[2] and when he was king his minstrels formed an indispensable part of his retinue, whether he went on progress through his kingdom, or crossed the seas on errands of peace or war.[3] He became an expert performer on the lute, the organ and the harpsichord, and all the cares of State could not divert him from practising on those instruments both day and night. He sent all over England in search of singing men and boys for the chapel royal, and sometimes appropriated choristers from Wolsey's chapel, which he thought better provided than his own.[4] From Venice he enticed to England the organist of St. Mark's, Dionysius Memo, and on occasion Henry and his Court

[1] *Cotton MS. Vitellius A.* xvi. f. 172.
[2] *Hist. MSS. Comm.* 5th Rep. App. p. 549.
[3] *L. and P.* i. 4314.
[4] *Ibid.* ii. 410, 4024.

listened four hours at a stretch to Memo's organ recitals.[1]
Not only did he take delight in the practice of music by
himself and others ; he also studied its theory and wrote
with the skill of an expert. Vocal and instrumental
pieces of his own composition, preserved among the
manuscripts at the British Museum,[2] rank among the
best productions of the time ; and one of his anthems,
" O Lorde, the Maker of all thyng," is of the highest
order of merit, and still remains a favourite in English
cathedrals.

In April, 1502, at the age of ten, Henry became the
heir-apparent to the English throne. He succeeded at
once to the dukedom of Cornwall, but again a precedent
was set which was followed but yesterday ; and ten
months were allowed to elapse before he was, on 18th
February, 1503, created Prince of Wales and Earl of
Chester, the dukedom of York becoming void until a
king or an heir-apparent should again have a second son.[3]
The first sign of his increased importance was his implication in the maze of matrimonial intrigues which formed
so large a part of sixteenth-century diplomacy. The last
thing kings considered was the domestic felicity of their
children ; their marriages were pieces in the diplomatic
game and sometimes the means by which States were
built up. While Duke of York, Henry had been proposed
as a husband for Eleanor,[4] daughter of the Archduke
Philip ; and his sister Mary as the bride of Philip's son
Charles, who, as the heir of the houses of Castile and of
Aragon, of Burgundy and of Austria, was from the cradle
destined to wield the imperial sceptre of Cæsar. No
further steps were taken at the time, and Prince Arthur's
death brought other projects to the front.

Immediately on receiving the news, and two days
before they dated their letter of condolence to Henry

---

[1] *Ven. Cal.* ii. 780 ; *L. and P.* ii. 2401, 3455.

[2] E.g. *Add. MS.* 31922.

[3] The next prince to hold the title was Charles, afterwards Charles I,
who was created Duke of York on 6th Jan., 1605.

[4] Afterwards Queen of Portugal and then of France. *L. and P. Henry
VII*, i. 285, 425.

VII, Ferdinand and Isabella commissioned the Duke of
Estrada to negotiate a marriage between the widowed
Catherine and her youthful brother-in-law.[1] No doubt
was entertained but that the Pope would grant the
necessary dispensation, for the spiritual head of Christendom was apt to look tenderly on the petitions of the
powerful princes of this world. A more serious difficulty
was the question of the widow's dower. Part only had
been paid, and Ferdinand not merely refused to hand
over the rest, but demanded the return of his previous
instalments. Henry, on the other hand, considered
himself entitled to the whole, refused to refund a penny
and gave a cold reception to the proposed marriage
between Catherine and his sole surviving son. He was,
however, by no means blind to the advantages of the
Spanish matrimonial and political alliance, and still less
to the attractions of Catherine's dower ; he declined to
send back the Princess, when Isabella, shocked at Henry
VII's proposal to marry his daughter-in-law himself,
demanded her return ; and eventually, when Ferdinand
reduced his terms, he suffered the marriage treaty to be
signed. On 25th June, 1503, Prince Henry and Catherine
were solemnly betrothed in the Bishop of Salisbury's
house in Fleet Street.

The papal dispensation arrived in time to solace
Isabella on her death-bed in November, 1504 ; but that
event once more involved in doubt the prospects of the
marriage. The crown of Castile passed from Isabella to
her daughter Juaña ; the government of the kingdom was
claimed by Ferdinand and by Juaña's husband, Philip of
Burgundy. On their way from the Netherlands to claim
their inheritance, Philip and Juaña were driven on
English shores. Henry VII treated them with all possible
courtesy, and made Philip a Knight of the Garter, while
Philip repaid the compliment by investing Prince Henry
with the Order of the Golden Fleece.[2] But advantage
was taken of Philip's plight to extort from him the
surrender of the Earl of Suffolk, styled the White Rose,

[1] *Sp. Cal.* i. 267.

[2] *L. and P. Henry VII*, ii. 158 ; *Ven. Cal.* i. 867.

and a commercial treaty with the Netherlands, which the Flemings named the Malus Intercursus. Three months after his arrival in Castile, Philip died, and Henry began to fish in the troubled waters for a share in his dominions. Two marriage schemes occurred to him ; he might win the hand of Philip's sister Margaret, now Regent of the Netherlands, and with her hand the control of those provinces ; or he might marry Juaña and claim in her right to administer Castile. On the acquisition of Castile he set his mind. If he could not gain it by marriage with Juaña, he thought he could do so by marrying her son and heir, the infant Charles, to his daughter Mary. Which-ever means he took to further his design, it would naturally irritate Ferdinand and make him less anxious for the completion of the marriage between Catherine and Prince Henry. Henry VII was equally averse from the consummation of the match. Now that he was scheming with Charles's other grandfather, the Emperor Maxi-milian, to wrest the government of Castile from Ferdinand's grasp, the alliance of the King of Aragon had lost its attraction, and it was possible that the Prince of Wales might find elsewhere a more desirable bride. Henry's marriage with Catherine was to have been accomplished when he completed the age of fourteen ; but on the eve of his fifteenth birthday he made a solemn protestation that the contract was null and void, and that he would not carry out his engagements.[1] This protest left him free to consider other proposals, and enhanced his value as a negotiable asset. More than once negotiations were started for marrying him to Marguerite de Valois, sister of the Duke of Angoulême, afterwards famous as Francis I ;[2] and in the last months of his father's reign, the Prince of Wales was giving audience to ambassadors from Maximilian, who came to suggest matrimonial alliances between the prince and a daughter of Duke Albert of Bavaria, and between Henry VII and the Lady Margaret of Savoy, Regent of the Netherlands.[3]

[1] *Sp. Cal.* i. 458 ; *L. and P.* iv. 5791.
[2] *L. and P. Henry VII*, i. 241-47 ; ii. 342-43.
[3] *Sp. Cal.* Suppl. p. 23.

Meanwhile, Ferdinand, threatened on all sides, first came
to terms with France ; he married a French princess,
Germaine de Foix, abandoned his claim to Navarre, and
bought the security of Naples by giving Louis XII a free
hand in the north of Italy. He then diverted Maximilian
from his designs on Castile by humouring his hostility to
Venice. By that bait he succeeded in drawing off his
enemies, and the league of Cambrai united them all,
Ferdinand and Louis, Emperor and Pope, in an iniquitous
attack on the Italian Republic. Henry VII, fortunately
for his reputation, was left out of the compact. He was
still cherishing his design on Castile, and in December,
1508, the treaty of marriage between Mary and Charles
was formally signed. It was the last of his worldly
triumphs ; the days of his life were numbered, and in the
early months of 1509 he was engaged in making a peace
with his conscience.

The twenty-four years during which Henry VII had
guided the destinies of England were a momentous epoch
in the development of Western civilisation. It was the
dawn of modern history, of the history of Europe in the
form in which we know it to-day. The old order was in
a state of liquidation. The mediæval ideal, described by
Dante, of a universal monarchy with two aspects, spiritual
and temporal, and two heads, emperor and pope, was
passing away. Its place was taken by the modern but
narrower ideal of separate polities, each pursuing its own
course, independent of, and often in conflict with, other
societies. Unity gave way to diversity of tongues, of
churches, of states ; and the cosmopolitan became
nationalist, patriot, separatist. Imperial monarchy shrank
to a shadow ; and kings divided the emperor's power at
the same time that they consolidated their own. They
extended their authority on both sides, at the expense of
their superior, the emperor, and at the expense of their
subordinate feudal lords. The struggle between the dis-
ruptive forces of feudalism and the central power of
monarchy ended at last in monarchical triumph ; and
internal unity prepared the way for external expansion.

France under Louis XI was first in the field. She had surmounted her civil troubles half a century earlier than England. She then expelled her foreign foes, crushed the remnants of feudal independence, and began to expand at the cost of weaker States. Parts of Burgundy, Provence, and Brittany became merged in France; the exuberant strength of the new-formed nation burst the barriers of the Alps and overflowed into the plains of Italy. The time of universal monarchy was past, but the dread of it remained; and from Charles VIII's invasion of Italy in 1494 to Francis I's defeat at Pavia in 1525, French dreams of world-wide sovereignty were the nightmare of other kings. Those dreams might, as Europe feared, have been realised, had not other States followed France in the path of internal consolidation. Ferdinand of Aragon married Isabella of Castile, drove out the Moors and founded the modern Spanish kingdom. Maximilian married Mary, the daughter of Charles the Bold, and joined the Netherlands to Austria. United France found herself face to face with other united States, and the political system of modern Europe was roughly sketched out. The boundaries of the various kingdoms were fluctuating. There still remained minor principalities and powers, chiefly in Italy and Germany, which offered an easy prey to their ambitious neighbours; for both nations had sacrificed internal unity to the shadow of universal dominion, Germany in temporal, and Italy in spiritual, things. Mutual jealousy of each other's growth at the expense of these States gave rise to the theory of the balance of power; mutual adjustment of each other's disputes produced international law; and the necessity of watching each other's designs begat modern diplomacy.[1]

Parallel with these developments in the relations between one State and another marched a no less momentous revolution in the domestic position of their sovereigns. National expansion abroad was marked by a corresponding growth in royal authority at home. The process was not new in England; every step in the path of the tribal

[1] Cf. A. O. Meyer, *Die Englische Diplomatie*, Breslau, 1901.

chief of Saxon pirates to the throne of a united England
denoted an advance in the nature of kingly power. Each
extension of his sway intensified his authority, and his
power grew in degree as it increased in area. So with
fifteenth-century sovereigns. Local liberties and feudal
rights which had checked a Duke of Brittany or a King
of Aragon were powerless to restrain the King of France
or of Spain. The sphere of royal authority encroached
upon all others; all functions and all powers tended to
concentrate in royal hands. The king was the emblem
of national unity, the centre of national aspirations, and
object of national reverence. The Renaissance gave
fresh impetus to the movement. Men turned not only to
the theology, literature, and art of the early Christian
era; they began to study anew its political organisation
and its system of law and jurisprudence. The code of
Justinian was as much a revelation as the original Greek
of the New Testament. Roman imperial law seemed as
superior to the barbarities of common law as classical
was to mediæval Latin; and Roman law supplanted
indigenous systems in France and in Germany, in Spain
and in Scotland. Both the Roman imperial law and the
Roman imperial constitution were useful models for kings
of the New Monarchy; the Roman Empire was a despotism; *quod principi placuit legis habet vigorem* ran the
fundamental principle of Roman Empire.[1] Nor was this
all; Roman emperors were habitually deified, and men
in the sixteenth century seemed to pay to their kings
while alive the Divine honours which Romans paid to
their emperors when dead. "Le nouveau Messie," says
Michelet, "est le roi."[2]

Nowhere was the king more emphatically the saviour
of society than in England. The sixty years of Lancastrian rule were in the seventeenth century represented
as the golden age of parliamentary government, a sort of

[1] The conclusion of the maxim *utpote cum lege regia quae de imperio
ejus lata est, populus ei et in eum omne suum imperium at potestatem conferat*
(Ulpian, *Digest* I. iv. 1), was conveniently forgotten by apologists for
absolutism, though the Tudors respected it in practice.

[2] *Hist. de France*, ed. 1879, ix. 301.

time before the fall to which popular orators appealed
when they wished to paint in vivid colours the evils of
Stuart tyranny. But to keen observers of the time the
pre-eminent characteristic of Lancastrian rule appeared
to be its " lack of governance " or, in modern phrase,
administrative anarchy.[1] There was no subordination in
the State. The weakness of the Lancastrian title left the
king at the mercy of Parliament, and the limitations of
Parliament were never more apparent than when its
powers stood highest. Even in the realm of legislation,
the statute book has seldom been so barren. Its principal
acts were to narrow the county electorate to an oligarchy,
to restrict the choice of constituencies to resident knights
and burgesses, and to impair its own influence as a focus
of public opinion. It was not content with legislative
authority ; it interfered with an executive which it could
hamper but could not control. It was possessed by the
inveterate fallacy that freedom and strong government
are things incompatible ; that the executive is the natural
enemy of the Legislature ; that if one is strong, the other
must be weak ; and of the two alternatives it vastly preferred a weak executive. So, to limit the king's power
it sought to make him " live of his own," when " his own "
was absolutely inadequate to meet the barest necessities
of government. Parliament was in fact irresponsible ;
the connecting link between it and the executive had yet
to be found. Hence the Lancastrian " lack of governance " ; it ended in a generation of civil war, and the
memory of that anarchy explains much in Tudor history.

The problems of Henry VIII's reign can indeed only
be solved by realising the misrule of the preceding century,
the failure of parliamentary government, and the strength
of the popular demand for a firm and masterful hand. It
is a modern myth that Englishmen have always been
consumed with enthusiasm for parliamentary government
and with a thirst for a parliamentary vote. The interpretation of history, like that of the Scriptures, varies
from age to age ; and present political theories colour our
views of the past. The political development of the

[1] Fortescue, *Governance of England*, ed. Plummer, 1885.

nineteenth century created a parliamentary legend ; and civil and religious liberty became the inseparable stage properties of the Englishman. Whenever he appeared on the boards, he was made to declaim about the rights of the subject and the privileges of Parliament. It was assumed that the desire for a voice in the management of his own affairs had at all times and all seasons been the mainspring of his actions ; and so the story of Henry's rule was made into a political mystery. In reality, love of freedom has not always been, nor will it always remain, the predominant note in the English mind. At times the English people have pursued it through battle and murder with grim determination, but other times have seen other ideals. On occasion the demand has been for strong government irrespective of its methods, and good government has been preferred to self-government. Wars of expansion and wars of defence have often cooled the love of liberty and impaired the faith in parliaments ; and generally English ideals have been strictly subordinated to a passion for material prosperity.

Never was this more apparent than under the Tudors. The parliamentary experiment of the Lancastrians was premature and had failed. Parliamentary institutions were discredited and people were indifferent to parliamentary rights and privileges : " A plague on both your Houses," was the popular feeling, " give us peace, above all peace at home to pursue new avenues of wealth, new phases of commercial development, peace to study new problems of literature, religion, and art " ; and both Houses passed out of the range of popular imagination, and almost out of the sphere of independent political action. Parliament played during the sixteenth century a modester part than it had played since its creation. Towards the close of the period Shakespeare wrote his play of *King John*, and in that play there is not the faintest allusion to Magna Carta.[1] Such an omission

[1] Magna Carta may almost be said to have been " discovered " by the parliamentary opponents of the Stuarts ; and in discovering it, they misinterpreted several of its clauses such as the *judicium parium*. Allusion was, however, made to Magna Carta in the proceedings against Wolsey for *Præmunire* (Fox vi. 43).

would be inconceivable now or at any time since the
death of Elizabeth ; for the Great Charter is enshrined
in popular imagination as the palladium of the British
constitution. It was the fetish to which Parliament
appealed against the Stuarts. But no such appeal would
have touched a Tudor audience. It needed and desired
no weapon against a sovereign who embodied national
desires, and ruled in accord with the national will.
References to the charter are as rare in parliamentary
debates as they are in the pages of Shakespeare. The
best hated instruments of Stuart tyranny were popular
institutions under the Tudors ; and the Star Chamber
itself found its main difficulty in the number of suitors
which flocked to a court where the king was judge, the
law's delays minimised, counsel's fees moderate, and
justice rarely denied merely because it might happen to
be illegal. England in the sixteenth century put its
trust in its princes far more than it did in its parliaments ;
it invested them with attributes almost Divine. By
Tudor majesty the poet was inspired with thoughts of
the divinity that doth hedge a king. " Love for the
King," wrote a Venetian of Henry VIII in the early
years of his reign, " is universal with all who see him,
for his Highness does not seem a person of this world,
but one descended from heaven."[1] *Le nouveau Messie
est le Roi.*

Such were the tendencies which Henry VII and Henry
VIII crystallised into practical weapons of absolute
government. Few kings have attained a greater measure
of permanent success than the first of the Tudors ; it
was he who laid the unseen foundations upon which
Henry VIII erected the imposing edifice of his personal
authority. An orphan from birth and an exile from
childhood, he stood near enough to the throne to invite
Yorkist proscription, but too far off to unite in his favour
Lancastrian support. He owed his elevation to the mistakes of his enemies and to the cool, calculating craft
which enabled him to use those mistakes without making
mistakes of his own. He ran the great risk of his life in

[1] *Ven. Cal.* ii. 336.

his invasion of England, but henceforth he left nothing to chance. He was never betrayed by passion or enthusiasm into rash adventures, and he loved the substance, rather than the pomp and circumstance of power. Untrammelled by scruples, unimpeded by principles, he pursued with constant fidelity the task of his life, to secure the throne for himself and his children, to pacify his country, and to repair the waste of the civil wars. Folly easily glides into war, but to establish a permanent peace required all Henry's patience, clear sight and far sight, caution and tenacity. A full exchequer, not empty glory, was his first requisite, and he found in his foreign wars a mine of money. Treason at home was turned to like profit, and the forfeited estates of rebellious lords accumulated in the hands of the royal family and filled the national coffers. Attainder, the characteristic instrument of Tudor policy, was employed to complete the ruin of the old English peerage which the Wars of the Roses began : and by 1509 there was only one duke and one marquis left in the whole of England.[1] Attainder not only removed the particular traitor, but disqualified his family for place and power ; and the process of eliminating feudalism from the region of government, started by Edward I, was finished by Henry VII. Feudal society has been described as a pyramid ; the upper slopes were now washed away leaving an impassable precipice, with the Tudor monarch alone in his glory at its summit. Royalty had become a caste apart. Marriages between royal children and English peers had hitherto been no uncommon thing ; since Henry VII's accession there have been but four, two of them in our own day. Only one took place in the sixteenth century, and the Duke of Suffolk was by some thought worthy of death for his presumption in marrying the sister of Henry VIII. The peerage was weakened not only by diminishing numbers, but by the systematic depression of those who remained. Henry VII, like Ferdinand of Aragon,[2] preferred to

[1] The Duke was Buckingham, and the Marquis was Dorset.
[2] See a description of Ferdinand's court by John Stile, the English envoy, in *L. and P.* i. 490.

govern by means of lawyers and churchmen ; they could be rewarded by judgeships and bishoprics, and required no grants from the royal estates. Their occupancy of office kept out territorial magnates who abused it for private ends. Of the sixteen regents nominated by Henry VIII in his will, not one could boast a peerage of twelve years' standing ;[1] and all the great Tudor ministers, Wolsey and Cromwell, Cecil and Walsingham, were men of comparatively humble birth. With similar objects Henry VII passed laws limiting the number of retainers and forbidding the practice of maintenance. The courts of Star Chamber and Requests were developed to keep in order his powerful subjects and give poor men protection against them. Their civil law procedure, influenced by Roman imperial maxims, served to enhance the royal power and dignity, and helped to build up the Tudor autocracy.

To the office of king thus developed and magnified, the young Prince who stood upon the steps of the throne brought personal qualities of the highest order, and advantages to which his father was completely a stranger. His title was secure, his treasury overflowed, and he enjoyed the undivided affections of his people. There was no alternative claimant. The White Rose, indeed, had languished in the Tower since his surrender by Philip, and the Duke of Buckingham had some years before been mentioned as a possible successor to the throne ;[2] but their claims only served to remind men that nothing but Henry's life stood between them and anarchy, for his young brother Edmund, Duke of Somerset, had preceded Arthur to an early grave. Upon the single thread of Henry's life hung the peace of the realm ; no other could have secured the throne without a second civil war. It was small wonder if England regarded Henry with a somewhat extravagant loyalty. Never had king ascended the throne more richly endowed with mental and physical gifts. He was ten weeks short of

[1] See the present writer's *England under Protector Somerset* p. 38.
[2] *L. and P. Henry VII*, i. 180, 233, 319.

his eighteenth year. From both his parents he inherited grace of mind and of person. His father in later years was broken in health and soured in spirit, but in the early days of his reign he had charmed the citizens of York with his winning smile. His mother is described by the Venetian ambassador as a woman of great beauty and ability. She transmitted to Henry many of the popular characteristics of her father, Edward IV, though little of the military genius of that consummate commander who fought thirteen pitched battles and lost not one. Unless eye-witnesses sadly belied themselves, Henry VIII must have been the desire of all eyes. " His Majesty," wrote one a year or two later,[1] " is the handsomest potentate I ever set eyes on ; above the usual height, with an extremely fine calf to his leg ; his complexion fair and bright, with auburn hair combed straight and short in the French fashion, and a round face so very beautiful that it would become a pretty woman, his throat being rather long and thick. . . . He speaks French, English, Latin, and a little Italian ; plays well on the lute and harpsichord, sings from the book at sight, draws the bow with greater strength than any man in England, and jousts marvellously." Another foreign resident in 1519[2] described him as " extremely handsome. Nature could not have done more for him. He is much handsomer than any other sovereign in Christendom ; a great deal handsomer than the King of France ; very fair and his whole frame admirably proportioned. On hearing that Francis I wore a beard, he allowed his own to grow, and as it is reddish, he has now got a beard that looks like gold. He is very accomplished, a good musician. composes well, is a capital horseman, a fine jouster, speaks French, Latin, and Spanish. . . . He is very fond of hunting, and never takes his diversion without tiring eight or ten horses which he causes to be stationed beforehand along the line of country he means to take, and when one is tired he mounts another, and before he gets home they are all exhausted. He is extremely fond

[1] *L. and P.* ii. 395.
[2] Giustinian, *Despatches*, ii. 312 ; *Ven. Cal.* ii. 1287 ; *L. and P.* iii. 402.

of tennis, at which game it is the prettiest thing in the world to see him play, his fair skin glowing through a shirt of the finest texture."

The change from the cold suspicious Henry VII to such a king as this was inevitably greeted with a burst of rapturous enthusiasm. " I have no fear," wrote Mountjoy to Erasmus,[1] " but when you heard that our Prince, now Henry the Eighth, whom we may well call our Octavius, had succeeded to his father's throne, all your melancholy left you at once. For what may you not promise yourself from a Prince with whose extraordinary and almost Divine character you are well acquainted. . . . But when you know what a hero he now shows himself, how wisely he behaves, what a lover he is of justice and goodness, what affection he bears to the learned, I will venture to swear that you will need no wings to make you fly to behold this new and auspicious star. If you could see how all the world here is rejoicing in the possession of so great a Prince, how his life is all their desire, you could not contain your tears for joy. The heavens laugh, the earth exults, all things are full of milk, of honey, of nectar ! Avarice is expelled the country. Liberality scatters wealth with a bounteous hand. Our King does not desire gold or gems or precious metals, but virtue, glory, immortality." The picture is over-drawn for modern taste, but making due allowance for Mountjoy's turgid efforts to emulate his master's elo-quence, enough remains to indicate the impression made by Henry on a peer of liberal education. His unrivalled skill in national sports and martial exercises appealed at least as powerfully to the mass of his people. In archery, in wrestling, in joust and in tourney, as well as in the tennis court or on the hunting field, Henry was a match for the best in his kingdom. None could draw a bow, tame a steed, or shiver a lance more deftly than he, and his single-handed tournaments on horse and foot with his brother-in-law, the Duke of Suffolk, are likened by one who watched them to the combats of Achilles and Hector. These are no mere trifles below the dignity of

[1] F. M. Nichols, *Epistles of Erasmus*, i. 457.

history; they help to explain the extraordinary hold Henry obtained over popular imagination. Suppose there ascended the throne to-day a young prince, the hero of the athletic world, the finest oar, the best bat, the crack marksman of his day, it is easy to imagine the enthusiastic support he would receive from thousands of his people who care much for sport, and nothing at all for politics. Suppose also that that prince were endowed with the iron will, the instinctive insight into the hearts of his people, the profound aptitude for government that Henry VIII displayed, he would be a rash man who would guarantee even now the integrity of parliamentary power or the continuance of cabinet rule. In those days, with thirty years of civil war and fifteen more of conspiracy fresh in men's mind, with no alternative to anarchy save Henry VIII, with a peerage fallen from its high estate, and a Parliament almost lost to respect, royal autocracy was not a thing to dread or distrust. "If a lion knew his strength," said Sir Thomas More of his master to Cromwell, "it were hard for any man to rule him." Henry VIII had the strength of a lion; it remains to be seen how soon he learnt it, and what use he made of that strength when he discovered the secret.

CHAPTER III

THE APPRENTICESHIP OF HENRY VIII

QUIETLY and peacefully, without a threat from abroad or
a murmur at home, the crown, which his father had won
amid the storm and stress of the field of battle, devolved
upon Henry VIII. With an eager profusion of zeal
Ferdinand of Aragon placed at Henry's disposal his
army, his fleet, his personal services.[1] There was no
call for this sacrifice. For generations there had been
no such tranquil demise of the crown. Not a ripple
disturbed the surface of affairs as the old King lay sick in
April, 1509, in Richmond Palace at Sheen. By his bedside
stood his only surviving son ; and to him the dying
monarch addressed his last words of advice. He desired
him to complete his marriage with Catherine, he exhorted
him to defend the Church, and to make war on the infidel ;
he commended to him his faithful councillors, and is
believed to have urged upon him the execution of De la
Pole, Earl of Suffolk, the White Rose of England. On
the 22nd he was dead. A fortnight later the funeral
procession wended its way from Sheen to St. Paul's, where
the illustrious John Fisher, cardinal and martyr, preached
the *éloge*. Thence it passed down the Strand, between
hedges and willows clad in the fresh green of spring, to

> That acre sown indeed
> With the richest, royallest seed
> That the earth did e'er drink in.

There, in the vault beneath the chapel in Westminster
Abbey which bears his name and testifies to his magnificence in building, Henry VII was laid to rest beside
his Queen ; dwelling, says Bacon, " more richly dead in
the monument of his tomb than he did alive in Richmond
or any of his palaces ". For years before and after,
Torrigiano, the rival of Buonarotti, wrought at its

[1] *Sp. Cal.* ii. 4.

" matchless altar," not a stone of which survived the Puritan fury of the civil war.

On the day of his father's death, or the next, the new King removed from Richmond Palace to the Tower, whence, on 23rd April, was dated the first official act of his reign. He confirmed in ampler form the general pardon granted a few days before by Henry VII; but the ampler form was no bar to the exemption of four-score offenders from the act of grace.[1] Foremost among them were the three brothers De la Pole, Sir Richard Empson and Edmund Dudley. The exclusion of Empson and Dudley from the pardon was more popular than the pardon itself. If anything could have enhanced Henry's favour with his subjects, it was the condign punishment of the tools of his father's extortion. Their death was none the less welcome for being unjust. They were not merely refused pardon and brought to the block; a more costly concession was made when their bonds for the payment of loans were cancelled.[2] Their victims, so runs the official record, had been " without any ground or matter of truth, by the undue means of certain of the council of our said late father, thereunto driven contrary to law, reason and good conscience, to the manifest charge and peril of the soul of our said late father ".

If filial piety demanded the delivery of his father's soul from peril, it counselled no less the fulfilment of his dying requests, and the arrangements for Catherine's marriage were hurried on with an almost indecent haste. The instant he heard rumours of Henry VII's death, Ferdinand sent warning to his envoy in England that Louis of France and others would seek by all possible means to break off the match.[3] To further it, he would withdraw his objections to the union of Charles and Mary; and a few days later he wrote again to remove any scruples Henry might entertain about marrying his deceased brother's wife; while to Catherine herself he declared with brutal frankness that she would get no other husband than Henry.[4] All his paternal anxiety

[1] *L. and P.* i. 2, 12.   [2] Cf. *L. and P.* i. 1004.
[3] *Sp. Cal.* ii. 3.   [4] *Ibid.* ii. 8, 15.

might have been spared. Long before Ferdinand's persuasions could reach Henry's ears, he had made up his
mind to consummate the marriage. He would not, he
wrote to Margaret of Savoy,[1] disobey his father's commands, reinforced as they were by the dispensation of
the Pope and by the friendship between the two families
contracted by his sister Mary's betrothal to Catherine's
nephew Charles. There were other reasons besides those
he alleged. A council trained by Henry VII was loth to
lose the gold of Catherine's dower ; it was of the utmost
importance to strengthen at once the royal line ; and a
full-blooded youth of Henry's temperament was not likely
to repel a comely wife ready to his hand, when the
dictates of his father's policy no longer stood between
them. So on 11th June, barely a month after Henry VII's
obsequies, the marriage, big with destinies, of Henry VIII
and Catherine of Aragon was privately solemnised by
Archbishop Warham " in the Queen's closet " at Greenwich.[2] On the same day the commission of claims was
appointed for the King's and Queen's coronation. A week
then sufficed for its business, and on Sunday, 24th June,
the Abbey was the scene of a second State function
within three months. Its splendour and display were
emblematic of the coming reign. Warham placed the
crown on the King's head ; the people cried, " Yea, yea ! "
in a loud voice when asked if they would have Henry
as King ; Sir Robert Dymock performed the office of
champion ; and a banquet, jousts and tourneys concluded
the ceremonies.

Though he had wedded a wife and been crowned a king,
Henry was as yet little more than a boy. A powerful
mind ripens slowly in a vigorous frame, and Henry's
childish precocity had given way before a youthful
devotion to physical sports. He was no prodigy of early
development. His intellect, will and character were of
a gradual, healthier growth ; they were not matured for
many years after he came to the throne. He was still

[1] *L. and P.* i. 224   [2] *Ibid.* iv. 5774.

in his eighteenth year ; and like most young Englishmen
of means and muscle, his interests centred rather in the
field than in the study. Youth sat on the prow and
pleasure at the helm. "Continual feasting" was the
phrase in which Catherine described their early married
life. In the winter evenings there were masks and
comedies, romps and revels, in which Henry himself,
Bessie Blount and other young ladies of his Court played
parts.[1] In the spring and summer there were archery
and tennis. Music, we are told, was practised day and
night. Two months after his accession Henry wrote to
Ferdinand that he diverted himself with jousts, birding,
hunting, and other innocent and honest pastimes, in
visiting various parts of his kingdom, but that he did
not therefore neglect affairs of State.[2] Possibly he was
as assiduous in his duties as modern university athletes
in their studies ; the neglect was merely comparative.
But Ferdinand's ambassador remarked on Henry's aver-
sion to business, and his councillors complained that he
cared only for the pleasures of his age. Two days a
week, said the Spaniard, were devoted to single combats
on foot, initiated in imitation of the heroes of romance,
Amadis and Lancelot ;[3] and if Henry's other innocent
and honest pastimes were equally exacting, his view of
the requirements of State may well have been modest.
From the earliest days of his reign the general outline of
policy was framed in accord with his sentiments, and he
was probably consulted on most questions of importance.
But it was not always so ; in August, 1509, Louis XII
acknowledged a letter purporting to come from the
English King with a request for friendship and peace.
"Who wrote this letter ?" burst out Henry. "I ask
peace of the King of France, who dare not look me in
the face, still less make war on me !"[4] His pride at the
age of eighteen was not less than his ignorance of what
passed in his name. He had yet to learn the secret that
painful and laborious mastery of detail is essential to him
who aspires not merely to reign but to rule ; and matters

[1] L. and P. ii. p. 1461.   [2] Sp. Cal. ii. 19.
[3] Ibid. ii. 44, 45.   [4] Ven. Cal. ii. 11.

of detail in administration and diplomacy were still left
in his ministers' hands.

With the exception of Empson and Dudley, Henry
made little or no change in the council his father bequeathed him. Official precedence appertained to his
Chancellor, Warham, Archbishop of Canterbury. Like
most of Henry VII's prelates, he received his preferment
in the Church as a reward for services to the State.
Much of the diplomatic work of the previous reign had
passed through his hands; he helped to arrange the
marriage of Arthur and Catherine, and was employed in
the vain attempt to obtain Margaret of Savoy as a bride
for Henry VII. As Archbishop he crowned and married
Henry VIII, and as Chancellor he delivered orations at
the opening of the young King's first three Parliaments.[1]
They are said to have given general satisfaction, but
apart from them, Warham, for some unknown reason,
took little part in political business. So far as Henry
can be said at this time to have had a Prime Minister,
that title belongs to Fox, his Lord Privy Seal and Bishop
of Winchester. Fox had been even more active than
Warham in politics, and more closely linked with the
personal fortunes of the two Tudor kings. He had
shared the exile of Henry of Richmond; the treaty of
Étaples, the Intercursus Magnus, the marriage of Henry's
elder daughter to James IV, and the betrothal of his
younger to Charles, were largely the work of his hands.
Malicious gossip described him as willing to consent to
his own father's death to serve the turn of his king, and
a better founded belief ascribed to his wit the invention of
" Morton's fork ".[2] He was Chancellor of Cambridge in
1500, as Warham was of Oxford, but won more enduring
fame by founding the college of Corpus Christi in the
university over which the Archbishop presided. He had
baptised Henry VIII and advocated his marriage to
Catherine; and to him the King extended the largest
share in his confidence. Badoer, the Venetian ambassador,
called him " alter rex,"[3] and Carroz, the Spaniard, said

---

[1] *L. and P.* i. 811, 2082 ; ii. 114.
[2] *D.N.B.* xx. 152.   [3] *Ven. Cal.* ii. 63.

Henry trusted him most ; but Henry was not blind to
the failings of his most intimate councillors, and he warned
Carroz that the Bishop of Winchester was, as his name
implied, a fox indeed.[1] A third prelate, Ruthal of
Durham, divided with Fox the chief business of State ;
and these clerical advisers were supposed to be eager to
guide Henry's footsteps in the paths of peace, and
counteract the more adventurous tendencies of their lay
colleagues.

At the head of the latter stood Thomas Howard, Earl
of Surrey, soon to be rewarded for his victory at Flodden
by his restoration to the dukedom of Norfolk. He and
his son, the third duke, were Lord High Treasurers
throughout Henry's reign ; but jealousy of their past,
Tudor distrust of their rank, or personal limitations, impaired the authority that would otherwise have attached
to their official position ; and Henry never trusted them
as he did ministers whom he himself had raised from the
dust. Surrey had served under Edward IV and Richard
III ; he had fought against Henry at Bosworth, been
attainted and sent to the Tower. Reflecting that it was
better to be a Tudor official at Court than a baronial
magnate in prison, he submitted to the King and was
set up as a beacon to draw his peers from their feudal
ways. The rest of the council were men of little distinction. Shrewsbury, the Lord High Steward, was a pale
reflex of Surrey, and illustrious in nought but descent.
Charles Somerset, Lord Herbert, who was Chamberlain
and afterwards Earl of Worcester, was a Beaufort bastard,[2]
and may have derived some little influence from his
harmless kinship with Henry VIII. Lovell, the Treasurer,
Poynings, the Controller of the Household, and Harry
Marney, Chancellor of the Duchy of Lancaster, were
tried and trusty officials. Bishop Fisher was great as a
Churchman, a scholar, a patron of learning, but not
as a man of affairs ; while Buckingham, the only duke in
England, and his brother, the Earl of Wiltshire, were

[1] *Sp. Cal.* ii. 44.
[2] He is a link in the hereditary chain which began with Beauforts,
Dukes of Somerset and ended in Somersets, Dukes of Beaufort.

rigidly excluded by dynastic jealousy from all share in
political authority.

The most persistent of Henry's advisers was none of
his council. He was Ferdinand, the Catholic King of
Aragon ; and to his inspiration has been ascribed [1] the
course of foreign policy during the first five years of his
son-in-law's reign. He worked through his daughter ;
the only thing she valued in life, wrote Catherine a month
after her marriage, was her father's confidence. When
Membrilla was recalled because he failed to satisfy
Catherine's somewhat exacting temper, she was herself
formally commissioned to act in his place as Ferdinand's
ambassador at Henry's Court ; Henry was begged to
give her implicit credence and communicate with Spain
through her mediation ! " These kingdoms of *your* highness," she wrote to her father, " are in great tranquility." [2]
Well might Ferdinand congratulate himself on the result
of her marriage, and the addition of fresh, to his already
extensive, domains. He needed them all to ensure the
success of his far-reaching schemes. His eldest grandson,
Charles, was heir not only to Castile and Aragon, Naples
and the Indies, which were to come to him from his
mother, Ferdinand's imbecile daughter, Juaña, but to
Burgundy and Austria, the lands of his father, Philip,
and of Philip's father, the Emperor Maximilian. This
did not satisfy Ferdinand's grasping ambition ; he sought
to carve out for his second grandson, named after himself,
a kingdom in Northern Italy.[3] On the Duchy of Milan,

[1] By Bergenroth in his prefaces to the *Calendar of Spanish State Papers.*
He greatly exaggerates Ferdinand's influence.

[2] *Sp. Cal.* ii. 12, 21 ; *L. and P.* i. 368.

[3] *Ibid.* ii. 153, 159. The following predigree may be useful for
reference :—

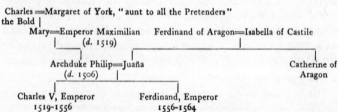

```
Charles ══Margaret of York, " aunt to all the Pretenders "
the Bold |
       Mary══Emperor Maximilian    Ferdinand of Aragon══Isabella of Castile
        |____(d. 1519)                        |
        |                          |                              |
     Archduke Philip══Juaña                               Catherine of
        (d. 1506)  |                                        Aragon
        |                          |
  Charles V, Emperor        Ferdinand, Emperor
   1519-1556                  1556-1564
```

the republics of Venice, Genoa and Florence, his greedy
eyes were fixed. Once conquered, they would bar the
path of France to Naples ; compensated by these possessions, the younger Ferdinand might resign his share
in the Austrian inheritance to Charles ; while Charles
himself was to marry the only daughter of the King of
Hungary, add that to his other dominions, and revive
the empire of Charlemagne. Partly with these objects
in view, partly to draw off the scent from his own track,
Ferdinand had, in 1508, raised the hue and cry after
Venice. Pope and Emperor, France and Spain, joined
in the chase, but of all the parties to the league of
Cambrai, Louis XII was in a position to profit the most.
His victory over Venice at Agnadello (14th May, 1509),
secured him Milan and Venetian territory as far as the
Mincio ; it also dimmed the prospects of Ferdinand's
Italian scheme and threatened his hold on Naples ; but
the Spanish King was restrained from open opposition
to France by the fact that Louis was still mediating
between him and Maximilian on their claims to the
administration of Castile, the realm of their daughter and
daughter-in-law, Juaña.

Such was the situation with which Henry VIII and
his council were required to deal. The young King
entered the arena of Europe, a child of generous impulse
in a throng of hoary intriguers—Ferdinand, Maximilian,
Louis XII, Julius II—each of whom was nearly three
times his age. He was shocked to see them leagued to
spoil a petty republic, a republic, too, which had been for
ages the bulwark of Christendom against the Turk and
from time immemorial the ally of England. Venice had
played no small part in the revival of letters which
appealed so strongly to Henry's intellectual sympathies.
Scholars and physicians from Venice, or from equally
threatened Italian republics, frequented his Court and
Cabinet. Venetian merchants developed the commerce
of London ; Venetian galleys called twice a year at
Southampton on their way to and from Flanders and
their trade was a source of profit to both nations. Inevitably Henry's sympathies went out to the sore-pressed

republic. They were none the less strong because the chief of the spoilers was France, for Henry and his people were imbued with an inborn antipathy to everything French.[1] Before he came to the throne he was reported to be France's enemy; and speculations were rife as to the chances of his invading it and imitating the exploits of his ancestor Henry V. It needed no persuasion from Ferdinand to induce him to intervene in favour of Venice. Within a few weeks of his accession he refused to publish the papal bull which cast the halo of crusaders over the bandits of Cambrai. The day after his coronation he deplored to Badoer Louis' victory at Agnadello, and a week later he wrote to the sovereigns of Europe urging the injustice of their Venetian crusade. In September he sent Bainbridge, Cardinal-Archbishop of York, to reside at the Papal Court, and watch over the interests of Venice as well as of England. " Italy," wrote Badoer, " was entirely rescued from the barbarians by the movements of the English King; and, but for that, Ferdinand would have done nothing."[2] Henry vainly endeavoured to persuade Maximilian, the Venetian's lifelong foe, to accept arbitration; but he succeeded in inducing the Doge to make his peace with the Pope, and Julius to remove his ecclesiastical censures. To Ferdinand he declared that Venice must be preserved as a wall against the Turk, and he hinted that Ferdinand's own dominions in Italy would, if Venice were destroyed, " be unable to resist the ambitious designs of certain Christian princes."[3] The danger was as patent to Julius and Ferdinand as it was to Henry; and as soon as Ferdinand had induced Louis to give a favourable verdict in his suit with the Emperor, the Catholic King was ready to join Henry and the Pope in a league of defence.

But, in spite of Venetian, Spanish and papal instigations to " recover his noble inheritance in France," in spite of his own indignation at the treatment of Venice, and the orders issued in the first year of his reign to his

[1] *Ven. Cal.* i. 941, 942, 945; ii. 1.
[2] *L. and P.* i. 922, 932, 3333; *Ven. Cal.* ii. 5, 7, 9, 19-22, 28, 32, 39, 40, 45, 51.   [3] *Sp. Cal.* ii. 23.

subjects to furnish themselves with weapons of war, for which the long peace had left them unprepared,[1] Henry, or the peace party in his council, was unwilling to resort to the arbitrament of arms. He renewed his father's treaties not only with other powers, but, much to the disgust of Ferdinand, Venice and the Pope, with Louis himself. His first martial exploit, apart from 1,500 archers whom he was bound by treaty to send to aid the Netherlands against the Duke of Guelders,[2] was an expedition for the destruction of the enemies of the faith.[3] Such an expedition, he once said, he owed to God for his peaceful accession ; at another time he declared [4] that he cherished, like an heirloom, the ardour against the infidel which he inherited from his father. He repressed that ardour, it must be added, with as much success as Henry VII ; and apart from this one youthful indiscretion, he did not suffer his ancestral zeal to escape into action. His generous illusions soon vanished before the sordid realities of European statecraft ; and the defence of Christendom became with him, as with others, a hollow pretence, a diplomatic fiction, the infinite varieties of which age could not wither nor custom stale. Did a monarch wish for peace ? Peace at once was imperative to enable Christian princes to combine against the Turk. Did he desire war ? War became a disagreeable necessity to restrain the ambition of Christian princes who, " worse than the infidel," disturbed the peace of Christendom and opened a door for the enemies of the Church. Nor did the success of Henry's first crusade encourage him to persist in similar efforts. It sailed from Plymouth in May, 1511, to join in Ferdinand's attack on the Moors, but it had scarcely landed when bickerings broke out between the Christian allies, and Ferdinand informed the English commanders that he had made peace with the Infidel, to gird his loins for war with the Most Christian King.

In the midst of their preparation against infidels, so runs the preamble to the treaty in which Henry and

[1] *L. and P.* i. 679. [2] *Ven. Cal.* ii. 16 ; *L. and P.* i. 1740.
[3] *Ibid.* i. 1531. [4] *Ibid.* ii. 4688 ; *Ven. Cal.* ii. 178.

Ferdinand signified their adhesion to the Holy League, they heard that Louis was besieging the Pope in Bologna.[1] The thought of violent hands being laid on the Vicar of Christ stirred Henry to a depth of indignation which no injuries practised against a temporal power could rouse. His ingenuous deference to the Papacy was in singular contrast to the contempt with which it was treated by more experienced sovereigns, and they traded on the weight which Henry always attached to the words of the Pope. He had read Maximilian grave lectures on his conduct in countenancing the schismatic *conciliabulum* assembled by Louis at Pisa.[2] He wrote to Bainbridge at the Papal Court that he was ready to sacrifice goods, life and kingdom for the Pope and the Church ;[3] and to the Emperor that at the beginning of his reign he thought of nothing else than an expedition against the Infidel. But now he was called by the Pope and the danger of the Church in another direction ; and he proceeded to denounce the impiety and schism of the French and their atrocious deeds in Italy. He joined Ferdinand in requiring Louis to desist from his impious work. Louis turned a deaf ear to their demands ; and in November, 1511, they bound themselves to defend the Church against all aggression and make war upon the aggressor.

This reversal of the pacific policy which had marked the first two and a half years of Henry's reign was not exclusively due to the King's zeal for the Church. The clerical party of peace in his council was now divided by the appearance of an ecclesiastic who was far more remarkable than any of his colleagues, and to whose turbulence and energy the boldness of English policy must, henceforth, for many years be mainly ascribed. Thomas Wolsey had been appointed Henry's almoner at the beginning of his reign, but he exercised no apparent influence in public affairs. It was not till 1511 that he joined the council, though during the interval he must have been gradually building up his ascendancy over the

[1] *Sp. Cal.* ii. 59.　　　　　[2] *L. and P.* i. 1828.
[3] *Ven. Cal.* ii. 177.

King's mind. To Wolsey, restlessly ambitious for himself, for Henry, and England, was attributed the responsibility for the sudden adoption of a spirited foreign policy ; and it was in the preparations for the war of 1512 that his marvellous industry and grasp of detail first found full scope.

The main attack of the English and Spanish monarchs was to be on Guienne,[1] and in May, 1512, Henry went down to Southampton to speed the departing fleet.[2] It sailed from Cowes under Dorset's command on 3rd June, and a week later the army disembarked on the coast of Guipuscoa.[3] There it remained throughout the torrid summer, awaiting the Spanish King's forces to co-operate in the invasion of France. But Ferdinand was otherwise occupied. Navarre was not mentioned in the treaty with Henry, but Navarre was what Ferdinand had in his mind. It was then an independent kingdom, surrounded on three sides by Spanish territory, and an easy prey which would serve to unite all Spain beyond the Pyrenees under Ferdinand's rule. Under pretence of restoring Guienne to the English crown, Dorset's army had been enticed to Passages, and there it was used as a screen against the French, behind which Ferdinand calmly proceeded to conquer Navarre. It was, he said, impossible to march into France with Navarre unsubdued in his rear. Navarre was at peace, but it might join the French, and he invited Dorset to help in securing the prey. Dorset refused to exceed his commission, but the presence of his army at Passages was admitted by the Spaniards to be " quite providential,"[4] as it prevented the French from assisting Navarre. English indignation was loud and deep ; men and officers vowed that, but for Henry's displeasure, they would have called to account the perfidious King. Condemned to inactivity, the troops almost mutinied ; they found it impossible to live on their wages of sixpence a day (equivalent now to at least six shillings), drank Spanish wine as if it were English beer, and died of dysentery like flies in the autumn.

[1] L. and P. i. 1980 ; Sp. Cal. ii. 59 ; Ven. Cal. ii. 122.
[2] Ibid. ii. 159. [3] L. and P. i. 3243. [4] Ibid. i. 3352.

C

Discipline relaxed ; drill was neglected. Still Ferdinand tarried, and in October, seeing no hope of an attempt on Guienne that year, the army took matters into its own hands and embarked for England.[1]

Henry's first military enterprise had ended in disgrace and disaster. The repute of English soldiers, dimmed by long peace, was now further tarnished. Henry's own envoys complained of the army's insubordination, its impatience of the toils, and inexperience of the feats, of war ; and its ignominious return exposed him to the taunts of both friends and foes. He had been on the point of ordering it home, when it came of its own accord ; but the blow to his authority was not, on that account, less severe. His irritation was not likely to be soothed when he realised the extent to which he had been duped by his father-in-law. Ferdinand was loud in complaints and excuses.[2] September and October were, he said, the proper months for a campaign in Guienne, and he was marching to join the English army at the moment of its desertion. In reality, it had served his purpose to perfection. Its presence had diverted French levies from Italy, and enabled him, unmolested, to conquer Navarre. With that he was content. Why should he wish to see Henry in Guienne ? He was too shrewd to involve his own forces in that hopeless adventure, and the departure of the English furnished him with an excuse for entering into secret negotiations with Louis. His methods were eloquent of sixteenth-century diplomacy. He was, he ordered Carroz to tell Henry many months later,[3] when concealment was no longer possible or necessary, sending a holy friar to his daughter in England ; the friar's health did not permit of his going by sea ; so he went through France, and was taken prisoner. Hearing of his fame for piety, the French Queen desired his ghostly advice, and took the opportunity of the interview to persuade the friar to return to Spain

---

[1] *L. and P.* i. 3298, 3355 ; *Ven. Cal.* ii. 198, 205. The financial accounts for the expedition are in *L. and P.* i. 3762.

[2] *Sp. Cal.* ii. 68, 70, 72 ; cf. *L. and P.* i. 3350, 3356.

[3] *Sp. Cal.* ii. 89, 118 ; *L. and P.* i. 3839.

with proposals of peace. Ferdinand was suddenly convinced that death was at hand ; his confessor exhorted him to forgive and make peace with his enemies. This work of piety he could not in conscience neglect. So he agreed to a twelvemonth's truce, which secured Navarre. In spite of his conscience he would never have consented, had he not felt that the truce was really in Henry's interests   But what weighed with him most was, he said, the reformation of the Church. That should be Henry's first and noblest work ; he could render no greater service to God. No reformation was possible without peace, and so long as the Church was unreformed, wars among princes would never cease.

Such reasoning, he thought, would appeal to the pious and unsophisticated Henry. To other sovereigns he used arguments more suited to their experience of his diplomacy. He told Maximilian [1] that his main desire was to serve the Emperor's interests, to put a curb on the Italians, and to frustrate their design of driving himself, Louis and Maximilian across the Alps. But the most monumental falsehood he reserved for the Pope ; his ambassador at the Papal Court was to assure Julius that he had failed in his efforts to concert with Henry a joint invasion of France, that Henry was not in earnest over the war and that he had actually made a truce [2] with France. This had enabled Louis to pour fresh troops into Italy, and compelled him, Ferdinand, to consult his own interests and make peace ! Two days later he was complaining to Louis that Henry refused to join in the truce.[3] To punish Henry for his refusal he was willing to aid Louis against him, but he would prefer to settle the differences between the French and the English kings by a still more treacherous expedient. Julius was to be induced to give a written promise that, if the points at issue were submitted to his arbitration, he would pronounce no verdict till it had been secretly sanctioned by Ferdinand and Louis. This promise obtained, Louis was publicly to appeal to the Pope ; Henry's devotion to

[1] *L. and P.* ii. 96, 101.   [2] *Sp. Cal.* ii. 106.
[3] *Ibid.* ii. 107.

the Church would prevent his refusing the Supreme
Pontiff's mediation ; if he did, ecclesiastical censures
could be invoked against him.[1] Such was the plot
Ferdinand was hatching for the benefit of his daughter's
husband. The Catholic King had ever deceit in his heart
and the name of God on his lips. He was accused by a
rival of having cheated him twice ; the charge was
repeated to Ferdinand. "He lies," he broke out, "I
cheated him three times". He was faithful to one
principle only, self-aggrandisement by fair means or
foul. His favourite scheme was a kingdom in Northern
Italy ; but in the way of its realisation his own over-
reaching ambition placed an insuperable bar. Italy had
been excluded from his truce with France to leave him
free to pursue that design ;[2] but in July, 1512, the
Italians already suspected his motives, and a papal legate
declared that they no more wished to see Milan Spanish
than French.[3] In the following November, Spanish
troops in the pay and alliance of Venice drove the French
out of Brescia. By the terms of the Holy League, it
should have been restored to its owner, the Venetian
Republic. Ferdinand kept it himself ; it was to form the
nucleus of his North Italian dominion. Venice at once
took alarm and made a compact with France which kept
the Spaniards at bay until after Ferdinand's death.[4] The
friendship between Venice and France severed that between France and the Emperor ; and in 1513 the war
went on with a rearrangement of partners, Henry and
Maximilian on one side,[5] against France and Venice on the
other, with Ferdinand secretly trying to trick them all.

---

[1] *Sp. Cal.* ii. 104.   [2] *Ibid.* ii. 70.   [3] *L. and P.* i. 3325.
[4] *Ven. Cal.* ii. 208, 234, 254, 283, 298. Bergenroth, in his zeal for
Ferdinand, represents the Pope and not Ferdinand as being responsible
for driving Venice into the arms of France.
[5] *L. and P.* i. 3649, 3859-61. The league between Henry and Maximilian was concluded 5th April, 1513 ; Carroz ratified it on Ferdinand's
behalf on 25th April, though Ferdinand had already signed a truce with
France. A good instance of Ferdinand's duplicity may be found in *Sp.
Cal.* ii. 104, 207 ; in the former he is asking for the hand of Renée for his
grandson Ferdinand, in the latter he tells the Pope that the report that
he had made this request was pure invention.

For many months Henry knew not, or refused to credit, his father-in-law's perfidy. To outward appearance, the Spanish King was as eager as ever for the war in Guienne. He was urging Henry to levy 6,000 Germans to serve for that purpose in conjunction with Spanish forces ; and, in April, Carroz, in ignorance of his master's real intentions, signed on his behalf a treaty for the joint invasion of France.[1] This forced the Catholic King to reveal his hand. He refused his ratification ;[2] now he declared the conquest of Guienne to be a task of such magnitude that preparations must be complete before April, a date already past ; and he recommended Henry to come into the truce with Louis, the existence of which he had now to confess. Henry had not yet fathomed the depths ; he even appealed to Ferdinand's feelings and pathetically besought him, as a good father, not to forsake him entirely.[3] But in vain ; his father-in-law deserted him at his sorest hour of need. To make peace was out of the question. England's honour had suffered a stain that must at all costs be removed. No king with an atom of spirit would let the dawn of his reign be clouded by such an admission of failure. Wolsey was there to stiffen his temper in case of need ; with him it was almost a matter of life and death to retrieve the disaster. His credit was pledged in the war. In their moments of anger under the Spanish sun, the English commanders had loudly imputed to Wolsey the origin of the war and the cause of all the mischief.[4] Surrey, for whose banishment from Court the new favourite had expressed to Fox a wish, and other " great men " at home, repeated the charge.[5] Had Wolsey failed to bring honour with peace, his name would not have been numbered among the greatest of England's statesmen.

Henry's temper required no spur. Tudors never flinched in the face of danger, and nothing could have made Henry so resolved to go on as Ferdinand's desertion and advice to desist. He was prepared to avenge his army in person. There were to be no expeditions to

---

[1] *Sp. Cal.* ii. 101.   [2] *Ibid.* ii. 118, 122.   [3] *Ibid.* ii. 125.
[4] *L. and P.* i. 3356, 3451.   [5] *Ibid.* i. 3443.

distant shores; there was to be war in the Channel, where Englishmen were at home on the sea; and Calais was to be the base of an invasion of France over soil worn by the tramp of English troops. In March, 1513, Henry, to whom the navy was a weapon, a plaything, a passion, watched his fleet sail down the Thames; its further progress was told him in letters from its gallant admiral, Sir Edmund Howard, who had been strictly charged to inform the King of the minutest details in the behaviour of every one of the ships.[1] Never had such a display of naval force left the English shores; twenty-four ships ranging downwards from the 1,600 tons of the *Henry Imperial*, bore nearly 5,000 marines and 3,000 mariners.[2] The French dared not venture out, while Howard swept the Channel, and sought them in their ports. Brest was blockaded. A squadron of Mediterranean galleys coming to its relief anchored in the shallow water off Conquêt. Howard determined to cut them out; he grappled and boarded their admiral's galley. The grappling was cut away, his boat swept out in the tide, and Howard, left unsupported, was thrust overboard by the Frenchmen's pikes.[3] His death was regarded as a national disaster, but he had retrieved England's reputation for foolhardy valour.

Meanwhile, Henry's army was gathering at Calais.[4] On 30th June, at 7 p.m., the King himself landed. Before his departure, the unfortunate Edmund de la Pole, Earl of Suffolk, was brought to the block for an alleged correspondence with his brother in Louis' service, but really because rumours were rife of Louis' intention to proclaim the White Rose as King of England.[5] On 21st July, Henry left Calais to join his army, which had already

---

[1] *L. and P.* i. 3809, 3820.   [2] *Ibid.* i. 3977.

[3] *Ibid.* i. 4005; see also *The War of 1512-13* (Navy Records Society) where the documents are printed in full.

[4] *L. and P.* i. 3885, 3915. There are three detailed diaries of the campaign in *L. and P.*, two anonymous (Nos. 4253 and 4306), and the other (No. 4284) by John Taylor, afterwards Master of the Rolls, for whom see the present writer in *D.N.B.* lv. 429; the original of his diary is in *Cotton MS.*, Cleopatra, C. v. 64.

[5] *Ibid.* i. 4324, 4328-29.

advanced into French territory. Heavy rains impeded
its march and added to its discomfort. Henry, we are
told, did not put off his clothes, but rode round the camp
at three in the morning, cheering his men with the
remark, " Well, comrades, now that we have suffered in
the beginning, fortune promises us better things, God
willing ".[1] Near Ardres some German mercenaries, of
whom there were 8,000 with Henry's forces, pillaged the
church ; Henry promptly had three of them hanged.
On 1st August the army sat down before Thérouanne ;
on the 10th, the Emperor arrived to serve as a private
at a hundred crowns a day under the English banners.
Three days later a large French force arrived at Guinegate
to raise the siege ; a panic seized it, and the bloodless
rout that followed was named the Battle of Spurs.
Louis d'Orléans, Duc de Longueville, the famous
Chevalier Bayard, and others of the noblest blood in
France, were among the captives.[2] Ten days after this
defeat Thérouanne surrendered ; and on the 24th Henry
made his triumphal entry into the first town captured by
English arms since the days of Jeanne Darc. On the 26th
he removed to Guinegate, where he remained a week,
" according," says a curious document, " to the laws of
arms, for in case any man would bid battle for the
besieging and getting of any city or town, then the winner
(has) to give battle, and to abide the same certain days ".[3]
No challenge was forthcoming, and on 15th September
Henry besieged Tournay, then said to be the richest city
north of Paris. During the progress of the siege the Lady
Margaret of Savoy, the Regent of the Netherlands,
joined her father, the Emperor, and Henry, at Lille.
They discussed plans for renewing the war next year and
for the marriage of Charles and Mary. To please the
Lady Margaret and to exhibit his skill Henry played the
gitteron, the lute and the cornet, and danced and jousted
before her.[4] He " excelled every one as much in agility
in breaking spears as in nobleness of stature ". Within a

[1] Taylor's *Diary*.
[2] Besides the English accounts referred to, see *L. and P.* i. 4401.
[3] *L. and P.* i. 4431.   [4] *Ven. Cal.* ii. 328.

week Tournay fell ; on 13th October Henry commenced his return, and on the 21st he re-embarked at Calais.

Thérouanne, the Battle of Spurs, and Tournay were not the only, or the most striking, successes in this year of war. In July, Catherine, whom Henry had left as Regent in England, wrote that she was " horribly busy with making standards, banners, and badges "[1] for the army in the North ; for war with France had brought, as usual, the Scots upon the English backs. James IV, though Henry's brother-in-law, preferred to be the cat's paw of the King of France ; and in August the Scots forces poured over the Border under the command of James himself. England was prepared ; and on 9th September, " at Flodden hills," sang Skelton, " our bows and bills slew all the flower of their honour ". James IV was left a mutilated corpse upon the field of battle.[2] " He has paid," wrote Henry, " a heavier penalty for his perfidy than we would have wished." There was some justice in the charge. James was bound by treaty not to go to war with England ; he had not even waited for the Pope's answer to his request for absolution from his oath ; and his challenge to Henry, when he was in France and could not meet it, was not a knightly deed. Henry wrote to Leo for permission to bury the excommunicated Scottish King with royal honours in St. Paul's.[3] The permission was granted, but the interment did not take place. In Italy, Louis fared no better ; at Novara, on 6th June, the Swiss infantry broke in pieces the grand army of France, drove the fragments across the Alps, and restored the Duchy of Milan to the native house of Sforza.

The results of the campaign of 1513 were a striking vindication of the refusal of Henry VIII and Wolsey to rest under the stigma of their Spanish expedition of 1512. English prestige was not only restored, but raised higher than it had stood since the death of Henry V, whose " name," said Pasqualigo, a Venetian in London, " Henry

---

[1] L. and P. i. 4398 ; Ellis, Original Letters, 1st ser. i. 83.
[2] L. and P. i. 4439, 4441, 4461 ; cf. popular ballads in Weber's Flodden Field, and La Rotta de Scocese (Bannatyne Club).
[3] Ven. Cal. ii. 909 ; Sp. Cal. i. 137 ; L. and P. i. 4502, 4582.

VIII would now renew ". He styled him " our great King ".[1] Peter Martyr, a resident at Ferdinand's Court, declared that the Spanish King was " afraid of the overgrowing power of England ".[2] Another Venetian in London reported that " were Henry ambitious of dominion like others, he would soon give law to the world ". But, he added, " he is good and has a good council. His quarrel was a just one, he marched to free the Church, to obtain his own, and to liberate Italy from the French."[3] The pomp and parade of Henry's wars have, indeed, somewhat obscured the fundamentally pacific character of his reign. The correspondence of the time bears constant witness to the peaceful tendencies of Henry and his council. " I content myself," he once said to Giustinian, " with my own, I only wish to command my own subjects ; but, on the other hand, I do not choose that any one shall have it in his power to command me."[4] On another occasion he said : " We want all potentates to content themselves with their own territories ; we are content with this island of ours " ; and Giustinian, after four years' residence at Henry's Court, gave it as his deliberate opinion to his Government, that Henry did not covet his neighbours' goods, was satisfied with his own dominions, and " extremely desirous of peace ".[5] Ferdinand said, in 1513, that his pensions from France and a free hand in Scotland were all that Henry really desired ;[6] and Carroz, his ambassador, reported that Henry's councillors did not like to be at war with any one.[7] Peace, they told Badoer, suited England better than war.[8]

But Henry's actions proclaimed louder than the words of himself or of others that he believed peace to be the first of English interests. He waged no wars on the continent except against France ; and though he reigned thirty-eight years, his hostilities with France were

[1] *Ven. Cal.* ii. 340. [2] *L. and P.* i. 4864.
[3] *Ven. Cal.* ii. 362. [4] *L. and P.* ii. 1991.
[5] *Ven. Cal.* ii. 1287 ; Giustinian, *Desp.* App. ii. 309.
[6] *Sp. Cal.* ii. 142. [7] *Ibid.* ii. 201.
[8] *Ven. Cal.* ii. 298 ; cf. *L. and P.* i. 3081.

compressed into as many months. The campaigns of
1512-13, Surrey's and Suffolk's inroads of 1522 and 1523,
and Henry's invasion of 1544, represent the sum of his
military operations outside Great Britain and Ireland.
He acquired Tournay in 1513 and Boulogne in 1544, but
the one was restored in five years for an indemnity, and
the other was to be given back in eight for a similar consideration. These facts are in curious contrast with the
high-sounding schemes of recovering the crown of France,
which others were always suggesting to Henry, and which
he, for merely conventional reasons, was in the habit of
enunciating before going to war ; and in view of the
tenacity which Henry exhibited in other respects, and the
readiness with which he relinquished his regal pretensions
to France, it is difficult to believe that they were any real
expression of settled policy. They were, indeed, impossible of achievement, and Henry saw the fact clearly
enough.[1] Modern phenomena such as huge armies
sweeping over Europe, and capitals from Berlin to Mos-
cow, Paris to Madrid, falling before them, were quite
beyond military science of the sixteenth century. Armies
fought, as a rule, only in the five summer months ; it was
difficult enough to victual them for even that time ; and
lack of commissariat or transport crippled all the
invasions of Scotland. Hertford sacked Edinburgh, but
he went by sea. No other capital except Rome saw an invading army. Neither Henry nor Maximilian, Ferdinand
nor Charles, ever penetrated more than a few miles into
France, and French armies got no further into Spain, the
Netherlands, or Germany. Machiavelli points out that
the chief safeguard of France against the Spaniards was
that the latter could not victual their army sufficiently to
pass the Pyrenees.[2] If in Italy it was different, it was
because Italy herself invited the invaders, and was mainly
under foreign dominion. Henry knew that with the
means at his disposal he could never conquer France ; his

[1] In 1520 he described his title " King of France " as a title given him
by others which was " good for nothing " (*Ven. Cal.* iii. 45). Its value
consisted in the pensions he received as a sort of commutation.

[2] Machiavelli, *Opera* iv. 139.

claims to the crown were transparent conventions, and he
was always ready for peace in return for the *status quo* and
a money indemnity, with a town or so for security.

The fact that he had only achieved a small part of the
conquest he professed to set out to accomplish was, therefore, no bar to negotiations for peace. There were many
reasons for ending the war ; the rapid diminution of his
father's treasures ; the accession to the papal throne of
the pacific Leo in place of the warlike Julius ; the absolution of Louis as a reward for renouncing the council
of Pisa ; the interruption of the trade with Venice ; the
attention required by Scotland now that her king was
Henry's infant nephew ; and lastly, his betrayal first by
Ferdinand and now by the Emperor. In October, 1513,
at Lille, a treaty had been drawn up binding Henry,
Maximilian and Ferdinand to a combined invasion of
France before the following June.[1] On 6th December,
Ferdinand wrote to Henry to say he had signed the
treaty. He pointed out the sacrifices he was making in
so doing ; he was induced to make them by considering
that the war was to be waged in the interests of the Holy
Church, of Maximilian, Henry, and Catherine, and by
his wish and hope to live and die in friendship with the
Emperor and the King of England. He thought, however, that to make sure of the assistance of God, the
allies ought to bind themselves, if He gave them the
victory, to undertake a general war on the infidel.[2]
Ferdinand seems to have imagined that he could dupe
the Almighty as easily as he hoped to cheat his allies,
by a pledge which he never meant to fulfil. A fortnight
after this despatch he ordered Carroz not to ratify the
treaty he himself had already signed.[3] The reason was
not far to seek. He was deluding himself with the hope,
which Louis shrewdly encouraged, that the French King
would, after his recent reverses, fall in with the Spaniard's
Italian plans.[4] Louis might even, he thought, of his own
accord cede Milan and Genoa, which would annihilate the

[1] *Sp. Cal.* ii. 138, 143 ; *L. and P.* i. 4511, 4560.
[2] *Sp. Cal.* ii. 132.   [3] *Ibid.* ii. 159.
[4] *Ibid.* ii. 158, 163.

French King's influence in Italy, and greatly facilitate the attack on Venice.

That design had occupied him throughout the summer, before Louis had become so amenable ; then he was urging Maximilian that the Pope must be kept on their side and persuaded " not to forgive the great sins committed by the King of France " ; for if he removed his ecclesiastical censures, Ferdinand and Maximilian " would be deprived of a plausible excuse for confiscating the territories they intended to conquer ".[1] Providence was, as usual, to be bribed into assisting in the robbery of Venice by a promise to make war on the Turk. But now that Louis was prepared to give his daughter Renée in marriage to young Ferdinand and to endow the couple with Milan and Genoa and his claims on Naples, his sins might be forgiven. The two monarchs would not be justified in making war upon France in face of these offers. Venice remained a difficulty, for Louis was not likely to help to despoil his faithful ally ; but Ferdinand had a suggestion. They could all make peace publicly guaranteeing the Republic's possessions, but Maximilian and he could make a " mental reservation " enabling them to partition Venice, when France could no longer prevent it.[2]

So on 13th March, 1514, Ferdinand renewed his truce with France, and Maximilian joined it soon after.[3] The old excuses about the reformation of the Church, his death-bed desire to make peace with his enemies, could scarcely be used again ; so Ferdinand instructed his agent to say, if Henry asked for an explanation, that there was a secret conspiracy in Italy.[4] If he had said no more, it would have been literally true, for the conspiracy was his own ; but he went on to relate that the conspiracy was being hatched by the Italians to drive him and the Emperor out of the peninsula. The two were alike in their treachery ; both secretly entered the truce with France and broke their promise to Henry. Another

[1] *Sp. Cal.* ii. 131.   [2] *Ibid.* ii. 153.
[3] *Ibid.* ii. 164 ; *Ven. Cal.* ii. 389, 391, 401, 405.
[4] *Sp. Cal.* ii. 167.

engagement of longer standing was ruptured. Since 1508, Henry's sister Mary had been betrothed to Maximilian's grandson Charles. The marriage was to take place when Charles was fourteen ; the pledge had been renewed at Lille, and the nuptials fixed not later than 15th May, 1514.[1] Charles wrote to Mary signing himself *votre mari*, while Mary was styled Princess of Castile, carried about a bad portrait of Charles,[2] and diplomatically sighed for his presence ten times a day. But winter wore on and turned to spring ; no sign was forthcoming of Maximilian's intention to keep his grandson's engagement, and Charles was reported as having said that he wanted a wife and not a mother.[3] All Henry's inquiries were met by excuses ; the Ides of May came and went, but they brought no wedding between Mary and Charles.

Henry was learning by bitter experience. Not only was he left to face single-handed the might of Louis ; but Ferdinand and Maximilian had secretly bound themselves to make war on him, if he carried out the treaty to which they had all three publicly agreed. The man whom he said he loved as a natural father, and the titular sovereign of Christendom, had combined to cheat the boy-king who had come to the throne with youthful enthusiasms and natural, generous instincts. " Nor do I see," said Henry to Giustinian, " any faith in the world save in me, and therefore God Almighty, who knows this, prospers my affairs ".[4] This absorbing belief in himself and his righteousness led to strange aberrations in later years, but in 1514 it had some justification. " Je vous assure," wrote Margaret of Savoy to her father, the Emperor, " qu'en lui n'a nulle faintise." " At any rate," said Pasqualigo, " King Henry has done himself great honour, and kept faith single-handed ".[5] A more striking testimony was forthcoming a year or two later. When Charles succeeded Ferdinand, the Bishop of Badajos drew up for Cardinal Ximenes a report on the state of the Prince's affairs. In it he says : " The King of England

[1] *L. and P.* i. 4560.   [2] *Ibid.* i. 5203.
[3] *Ven. Cal.* ii. 295. Charles was fourteen, Mary eighteen years of age.
[4] *L. and P.* ii. 3163.   [5] *Ven. Cal.* ii. 406.

has been truer to his engagements towards the House of
Austria than any other prince. The marriage of the
Prince with the Princess Mary, it must be confessed, did
not take place, but it may be questioned whether it was
the fault of the King of England or of the Prince and his
advisers. However that may be, with the exception of
the marriage, the King of England has generally fulfilled
his obligations towards the Prince, and has behaved as a
trusty friend. An alliance with the English can be
trusted most of all."[1]

But the meekest and saintliest monarch could scarce
pass unscathed through the baptism of fraud practised
on Henry; and Henry was at no time saintly or meek.
Ferdinand, he complained, induced him to enter upon
the war, and urged the Pope to use his influence with
him for that purpose; he had been at great expense, had
assisted Maximilian, taken Tournay, and reduced France
to extremities; and now, when his enemy was at his feet,
Ferdinand talked of truce: he would never trust any one
again.[2] "Had the King of Spain," wrote a Venetian
attaché, "kept his promise to the King of England, the
latter would never have made peace with France; and
the promises of the Emperor were equally false, for he had
received many thousands of pounds from King Henry, on
condition that he was to be in person at Calais in the
month of May, with a considerable force in the King's
pay; but the Emperor pocketed the money and never
came. His failure was the cause of all that took place, for,
as King Henry was deceived in every direction, he
thought fit to take this other course."[3] He discovered
that he, too, could play at the game of making peace
behind the backs of his nominal friends; and when once
he had made up his mind, he played the game with vastly
more effect than Maximilian or Ferdinand. It was he
who had been really formidable to Louis, and Louis was
therefore prepared to pay him a higher price than to
either of the others. In February Henry had got wind of
his allies' practice with France. In the same month a

[1] *Sp. Cal.* ii. 246.   [2] *L. and P.* i. 4864.
[3] *Ven. Cal.* ii. 505.

nuncio started from Rome to mediate peace between Henry and Louis ;[1] but, before his arrival, informal advances had probably been made through the Duc de Longueville, a prisoner in England since the Battle of Spurs.[2] In January Louis' wife, Anne of Brittany, had died. Louis was fifty-two years old, worn out and decrepit ; but at least half a dozen brides were proposed for his hand. In March it was rumoured in Rome that he would choose Henry's sister Mary, the rejected of Charles.[3] But Henry waited till May had passed, and Maximilian had proclaimed to the world his breach of promise. Negotiations for the alliance and marriage with Louis then proceeded apace. Treaties for both were signed in August. Tournay remained in Henry's hands, Louis increased the pensions paid by France to England since the Treaty of Étaples, and both kings bound themselves to render mutual aid against their common foes.[4]

Maximilian and Ferdinand were left out in the cold. Louis not only broke off his negotiations with them, but prepared to regain Milan and discussed with Henry the revival of his father's schemes for the conquest of Castile. Henry was to claim part of that kingdom in right of his wife, the late Queen's daughter ; later on a still more shadowy title by descent was suggested. As early as 5th October, the Venetian Government wrote to its ambassador in France, " commending extremely the most sage proceeding of Louis in exhorting the King of England to attack Castile ".[5] Towards the end of the year it declared that Louis had wished to attack Spain, and sought to arrange details in an interview with Henry ; but the English King would not consent, delayed the interview, and refused the six thousand infantry required for the purpose.[6] But Henry had certainly urged Louis to reconquer Navarre,[7] and from the tenor of Louis' reply to Henry, late in November, it would be inferred that the

[1] *Ven. Cal.* ii. 372.   [2] *Ibid.* ii. 505 ; *L. and P.* i. 5173, 5278.
[3] *Ven. Cal.* ii. 383.
[4] *L. and P.* i. 5305 ; *Ven. Cal.* ii. 482, 483.
[5] *Ven. Cal.* ii. 495.   [6] *Ibid.* ii. 532, 542.
[7] *Sp. Cal.* ii. 192 ; *L. and P.* i. 5637.

proposed conquest of Castile also emanated from the
English King or his ministers. Louis professed not to
know the laws of succession in Spain, but he was willing
to join the attack, apart from the merits of the case on
which it was based. Whether the suggestion originated
in France or in England, whether Henry eventually
refused it or not, its serious discussion shows how far
Henry had travelled in his resentment at the double
dealing of Ferdinand. Carroz complained that he was
treated by the English " like a bull at whom every one
throws darts,"[1] and that Henry himself behaved in a most
offensive manner whenever Ferdinand's name was mentioned. " If," he added, " Ferdinand did not put a bridle
on this young colt," it would afterwards become impossible to control him. The young colt was, indeed,
already meditating a project, to attain which he, in later
years, took the bit in his teeth and broke loose from
control. He was not only betrayed into casting in
Catherine's teeth her father's ill faith, but threatening
her with divorce.[2]

Henry had struck back with a vengeance. His blow
shivered to fragments the airy castles which Maximilian
and Ferdinand were busy constructing. Their plans for
reviving the empire of Charlemagne, creating a new
kingdom in Italy, inducing Louis to cede Milan and
Genoa and assist in the conquest of Venice, disappeared
like empty dreams. The younger Ferdinand found no
provision in Italy ; he was compelled to retain his
Austrian inheritance, and thus to impair the power of
the future Charles V ; while the children's grandparents
were left sadly reflecting on means of defence against the
Kings of England and France. The blot on the triumph
was Henry's desertion of Sforza,[3] who, having gratefully
acknowledged that to Henry he owed his restoration of
Milan,[4] was now left to the uncovenanted mercies of

---

[1] Sp. Cal. ii. 201. A Venetian reports that the English were so enraged
that they would have killed Carroz had it not been for Henry (Ven. Cal.
ii. 248), and Carroz was actually placed in confinement.

[2] L. and P. i. 5718 ; Ven. Cal. ii. 464.

[3] L. and P. i. 5319.   [4] Ibid. i. 4499, 4921.

Louis. But neither the credit nor discredit is due mainly to Henry. He had learnt much, but his powers were not yet developed enough to make him a match for the craft and guile of his rivals. The consciousness of the fact made him rely more and more upon Wolsey, who could easily beat both Maximilian and Ferdinand at their own game. He was not more deceitful than they, but in grasp of detail, in boldness and assiduity, he was vastly superior. While Ferdinand hawked, and Maximilian hunted the chamois, Wolsey worked often for twelve hours together at the cares of the State. Possibly, too, his clerical profession and the cardinalate which he was soon to hold gave him an advantage which they did not possess ; for, whenever he wanted to obtain credence for a more than usually monstrous perversion of truth, he swore, " as became a cardinal and on the honour of the cardinalate ".[1] His services were richly rewarded ; besides livings, prebends, deaneries and the Chancellorship of Cambridge University, he received the Bishoprics of Lincoln and of Tournay, the Archbishopric of York, and finally, in 1515, Cardinalate. This dignity he had already, in May of the previous year, sent Polydore Vergil to claim from the Pope ; Vergil's mission was unknown to Henry, to whom the grant of the Cardinal's hat was to be represented as Leo's own idea.[2]

[1] Cf. *Ven. Cal.* ii. 695 ; *L. and P.* ii. 1380. Giustinian complains that Wolsey " never said what he meant but the reverse of what he intended to do " (*Ibid.* ii. 3081). This perhaps is no great crime in a diplomatist.

[2] *L. and P.* i. 5110, 5121. Henry's request that Leo should make Wolsey a Cardinal was not made till 12th Aug., 1514 (*L. and P.* i. 5318), at least six months after Wolsey had instructed Pace to negotiate for that honour.

CHAPTER IV

THE THREE RIVALS

THE edifice which Wolsey had so laboriously built up was, however, based on no surer foundation than the feeble life of a sickly monarch already tottering to his grave. In the midst of his preparations for the conquest of Milan and his negotiations for an attack upon Spain, Louis XII died on 1st January, 1515; and the stone which Wolsey had barely rolled up the hill came down with a rush. The bourgeois Louis was succeeded by the brilliant, ambitious and warlike Francis I, a monarch who concealed under the mask of chivalry and the culture of arts and letters a libertinism beside which the peccadilloes of Henry or Charles seem virtue itself; whose person was tall and whose features were described as handsome; but of whom an observer wrote with unwonted candour that he " looked like the Devil ".[1] The first result of the change was an episode of genuine romance. The old King's widow, " la reine blanche," was one of the most fascinating women of the Tudor epoch. " I think," said a Fleming, " never man saw a more beautiful creature, nor one having so much grace and sweetness ".[2] " He had never seen so beautiful a lady," repeated Maximilian's ambassador, " her deportment is exquisite, both in conversation and in dancing, and she is very lovely ".[3] " She is very beautiful," echoed the staid old Venetian, Pasqualigo, " and has not her match in England; she is tall, fair, of a light complexion with a colour, and most affable and graceful "; he was warranted, he said, in describing her as " a nymph from heaven ".[4] A more critical observer of feminine beauty thought her eyes and eyebrows too light,[5] but, as an Italian, he may have been biased in favour of

[1] *Ven. Cal.* ii. 582.
[2] *L. and P.* i. 4953
[3] *Ibid.* i. 5203.
[4] *Ven. Cal.* ii. 499, 500.
[5] *Ibid.* ii. 511.

brunettes, and even he wound up by calling Mary " a Paradise ". She was eighteen at the time ; her marriage with a dotard like Louis had shocked public opinion ;[1] and if, as was hinted, the gaieties in which his youthful bride involved him, hastened the French King's end, there was some poetic justice in the retribution. She had, as she reminded Henry herself, only consented to marry the " very aged and sickly " monarch on condition that, if she survived him, she should be allowed to choose her second husband herself. And she went on to declare, that " remembering the great virtue " in him, she had, as Henry himself was aware, " always been of good mind to my Lord of Suffolk ".[2]

She was probably fascinated less by Suffolk's virtue than by his bold and handsome bearing. A bluff Englishman after the King's own heart, he shared, as none else did, in Henry's love of the joust and tourney, in his skill with the lance and the sword ; he was the Hector of combat, on foot and on horse, to Henry's Achilles. His father, plain William Brandon, was Henry of Richmond's standard-bearer on Bosworth field ; and as such he had been singled out and killed in personal encounter by Richard III. His death gave his son a claim on the gratitude of Henry VII and Henry VIII ; and similarity of tastes secured him rapid promotion at the young King's Court. Created Viscount Lisle, he served in 1513 as marshal of Henry's army throughout his campaign in France. With the King there were said to be " two obstinate men who governed everything " ;[3] one was Wolsey, the other was Brandon. In July he was offering his hand to Margaret of Savoy, who was informed that Brandon was " a second king," and that it would be well to write him " a kind letter, for it is he who does and undoes ".[4] At Lille, in October, he continued his assault on Margaret as a relief from the siege of Tournay ; Henry favoured his suit, and when Margaret called Brandon a *larron* for stealing a ring from her finger, the King was called in to help Brandon out with his French. Possibly

---

[1] *L. and P.* i. 5470.
[2] *Ibid.* ii. 227.
[3] *Ibid.* i. 4386.
[4] *Ibid.* i. 4405.

it was to smooth the course of his wooing that Brandon, early in 1514, received an extraordinary advancement in rank. There was as yet only one duke in England, but now Brandon was made Duke of Suffolk, at the same time that the dukedom of Norfolk was restored to Surrey for his victory at Flodden. Even a dukedom could barely make the son of a simple esquire a match for an emperor's daughter, and the suit did not prosper. Political reasons may have interfered. Suffolk, too, is accused by the Venetian ambassador of having already had three wives.[1] This seems to be an exaggeration, but the intricacy of the Duke's marital relationships, and the facility with which he renounced them might well have served as a precedent to his master in later years.

In January, 1515, the Duke was sent to Paris to condole with Francis on Louis' death, to congratulate him on his own accession, and renew the league with England. Before he set out, Henry made him promise that he would not marry Mary until their return. But Suffolk was not the man to resist the tears of a beautiful woman in trouble, and he found Mary in sore distress. No sooner was Louis dead than his lascivious successor became, as Mary said, " importunate with her in divers matters not to her honour," in suits " the which," wrote Suffolk, " I and the Queen had rather be out of the world than abide ".[2] Every evening Francis forced his attentions upon the beautiful widow.[3] Nor was this the only trouble which threatened the lovers. There were reports that the French would not let Mary go, but marry her somewhere to serve their own political purposes.[4] Henry, too, might want to betroth her again to Charles ; Maximilian was urging this course, and telling Margaret that Mary must be recovered for Charles, even at the point of the sword.[5] Early in January, Wolsey had

---

[1] *Ven. Cal.* ii. 464. He had made contracts with three different ladies, but had not actually married them all. See below, p. 199 and *D.N.B.*, *s.v.* " Brandon ".

[2] *L. and P.* ii. 134, 138, 163.   [3] *Ven. Cal.* ii. 574.

[4] *L. and P.* ii. 70, 85, 114.

[5] *Ven. Cal.* ii. 594 ; *L. and P.* ii. 124.

written to her, warning her not to make any fresh promise of marriage. Two friars from England, sent apparently by Suffolk's secret enemies, told Mary the same tale, that if she returned to England she would never be suffered to marry the Duke, but made to take Charles for her husband, " than which," she declared, " I would rather be torn in pieces ".[1] Suffolk tried in vain to soothe her fears. She refused to listen, and brought him to his knees with the announcement that unless he would wed her there and then, she would continue to believe that he had come only to entice her back to England and force her into marriage with Charles. What was the poor Duke to do, between his promise to Henry and the pleading of Mary ? He did what every other man with a heart in his breast and warm blood in his veins would have done, he cast prudence to the winds and secretly married the woman he loved.

The news could not be long concealed, but unfortunately we have only Wolsey's account of how it was received by Henry. He took it, wrote the cardinal to Suffolk, " grievously and displeasantly," not only on account of the Duke's presumption, but of the breach of his promise to Henry.[2] " You are," he added, " in the greatest danger man was ever in ; " the council were calling for his ruin. To appease Henry and enable the King to satisfy his council, Suffolk must induce Francis to intervene in his favour, to pay Henry two hundred thousand crowns as Mary's dowry, and to restore the plate and jewels she had received ; the Duke himself was to return the fortune with which Henry had endowed his sister and pay twenty-four thousand pounds in yearly instalments for the expenses of her marriage. Francis proved unexpectedly willing ; perhaps his better nature was touched by the lovers' distress. He also saw that Mary's marriage with Suffolk prevented her being used as a link to bind Charles to Henry ; and he may have thought that a service to Suffolk would secure him a

[1] L. and P. ii. 80, Suffolk to Henry VIII. This letter is placed under January in the Calendar, but it was obviously written about 6th March, 1514-15. [2] L. and P. ii. 224.

powerful friend at the English Court, a calculation that was partly justified by the suspicion under which Suffolk henceforth laboured, of being too partial to Francis. Yet it was with heavy hearts that the couple left Paris in April and wended their way towards Calais. Henry had given no sign ; from Calais, Mary wrote to him saying she would go to a nunnery rather than marry against her desire.[1] Suffolk threw himself on the King's mercy ; all the council, he said, except Wolsey, were determined to put him to death.[2] Secretly, against his promise, and without Henry's consent, he had married the King's sister, an act the temerity of which no one has since ventured to rival. He saw the executioner's axe gleam before his eyes, and he trembled.

At Calais, Mary said she would stay until she heard from the King.[3] His message has not been preserved, but fears were never more strangely belied than when the pair crossed their Rubicon. So far from any attempt being made to separate them, their marriage was publicly solemnised before Henry and all his Court on 13th May, at Greenwich.[4] In spite of all that happened, wrote the Venetian ambassador, Henry retained his friendship for Suffolk ;[5] and a few months later he asserted, with some exaggeration, that the Duke's authority was scarcely less than the King's.[6] He and Mary were indeed required to return all the endowment, whether in money, plate, jewels or furniture, that she received on her marriage. But both she and the Duke had agreed to these terms before their offence.[7] They were not unreasonable. Henry's money had been laid out for political purposes which could no longer be served ; and Mary did not expect the splendour, as Duchess of Suffolk, which she had enjoyed as Queen of France. The only stipulation that looks like a punishment was the bond to repay the cost of

---

[1] L. and P. ii. 228.   [2] Ibid. ii. 367.
[3] Ibid. ii. 367, 226. The letters relating to this episode in L. and P. are often undated and sometimes misplaced ; e.g. this last is placed under March, although from Nos. 295, 296, 319, 327, 331, we find that Mary did not leave Paris till 16th April.
[4] Ibid. ii. 468.   [5] Ven. Cal. ii. 618.
[6] Ibid. 638.   [7] L. and P. ii. 436.

her journey to France ; though not only was this modified later on, but the Duke received numerous grants of land to help to defray the charge. They were indeed required to live in the country ; but the Duke still came up to joust as of old with Henry on great occasions, and Mary remained his favourite sister, to whose issue, in preference to that of Margaret, he left the crown by will. The vindictive suspicions which afterwards grew to rank luxuriance in Henry's mind were scarcely budding as yet ; his favour to Suffolk and affection for Mary were proof against the intrigues in his Court. The contrast was marked between the event and the terrors which Wolsey had painted ; and it is hard to believe that the Cardinal played an entirely disinterested part in the matter.[1] It was obviously his cue to exaggerate the King's anger, and to represent to the Duke that its mitigation was due to the Cardinal's influence ; and it is more than possible that Wolsey found in Suffolk's indiscretion the means of removing a dangerous rival. The " two obstinate men " who had ruled in Henry's camp were not likely to remain long united ; Wolsey could hardly approve of any " second king " but himself, especially a " second king " who had acquired a family bond with the first. The Venetian ambassador plainly hints that it was through Wolsey that Suffolk lost favour.[2] In the occasional notices of him during the next few years it is Wolsey, and not Henry, whom Suffolk is trying to appease, and we even find the Cardinal secretly warning the King against some designs of the Duke that probably existed only in his own imagination.[3]

This episode threw into the shade the main purpose of Suffolk's embassy to France. It was to renew the treaty concluded the year before, and apparently also the discussions for war upon Spain. Francis was ready enough to confirm the treaty, particularly as it left him free to pursue his designs on Milan. With a similar object he made terms with the Archduke Charles, who this year

[1] Brewer's view is that Wolsey saved Suffolk from ruin on this occasion
[2] *Ven. Cal.* ii. 919.   [3] *L. and P.* ii. 4507, 4308 ; iii. 1.

assumed the government of the Netherlands, but was completely under the control of Chièvres, a Frenchman by birth and sympathy, who signed his letters to Francis "your humble servant and vassal ".[1] Charles bound himself to marry Louis XII's daughter Renée, and to give his grandfather Ferdinand no aid unless he restored Navarre to Jean d'Albret. Thus safeguarded from attack on his rear, Francis set out for Milan. The Swiss had locked all the passes they thought practicable ; but the French generals, guided by chamois hunters and over-coming almost insuperable obstacles, transported their artillery over the Alps near Embrun ; and on 13th September, at Marignano, the great "Battle of the Giants" laid the whole of Northern Italy at the French King's feet. At Bologna he met Leo X, whose lifelong endeavour was to be found on both sides at once, or at least on the side of the bigger battalions ; the Pope recognised Francis's claim to Milan, while Francis undertook to support the Medici in Florence, and to countenance Leo's project for securing the Duchy of Urbino to his nephew Lorenzo.

Henry watched with ill-concealed jealousy his rival's victorious progress ; his envy was personal, as well as political. " Francis," wrote the Bishop of Worcester in describing the interview between the French King and the Pope at Bologna, " is tall in stature, broad-shouldered, oval and handsome in face, very slender in the legs and much inclined to corpulence ".[2] His appearance was the subject of critical inquiry by Henry himself. On May Day, 1515, Pasqualigo[3] was summoned to Greenwich by the King, whom he found dressed in green, " shoes and all," and mounted on a bay Frieslander sent him by the Marquis of Mantua ; his guard were also dressed in green and armed with bows and arrows for the usual May Day sports. They breakfasted in green bowers some distance from the palace. " His Majesty," con-tinues Pasqualigo, " came into our arbor, and addressing me in French, said : ' Talk with me awhile. The King

[1] Sp. Cal. ii. 246.   [2] L. and P. ii. 1281.
[3] Ibid. ii. 411 ; Giustinian, Desp. i. 90 ; Ven. Cal. ii. 624.

of France, is he as tall as I am ? ' I told him there was but little difference. He continued, ' Is he as stout ? ' I said he was not ; and he then inquired, ' What sort of legs has he ? ' I replied ' Spare '. Whereupon he opened the front of his doublet, and placing his hand on his thigh, said : ' Look here ; and I also have a good calf to my leg '. He then told me he was very fond of this King of France, and that on more than three occasions he was very near him with his army, but that he would never allow himself to be seen, and always retreated, which His Majesty attributed to deference for King Louis, who did not choose an engagement to take place." After dinner, by way of showing his prowess, Henry " armed himself *cap-à-pie* and ran thirty courses, capsizing his opponent, horse and all ". Two months later, he said to Giustinian : " I am aware that King Louis, although my brother-in-law, was a bad man. I know not what this youth may be ; he is, however, a Frenchman, nor can I say how far you should trust him ; "[1] and Giustinian says he at once perceived the great rivalry for glory between the two young kings.

Henry now complained that Francis had concealed his Italian enterprise from him, that he was ill-treating English subjects, and interfering with matters in Scotland. The last was his real and chief ground for resentment. Francis had no great belief that Henry would keep the peace, and resist the temptation to attack him, if a suitable opportunity were to arise. So he had sent the Duke of Albany to provide Henry with an absorbing disturbance in Scotland. Since the death of James IV at Flodden, English influence had, in Margaret's hands, been largely increased. Henry took upon himself to demand a voice in Scotland's internal affairs. He claimed the title of " Protector of Scotland " ; and wrote to the Pope asking him to appoint no Scottish bishops without his consent, and to reduce the Archbishopric of St. Andrews to its ancient dependence on York.[2] Many urged him to complete the conquest of Scotland, but this apparently he refused on the ground that his own sister was really

[1] *Ven. Cal.* ii. 652.   [2] *L. and P.* i. 4483, 4502 ; ii. 654.

its ruler and his own infant nephew its king. Margaret,
however, as an Englishwoman, was hated in Scotland,
and she destroyed much of her influence by marrying the
Earl of Angus. So the Scots clamoured for Albany, who
had long been resident at the French Court and was
heir to the Scottish throne, should James IV's issue fail.
His appearance was the utter discomfiture of the party
of England; Margaret was besieged in Stirling and
ultimately forced to give up her children to Albany's
keeping, and seek safety in flight to her brother's
dominions.[1]

Technically, Francis had not broken his treaty with
England, but he had scarcely acted the part of a friend;
and if Henry could retaliate without breaking the peace,
he would eagerly seize any opportunity that offered. The
alliance with Ferdinand and Maximilian was renewed,
and a new Holy League formed under Leo's auspices.
But Leo soon afterwards made his peace at Bologna with
France. Charles was under French influence, and Henry's
council and people were not prepared for war. So he
refused, says Giustinian, Ferdinand's invitations to join
in an invasion of France. He did so from no love of
Francis, and it was probably Wolsey's ingenuity which
suggested the not very scrupulous means of gratifying
Henry's wish for revenge. Maximilian was still pursuing
his endless quarrel with Venice; and the seizure of
Milan by the French and Venetian allies was a severe
blow to Maximilian himself, to the Swiss, and to their
protégé, Sforza. Wolsey now sought to animate them
all for an attempt to recover the duchy, and Sforza
promised him 10,000 ducats a year from the date of his
restoration. There was nothing but the spirit of his
treaty with France to prevent Henry spending his money
as he thought fit; and it was determined to hire 20,000
Swiss mercenaries to serve under the Emperor in order
to conquer Milan and revenge Marignano.[2] The negotia-
tion was one of great delicacy; not only was secrecy

---

[1] It was said by the Scots Estates that she had forfeited her claim to
their custody by her marriage with Angus (*L. and P.* ii. 1011).

[2] *Ibid.* ii. 1065.

absolutely essential, but the money must be carefully
kept out of Maximilian's reach. "Whenever," wrote
Pace, "the King's money passed where the Emperor
was, he would always get some portion of it by force
or false promises of restitution".[1] The accusation was
justified by Maximilian's order to Margaret, his daughter,
to seize Henry's treasure as soon as he heard it was on
the way to the Swiss.[2] "The Emperor," said Julius II,
" is light and inconstant, always begging for other men's
money, which he wastes in hunting the chamois ".[3]

The envoy selected for this difficult mission was
Richard Pace, scholar and author, and friend of Erasmus
and More. He had been in Bainbridge's service at Rome,
was then transferred to that of Wolsey and Henry, and,
as the King's secretary, was afterwards thought to be
treading too close on the Cardinal's heels. He set out
in October, and arrived in Zurich just in time to prevent
the Swiss from coming to terms with Francis. Before
winter had ended the plans for invasion were settled.
Maximilian came down with the snows from the moun-
tains in March ; on the 23rd he crossed the Adda ;[4] on
the 25th he was within nine miles of Milan, and almost in
sight of the army of France. On the 26th he turned and
fled without striking a blow. Back he went over the Adda,
over the Oglio, up into Tyrol, leaving the French and
Venetians in secure possession of Northern Italy. A year
later they had recovered for Venice the last of the places
of which it had been robbed by the League of Cambrai.

Maximilian retreated, said Pace, voluntarily and shame-
fully, and was now so degraded that it signified little
whether he was a friend or an enemy.[5] The cause of his
ignominious flight still remains a mystery ; countless
excuses were made by Maximilian and his friends. He
had heard that France and England had come to terms ;
6,000 of the Swiss infantry deserted to the French on
the eve of the battle. Ladislaus of Hungary had died,
leaving him guardian of his son, and he must go to

[1] L. and P. ii. 1817.   [2] Ibid. ii. 1231.   [3] Ibid. ii. 1877.
[4] Ibid. 1697, 1699, 1721, 1729, 1736, 1754, 1831, 2011, 2034, 2114.
[5] Ibid. ii. 1877.

arrange matters there. He had no money to pay his
troops. The last has an appearance of verisimilitude.
Money was at the bottom of all his difficulties, and drove
him to the most ignominious shifts. He had served as a
private in Henry's army for 100 crowns a day. His
councillors robbed him ; on one occasion he had not
money to pay for his dinner ;[1] on another he sent down
to Pace, who was ill in bed, and extorted a loan by force.
He had apparently seized 30,000 crowns of Henry's pay
for the Swiss ;[2] the Fuggers, Welzers and Frescobaldi,
were also accused of failing to keep their engagements,
and only the first month's pay had been received by the
Swiss when they reached Milan. On the Emperor's
retreat the wretched Pace was seized by the Swiss and
kept in prison as security for the remainder.[3] His task
had been rendered all the more difficult by the folly of
Wingfield, ambassador at Maximilian's Court, who, said
Pace, " took the Emperor for a god and believed that all
his deeds and thoughts proceeded *ex Spiritu Sancto* ".[4]
There was no love lost between them ; the lively Pace
nicknamed his colleague " Summer shall be green," in
allusion perhaps to Wingfield's unending platitudes, or to
his limitless belief in the Emperor's integrity and wisdom.[5]
Wingfield opened Pace's letters and discovered the gibe,
which he parried by avowing that he had never known
the time when summer was not green.[6] On another
occasion he forged Pace's signature, with a view of
obtaining funds for Maximilian ;[7] and he had the hardi-
hood to protest against Pace's appointment as Henry's
secretary. At last his conduct brought down a stinging
rebuke from Henry ;[8] but the King's longsuffering was
not yet exhausted, and Wingfield continued as ambassador
to the Emperor's Court.

The failure of the Milan expedition taught Wolsey and
Henry a bitter but salutary lesson. It was their first

[1] *L. and P.* ii. 2152, 1892, 1896, 2034, 2035.
[2] *Ibid.* ii. 1231, 1792, 1854.   [3] *Ibid.* ii. 1877.
[4] *Ibid.* ii. 1817.   [5] *Ibid.* ii. 1566, 1567.
[6] *Ibid.* ii. 1775.   [7] *Ibid.* ii. 1813.   [8] *Ibid.* ii 2177.

attempt to intervene in a sphere of action so distant from English shores and so remote from English interests as the affairs of Italian States. Complaints in England were loud against the waste of money ; the sagacious Tunstall wrote that he did not see why Henry should bind himself to maintain other men's causes.[1] All the grandees, wrote Giustinian, were opposed to Wolsey's policy, and its adoption was followed by what Giustinian called a change of ministry in England.[2] Warham relinquished the burdens of the Chancellorship which he had long un- willingly borne ; Fox sought to atone for twenty-eight years' neglect of his diocese by spending in it the rest of his days.[3] Wolsey succeeded Warham as Chancellor, and Ruthal, who " sang treble to Wolsey's bass,"[4] became Lord Privy Seal in place of Fox. Suffolk was out of favour, and the neglect of his and Fox's advice was, according to the Venetian, resented by the people, who murmured against the taxes which Wolsey's intervention in foreign affairs involved.

But Wolsey still hoped that bribes would keep Maxi- milian faithful to England and induce him to counteract the French influences with which his grandson Charles was surrounded. Ferdinand had died in January, 1516,[5] having, said the English envoy at his Court, wilfully shortened his life by hunting and hawking in all weathers, and following the advice of his falconers rather than that of his physicians. Charles thus succeeded to Castile, Ara- gon and Naples ;[6] but Naples was seriously threatened by the failure of Maximilian's expedition and the om- nipotence of Francis in Italy. " The Pope is French," wrote an English diplomatist, " and everything from

[1] *L. and P.* ii. 2270.

[2] *Ibid.* ii. 1814, 2487, 2500.

[3] *Ven. Cal.* ii. 750, 798, 801 ; *L. and P.* ii. 2183.

[4] *Ibid.* ii. 2205.

[5] On 23rd Jan. (*L. and P.* ii. 1541, 1610). Brewer in his introduction to vol. ii. of the *L. and P.* says " in February ".

[6] His mother Juaña was rightfully Queen, but she was regarded as mad ; she thought her husband, the Archduke Philip, might come to life again, and carried him about in a coffin with her wherever she went (*Ven. Cal.* ii. 564).

Rome to Calais."[1] To save Naples, Charles, in July,
1516, entered into the humiliating Treaty of Noyon with
France.[2] He bound himself to marry Francis's infant
daughter, Charlotte, to do justice to Jean d'Albret in the
matter of Navarre, and to surrender Naples, Navarre,
and Artois, if he failed to keep his engagement. Such a
treaty was not likely to stand ; but, for the time, it was
a great feather in Francis's cap, and a further step
towards the isolation of England. It was the work of
Charles's Gallicised ministry, and Maximilian professed
the utmost disgust at their doings. He was eager to
come down to the Netherlands with a view to breaking
the Treaty of Noyon and removing his grandson's
advisers, but of course he must have money from England
to pay his expenses. The money accordingly came from
the apparently bottomless English purse ;[3] and in January,
1517, the Emperor marched down to the Netherlands,
breathing, in his dispatches to Henry, threatenings and
slaughter against Charles's misleaders. His descent on
Flanders eclipsed his march on Milan. " Mon fils," he
said to Charles, " vous allez tromper les Français, et
moi, je vais tromper les Anglais."[4] So far from breaking
the Treaty of Noyon, he joined it himself, and at Brussels
solemnly swore to observe its provisions. He probably
thought he had touched the bottom of Henry's purse,
and that it was time to dip into Francis's. Seventy-five
thousand crowns was his price for betraying Henry.[5]

In conveying the news to Wolsey, Tunstall begged
him to urge Henry " to refrain from his first passions "
and " to draw his foot out of the affair as gently as if he
perceived it not, giving good words for good words which
they yet give us, thinking our heads to be so gross that
we perceive not their abuses ".[6] Their persistent advances
to Charles had, he thought, done them more harm than
good ; let the King shut his purse in time, and he would
soon have Charles and the Emperor again at his feet.[7]

---

[1] *L. and P.* ii. 2930.
[2] *Ibid.* ii. 2303, 2327, 2387 ; *Ven. Cal.* ii. 769, 773.
[3] *L. and P.* ii. 2406, 2573, 2626, 2702.   [4] *Ibid.* ii. 2930.
[5] *Ibid.* ii. 2891.   [6] *Ibid.* ii. 2923, 2940.   [7] *Ibid.* ii. 2910.

Tunstall was ably seconded by Dr. William Knight, who
thought it would be foolish for England to attempt to
undo the Treaty of Noyon; it contained within itself
the seeds of its own dissolution. Charles would not
wait to marry Francis's daughter, and then the breach
would come.[1] Henry and Wolsey had the good sense to
act on this sound advice. Maximilian, Francis and Charles
formed at Cambrai a fresh league for the partition of
Italy,[2] but they were soon at enmity and too much
involved with their own affairs to think of the conquest
of others. Disaffection was rife in Spain, where a party
wished Ferdinand, Charles's brother, to be King.[3] If
Charles was to retain his Spanish kingdoms, he must
visit them at once. He could not go unless England
provided the means. His request for a loan was graciously
accorded and his ambassadors were treated with magnificent courtesy.[4] " One day," says Chieregati,[5] the papal
envoy in England, " the King sent for these ambassadors,
and kept them to dine with him privately in his chamber
with the Queen, a very unusual proceeding. After dinner
he took to singing and playing on every musical instrument,
and exhibited a part of his very excellent endowments.
At length he commenced dancing," and, continues
another narrator, " doing marvellous things, both in
dancing and jumping, proving himself, as he is in truth,
indefatigable ". On another day there was " a most
stately joust ". Henry was magnificently attired in
" cloth of silver with a raised pile, and wrought throughout with emblematic letters ". When he had made the
usual display in the lists, the Duke of Suffolk entered
from the other end, with well-nigh equal array and pomp.
He was accompanied by fourteen other jousters. " The
King wanted to joust with all of them; but this was
forbidden by the council, which, moreover, decided that
each jouster was to run six courses and no more, so that

[1] L. and P. ii. 2930.
[2] Ibid. ii. 2632, 3008; Monumenta Habsburgica ii. 37.
[3] L. and P. ii. 3076, 3077, 3081.
[4] Ibid. ii. 3402, 3439-41.
[5] Ven. Cal. ii. 918; L. and P. ii. 3455, 3462.

the entertainment might be ended on that day. . . .
The competitor assigned to the King was the Duke of
Suffolk ; and they bore themselves so bravely that the
spectators fancied themselves witnessing a joust between
Hector and Achilles." "They tilted," says Sagudino,
" eight courses, both shivering their lances at every time,
to the great applause of the spectators." Chieregati
continues : " On arriving in the lists the King presented
himself before the Queen and the ladies, making a
thousand jumps in the air, and after tiring one horse, he
entered the tent and mounted another . . . doing this
constantly, and reappearing in the lists until the end of
the jousts ". Dinner was then served amid a scene of
unparalleled splendour, and Chieregati avers that the
" guests remained at table for seven hours by the clock ".
The display of costume on the King's part was equally
varied and gorgeous. On one occasion he wore " stiff
brocade in the Hungarian fashion," on another, he " was
dressed in white damask in the Turkish fashion, the above-
mentioned robe all embroidered with roses, made of
rubies and diamonds " ; on a third, he " wore royal robes
down to the ground, of gold brocade lined with ermine " ;
while " all the rest of the Court glittered with jewels and
gold and silver, the pomp being unprecedented ".

All this riot of wealth would no doubt impress the
impecunious Charles. In September he landed in Spain,
so destitute that he was glad to accept the offer of a hobby
from the English ambassador.[1] At the first meeting of
his Cortes, they demanded that he should marry at once,
and not wait for Francis's daughter ; the bride his
subjects desired was the daughter of the King of
Portugal.[2] They were no more willing to part with
Navarre ; and Charles was forced to make to Francis the
feeble excuse that he was not aware, when he was in the
Netherlands, of his true title to Navarre, but had learnt
it since his arrival in Spain ; he also declined the personal
interview to which Francis invited him.[3] A rupture
between Francis and Charles was only a question of time ;

[1] L. and P. ii. 3705. [2] Ibid. ii. 4022.
[3] Ibid. ii. 4164, 418.

and, to prepare for it, both were anxious for England's alliance. Throughout the autumn of 1517 and spring of 1518, France and England were feeling their way towards friendship. Albany had left Scotland, so that source of irritation was gone. Henry had now a daughter, Mary, and Francis a son. " I will unite them," said Wolsey ;[1] and in October, 1518, not only was a treaty of marriage and alliance signed between England and France, but a general peace for Europe. Leo X sent Campeggio with blessings of peace from the Vicar of Christ, though he was kept chafing at Calais for three months, till he could bring with him Leo's appointment of Wolsey as legate and the deposition of Wolsey's enemy, Hadrian, from the Bishopric of Bath and Wells.[2] The ceremonies exceeded in splendour even those of the year before. They included, says Giustinian, a " most sumptuous supper " at Wolsey's house, " the like of which, I fancy, was never given by Cleopatra or Caligula ; the whole banqueting hall being so decorated with huge vases of gold and silver, that I fancied myself in the tower of Chosroes,[3] when that monarch caused Divine honours to be paid him. After supper . . . twelve male and twelve female dancers made their appearance in the richest and most sumptuous array possible, being all dressed alike. . . . They were disguised in one suit of fine green satin, all over covered with cloth of gold, undertied together with laces of gold, and had masking hoods on their heads ; the ladies had tires made of braids of damask gold with long hairs of white gold. All these maskers danced at one time, and after they had danced they put off their visors, and then they were all known. . . . The two leaders were the King and the Queen Dowager of France, and all the others were lords and ladies."[4] These festivities were followed by the formal ratification of peace.[5] Approval of it was general, and the old councillors who had been alienated by Wolsey's Milan expedition,

---

[1] *L. and P.* ii. 4047.   [2] *Ibid.* ii. 4348.
[3] Chosroes I (Nushirvan) of Persia.
[4] *Ven. Cal.* ii. 1085, 1088 ; cf. Shakespeare, *Henry VIII.*
[5] *L. and P.* ii. 4468, 4483, 4564, 4669.

D

hastened to applaud. " It was the best deed," wrote Fox
to Wolsey, " that ever was done for England, and, next
to the King, the praise of it is due to you ".[1] Once more
the wheel had come round, and the stone of Sisyphus was
lodged more secure than before some way up the side of
the hill.

This general peace, which closed the wars begun ten
years before by the League of Cambrai, was not entirely
due to a universal desire to beat swords into ploughshares
or to even turn them against the Turk. That was
the everlasting pretence, but eighteen months before,
Maximilian had suffered a stroke of apoplexy ; men, said
Giustinian, commenting on the fact, did not usually
survive such strokes a year, and rivals were preparing to
enter the lists for the Empire. Maximilian himself,
faithful to the end to his guiding principle, found a last
inspiration in the idea of disposing of his succession for
ready money. He was writing to Charles that it was
useless to expect the Empire unless he would spend at
least as much as the French.[2] " It would be lamentable,"
he said, " if we should now lose all through some pitiful
omission or penurious neglect ; " and Francis was " going
about covertly and laying many baits,"[3] to attain the
imperial crown. To Henry himself Maximilian had more
than once offered the prize, and Pace had declared that
the offer was only another design for extracting Henry's
gold " for the electors would never allow the crown to
go out of their nation ".[4] The Emperor had first proposed
it while serving under Henry's banners in France.[5] He
renewed the suggestion in 1516, inviting Henry to meet
him at Coire. The brothers in arms were thence to cross
the Alps to Milan, where the Emperor would invest the
English King with the duchy ; he would then take him
on to Rome, resign the Empire himself, and have Henry
crowned. Not that Maximilian desired to forsake all
earthly authority ; he sought to combine a spiritual with

[1] L. and P. ii. 4540.   [2] Ibid. ii. 4172.
[3] Ibid. ii. 4159.   [4] Ibid. ii. 1923.
[5] Ibid. ii. 1398, 1878, 1902, 2218, 2911, 4257.

a temporal glory ; he was to lay down the imperial crown
and place on his brows the papal tiara.[1] Nothing was
too fantastic for the Emperor Maximilian ; the man who
could not wrest a few towns from Venice was always
deluding himself with the hope of leading victorious hosts
to the seat of the Turkish Empire and the Holy City of
Christendom ; the sovereign whose main incentive in
life was gold, informed his daughter that he intended to
get himself canonised, and that after his death she would
have to adore him. He died at Welz on 12th January,
1519, neither Pope nor saint, with Jerusalem still in the
hands of the Turk, and the succession to the Empire
still undecided.

The contest now broke out in earnest, and the electors
prepared to garner their harvest of gold. The price of
a vote was a hundredfold more than the most corrupt
parliamentary elector could conceive in his wildest dreams
of avarice. There were only seven electors and the prize
was the greatest on earth. Francis I said he was ready to
spend 3,000,000 crowns, and Charles could not afford to
lag far behind.[2] The Margrave of Brandenburg, "the
father of all greediness," as the Austrians called him, was
particularly influential because his brother, the Archbishop of Mainz, was also an elector and he required an
especially exorbitant bribe. He was ambitious as well
as covetous, and the rivals endeavoured to satisfy his
ambitions with matrimonial prizes. He was promised
Ferdinand's widow, Germaine de Foix ; Francis sought
to parry this blow by offering to the Margrave's son the
French Princess Renée ; Charles bid higher by offering
his sister Catherine.[3] Francis relied much on his personal
graces, the military renown he had won by the conquest
of Northern Italy, and the assistance of Leo. With the
Pope he concluded a fresh treaty that year for the

---

[1] Cf. W. Boehm, *Hat Kaiser Maximilian I im Jahre 1511 Papst werden
wollen?* 1873.

[2] For details of the sums promised to the various German princes see
L. and P. iii. 36, etc. ; it has been said that there was really little or no
bribery at this election.

[3] *Ven. Cal.* ii. 1165, 1187 ; *L. and P.* ii. 4159 ; iii. 130.

conquest of Ferrara, the extension of the papal States, and the settlement of Naples on Francis's second son, on condition that it was meanwhile to be administered by papal legates,[1] and that its king was to abstain from all interference in spiritual matters. Charles, on the other hand, owed his advantages to his position and not to his person. Cold, reserved and formal, he possessed none of the physical or intellectual graces of Francis I and Henry VIII. He excelled in no sport, was unpleasant in features and repellent in manners. No gleam of magnanimity or chivalry lightened his character, no deeds in war or statecraft yet sounded his fame. He was none the less heir of the Austrian House, which for generations had worn the imperial crown ; as such, too, he was a German prince, and the Germanic constitution forbade any other the sovereignty of the Holy Roman Empire. Against this was the fact that his enormous dominions, including Naples and Spain, would preclude his continued residence in Germany and might threaten the liberties of the German people.

But was there no third candidate ? Leo at heart regarded the election of either as an absolute evil.[2] He had always dreaded Maximilian's claims to the temporal power of the Church, though Maximilian held not a foot of Italian soil. How much more would he dread those claims in the hands of Francis or Charles ! One threatened the papal States from Milan, and the other from Naples. Of the two, he feared Francis the less ;[3] for the union of Naples with the Empire had been such a terror to the Popes, that before granting the investiture of that kingdom, they bound its king by oath not to compete for the Empire.[4] But a third candidate would offer an escape from between the upper and the nether millstone ; and Leo suggested at one time Charles's brother Ferdinand,[5] at another a German elector. Precisely the same recommendations had been secretly made by Henry VIII. In public he followed the course he commended

[1] *Sp. Cal.* ii. 267.   [2] *L. and P.* iii. 149.
[3] *Ven. Cal.* ii. 1227.   [4] *Ibid.* ii. 1246.
[5] *Ibid.* ii. 1163.

to Leo; he advocated the claims of both Charles and Francis, when asked so to do, but sent trusty envoys with his testimonials to explain that no credence was to be given them.[1] He told the French King that he favoured the election of Francis, and the Spanish King the election of Charles, but like Leo he desired in truth the election of neither. Why should he not come forward himself? His dominions were not so extensive that, when combined with the imperial dignity, they would threaten to dominate Europe; and his election might seem to provide a useful check in the balance of power. In March he had already told Francis that his claims were favoured by some of the electors, though he professed a wish to promote the French King's pretensions. In May, Pace was sent to Germany with secret instructions to endeavour to balance the parties and force the electors into a deadlock, from which the only escape would be the election of a third candidate, either Henry himself or some German prince. It is difficult to believe that Henry really thought his election possible or was seriously pushing his claim. He had repeatedly declined Maximilian's offers; he had been as often warned by trusty advisers that no non-German prince stood a chance of election; he had expressed his content with his own islands, which, Tunstall told him with truth, were an Empire worth more than the barren imperial crown.[2] Pace went far too late to secure a party for Henry, and, what was even more fatal, he went without the persuasive of money. Norfolk told Giustinian, after Pace's departure, that the election would fall on a German prince, and such, said the Venetian, was the universal belief and desire in England.[3] After the election, Leo expressed his " regret that Henry gave no attention to a project which would have made him a near, instead of a distant, neighbour of the papal States ". Under the circumstances, it seems more probable that the first alternative in Pace's instructions no more represented a settled design in Henry's mind than his often-professed intention of

[1] L. and P. iii. 137.　　　[2] Ibid. ii. 2911.
[3] Ven. Cal. ii. 1220.

conquering France, and that the real purport of his mission was to promote the election of the Duke of Saxony or another German prince.[1]

Whether that was its object or not the mission was foredoomed to failure. The conclusion was never really in doubt. Electors might trouble the waters in order to fish with more success. They might pretend to Francis that if he was free with his money he might be elected, and to Charles that unless he was free with his money he would not, but no sufficient reason had been shown why they should violate national prejudices, the laws of the Empire, and prescriptive hereditary right, in order to place Henry or Francis instead of a German upon the imperial throne. Neither people nor princes nor barons, wrote Leo's envoys, would permit the election of the Most Christian King ;[2] and even if the electors wished to elect him, it was not in their power to do so. The whole of the nation, said Pace, was in arms and furious for Charles ; and had Henry been elected, they would in their indignation have killed Pace and all his servants.[3] The voice of the German people spoke in no uncertain tones ; they would have Charles and no other to be their ruler. Leo himself saw the futility of resistance, and making a virtue of necessity, he sent Charles an absolution from his oath as King of Naples. As soon as it arrived, the electors unanimously declared Charles their Emperor on 28th June.[4]

Thus was completed the shuffling of the cards for the struggle which lasted till Henry's death. Francis had now succeeded to Louis, Charles to both his grandfathers, and Henry at twenty-eight was the *doyen* of the princes of Europe. He was two years older than Francis and eight years older than Charles. Europe had passed under the rule of youthful triumvirs whose rivalry troubled its peace and guided its destinies for nearly thirty years. The youngest of all was the greatest in power. His dominions, it is true, were disjointed, and funds were often to seek, but these defects have been overrated. It

[1] *L. and P.* iii. 241.   [2] *Ven. Cal.* ii. 1227.
[3] *L. and P.* iii. 326.   [4] *Ibid.* iii. 339.

was neither of these which proved his greatest embarrassment. It was a cloud in Germany, as yet no bigger than a man's hand, but soon to darken the face of Europe. Ferdinand and Maximilian had at times been dangerous; Charles wielded the power of both. He ruled over Castile and Aragon, the Netherlands and Naples, Burgundy and Austria; he could command the finest military forces in Europe; the infantry of Spain, the science of Italy, the lance-knights of Germany, for which Ferdinand sighed, were at his disposal; and the wealth of the Indies was poured out at his feet. He bestrode the narrow world like a Colossus, and the only hope of lesser men lay in the maintenance of Francis's power. Were that to fail, Charles would become arbiter of Christendom, Italy a Spanish kingdom, and the Pope little more than the Emperor's chaplain. " Great masters," said Tunstall, with reference to a papal brief urged by Charles in excuse for his action in 1517, " could get great clerks to say what they liked ".[1] The mastery of Charles in 1517 was but the shadow of what it became ten years later; and if under its dominance the " great clerk " were called upon to decide between " the great master " and Henry, it was obvious already that all Henry's services to the Papacy would count for nothing.

For the present, those services were to be remembered. They were not, indeed, inconsiderable. It would be absurd to maintain that, since his accession, Henry had been actuated by respect for the Papacy more than by another motive; but it is indisputable that that motive had entered more largely into his conduct than into that of any other monarch. James IV and Louis had been excommunicated, Maximilian had obstinately countenanced a schismatic council and wished to arrogate to himself the Pope's temporal power. Ferdinand's zeal for his house had eaten him up and left little room for less selfish impulses; his anxiety for war with the Moor or the Turk was but a cloak; and the value of his frequent demands for a Reformation may be gauged by his opinion

[1] L. and P. ii. 3054.

that never was there more need for the Inquisition, and
by his anger with Leo for refusing the Inquisitors the
preferments he asked.[1] From hypocrisy like Ferdinand's
Henry was, in his early years, singularly free, and the
devotion to the Holy See, which he inherited, was of a
more than conventional type. " He is very religious,"
wrote Giustinian, " and hears three masses daily when
he hunts, and sometimes five on other days. He hears
the office every day in the Queen's chamber, that is to
say, vesper and compline."[2] The best theologians and
doctors in his kingdom were regularly required to preach
at his Court, when their fee for each sermon was equivalent
to ten or twelve pounds. He was generous in his alms-
giving, and his usual offering on Sundays and saints'
days was six shillings and eightpence or, in modern
currency, nearly four pounds ; often it was double that
amount, and there were special offerings besides, such as
the twenty shillings he sent every year to the shrine of
St. Thomas at Canterbury. In January, 1511, the gentlemen of the King's chapel were paid what would now be
seventy-five pounds for praying for the Queen's safe
delivery, and similar sums were no doubt paid on other
occasions.[3] In 1513, Catherine thought Henry's success
was all due to his zeal for religion,[4] and a year or two later
Erasmus wrote that Henry's Court was an example to all
Christendom for learning and piety.[5]

Piety went hand in hand with a filial respect for the
head of the Church. Not once in the ten years is there
to be found any expression from Henry of contempt for
the Pope, whether he was Julius II or Leo X. There
had been no occasion on which Pope and King had been
brought into conflict, and almost throughout they had
acted in perfect harmony. It was the siege of Julius by
Louis that drew Henry from his peaceful policy to intervene as the champion of the Papal See, and it was as

[1] *Sp. Cal.* ii. 80, 89, 167, 175.
[2] *Ven. Cal.* ii. 1287; Giustinian, *Desp.* ii. App. 309; *L. and P.* iii. 402.
[3] These details are from the King's " Book of Payments " calendared
at the end of *L. and P.* vol. ii.
[4] *L. and P.* i. 4417.   [5] *Ibid.* ii. 4115.

the executor of papal censures that he made war on
France.[1] If he had ulterior views on that kingdom, he
could plead the justification of a brief, drawn up if not
published, by Julius II, investing him with the French
crown.[2] A papal envoy came to urge peace in 1514,
and a Pope claimed first to have suggested the marriage
between Mary and Louis.[3] The Milan expedition of 1516
was made under cover of a new Holy League concluded
in the spring of the previous year, and the peace of 1518
was made with the full approval and blessings of Leo.
Henry's devotion had been often acknowledged in words,
and twice by tangible tokens of gratitude, in the gift of
the golden rose in 1510 and of the sword and cap in 1513.[4]
But did not his services merit some more signal mark of
favour ? If Ferdinand was " Catholic," and Louis " Most
Christian," might not some title be found for a genuine
friend ? And, as early as 1515, Henry was pressing the
Pope for " some title as protector of the Holy See ".[5]
Various names were suggested, " King Apostolic," " King
Orthodox," and others ; and in January, 1516, we find
the first mention of " Fidei Defensor ".[6] But the prize
was to be won by services more appropriate to the title
than even ten years' maintenance of the Pope's temporal
interests. His championship of the Holy See had been
the most unselfish part of Henry's policy since he came
to the throne ; and his whole conduct had been an
example, which others were slow to follow, and which
Henry himself was soon to neglect.

[1] *L. and P.* i. 3876, 4283.   [2] *Arch. R. Soc. Rom.* xix. 3, 4.
[3] *L. and P.* i. 5543.
[4] *Ven. Cal.* ii. 53-54, 361 ; *L. and P.* i. 976, 4621.
[5] *Ibid.* ii. 887, 967.   [6] *Ibid.* ii. 1456, 1928 ; iii. 1369.

CHAPTER V

KING AND CARDINAL

"Nothing," wrote Giustinian of Wolsey in 1519, "pleases him more than to be called the arbiter of Christendom ".[1] Continental statesmen were inclined to ridicule and resent the Cardinal's claim. But the title hardly exaggerates the part which the English minister was enabled to play during the next few years by the rivalry of Charles and Francis, and by the apparently even balance of their powers. The position which England held in the councils of Europe in 1519 was a marvellous advance upon that which it had occupied in 1509. The first ten years of Henry's reign had been a period of fluctuating, but continual, progress. The campaign of 1513 had vindicated England's military prowess, and had made it possible for Wolsey, at the peace of the following year, to place his country on a level with France and Spain and the Empire. Francis's conquest of Milan, and the haste with which Maximilian, Leo and Charles sought to make terms with the victor, caused a temporary isolation of England and a consequent decline in her influence. But the arrangements made between Charles and Francis contained, in themselves, as acute English diplomatists saw, the seeds of future disruption ; and, in 1518, Wolsey was able so to play off these mutual jealousies as to reassert England's position. He imposed a general peace, or rather a truce, which raised England even higher than the treaties of 1514 had done, and made her appear as the conservator of the peace of Europe. England had almost usurped the place of the Pope as mediator between rival Christian princes.[2]

[1] L. and P. iii. 125 ; Giustinian, Desp. ii. 256.
[2] L. and P. iii. 125. Men were shocked when the Pope was styled "comes" instead of "princeps confederationis" of 1518. "The chief author of these proceedings," says Giustinian, "is Wolsey, whose sole aim is to procure incense for his king and himself " (Desp. ii. 256).

These brilliant results were achieved with the aid of very moderate military forces and an only respectable navy. They were due partly to the lavish expenditure of Henry's treasures, partly to the extravagant faith of other princes in the extent of England's wealth, but mainly to the genius for diplomacy displayed by the great English Cardinal. Wolsey had now reached the zenith of his power ; and the growth of his sense of his own importance is graphically described by the Venetian ambassador. When Giustinian first arrived in England, Wolsey used to say, " His Majesty will do so and so ". Subsequently, by degrees, forgetting himself, he commenced saying, " We shall do so and so ". In 1519 he had reached such a pitch that he used to say, " I shall do so and so ".[1] Fox had been called by Badoer " a second King," but Wolsey was now " the King himself ".[2] " We have to deal," said Fox, " with the Cardinal, who is not Cardinal, but King ; and no one in the realm dares attempt aught in opposition to his interests ".[3] On another occasion Giustinian remarks : " This Cardinal is King, nor does His Majesty depart in the least from the opinion and counsel of his lordship ".[4] Sir Thomas More, in describing the negotiations for the peace of 1518, reports that only after Wolsey had concluded a point did he tell the council, " so that even the King hardly knows in what state matters are ".[5] A month or two later there was a curious dispute between the Earl of Worcester and West, Bishop of Ely, who were sent to convey the Treaty of London to Francis. Worcester, as a layman, was a partisan of the King, West of the Cardinal. Worcester insisted that their detailed letters should be addressed to Henry, and only general ones to Wolsey. West refused ; the important letters, he thought, should go to the Cardinal, the formal ones to the King ; and, eventually, identical despatches were sent to both.[6] In

---

[1] *Ven. Cal.* ii. 1287.   [2] *L. and P.* ii. 1380.
[3] *Ibid.* ii. 3558.   [4] Cf. *Ven. Cal.* ii. 671, 875, 894.
[5] *L. and P.* ii. 4438.
[6] *Ibid.* ii. 4664. On other occasions Wolsey took it upon himself to open letters addressed to the King (*Ibid.* iii. 2126).

negotiations with England, Giustinian told his Government, " if it were necessary to neglect either King or Cardinal, it would be better to pass over the King ; he would therefore make the proposal to both, but to the Cardinal first, *lest he should resent the precedence conceded to the King* ".[1] The popular charge against Wolsey, repeated by Shakespeare, of having written *Ego et rex meus*, though true in fact,[2] is false in intention, because no Latin scholar could put the words in any other order ; but the Cardinal's mental attitude is faithfully represented in the meaning which the familiar phrase was supposed to convey.

His arrogance does not rest merely on the testimony of personal enemies like the historian, Polydore Vergil, and the poet Skelton, or of chroniclers like Hall, who wrote when vilification of Wolsey pleased both king and people, but on the despatches of diplomatists with whom he had to deal, and on the reports of observers who narrowly watched his demeanour. " He is," wrote one, " the proudest prelate that ever breathed ".[3] During the festivities of the Emperor's visit to England, in 1520, Wolsey alone sat down to dinner with the royal party, while peers, like the Dukes of Suffolk and Buckingham, performed menial offices for the Cardinal, as well as for Emperor, King and Queen.[4] When he celebrated mass at the Field of Cloth of Gold, bishops invested him with his robes and put sandals on his feet, and " some of the chief noblemen in England " brought water to wash his hands.[5] A year later, at his meeting with Charles at Bruges, he treated the Emperor as an equal. He did not dismount from his mule, but merely doffed his cap, and embraced as a brother the temporal head of Christendom.[6] When, after a dispute with the Venetian ambassador, he wished to be friendly, he allowed Giustinian, with royal condescension, and as a special mark of

---

[1] *Ven. Cal.* ii. 1215.

[2] It will be found in *Ven. Cal.* iii. p. 43 ; Shakespeare, *Henry VIII* Act III. Sc. ii.

[3] *Ven. Cal.* iii. 56.   [4] *Ibid.* iii. 50.

[5] *Ibid.* vol. iii. p. 29.   [6] *Ibid.* iii. 298.

favour, to kiss his hand.[1] He never granted audience
either to English peers or foreign ambassadors until the
third or fourth time of asking.[2] In 1515 it was the
custom of ambassadors to dine with Wolsey before
presentation at Court, but four years later they were
never served until the viands had been removed from
the Cardinal's table.[3] A Venetian, describing Wolsey's
embassy to France in 1527, relates that his " attendants
served cap in hand, and, when bringing the dishes,
knelt before him in the act of presenting them. Those
who waited on the Most Christian King, kept their caps
on their heads, dispensing with such exaggerated ceremonies."[4]

Pretenders to royal honours seldom acquire the grace
of genuine royalty, and the Cardinal pursued with
vindictive ferocity those who offended his sensitive
dignity. In 1515, Polydore Vergil said, in writing to his
friend, Cardinal Hadrian, that Wolsey was so tyrannical
towards all men that his influence could not last, and that
all England abused him.[5] The letter was copied by
Wolsey's secretary, Vergil was sent to the Tower,[6] and
only released after many months at the repeated inter-
cession of Leo X. His correspondent, Cardinal Hadrian,
was visited with Wolsey's undying hatred. A pretext
for his ruin was found in his alleged complicity in a plot
to poison the Pope ; the charge was trivial, and Leo
forgave him.[7] Not so Wolsey, who procured Hadrian's
deprivation of the Bishopric of Bath and Wells, appropriated the see for himself, and in 1518 kept Campeggio,
the Pope's legate, chafing at Calais until he could bring
with him the papal confirmation of these measures.[8]
Venice had the temerity to intercede with Leo on
Hadrian's behalf ; Wolsey thereupon overwhelmed Giustinian with " rabid and insolent language " ; ordered him
not to put anything in his despatches without his consent ;

[1] L. and P. ii. 3733.   [2] Giustinian, Desp. App. ii. 309.
[3] Ibid.   [4] Ven. Cal. iii. p. 84.
[5] L. and P. ii. 215.   [6] Ibid. ii. 491, 865, 1229.
[7] Ibid. ii. 3581, 3584 ; Ven. Cal. ii. 902, 951.
[8] L. and P. ii. 4348.

and revoked the privileges of Venetian merchants in England.[1] In these outbursts of fury, he paid little respect to the sacrosanct character of ambassadors. He heard that the papal nuncio, Chieregati, was sending to France unfavourable reports of his conduct. The nuncio " was sent for by Wolsey, who took him into a private chamber, laid rude hands upon him, fiercely demanding what he had written to the King of France, and what intercourse he had held with Giustinian and his son, adding that he should not quit the spot until he had confessed everything, and, if fair means were not sufficient, he should be put upon the rack ".[2] Nine years later, Wolsey nearly precipitated war between England and the Emperor by a similar outburst against Charles's ambassador, De Praet. He intercepted De Praet's correspondence, and confined him to his house. It was a flagrant breach of international law. Tampering with diplomatic correspondence was usually considered a sufficient cause for war ; on this occasion war did not suit Charles's purpose, but it was no fault of Wolsey's that his fury at an alleged personal slight did not provoke hostilities with the most powerful prince in Christendom.[3]

Englishmen fared no better than others at Wolsey's hands. He used the coercive power of the State to revenge his private wrongs as well as to secure the peace of the realm. In July, 1517, Sir Robert Sheffield,[4] who had been Speaker in two Parliaments, was sent to the Tower for complaining of Wolsey, and to point the moral of Fox's assertion, that none durst do ought in opposition to the Cardinal's interests.[5] Again, the idea reflected by Shakespeare, that Wolsey was jealous of Pace, has been described as absurd ; but it is difficult to draw any other inference from the relations between them after 1521. While Wolsey was absent at Calais, he accused Pace, without ground, of misrepresenting his letters to Henry, and of obtaining Henry's favour on behalf of a canon of

[1] *Ven. Cal.* ii. 951, 953, 978 ; *L. and P.* ii. 3584.
[2] *L. and P.* ii. 2643.   [3] *Sp. Cal.* iii. pp. 50, 76, 78, 92.
[4] *L. and P.* ii. 3487.   [5] *Ibid.* ii. 3558.

York ;[1] he complained that foreign powers were trusting
to another influence than his over the King ; and, when
he returned, he took care that Pace should henceforth be
employed, not as secretary to Henry, but on almost
continuous missions to Italy. In 1525, when the Venetian
ambassador was to thank Henry for making a treaty
with Venice, which Pace had concluded, he was instructed
not to praise him so highly, if the Cardinal were present,
as if the oration were made to Henry alone ;[2] and, four
years later, Wolsey found an occasion for sending Pace
to the Tower—treatment which eventually caused Pace's
mind to become unhinged.[3]

Wolsey's pride in himself, and his jealousy of others,
were not more conspicuous than his thirst after riches.
His fees as Chancellor were reckoned by Giustinian at
five thousand ducats a year. He made thrice that sum
by New Year's presents, " which he receives like the
King ".[4] His demand for the Bishopric of Bath and
Wells, coupled with the fact that it was he who petitioned

---

[1] *L. and P.* iii. 1713. [2] *Ven. Cal.* iii. 975.

[3] Brewer (Henry VIII. ii. 388 ; *L. and P.* vol. iv. Introd. p. dxxxv. *n.*)
is very indignant at this allegation, and when recording Chapuys' statement in 1529 that Pace had been imprisoned for two years in the Tower
and elsewhere by Wolsey, declares that " Pace was never committed to
the Tower, nor kept in prison by Wolsey " but was " placed under the
charge of the Bishop of Bangor," and that Chapuys' statement is " an
instance how popular rumour exaggerates facts, or how Spanish ambassadors were likely to misrepresent them ". It is rather an instance of the
lengths to which Brewer's zeal for Wolsey carried him. He had not seen
the despatch from Mendoza recording Pace's committal to the Tower
on 25th Oct., 1527, " for speaking to the King in opposition to Wolsey
and the divorce " (*Sp. Cal.*, 1527-29, p. 440). It is true that Pace was in
the charge of the Bishop of Bangor, but he was not transferred thither
until 1528 (Ellis, *Orig. Letters*, 3rd ser. ii. 151) ; he was released immediately upon Wolsey's fall. Erasmus, thereupon, congratulating him on the
fact, remarked that he was consoled by Pace's experience for his own
persecution and that God rescued the innocent and cast down the proud
(*ibid.* iv. 6283). The *D.N.B.* (xliii. 24), has been misled by Brewer.
Wolsey had long had a grudge against Pace, and in 1514 was anxious to
make " a fearful example " of him (*L. and P.* i. 5465) ; and his treatment
of Pace was one of the charges brought against him in 1529 (*ibid.* iv.
p. 2552).

[4] Giustinian, *Desp.* App. ii. 309.

for Hadrian's deprivation, amazed even the Court
at Rome, and, "to avoid murmurs,"[1] compliance was
deferred for a time. But these scruples were allowed
no more than ecclesiastical law to stand in the way of
Wolsey's preferment. One of the small reforms decreed
by the Lateran Council was that no bishoprics should
be held *in commendam*; the ink was scarcely dry when
Wolsey asked *in commendam* for the see of the recently
conquered Tournay.[2] Tournay was restored to France
in 1518, but the Cardinal took care that he should not be
the loser. A *sine qua non* of the peace was that Francis
should pay him an annual pension of twelve thousand
livres as compensation for the loss of a bishopric of
which he had never obtained possession.[3] He drew
other pensions for political services, from both Francis
and Charles; and, from the Duke of Milan, he obtained
the promise of ten thousand ducats a year before Pace
set out to recover the duchy.[4] It is scarcely a matter
for wonder that foreign diplomatists, and Englishmen,
too, should have accused Wolsey of spending the King's
money for his own profit, and have thought that the
surest way of winning his favour was by means of a
bribe.[5] When England, in 1521, sided with Charles
against Francis, the Emperor bound himself to make
good to Wolsey all the sums he would lose by a breach
with France; and from that year onwards Charles paid
—or owed—Wolsey eighteen thousand livres a year.[6]
It was nine times the pensions considered sufficient for
the Dukes of Norfolk and Suffolk; and even so it does

---

[1] *Ven. Cal.* ii. 1045.   [2] *L. and P.* i. 5457.
[3] *Ibid.* ii. 4354.   [4] *Ibid.* ii. 1053, 1066.
[5] *Ibid.* ii. 1931; cf. Shakespeare, *Henry VIII*, Act I, Sc. i.:—

> Thus the Cardinal
> Does buy and sell his honour as he pleases
> And for his own advantage.

[6] *L. and P.* iii. 709, 2307 (where it is given as nine thousand " crowns
of the sun "); *Sp. Cal.* ii. 273, 600. In 1527 Charles instructed his
ambassador to offer Wolsey in addition to his pension of nine thousand
ducats with arrears a further pension of six thousand ducats and a
marquisate in Milan worth another twelve or fifteen thousand ducats a
year (*L. and P.* iv. 3464).

not include the revenue Wolsey derived from two Spanish bishoprics. These were not bribes in the sense that they affected Wolsey's policy; they were well enough known to the King; to spoil the Egyptians was considered fair game, and Henry was generous enough not to keep all the perquisites of peace or war for himself.

Two years after the agreement with Charles, Ruthal, Bishop of Durham, died, and Wolsey exchanged Bath and Wells for the richer see formerly held by his political ally and friend. But Winchester was richer even than Durham; so when Fox followed Ruthal to the grave, in 1528, Wolsey exchanged the northern for the southern see, and begged that Durham might go to his natural son, a youth of eighteen.[1] All these were held *in commendam* with the Archbishopric of York, but they did not satisfy Wolsey; and, in 1521, he obtained the grant of St. Albans, the greatest abbey in England. His palaces outshone in splendour those of Henry himself, and few monarchs have been able to display such wealth of plate as loaded the Cardinal's table. Wolsey is supposed to have conceived vast schemes of ecclesiastical reform, which time and opportunity failed him to effect.[2] If he had ever seriously set about the work, the first thing to be reformed would have been his own ecclesiastical practice. He personified in himself most of the clerical abuses of his age. Not merely an " unpreaching prelate ", he rarely said mass; his *commendams* and absenteeism were alike violations of canon law. Three of the bishoprics he held he never visited at all; York, which he had obtained fifteen years before, he did not visit till the year of his death, and then through no wish of his own. He was equally negligent of the vow of chastity; he cohabited with the daughter of " one Lark," a relative of the Lark who is mentioned in the correspondence of

---

[1] *L. and P.* iv. 4824.

[2] There is no doubt about his eagerness for the power which would have enabled him to carry out a reformation. As legate he demanded from the Pope authority to visit and reform the secular clergy as well as the monasteries; this was refused on the ground that it would have superseded the proper functions of the episcopate (*L. and P.* ii. 4399; ii. 149).

the time as "omnipotent" with the Cardinal, and as resident in his household.[1] By her he left two children, a son,[2] for whom he obtained a deanery, four arch-deaconries, five prebends, and a chancellorship, and sought the Bishopric of Durham, and a daughter who became a nun. The accusation brought against him by the Duke of Buckingham and others, of procuring objects for Henry's sensual appetite, is a scandal, to which no credence would have been attached but for Wolsey's own moral laxity, and the fact that the governor of Charles V performed a similar office.[3]

Repellent as was Wolsey's character in many respects, he was yet the greatest, as he was the last, of the ecclesiastical statesmen who have governed England. As a diplomatist, pure and simple, he has never been surpassed, and as an administrator he has had few equals. "He is," says Giustinian, "very handsome, learned, extremely eloquent, of vast ability and indefatigable. He alone transacts the same business as that which occupies all the magistracies, offices, and councils of Venice, both civil and criminal ; and all State affairs are managed by him, let their nature be what it may. He is thoughtful, and has the reputation of being extremely just ; he favours the people exceedingly, and especially the poor, hearing their suits and seeking to despatch them instantly. He also makes the lawyers plead gratis for all poor suitors. He is in very great repute, seven times more so than if he were Pope."[4] His sympathy with the poor was no idle sentiment, and his commission of 1517, and decree against enclosures in the following year, were the only steps taken in Henry's reign to mitigate that curse of the agricultural population.

The Evil May Day riots of 1517 alone disturbed the

[1] *L. and P.* ii. 629, 2637, 4068. Lark became prebendary of St. Stephen's (*ibid.* iv. *Introd.* p. xlvi.).

[2] Called Thomas Wynter, see the present writer's *Life of Cranmer* p. 324 *n.* Some writers have affected to doubt Wolsey's parentage of Wynter, but this son is often referred to in the correspondence of the time, e.g. *L. and P.* iv. p. 1407, Nos. 4824, 5581, 6026, 6075, Art. 27.

[3] *Ibid.* iii. 1284 ; iv. p. 2558 ; ii. 2930.

[4] *Ven. Cal.* ii. 1287 ; Giustinian, *Desp.* App. ii. 309 ; *L. and P.* iii. 402

peace of Wolsey's internal administration; and they were due merely to anti-foreign prejudice, and to the idea that strangers within the gates monopolised the commerce of England and diverted its profits to their own advantage. "Never," wrote Wolsey to a bishop at Rome in 1518, "was the kingdom in greater harmony and repose than now; such is the effect of my administration of justice and equity".[1] To Henry his strain was less arrogant. "And for your realm," he says, "our Lord be thanked, it was never in such peace nor tranquility; for all this summer I have had neither of riot, felony, nor forcible entry, but that your laws be in every place indifferently ministered without leaning of any manner. Albeit, there hath lately been a fray betwixt Pygot, your serjeant, and Sir Andrew Windsor's servants for the seisin of a ward, whereto they both pretend titles; in the which one man was slain. I trust the next term to learn them the law of the Star Chamber that they shall ware how from henceforth they shall redress their matter with their hands. They be both learned in the temporal law, and I doubt not good example shall ensue to see them learn the new law of the Star Chamber, which, God willing, they shall have indifferently administered to them, according to their deserts."[2]

Wolsey's "new law of the Star Chamber," his stern enforcement of the statutes against livery and maintenance, and his spasmodic attempt to redress the evils of enclosures,[3] probably contributed as much as his arrogance and ostentation to the ill-favour in which he stood with the nobility and landed gentry. From the beginning there were frequent rumours of plots to depose him, and his enemies abroad often talked of the universal hatred which he inspired in England. The classes which benefited by his justice complained bitterly of the impositions required to support his spirited foreign policy. Clerics

[1] *L. and P.* ii. 3973.
[2] *Ibid.* ii. App. No. 38; for the Star Chamber see Scofield, *Star Chamber*, 1902, and Leadam, *Select Cases* (Selden Soc., 1904).
[3] *L. and P.* App. No. 53; cf. Leadam, *Domesday of Enclosures* (Royal Hist. Soc.).

who regarded him as a bulwark on the one hand against heresy, and, on the other, against the extreme view which Henry held from the first of his authority over the Church, were alienated by the despotism Wolsey wielded by means of his legatine powers. Even the mild and aged Warham felt his lash, and was threatened with *Præmunire* for having wounded Wolsey's legatine authority by calling a council at Lambeth.[1] Peers, spiritual no less than temporal, regarded him as " the great tyrant ". Parliament he feared and distrusted ; he had urged the speedy dissolution of that of 1515 ; only one sat during the fourteen years of his supremacy, and with that the Cardinal quarrelled. He possessed no hold over the nation, but only over the King, in whom alone he put his trust.

For the time he seemed secure enough. No one could touch a hair of his head so long as he was shielded by Henry's power, and Henry seemed to have given over his royal authority to Wolsey's hands with a blind and undoubting confidence. " The King," said one, in 1515, " is a youngling, cares for nothing but girls and hunting, and wastes his father's patrimony ".[2] " He gambled," reported Giustinian in 1519, " with the French hostages, occasionally, it was said, to the amount of six or eight thousand ducats a day ".[3] In the following summer Henry rose daily at four or five in the morning and hunted till nine or ten at night ; " he spares," said Pace, " no pains to convert the sport of hunting into a martyrdom ".[4] " He devotes himself," wrote Chieregati, " to accomplishments and amusements day and night, is intent on nothing else, and leaves business to Wolsey, who rules everything ".[5] Wolsey, it was remarked by Leo X, made Henry go hither and thither, just as he liked,[6] and the King signed State papers without knowing their

---

[1] *L. and P.* iii. 77, 98 ; cf. ii. 3973 ; iii. 1142.

[2] *Ibid.* ii. 1105 ; cf. *ibid.* ii. 215.

[3] Giustinian, *Desp.* App. ii. 309.

[4] *L. and P.* iii. 950 ; cf. iii. 1160, where Fitzwilliam describes Henry as a " master " in deer-hunting.

[5] *Ven. Cal.* ii. 788.   [6] *Sp. Cal.* ii. 281.

contents. "Writing," admitted Henry, "is to me somewhat tedious and painful".[1] When Wolsey thought it
essential that autograph letters in Henry's hand should be
sent to other crowned heads, he composed the letters and
sent them to Henry to copy out.[2] Could the most
constitutional monarch have been more dutiful ? But
constitutional monarchy was not then invented, and it
is not surprising that Giustinian, in 1519, found it
impossible to say much for Henry as a statesman. *Agere
cum rege*, he said, *est nihil agere ;*[3] anything told to the
King was either useless or was communicated to Wolsey.
Bishop West was sure that Henry would not take the
pains to look at his and Worcester's despatches ; and
there was a widespread impression abroad and at home
that the English King was a negligible quantity in the
domestic and foreign affairs of his own kingdom.

For ten years Henry had reigned while first his council,
and then Wolsey, governed. Before another decade had
passed, Henry was King and Government in one ; and
nobody in the kingdom counted for much but the King.
He stepped at once into Wolsey's place, became his own
prime minister, and ruled with a vigour which was
assuredly not less than the Cardinal's. Such transforma-
tions are not the work of a moment, and Henry's would
have been impossible, had he in previous years been
so completely the slave of Vanity Fair, as most people
thought. In reality, there are indications that beneath
the superficial gaiety of his life, Henry was beginning to
use his own judgment, form his own conclusions, and
take an interest in serious matters. He was only twenty-
eight in 1519, and his character was following a normal
course of development.

From the earliest years of his reign Henry had at least
two serious preoccupations, the New Learning and his
navy. We learn from Erasmus that Henry's Court was
an example to Christendom for learning and piety ;[4] that
the King sought to promote learning among the clergy ;
and on one occasion defended " mental and *ex tempore*

---

[1] *L. and P.* iii. 1.   [2] *Ibid.* iii. 1453, 3377.
[3] *Ven. Cal.* ii. 1110.   [4] *L. and P.* ii. 4115.

prayer " against those who apparently thought laymen should, in their private devotions, confine themselves to formularies prescribed by the clergy.[1] In 1519 there were more men of learning at the English Court than at any university ;[2] it was more like a museum, says the great humanist, than a Court ;[3] and in the same year the King endeavoured to stop the outcry against Greek, raised by the reactionary " Trojans " at Oxford. " You would say," continues Erasmus, " that Henry was a universal genius. He has never neglected his studies ; and whenever he has leisure from his political occupations, he reads, or disputes—of which he is very fond—with remarkable courtesy and unruffled temper. He is more of a companion than a king. For these little trials of wit, he prepares himself by reading schoolmen, Thomas, Scotus or Gabriel."[4] His theological studies were encouraged by Wolsey, possibly to divert the King's mind from an unwelcome interference in politics, and it was at the Cardinal's instigation that Henry set to work on his famous book against Luther.[5] He seems to have begun it, or some similar treatise, which may afterwards have been adapted to Luther's particular case, before the end of the year in which the German reformer published his original theses. In September, 1517, Erasmus heard that Henry had returned to his studies,[6] and, in the following June, Pace writes to Wolsey that, with respect to the commendations given by the Cardinal to the King's book, though Henry does not think it worthy such great praise as it has had from him and from all other " great learned " men, yet he says he is very glad to have " noted in your grace's letters that his reasons be called inevitable, considering that your grace was sometime his adversary herein and of contrary opinion ".[7] It is obvious that this " book," whatever it may have been, was the fruit of Henry's own mind, and that he adopted a line of argument not entirely relished by Wolsey. But, if it was the

[1] L. and P. iii. 226.　　　　[2] Ibid. iii. 251.　　　　[3] Ibid. ii. 4340.
[4] Ibid. iv. 5412 ; for the freedom with which Cranmer in later days debated with Henry see the present writer's Cranmer, p. 169.
[5] L. and P. iii. 1659, 1772　　　[6] Ibid. ii. 3673.　　　[7] Ibid. ii. 4257.

book against Luther, it was laid aside and rewritten
before it was given to the world in its final form. Nothing
more is heard of it for three years. In April, 1521, Pace
explains to Wolsey the delay in sending him on some
news-letters from Germany " which his grace had not
read till this day after his dinner ; and thus he commanded me to write unto your grace, declaring he was
otherwise occupied ; *i.e., in scribendo contra Lutherum*,
as I do conjecture ".[1] Nine days later Pace found the
King reading a new book of Luther's, " which he dis-
praised " ; and he took the opportunity to show Henry
Leo's bull against the Reformer. " His grace showed
himself well contented with the coming of the same ;
howbeit, as touching the publication thereof, he said he
would have it well examined and diligently looked to
afore it were published."[2] Even in the height of his
fervour against heresy, Henry was in no mood to abate
one jot or one tittle of his royal authority in ecclesiastical
matters.

His book was finished before 21st May, 1521, when
the King wrote to Leo, saying that " ever since he knew
Luther's heresy in Germany, he had made it his study
how to extirpate it. He had called the learned of his
kingdom to consider these errors and denounce them,
and exhort others to do the same. He had urged the
Emperor and Electors, since this pestilent fellow would
not return to God, to extirpate him and his heretical
books. He thought it right still further to testify his
zeal for the faith by his writings, that all might see he
was ready to defend the Church, not only with his arms,
but with the resources of his mind. He dedicated therefore, to the Pope, the first offerings of his intellect and
his little erudition."[3] The letter had been preceded, on
12th May, by a holocaust of Luther's books in St. Paul's
Churchyard. Wolsey sat in state on a scaffold at St.
Paul's Cross, with the papal nuncio and the Archbishop
of Canterbury at his feet on the right, and the imperial
ambassador and Tunstall, Bishop of London, at his feet
on the left ; and while the books were being devoured by

[1] *L. and P.* iii. 1220.   [2] *Ibid.* 1233.   [3] *Ibid.* iii. 1297.

the flames, Fisher preached a sermon denouncing the errors contained therein.[1] But it was July before the fair copy of Henry's book was ready for presentation to Leo ; possibly the interval was employed by learned men in polishing Henry's style, but the substance of the work was undoubtedly of Henry's authorship. Such is the direct testimony of Erasmus, and there is no evidence to indicate the collaboration of others.[2] Pace was then the most intimate of Henry's counsellors, and Pace, by his own confession, was not in the secret. Nor is the book so remarkable as to preclude the possibility of Henry's authorship. Its arguments are respectable and give evidence of an intelligent and fairly extensive acquaintance with the writings of the fathers and schoolmen ; but they reveal no profound depth of theological learning nor genius for abstract speculation. It does not rank so high in the realm of theology, as do some of Henry's compositions in that of music. In August it was sent to Leo, with verses composed by Wolsey and copied out in the royal hand.[3] In September the English ambassador at Rome presented Leo his copy, bound in cloth of gold. The Pope read five leaves without interruption, and remarked that " he would not have thought such a book should have come from the King's grace, who hath been occupied, necessarily, in other feats, seeing that other men which hath occupied themselves in study all their lives cannot bring forth the like ".[4] On 2nd October it was formally presented in a consistory of cardinals ; and, on the 11th, Leo promulgated his bull conferring on Henry his coveted title, " Fidei Defensor ".

Proud as he was of his scholastic achievement and its reward at the hands of the Pope, Henry was doing more for the future of England by his attention to naval affairs than by his pursuit of high-sounding titles. His intuitive perception of England's coming needs in this respect is, perhaps, the most striking illustration of his political foresight. He has been described as the father of the

[1] *I.. and P.* iii. 1273.
[2] F. M. Nichols, *Epistles of Erasmus* p. 424 ; *L. and P.* iv. 5412.
[3] *Ibid.* iii. 1450.   [4] *Ibid.* iii. 1574, 1654, 1655, 1659.

British navy ; and, had he not laid the foundations of England's naval power, his daughter's victory over Spain and entrance on the path that led to empire would have been impossible. Under Henry, the navy was first organised as a permanent force ; he founded the royal dockyards at Woolwich and Deptford, and the corporation of Trinity House ;[1] he encouraged the planting of timber for shipbuilding, enacted laws facilitating inland navigation, dotted the coast with fortifications, and settled the constitution of the naval service upon a plan from which it has ever since steadily developed. He owed his inspiration to none of his councillors, least of all to Wolsey, who had not the faintest glimmering of the importance of securing England's naval supremacy, and who, during the war of 1522-23, preferred futile invasions on land to Henry's " secret designs " for destroying the navy of France.[2] The King's interest in ships and shipbuilding was strong, even amid the alluring diversions of the first years of his reign. He watched his fleet sail for Guienne in 1512, and for France in 1513 ; he knew the speed, the tonnage and the armament of every ship in his navy ; he supervised the minutest details of their construction. In 1520 his ambassador at Paris tells him that Francis is building a ship, " and reasoneth in this mystery of shipman's craft as one which had understanding in the same. But, sir, he approacheth not your highness in that science."[3] A French envoy records how, in 1515, the whole English Court went down to see the launch of the *Princess Mary*. Henry himself " acted as pilot and wore a sailor's coat and trousers, made of cloth of gold, and a gold chain with the inscription, ' Dieu *est* mon droit,' to which was suspended a whistle, which he blew nearly as loud as a trumpet ".[4] The launch of a ship was then almost a religious ceremony, and the place of the modern bottle of champagne was taken by a mass, which was said by the Bishop of Durham. In 1518 Giustinian tells how Henry went to Southampton to see the Venetian

[1] *L. and P.* i. 3807. In 1513 an English consul was appointed at Scio (*ibid.* i. 3854).   [2] *Ibid.* iii. 1440 ; cf. *ibid.* 2421.
[3] *Ibid.* iii. 748.   [4] *Ibid.* ii. 1113.

galleys, and caused some new guns to be " fired again and again, marking their range, as he is very curious about matters of this kind ".[1]

It was not long before Henry developed an active participation in serious matters other than theological disputes and naval affairs. It is not possible to trace its growth with any clearness because no record remains of the verbal communications which were sufficient to indicate his will during the constant attendance of Wolsey upon him. But, as soon as monarch and minister were for some cause or another apart, evidence of Henry's activity in political matters becomes more available. Thus, in 1515, we find Wolsey sending the King, at his own request, the Act of Apparel, just passed by Parliament, for Henry's " examination and correction ".[2] He also desires Henry's determination about the visit of the Queen of Scotland, that he may make the necessary arrangements. In 1518 Henry made a prolonged stay at Abingdon, partly from fear of the plague, and partly, as he told Pace, because at Abingdon people were not continually coming to tell him of deaths, as they did daily in London. During this absence from London, Henry insisted upon the attendance of sufficient councillors to enable him to transact business ; he established a relay of posts every seven hours between himself and Wolsey ; and we hear of his reading " every word of all the letters " sent by his minister.[3] Every week Wolsey despatched an account of such State business as he had transacted ; and on one occasion, " considering the importance of Wolsey's letters," Henry paid a secret and flying visit to London.[4] In 1519 there was a sort of revolution at Court, obscure enough now, but then a subject of some comment at home and abroad. Half a dozen of Henry's courtiers were removed from his person and sent into honourable exile, receiving posts at Calais, at Guisnes, and elsewhere.[5] Giustinian thought that Henry had

[1] L. and P. ii. 4232.　　　　[2] Ibid. ii. 1223.
[3] Ibid. ii. 4060, 4061, 4089.　　[4] Ibid. ii. 4276.
[5] Ven. Cal. ii. 1220, 1230 ; L. and P. iii. 246, 247, 249, 250. Francis I thought they were dismissed as being too favourable to him, and as a rule the younger courtiers favoured France and the older Spain.

been gambling too much and wished to turn over a new leaf. There were also rumours that these courtiers governed Henry after their own appetite, to the King's dishonour ; and Henry, annoyed at the report and jealous as ever of royal prestige, promptly cashiered them, and filled their places with grave and reverend seniors.

Two years later Wolsey was abroad at the conference of Calais, and again Henry's hand in State affairs becomes apparent. Pace, defending himself from the Cardinal's complaints, tells him that he had done everything " by the King's express commandment, who readeth all your letters with great diligence ". One of the letters which angered Wolsey was the King's, for Pace " had devised it very different " ; but the King would not approve of it ; " and commanded me to bring your said letters into his privy chamber with pen and ink, and there he would declare unto me what I should write. And when his grace had your said letters, he read the same three times, and marked such places as it pleased him to make answer unto, and commanded me to write and rehearse as liked him, and not further to meddle with that answer ; so that I herein nothing did but obeyed the King's commandment, and especially at such time *as he would upon good grounds be obeyed, whosoever spake to the contrary*."[1] Wolsey might say in his pride " I shall do so and so," and foreign envoys might think that the Cardinal made the King " go hither and thither, just as he liked " ; but Wolsey knew perfectly well that when he thought fit, Henry " would be obeyed, whosoever spake to the contrary ". He might delegate much of his authority, but men were under no misapprehension that he could and would revoke it whenever he chose. For the time being, King and Cardinal worked together in general harmony, but it was a partnership in which Henry could always have the last word, though Wolsey did most of the work. As early as 1518 he had nominated Standish to the bishopric of St. Asaph, disregarding Wolsey's candidate and the opposition of the clerical party at Court, who detested Standish for his advocacy of Henry's authority

[1] *L. and P.* iii. 1713.

in ecclesiastical matters, and dreaded his promotion as an
evil omen for the independence of the Church.[1]

Even in the details of administration, the King was
becoming increasingly vigilant. In 1519 he drew up
a "remembrance of such things" as he required the
Cardinal to "put in effectual execution".[2] They were
twenty-one in number and ranged over every variety of
subject. The household was to be arranged; "views
to be made and books kept"; the ordnance seen to;
treasurers were to make monthly reports of their receipts
and payments, and send counterparts to the King; the
surveyor of lands was to make a yearly declaration; and
Wolsey himself and the judges were to make quarterly
reports to Henry in person. There were five points
"which the King will debate with his council," the
administration of justice, reform of the exchequer,
Ireland, employment of idle people, and maintenance of
the frontiers. The general plan of Wolsey's negotiations
at Calais in 1521 was determined by King and Cardinal
in consultation, and every important detail in them and
in the subsequent preparations for war was submitted to
Henry. Not infrequently they differed. Wolsey wanted
Sir William Sandys to command the English contingent;
Henry declared it would be inconsistent with his dignity
to send a force out of the realm under the command of
any one of lower rank than an earl. Wolsey replied that
Sandys would be cheaper than an earl,[3] but the command
was entrusted to the Earl of Surrey. Henry thought it
unsafe, considering the imminence of a breach with
France, for English wine ships to resort to Bordeaux;
Wolsey thought otherwise, and they disputed the point
for a month. Honours were divided; the question was
settled for the time by twenty ships sailing while the
dispute was in progress.[4] Apparently they returned in
safety, but the seizure of English ships at Bordeaux in
the following March justified Henry's caution.[5] The
King was already an adept in statecraft, and there was

[1] L. and P. ii. 4074, 4083, 4089.   [2] Ibid. iii. 576.
[3] Ibid. iii. 1454, 1473, 1474.   [4] Ibid. iii. 1629, 1630.
[5] Ibid. iii. 2224.

at least an element of truth in the praise which Wolsey bestowed on his pupil. " No man," he wrote, " can more groundly consider the politic governance of your said realm, nor more assuredly look to the preservation thereof, than ye yourself." And again, " surely, if all your whole council had been assembled together, they could not have more deeply perceived or spoken therein ".[1]

The Cardinal " could not express the joy and comfort with which he noted the King's prudence " ; but he can scarcely have viewed Henry's growing interference without some secret misgivings. For he was developing not only Wolsey's skill and lack of scruple in politics, but also a choleric and impatient temper akin to the Cardinal's own. In 1514 Carroz had complained of Henry's offensive behaviour, and had urged that it would become impossible to control him, if the " young colt " were not bridled. In the following year Henry treated a French envoy with scant civility, and flatly contradicted him twice as he described the battle of Marignano. Giustinian also records how Henry went " pale with anger " at unpleasant news.[2] A few years later his successor describes Henry's " very great rage " when detailing Francis's injuries ; Charles made the same complaints against the French King, " but not so angrily, in accordance with his gentler nature ".[3] On another occasion Henry turned his back upon a diplomatist and walked away in the middle of his speech, an incident, we are told, on which much comment was made in Rome.[4]

But these outbursts were rare and they grew rarer ; in 1527 Mendoza, the Spanish ambassador, remarks that it was " quite the reverse of the King's ordinary manner " to be more violent than Wolsey ;[5] and throughout the period of strained relations with the Emperor, Chapuys constantly refers to the unfailing courtesy and graciousness with which Henry received him. He never forgot himself so far as to lay rude hands on an ambassador, as Wolsey did ; and no provocation betrayed him in his

[1] L. and P. iii. 1544, 1762.   [2] Ibid. ii. 1113, 1653.
[3] Ven. Cal. iii. 493.   [4] Sp. Cal. ii. 314.   [5] Ibid. iii. 109.

later years, passionate though he was, into a neglect of
the outward amenities of diplomatic and official intercourse. Outbursts of anger, of course, there were ; but
they were often like the explosions of counsel in law
courts, and were " to a great extent diplomatically controlled ".[1] Nor can we deny the consideration with which
Henry habitually treated his councillors, the wide discretion he allowed them in the exercise of their duties, and
the toleration he extended to contrary opinions. He was
never impatient of advice even when it conflicted with
his own views. His long arguments with Wolsey, and
the freedom with which the Cardinal justified his recommendations, even after Henry had made up his mind to
an opposite course, are a sufficient proof of the fact. In
1517, angered by Maximilian's perfidy, Henry wrote him
some very " displeasant " letters. Tunstall thought they
would do harm, kept them back, and received no censure
for his conduct. In 1522-23 Wolsey advised first the
siege of Boulogne and then its abandonment. " The
King," wrote More, " is by no means displeased that you
have changed your opinion, as his highness esteemeth
nothing in counsel more perilous than one to persevere in
the maintenance of his advice because he hath once given
it. He therefore commendeth and most affectuously
thanketh your faithful diligence and high wisdom in
advertising him of the reasons which have moved you
to change your opinion."[2] No king knew better than
Henry how to get good work from his ministers, and
his warning against persevering in advice, merely because it has once been given, is a political maxim for
all time.

A lesson might also be learnt from a story of Henry
and Colet told by Erasmus on Colet's own authority.[3]
In 1513 war fever raged in England. Colet's bishop
summoned him " into the King's Court for asserting,
when England was preparing for war against France, that
an unjust peace was preferable to the most just war ; but
the King threatened his persecutor with vengeance. After

---

[1] L. and P. xiii. p. xli.
[2] Ibid. iii. 2421, 3346.   [3] Ibid. iii. 303.

Easter, when the expedition was ready against France, Colet preached on Whitsunday before the King and the Court, exhorting men rather to follow the example of Christ their prince than that of Cæsar and Alexander. The King was afraid that this sermon would have an ill effect upon the soldiers and sent for the Dean. Colet happened to be dining at the Franciscan monastery near Greenwich. When the King heard of it, he entered the garden of the monastary, and on Colet's appearance dismissed his attendants ; then discussed the matter with him, desiring him to explain himself, lest his audience should suppose that no war was justifiable. After the conversation was over he dismissed him before them all, drinking to Colet's health and saying ' Let every man have his own doctor, this is mine ' ". The picture is pleasing evidence of Henry's superiority to some vulgar passions. Another instance of freedom from popular prejudice, which he shared with his father, was his encouragement of foreign scholars, diplomatists and merchants ; not a few of the ablest of Tudor agents were of alien birth. He was therefore intensely annoyed at the rabid fury against them that broke out in the riots of Evil May Day ; yet he pardoned all the ringleaders but one. Tolerance and clemency were no small part of his character in early manhood ;[1] and together with his other mental and physical graces, his love of learning and of the society of learned men, his magnificence and display, his supremacy in all the sports that were then considered the peculiar adornment of royalty, they contributed scarcely less than Wolsey's genius for diplomacy and administration to England's renown. " In short," wrote Chieregati to Isabella d'Este in 1517, " the wealth and civilisation of the world are here ; and those who call the English barbarians appear to me to render themselves such. I here perceive very elegant manners, extreme decorum, and very great politeness. And amongst other

---

[1] For the extraordinary freedom of speech which Henry permitted, see L. and P. xii. ii. 952, where Sir George Throckmorton relates how he accused Henry to his face of immoral relations with Mary Boleyn and her mother.

things there is this most invincible King, whose accomplishments and qualities are so many and excellent that I consider him to surpass all who ever wore a crown ; and blessed and happy may this country call itself in having as its lord so worthy and eminent a sovereign ; whose sway is more bland and gentle than the greatest liberty under any other." [1]

[1] *Ven. Cal.* ii 918.

CHAPTER VI

FROM CALAIS TO ROME

THE wonderful success that had attended Wolsey's policy during his seven years' tenure of power, and the influential position to which he had raised England in the councils of Christendom, might well have disturbed the mental balance of a more modest and diffident man than the Cardinal ; and it is scarcely surprising that he fancied himself, and sought to become, arbiter of the destinies of Europe. The condition of continental politics made his ambition seem less than extravagant. Power was almost monopolised by two young princes whose rivalry was keen, whose resources were not altogether unevenly matched, and whose disputes were so many and serious that war could only be averted by a pacific determination on both sides which neither possessed. Francis had claims on Naples, and his dependant, D'Albret, on Navarre. Charles had suzerain rights over Milan and a title to Burgundy, of which his great-grandfather Charles the Bold had been despoiled by Louis XI. Yet the Emperor had not the slightest intention of compromising his possession of Naples or Navarre, and Francis was quite as resolute to surrender neither Burgundy nor Milan. They both became eager competitors for the friendship of England, which, if its resources were inadequate to support the position of arbiter, was at least a most useful makeweight. England's choice of policy was, however, strictly limited. She could not make war upon Charles. It was not merely that Charles had a staunch ally in his aunt Catherine of Aragon, who is said to have " made such representations and shown such reasons against " the alliance with Francis " as one would not have supposed she would have dared to do, or even to imagine ".[1] It was not

[1] *L. and P.* iii. 728. Wolsey's opposition is attributed by the imperial ambassador to Francis I's promise to make him Pope, " which we might have done much better ".

merely that in this matter Catherine was backed by the whole council except Wolsey, and by the real inclinations of the King. It was that the English people were firmly imperialist in sympathy. The reason was obvious. Charles controlled the wool-market of the Netherlands, and among English exports wool was all-important. War with Charles meant the ruin of England's export trade, the starvation or impoverishment of thousands of Englishmen ; and when war was declared against Charles eight years later, it more nearly cost Henry his throne than all the fulminations of the Pope or religious discontents, and after three months it was brought to a summary end. England remained at peace with Spain so long as Spain controlled its market for wool ; when that market passed into the hands of the revolted Netherlands, the same motive dictated an alliance with the Dutch against Philip II. War with Charles in 1520 was out of the question ; and for the next two years Wolsey and Henry were endeavouring to make Francis and the Emperor bid against each other, in order that England might obtain the maximum of concession from Charles when it should declare in his favour, as all along was intended.

By the Treaty of London Henry was bound to assist the aggrieved against the aggressor. But that treaty had been concluded between England and France in the first instance ; Henry's only daughter was betrothed to the Dauphin ; and Francis was anxious to cement his alliance with Henry by a personal interview.[1] It was Henry's policy to play the friend for the time ; and, as a proof of his desire for the meeting with Francis, he announced, in August, 1519, his resolve to wear his beard until the meeting took place.[2] He reckoned without his wife. On 8th November Louise of Savoy, the queen-mother of France, taxed Boleyn, the English ambassador, with a report that Henry had put off his beard. " I said," writes Boleyn, " that, as I suppose, it hath been by the Queen's

[1] The interview had been agreed upon as early as October, 1518, when it was proposed that it should take place before the end of July, 1519 (*L. and P.* ii. 4483).   [2] *Ibid*. iii. 416.

desire ; for I told my lady that I have hereafore time
known when the King's grace hath worn long his beard,
that the Queen hath daily made him great instance, and
desired him to put it off for her sake ".[1] Henry's incon-
stancy in the matter of his beard not only caused diplomatic inconvenience, but, it may be parenthetically
remarked, adds to the difficulty of dating his portraits.
Francis, however, considered the Queen's interference a
sufficient excuse, or was not inclined to stick at such
trifles ; and on 10th January, 1520, he nominated Wolsey
his proctor to make arrangements for the interview.[2] As
Wolsey was also agent for Henry, the French King saw
no further cause for delay.

The delay came from England ; the meeting with
Francis would be a one-sided pronouncement without
some corresponding favour to Charles. Some time before
Henry had sent Charles a pressing invitation to visit
England on his way from Spain to Germany ; and the
Emperor, suspicious of the meeting between Henry and
Francis, was only too anxious to come and forestall it.
The experienced Margaret of Savoy admitted that
Henry's friendship was essential to Charles ;[3] but
Spaniards were not to be hurried, and it would be May
before the Emperor's convoy was ready. So Henry
endeavoured to postpone his engagement with Francis.
The French King replied that by the end of May his
Queen would be in the eighth month of her pregnancy,
and that if the meeting were further prorogued she must
perforce be absent.[4] Henry was nothing if not gallant,
at least on the surface. Francis's argument clinched the
matter. The interview, ungraced by the presence of
France's Queen, would, said Henry, be robbed of most of
its charm ;[5] and he gave Charles to understand that,
unless he reached England by the middle of May, his
visit would have to be cancelled. This intimation produced an unwonted despatch in the Emperor's movements ; but fate was against him, and contrary winds

[1] L. and P. iii. 514.   [2] Ibid. iii. 592.
[3] Ibid. iii. 672 ; cf. iii. 742.
[4] Ibid. iii. 681, 725.   [5] Ibid. iii. 697.

rendered his arrival in time a matter of doubt till the last possible moment. Henry must cross to Calais on the 31st of May, whether Charles came or not; and it was the 26th before the Emperor's ships appeared off the cliffs of Dover. Wolsey put out in a small boat to meet him, and conducted Charles to the castle where he lodged. During the night Henry arrived. Early next day, which was Whitsunday, the two sovereigns proceeded to Canterbury, where the Queen and Court had come on the way to France to spend their Pentecost. Five days the Emperor remained with his aunt, whom he now saw for the first time; but the days were devoted to business rather than to elaborate ceremonial and show, for which there had been little time to prepare.[1]

On the last day of May Charles took ship at Sandwich for Flanders. Henry embarked at Dover for France. The painting at Hampton Court depicting the scene has, like almost every other picture of Henry's reign, been ascribed to Holbein; but six years were to pass before the great artist visited England. The King himself is represented as being on board the four-masted *Henry Grâce à Dieu*, commonly called the *Great Harry*, the finest ship afloat; though the vessel originally fitted out for his passage was the *Katherine Pleasaunce*.[2] At eleven o'clock he landed at Calais. On Monday, the 4th of June, Henry and all his Court proceeded to Guisnes. There a temporary palace of art had been erected, the splendour of which is inadequately set forth in pages upon pages of contemporary descriptions. One Italian likened it to the palaces described in Boiardo's *Orlando Innamorato* and Ariosto's *Orlando Furioso;* another declared that it could not have been better designed by Leonardo da Vinci himself.[3] Everything was in harmony with this architectural pomp. Wolsey was accompanied, it was

---

[1] *Ven. Cal.* iii. 50; *Sp. Cal.* ii. 274.

[2] *L. and P.* iii. 558, an account-book headed " expense of making the *Kateryn Pleasaunce* for transporting the King to Calais 22 May, 10 Henry VIII ".

[3] *Ven. Cal.* iii. 81, 88; cf. *L. and P.* iii. 303-14; Hall, *Chronicle*, p. 604, etc.

said in Paris, by two hundred gentlemen clad in crimson
velvet, and had a body-guard of two hundred archers.
He was himself clothed in crimson satin from head to
foot, his mule was covered with crimson velvet, and her
trappings were all of gold. Henry, " the most goodliest
prince that ever reigned over the realm of England,"
appeared even to Frenchmen as a very handsome prince,
" honnête, hault et droit,"[1] in manner gentle and
gracious, rather fat, and—in spite of his Queen—with a
red beard, large enough and very becoming. Another
eye-witness adds the curious remark that, while Francis
was the taller of the two, Henry had the handsomer and
more *feminine* face ![2] On the 7th of June the two Kings
started simultaneously from Guisnes and Ardres for their
personal meeting in the valley midway between the two
towns, already known as the Val Doré. The obscure but
familiar phrase, Field of Cloth of Gold,[3] is a mistranslation
of the French Camp du Drap d'Or. As they came in
sight a temporary suspicion of French designs seized the
English, but it was overcome. Henry and Francis rode
forward alone, embraced each other first on horseback and
then again on foot, and made show of being the closest
friends in Christendom. On Sunday the 10th Henry
dined with the French Queen, and Francis with Catherine
of Aragon. The following week was devoted to tourneys,
which the two Kings opened by holding the field against
all comers. The official accounts are naturally silent on
the royal wrestling match, recorded in French memoirs
and histories.[4] On the 17th Francis, as a final effort to
win Henry's alliance, paid a surprise visit to him at
breakfast with only four attendants. The jousts were
concluded with a solemn mass said by Wolsey in a chapel
built on the field. The Cardinal of Bourbon presented
the Gospel to Francis to kiss ; he refused, offering it to
Henry who was too polite to accept the honour. The
same respect for each other's dignity was observed with

[1] *L. and P.* iii. 306.   [2] *Ven. Cal.* iii. 80.
[3] Erroneously called " Field of *the* Cloth of Gold " ; cloth of gold is
a material like velvet, and one does not talk about " a coat of *the* velvet ".
[4] See Michelet, x. 137-38.

the *Pax*, and the two Queens behaved with a similarly
courteous punctilio. After a friendly dispute as to who
should kiss the *Pax* first, they kissed each other instead.[1]
On the 24th Henry and Francis met to interchange gifts,
to make their final professions of friendship, and to bid
each other adieu. Francis set out for Abbeville, and
Henry returned to Calais.

The Field of Cloth of Gold was the last and most
gorgeous display of the departing spirit of chivalry; it
was also perhaps the most portentous deception on record.
"These sovereigns," wrote a Venetian, "are not at
peace. They adapt themselves to circumstances, but they
hate each other very cordially."[2] Beneath the profusion
of friendly pretences lay rooted suspicions and even
deliberate hostile intentions. Before Henry left England
the rumour of ships fitting out in French ports had
stopped preparations for the interview; and they were
not resumed till a promise under the broad seal of France
was given that no French ship should sail before Henry's
return.[3] On the eve of the meeting Henry is said to have
discovered that three or four thousand French troops
were concealed in the neighbouring country;[4] he insisted
on their removal, and Francis's unguarded visit to Henry
was probably designed to disarm the English distrust.[5]
No sooner was Henry's back turned than the French
began the fortification of Ardres,[6] while Henry on his
part went to Calais to negotiate a less showy but genuine
friendship with Charles. No such magnificence adorned
their meeting as had been displayed at the Field of Cloth
of Gold, but its solid results were far more lasting. On
10th July Henry rode to Gravelines where the Emperor
was waiting. On the 11th they returned together to
Calais, where during a three days' visit the negotiations
begun at Canterbury were completed. The ostensible
purport of the treaty signed on the 14th was to bind
Henry to proceed no further in the marriage between the
Princess Mary and the Dauphin, and Charles no further

[1] See Michelet, x. p. 312.   [2] *Ven. Cal.* iii. 119.
[3] *L. and P.* iii. 836, 842, 843.   [4] *Ven. Cal.* iii. 80.
[5] *Ibid.* iii. 90.   [6] *Ibid.* iii. 121.

in that between himself and Francis's daughter, Charlotte,[1] but more topics were discussed than appeared on the surface ; and among them was a proposal to marry Mary to the Emperor himself.[2] The design proves that Henry and Wolsey had already made up their minds to side with Charles, whenever his disputes with Francis should develop into open hostilities.

That consummation could not be far off. Charles had scarcely turned his back upon Spain when murmurs of disaffection were heard through the length and breadth of the land ; and while he was discussing with Henry at Calais the prospects of a war with France, his commons in Spain broke out into open revolt.[3] The rising had attained such dimensions by February, 1521, that Henry thought Charles was likely to lose his Spanish dominions. The temptation was too great for France to resist ; and in the early spring of 1521 French forces overran Navarre, and restored to his kingdom the exile D'Albret. Francis had many plausible excuses, and sought to prove that he was not really the aggressor. There had been confused fighting between the imperialist Nassau and Francis's allies, the Duke of Guelders and Robert de la Marck, which the imperialists may have begun. But Francis revealed his true motive, when he told Fitzwilliam that he had many grievances against Charles and could not afford to neglect this opportunity for taking his revenge.[4]

War between Emperor and King soon spread from Navarre to the borders of Flanders and to the plains of Northern Italy. Both sovereigns claimed the assistance of England in virtue of the Treaty of London. But Henry would not be prepared for war till the following year at least ; and he proposed that Wolsey should go to Calais to mediate between the two parties and decide which had been the aggressor. Charles, either because he was unprepared or was sure of Wolsey's support, readily agreed ; but Francis was more reluctant, and only the knowledge

[1] *L. and P.* iii. 914.   [2] *Ibid.* iii. 1149, 1150.
[3] *Ibid.* iii. 883, 891, 964, 976, 988, 994.
[4] *Ibid.* iii. 1303, 1310, 1315.

that, if he refused, Henry would at once side with Charles, induced him to consent to the conference. So on 2nd August, 1521, the Cardinal again crossed the Channel.[1] His first interview was with the imperial envoys.[2] They announced that Charles had given them no power to treat for a truce. Wolsey refused to proceed without this authority; and he obtained the consent of the French chancellor, Du Prat, to his proposal to visit the Emperor at Bruges, and secure the requisite powers. He was absent more than a fortnight, and not long after his return fell ill. This served to pass time in September, and the extravagant demands of both parties still further prolonged the proceedings. Wolsey was constrained to tell them the story of a courtier who asked his King for the grant of a forest; when his relatives denounced his presumption, he replied that he only wanted in reality eight or nine trees.[3] The French and imperial chancellors not merely demanded their respective forests, but made the reduction of each single tree a matter of lengthy dispute; and as soon as a fresh success in the varying fortune of war was reported, they returned to their early pretensions. Wolsey was playing his game with consummate skill; delay was his only desire; his illness had been diplomatic; his objects were to postpone for a few months the breach and to secure the pensions from France due at the end of October.[4]

The conference at Calais was in fact a monument of perfidy worthy of Ferdinand the Catholic. The plan was Wolsey's, but Henry had expressed full approval. As early as July the King was full of his secret design for destroying the navy of France, though he did not propose to proceed with the enterprise till Wolsey had completed the arrangements with Charles.[5] The subterfuge about

[1] See his various and ample commissions, *L. and P*. iii. 1443.
[2] *Ibid*. iii. 1462.   [3] *Ibid*. iii. 1622.
[4] *Ibid*. iii. 1507. " The Cardinal apologised for not having met them so long on account of his illness, but said he could not otherwise have gained so much time without causing suspicion to the French " (Gattinara to Charles V, 24th September, 1521, *ibid*. iii. 1605).
[5] *Ibid*. iii. 1440.

Charles refusing his powers and the Cardinal's journey
to Bruges had been arranged between Henry, Wolsey and
Charles before Wolsey left England. The object of that
visit, so far from being to facilitate an agreement, was to
conclude an offensive and defensive alliance against one
of the two parties between whom Wolsey was pretending
to mediate. " Henry agrees," wrote Charles's ambassador
on 6th July, " with Wolsey's plan that he should be sent
to Calais under colour of hearing the grievances of both
parties : and when he cannot arrange them, he should
withdraw to the Emperor to treat of the matters aforesaid ".[1] The treaty was concluded at Bruges on 25th
August[2] before he returned to Calais ; the Emperor
promised Wolsey the Papacy ;[3] the details of a joint
invasion were settled. Charles was to marry Mary ; and
the Pope was to dispense the two from the disability of
their kinship, and from engagements with others which
both had contracted. The Cardinal might be profuse in
his protestations of friendship for France, of devotion to
peace, and of his determination to do justice to the
parties before him. But all his painted words could not
long conceal the fact that behind the mask of the judge
were hidden the features of a conspirator. It was an
unpleasant time for Fitzwilliam, the English ambassador
at the French Court. The King's sister, Marguerite de
Valois, taxed Fitzwilliam with Wolsey's proceedings,
hinting that deceit was being practised on Francis. The
ambassador grew hot, vowed Henry was not a dissembler,
and that he would prove it on any gentleman who dared
to maintain that he was.[4] But he knew nothing of
Wolsey's intrigues ; nor was the Cardinal, to whom
Fitzwilliam denounced the insinuation, likely to blush,
though he knew that the charge was true.

Wolsey returned from Calais at the end of November,

[1] L. and P. iii. 1395, 1433; cf. iii. 1574, where Henry VIII's envoy
tells Leo X that the real object of the conference was to gain time for
English preparations.

[2] Ibid. iii. 1508; Cotton MS., Galba, B vii. 102; see also an account of
the conference in L. and P. iii. 1816, 1817.

[3] Ibid. iii. 1868, 1876.   [4] Ibid. iii. 1581.

having failed to establish the truce to which the negotiations had latterly been in appearance directed. But the French half-yearly pensions were paid, and England had the winter in which to prepare for war. No attempt had been made to examine impartially the mutual charges of aggression urged by the litigants, though a determination of that point could alone justify England's intervention. The dispute was complicated enough. If, as Charles contended, the Treaty of London guaranteed the *status quo*, Francis, by invading Navarre, was undoubtedly the offender. But the French King pleaded the Treaty of Noyon, by which Charles had bound himself to do justice to the exiled King of Navarre, to marry the French King's daughter, and to pay tribute for Naples. That treaty was not abrogated by the one concluded in London, yet Charles had fulfilled none of his promises. Moreover, the Emperor himself had, long before the invasion of Navarre, been planning a war with France, and negotiating with Leo to expel the French from Milan, and to destroy the predominant French faction in Genoa.[1] His ministers were making little secret of Charles's warlike intentions, when the Spanish revolt placed irresistible temptation in Francis's way, and provoked that attack on Navarre, which enabled Charles to plead, with some colour, that he was not the aggressor. This was the ground alleged by Henry for siding with Charles, but it was not his real reason for going to war. Nearly a year before Navarre was invaded, he had discussed the rupture of Mary's engagement with the Dauphin and the transference of her hand to the Emperor.

The real motives of England's policy do not appear on the surface. "The aim of the King of England," said Clement VII in 1524,[2] "is as incomprehensible as the causes by which he is moved are futile. He may, perhaps, wish to revenge himself for the slights he has received from the King of France and from the Scots, or

[1] In July, 1521, Gattinara drew out seven reasons for peace and ten for war; the former he playfully termed the seven deadly sins, and the latter the ten commandments (*L. and P.* iii. 1446; *Sp. Cal.* ii. 337).

[2] *Sp. Cal.* ii. 626.

to punish the King of France for his disparaging language ;
or, seduced by the flattery of the Emperor, he may have
nothing else in view than to help the Emperor ; or he
may, perhaps, really wish to preserve peace in Italy, and
therefore declares himself an enemy of any one who
disturbs it. It is even not impossible that the King of
England expects to be rewarded by the Emperor after
the victory, and hopes, perhaps, to get Normandy."
Clement three years before, when Cardinal de Medici,
had admitted that he knew little of English politics ;[1]
and his ignorance may explain his inability to give a
more satisfactory reason for Henry's conduct than these
tentative and far-fetched suggestions. But after the
publication of Henry's State papers, it is not easy to
arrive at any more definite conclusion. The only motive
Wolsey alleges, besides the *ex post facto* excuses of
Francis's conduct, is the recovery of Henry's rights to
the crown of France ; and if this were the real object, it
reduces both King and Cardinal to the level of political
charlatans. To conquer France was a madcap scheme,
when Henry himself was admitting the impossibility of
raising 30,000 foot or 10,000 horse, without hired con-
tingents from Charles's domains ;[2] when, according to
Giustinian, it would have been hard to levy 100 men-at-
arms or 1000 light cavalry in the whole island ;[3] when
the only respectable military force was the archers,
already an obsolete arm. Invading hosts could never
be victualled for more than three months, or stand a
winter campaign ; English troops were ploughmen by
profession and soldiers only by chance ; Henry VII's
treasure was exhausted, and efforts to raise money for
fitful and futile inroads nearly produced a revolt. Henry
VIII himself was writing that to provide for these
inroads would prevent him keeping an army in Ireland ;
and Wolsey was declaring that for the same reason
English interests in Scotland must take care of themselves,
that border warfare must be confined to the strictest
defensive, and that a " cheap " deputy must be found

[1] *L. and P*. iii. 853.   [2] *Ibid*. iii. 2333 (iv).
[3] *Desp*. App. ii. 309.

for Ireland, who would rule it, like Kildare, without English aid.[1] It is usual to lay the folly of the pretence to the crown of France at Henry's door. But it is a curious fact that when Wolsey was gone, and Henry was his own prime minister, this spirited foreign policy took a very subordinate place, and Henry turned his attention to the cultivation of his own garden instead of seeking to annex his neighbour's. It is possible that he was better employed in wasting his people's blood and treasure in the futile devastation of France, than in placing his heel on the Church and sending Fisher and More to the scaffold ; but his attempts to reduce Ireland to order, and to unite England and Scotland, violent though his methods may have been, were at least more sane than the quest for the crown of France, or even for the possession of Normandy.[2]

Yet if these were not Wolsey's aims, what were his motives ? The essential thing for England was the maintenance of a fairly even balance between Francis and Charles ; and if Wolsey thought that would best be secured by throwing the whole of England's weight into the Emperor's scale, he must have strangely misread the political situation. He could not foresee, it may be said, the French debacle. If so, it was from no lack of omens. Even supposing he was ignorant, or unable to estimate the effects, of the moral corruption of Francis, the peculations of his mother Louise of Savoy, the hatred of the war, universal among the French lower classes, there were definite warnings from more careful observers.[3] As early as 1517 there were bitter complaints in France of the *gabelle* and other taxes, and a Cordelier denounced

[1] *L. and P.* iii. 1252, 1646, 1675.

[2] The policy of abstention was often urged at the council-table and opposed by Wolsey, who, according to More, used to repeat the fable of the men who hid in caves to keep out of the rain which was to make all whom it wetted fools, hoping thereby to have the rule over the fools (*L. and P.* vii. 1114 ; More, *English Works* p. 1434). It had cost England, says More, many a fair penny.

[3] " To hear how rich and poor lament the war would grieve any man's heart " (Fitzwilliam to Wolsey, 18th Jan., 1521-22, *L. and P.* iii 1971).

the French King as worse than Nero.[1] In 1519 an
anonymous Frenchman wrote that Francis had destroyed
his own people, emptied his kingdom of money, and that
the Emperor or some other would soon have a cheap
bargain of the kingdom, for he was more unsteady on his
throne than people thought.[2] Even the treason of
Bourbon, which contributed so much to the French
King's fall, was rumoured three years before it occurred,
and in 1520 he was known to be " playing the malcon-
tent ".[3] At the Field of Cloth of Gold Henry is said to
have told Francis that, had he a subject like Bourbon, he
would not long leave his head on his shoulders.[4] All these
details were reported to the English Government and
placed among English archives ; and, indeed, at the
English Court the general anticipation, justified by the
event, was that Charles would carry the day.

No possible advantage could accrue to England from
such a destruction of the balance of power ; her position
as mediator was only tenable so long as neither Francis
nor Charles had the complete mastery. War on the
Emperor was, no doubt, out of the question, but that was
no reason for war on France. Prudence counselled
England to make herself strong, to develop her resources,
and to hold her strength in reserve, while the two rivals
weakened each other by war. She would then be in a
far better position to make her voice heard in the settlement, and would probably have been able to extract from
it all the benefits she could with reason or justice demand.
So obvious was the advantage of this policy that for
some time acute French statesmen refused to credit
Wolsey with any other. They said, reported an English
envoy to the Cardinal, " that your grace would make your
profit with them and the Emperor both, and proceed
between them so that they might continue in war, and
that the one destroy the other, and the King's highness
may remain and be their arbiter and superior ".[5] If it is
urged that Henry was bent on the war, and that Wolsey

[1] *L. and P.* ii. 3702-3. [2] *Ibid.* iii. 378.
[3] *Ibid.* iii. 404 ; cf. iii. 2446 *ad fin.* [4] Michelet x. 131.
[5] *L. and P.* iii. 2026.

must satisfy the King or forfeit his power, even the
latter would have been the better alternative. His fall
would have been less complete and more honourable than
it actually was. Wolsey's failure to follow this course
suggests that, by involving Henry in dazzling schemes
of a foreign conquest, he was seeking to divert his attention
from urgent matters at home ; that he had seen a vision
of impending ruin ; and that his actions were the frantic
efforts of a man to turn a steed, over which he has
imperfect control, from the gulf he sees yawning ahead.
The only other explanation is that Wolsey sacrificed
England's interests in the hope of securing from Charles
the gift of the papal tiara.[1]

However that may be, it was not for Clement VII to
deride England's conduct. The keen-sighted Pace had
remarked in 1521 that, in the event of Charles's victory,
the Pope would have to look to his affairs in time.[2] The
Emperor's triumph was, indeed, as fatal to the Papacy as
it was to Wolsey. Yet Clement VII, on whom the full
force of the blow was to fall, had, as Cardinal de Medici,
been one of the chief promoters of the war. In August,
1521, the Venetian, Contarini, reports Charles as saying
that Leo rejected both the peace and the truce speciously
urged by Wolsey, and adds, on his own account, that he
believes it the truth.[3] In 1522 Francis asserted that
Cardinal de Medici " was the cause of all this war " ;[4] and
in 1527 Clement VII sought to curry favour with Charles
by declaring that as Cardinal de Medici he had in 1521
caused Leo X to side against France.[5] In 1525 Charles
declared that he had been mainly induced to enter on the
war by the persuasions of Leo,[6] over whom his cousin,
the Cardinal, then wielded supreme influence. So complete was his sway over Leo, that, on Leo's death, a
cardinal in the conclave remarked that they wanted a

[1] For another view see Busch, *Cardinal Wolsey und die Englisch-
Kaiserliche Allianz, 1522-25.* Bonn, 1886.
[2] *L. and P.* iii. 1370.   [3] *Ven. Cal.* iii. 312.
[4] *L. and P.* iii. 1947.   [5] *Sp. Cal.* iii. pp. 510-11.
[6] *Ibid.* ii. p. 717.

new Pope, not one who had already been Pope for years ;
and the gibe turned the scale against the future Clement
VII. Medici both, Leo and the Cardinal regarded the
Papacy mainly as a means for family aggrandisement.
In 1518 Leo had fulminated against Francis Maria della
Rovere, Duke of Urbino, as " the son of iniquity and
child of perdition,"[1] because he desired to bestow the
duchy on his nephew Lorenzo. In the family interest he
was withholding Modena and Reggio from Alfonso d'Este,
and casting envious eyes on Ferrara. In March, 1521,
the French marched to seize some Milanese exiles, who
were harboured at Reggio.[2] Leo took the opportunity to
form an alliance with Charles for the expulsion of Francis
from Italy. It was signed at Worms on the 8th of May,
the day on which Luther was outlawed ;[3] and a war
broke out in Italy, the effects of which were little foreseen
by its principal authors. A veritable Nemesis attended
this policy conceived in perfidy and greed. The battle
of Pavia made Charles more nearly dictator of Europe
than any ruler has since been, except Napoleon Bona-
parte. It led to the sack of Rome and the imprisonment
of Clement VII by Charles's troops. The dependence
of the Pope on the Emperor made it impossible for
Clement to grant Henry's petition for divorce, and his
failure to obtain the divorce precipitated Wolsey's fall.

Leo, meanwhile, had gone to his account on the night
of 1st-2nd December, 1521, singing " Nunc dimittis " for
the expulsion of the French from Milan ;[4] and amid the
clangour of war the cardinals met to choose his successor.
Their spirit belied their holy profession. " All here,"
wrote Manuel, Charles's representative, " is founded on
avarice and lies ; "[5] and again " there cannot be so much
hatred and so many devils in hell as among these cardinals ". " The Papacy is in great decay " echoed the

[1] L. and P. ii. 3617.   [2] Ibid. iii. 1209, 1400.
[3] Creighton, Papacy, ed. 1901, vi. 184 n. The edict was not issued
till 25th May, but there was an intimate connection between the two
events. It was in the same month that Luther's books were solemnly
burnt in England, the ally of Pope and Emperor, and the extirpation of
heresy was the first motive alleged for the alliance.
[4] Sp. Cal. ii. 365 ; L. and P. ii. 1795.   [5] Sp. Cal. ii. 370.

English envoy Clerk, " the cardinals brawl and scold ;
their malicious, unfaithful and uncharitable demeanour
against each other increases every day ".[1] Feeling between
the French and imperial factions ran high, and the only
question was whether an adherent of Francis or Charles
would secure election. Francis had promised Wolsey
fourteen French votes ; but after the conference of
Calais he would have been forgiving indeed had he
wielded his influence on behalf of the English candidate.
Wolsey built more upon the promise of Charles at
Bruges ;[2] but, if he really hoped for Charles's assistance,
his sagacity was greatly to seek. The Emperor at no
time made any effort on Wolsey's behalf ; he did him
the justice to think that, were Wolsey elected, he would
be devoted more to English than to imperial interests ;
and he preferred a Pope who would be undividedly imperialist at heart. Pace was sent to join Clerk at Rome
in urging Wolsey's suit, and they did their best ; but
English influence at the Court of Rome was infinitesimal.
In spite of Campeggio's flattering assurance that Wolsey's
name appeared in every scrutiny, and that sometimes he
had eight or nine votes, and Clerk's statement that he
had nine at one time, twelve at another, and nineteen at
a third,[3] Wolsey's name only appears in one of the eleven
scrutinies, and then he received but seven out of eighty-
one votes.[4] The election was long and keenly contested.
The conclave commenced on the 28th of December, and
it was not till the 9th of January, 1522, that the cardinals,
conscious of each other's defects, agreed to elect an
absentee, about whom they knew little. Their choice
fell on Adrian, Cardinal of Tortosa ; and it is significant
of the extent of Charles's influence, that the new Pope
had been his tutor, and was proposed as a candidate by
the imperial ambassador on the day that the conclave
opened.[5]

---

[1] *L. and P.* iii. 1960.   [2] *Ibid.* iii. 1884.
[3] *Ibid.* iii. 1952, 1960.
[4] *Sp. Cal.* ii. 375. It is not quite clear how these votes were recorded,
for there were not eighty-one cardinals.
[5] *Ibid.* ii. 371.

Neither the expulsion of the French from Milan, nor the election of Charles's tutor as Pope, opened Wolsey's eyes to the danger of further increasing the Emperor's power.[1] He seems rather to have thrown himself into the not very chivalrous design of completing the ruin of the weaker side, and picking up what he could from the spoils. During the winter of 1521-22 he was busily preparing for war, while endeavouring to delay the actual breach till his plans were complete. Francis, convinced of England's hostile intentions, let Albany loose upon Scotland and refused to pay the pensions to Henry and Wolsey. They made these grievances the excuse for a war on which they had long been determined. In March Henry announced that he had taken upon himself the protection of the Netherlands during Charles's impending visit to Spain. Francis asserted that this was a plain declaration of war, and seized the English wine-ships at Bordeaux. But he was determined not to take the formal offensive, and, in May, Clarencieux herald proceeded to France to bid him defiance.[2] In the following month Charles passed through England on his way to the south, and fresh treaties were signed for the invasion of France, for the marriage of Mary and for the extirpation of heresy. At Windsor[3] Wolsey constituted his legatine court to bind the contracting parties by oaths enforced by ecclesiastical censures. He arrogated to himself a function usually reserved for the Pope, and undertook to arbitrate between Charles and Henry if disputes arose about the observance of their engagements. But he obviously found difficulty in raising either money or men ; and one of the suggestions at Windsor was that a " dissembled peace " or a two years' truce should be made with France, to give England time for more preparations for war. Nothing came of this last nefarious suggestion. In

[1] Francis " begged Henry to consider what would happen now that a Pope had been elected entirely at Charles's devotion " (L. and P. iii. 1994) ; but Adrian's attitude was at first independent (Sp. Cal. ii. 494, 504, 533). In July, 1522, however, he joined the league against Francis. (ibid. ii. 574).   [2] L. and P. iii. 2140, 2224, 2290.

[3] Ibid. iii. 2322, 2333 ; Sp. Cal. ii. 430, 435, 561.

July Surrey captured and burnt Morlaix ;[1] but, as he
wrote from on board the *Mary Rose*, Fitzwilliam's ships
were without flesh or fish, and Surrey himself had only
beer for twelve days. Want of victuals prevented further
naval successes, and, in September, Surrey was sent into
Artois, where the same lack of organisation was equally
fatal. It did not, however, prevent him from burning
farms and towns wherever he went ; and his conduct
evoked from the French commander a just rebuke of his
" foul warfare ".[2] Henry himself was responsible ; for
Wolsey wrote on his behalf urging the destruction of
Doullens and the adjacent towns.[3] If Henry really
sought to make these territories his own, it was an odd
method of winning the affections and developing the
wealth of the subjects he hoped to acquire. Nothing
was really accomplished except devastation in France.
Even this useless warfare exhausted English energies,
and left the Borders defenceless against one of the largest
armies ever collected in Scotland. Wolsey and Henry
were only saved from what might have been a most
serious invasion by Dacre's dexterity and Albany's
cowardice. Dacre, the warden of the marches, signed
a truce without waiting for instructions, and before it
expired the Scots army disbanded. Henry and Wolsey
might reprimand Dacre for acting on his own responsibility, but they knew well enough that Dacre had done
them magnificent service.[4]

The results of the war from the English point of view
had as yet been contemptible, but great things were hoped
for the following year. Bourbon, Constable of France,
and the most powerful peer in the kingdom, intent on the
betrayal of Francis, was negotiating with Henry and
Charles the price of his treason.[5] The commons in
France, worn to misery by the taxes of Francis and the
ravages of his enemies, were eager for anything that might
promise some alleviation of their lot. They would even,

---

[1] *L. and P.* iii. 2362.   [2] *Ibid.* iii. 2541.
[3] *Ibid.* iii. 2551.   [4] *Ibid.* iii. 2537.
[5] *Sp. Cal.* ii. 584 ; *L. and P.* iii. 2450, 2567, 2770, 2772, 2879, 3154.
Bourbon had substantial grievances against Francis I and his mother.

it appears, welcome a change of dynasty; everywhere, Henry was told, they cried " Vive le roi d'Angleterre ! "[1] Never, said Wolsey, would there be a better opportunity for recovering the King's right to the French crown; and Henry exclaimed that he trusted to treat Francis as his father did Richard III. " I pray God," wrote Sir Thomas More to Wolsey, " if it be good for his grace and for this realm, that then it may prove so, and else in the stead thereof, I pray God send his grace an honourable and profitable peace ".[2] He could scarcely go further in hinting his preference for peace to the fantastic design which now occupied the minds of his masters. Probably his opinion of the war was not far from that of old Bishop Fox, who declared : " I have determined, and, betwixt God and me, utterly renounced the meddling with worldly matters, specially concerning war or anything to it appertaining (whereof, for the many intolerable enormities that I have seen ensue by the said war in time past, I have no little remorse in my conscience), thinking that if I did continual penance for it all the days of my life, though I should live twenty years longer than I may do, I could not yet make sufficient recompense therefor. And now, my good lord, to be called to fortifications of towns and places of war, or to any matter concerning the war, being of the age of seventy years and above, and looking daily to die, the which if I did, being in any such meddling of the war, I think I should die in despair ".[3] Protests like this and hints like More's were little likely to move the militant Cardinal, who hoped to see the final ruin of France in 1523. Bourbon was to raise the standard of revolt, Charles was to invade from Spain and Suffolk from Calais. In Italy French influence seemed irretrievably ruined. The Genoese revolution, planned before the war, was effected ; and the persuasions of Pace and the threats of Charles at last detached Venice and Ferrara from the alliance of France.[4]

The usual delays postponed Suffolk's invasion till late

[1] *L. and P.* iii. 2770.   [2] *Ibid.* iii. 2555.
[3] Ellis, *Orig. Letters*, 2nd series ii. 4 ; *L. and P.* iii. 2207.
[4] *L. and P.* iii. 3207, 3271, 3291 ; *Sp. Cal.* ii. 576, 594.

in the year. They were increased by the emptiness of
Henry's treasury. His father's hoard had melted away,
and it was absolutely necessary to obtain lavish supplies
from Parliament. But Parliament proved ominously
intractable. Thomas Cromwell, now rising to notice,
in a temperate speech urged the folly of indulging in
impracticable schemes of foreign conquest, while Scotland remained a thorn in England's side.[1] It was three
months from the meeting of Parliament before the subsidies were granted, and nearly the end of August before
Suffolk crossed to Calais with an army, " the largest
which has passed out of this realm for a hundred years ".[2]
Henry and Suffolk wanted it to besiege Boulogne, which
might have been some tangible result in English hands.[3]
But the King was persuaded by Wolsey and his imperial
allies to forgo this scheme, and to order Suffolk to
march into the heart of France. Suffolk was not a
great general, but he conducted the invasion with no
little skill, and desired to conduct it with unwonted
humanity. He wished to win the French by abstaining
from pillage and proclaiming liberty, but Henry thought
only the hope of plunder would keep the army together.[4]
Waiting for the imperial contingent under De Buren,
Suffolk did not leave Calais till 19th September. He
advanced by Bray, Roye and Montdidier, capturing all
the towns that offered resistance. Early in November
he reached the Oise at a point less than forty miles from
the French capital.[5] But Bourbon's treason had been
discovered ; instead of joining Suffolk with a large force,
he was a fugitive from his country. Charles contented
himself with taking Fuentarabia,[6] and made no effort
at invasion. The imperial contingent with Suffolk's
army went home ; winter set in with unexampled
severity, and Vendôme advanced.[7] The English were
compelled to retire ; their retreat was effected without

[1] Merriman, *Cromwell's Letters* i. 30-44 ; *L. and P.* iii. 2958, 3024 ;
Hall, *Chronicle* pp. 656, 657.
[2] *L. and P.* iii. 3281.   [3] *Ibid*. iii. 2360, 3319.
[4] *Ibid*. iii. 3346.   [5] *Ibid*. iii. 3452, 3485, 3505, 3516.
[6] *Ibid*. iii. 2798, 2869.   [7] *Ibid*. iii. 3559, 3580, 3601.

loss, and by the middle of December the army was
back at Calais. Suffolk is represented as being in disgrace
for this retreat, and Wolsey as saving him from the
effects of his failure.[1] But even Wolsey can hardly have
thought that an army of twenty-five thousand men could
maintain itself in the heart of France, throughout the
winter, without support and with unguarded communications. The Duke's had been the most successful
invasion of France since the days of Henry V from a
military point of view. That its results were negative is
due to the policy by which it was directed.

Meanwhile there was another papal election. Adrian,
one of the most honest and unpopular of Popes, died on
14th September, 1523, and by order of the cardinals
there was inscribed on his tomb : *Hic jacet Adrianus
Sextus cui nihil in vita infelicius contigit quam quod
imperaret.* With equal malice and keener wit the Romans
erected to his physician, Macerata, a statue with the
title *Liberatori Patriæ.*[2] Wolsey was again a candidate.
He told Henry he would rather continue in his service
than be ten Popes.[3] That did not prevent him instructing
Pace and Clerk to further his claims. They were to
represent to the cardinals Wolsey's " great experience in
the causes of Christendom, his favour with the Emperor,
the King, and other princes, his anxiety for Christendom,
his liberality, the great promotions to be vacated by his
election, his frank, pleasant and courteous inclinations,
his freedom from all ties of family or party, and the hopes
of a great expedition against the infidel ".[4] Charles was,
as usual, profuse in his promise of aid. He actually wrote
a letter in Wolsey's favour ; but he took the precaution
to detain the bearer in Spain till the election was over.[5]
He had already instructed his minister at Rome to
procure the election of Cardinal de Medici. That
ambassador mocked at Wolsey's hopes ; " as if God," he
wrote, " would perform a miracle every day ".[6] The
Holy Spirit, by which the cardinals always professed to be

[1] Brewer's Introd. to *L. and P.* vol. iv. p. ii., etc.
[2] *L. and P.* iii. 3464.   [3] *Ibid.* iii. 3372.   [4] *Ibid.* 3389.
[5] *Sp. Cal.* ii. 615.   [6] *Ibid.* ii. 604, 606.

moved, was not likely to inspire the election of another
absentee after their experience of Adrian. Wolsey had
not the remotest chance, and his name does not occur in
a single scrutiny. After the longest conclave on record,
the imperial influence prevailed; on 18th November De
Medici was proclaimed Pope, and he chose as his title
Clement VII.[1]

Suffolk's invasion was the last of England's active
participation in the war. Exhausted by her efforts, discontented with the Emperor's failure to render assistance
in the joint enterprise, or perceiving at last that she had
little to gain, and much to lose, from the overgrown
power of Charles, England, in 1524, abstained from
action, and even began to make overtures to Francis.
Wolsey repaid Charles's inactivity of the previous year
by standing idly by, while the imperial forces with
Bourbon's contingent invaded Provence and laid siege to
Marseilles. But Francis still held command of the sea;
the spirit of his people rose with the danger; Marseilles
made a stubborn and successful defence; and by October
the invading army was in headlong retreat towards Italy.[2]
Had Francis been content with defending his kingdom,
all might have been well; but ambition lured him on to
destruction. He thought he had passed the worst of the
trouble, and that the prize of Milan might yet be his.
So, before the imperialists were well out of France, he
crossed the Alps and sat down to besiege Pavia. It was
brilliantly defended by Antonio de Leyva. In November
Francis's ruin was thought to be certain; astrologers
predicted his death or imprisonment.[3] Slowly and surely
Pescara, the most consummate general of his age, was
pressing north with imperial troops to succour Pavia.
Francis would not raise the siege. On 24th February,
1525, he was attacked in front by Pescara and in the
rear by De Leyva. "The victory is complete," wrote the

---

[1] L. and P. iii. 3547, 3592; Sp. Cal. ii. 610. He thought of retaining
his name Julius, but was told that Popes who followed that practice
always had short pontificates.

[2] Sp. Cal. ii. 686; L. and P. iv. 751, 753, 773, 774, 776.

[3] Sp. Cal. ii. 692-94, 711.

Abbot of Najera to Charles from the field of battle, " the King of France is made prisoner. . . . The whole French army is annihilated. . . . To-day is feast of the Apostle St. Mathias, on which, five and twenty years ago, your Majesty is said to have been born. Five and twenty thousand times thanks and praise to God for His mercy ! Your Majesty is, from this day, in a position to prescribe laws to Christians and Turks, according to your pleasure."[1]

Such was the result of Wolsey's policy since 1521, Francis a prisoner, Charles a dictator, and Henry vainly hoping that he might be allowed some share in the victor's spoils. But what claim had he ? By the most extraordinary misfortune or fatuity, England had not merely helped Charles to a threatening supremacy, but had retired from the struggle just in time to deprive herself of all claim to benefit by her mistaken policy. She had looked on while Bourbon invaded France, fearing to aid lest Charles would reap all the fruits of success. She had sent no force across the channel to threaten Francis's rear. Not a single French soldier had been diverted from attacking Charles in Italy through England's interference. One hundred thousand crowns had been promised the imperial troops, but the money was not paid ; and secret negotiations had been going on with France. In spite of all, Charles had won, and he was naturally not disposed to divide the spoils. England's policy since 1521 had been disastrous to herself, to Wolsey, to the Papacy, and even to Christendom. For the falling out of Christian princes seemed to the Turk to afford an excellent opportunity for the faithful to come by his own. After an heroic defence by the knights of St. John, Rhodes, the bulwark of Christendom, had surrendered to Selim. Belgrade, the strongest citadel in Eastern Europe, followed. In August, 1526, the King and the flower of Hungarian nobility perished at the battle of Mohacz ; and the internecine strife of Christians seemed doomed to be sated only by their common subjugation to the Turk.

[1] *Sp. Cal.* ii. 722 ; cf. Hall's *Chron.* p. 693, which professes to give the " very words " of Francis I's much misquoted letter to his mother (*L. and P.* iv. 1120-24).

Henry and Wolsey began to pay the price of their policy at home as well as abroad. War was no less costly for being ineffective, and it necessitated demands on the purses of Englishmen to which they had long been unused. In the autumn of 1522 Wolsey was compelled to have recourse to a loan from both spiritualty and temporalty.[1] It seems to have met with a response which, compared with later receptions, may be described as almost cheerful. But the loan did not go far, and before another six months had elapsed it was found necessary to summon Parliament to make further provision.[2] The Speaker was Sir Thomas More, who did all he could to secure a favourable reception of Wolsey's demands. An unwonted spirit of independence animated the members ; the debates were long and stormy ; and the Cardinal felt called upon to go down to the House of Commons, and hector it in such fashion that even More was compelled to plead its privileges. Eventually, some money was reluctantly granted ; but it too was soon swallowed up, and in 1525 Wolsey devised fresh expedients. He was afraid to summon Parliament again, so he proposed what he called an Amicable Grant. It was necessary, he said, for Henry to invade France in person ; if he went, he must go as a prince ; and he could not go as a prince without lavish supplies. So he required what was practically a graduated income-tax. The Londoners resisted till they were told that resistance might cost them their heads. In Suffolk and elsewhere open insurrection broke out. It was then proposed to withdraw the fixed ratio, and allow each individual to pay what he chose as a benevolence. A common councillor of London promptly retorted that benevolences were illegal by statute of Richard III. Wolsey cared little for the constitution, and was astonished that any one should quote the laws of a wicked usurper ; but the common councillor was a sound constitutionalist, if Wolsey was not. " An it please your grace," he replied, " although King Richard did evil, yet in his time were many good acts made, not by him only, but by the

[1] *L. and P.* iii. 2483.   [2] *Ibid.* iii. 2956, 2958, 3249.

consent of the body of the whole realm, which is Parliament."[1] There was no answer ; the demand was withdrawn. Never had Henry suffered such a rebuff, and he
never suffered the like again. Nor was this all ; the whole
of London, Wolsey is reported to have said, were traitors
to Henry.[2] Informations of " treasonable words "—that
ominous phrase—became frequent.[3] Here, indeed, was
a contrast to the exuberant loyalty of the early years of
Henry's reign. The change may not have been entirely
due to Wolsey, but he had been minister, with a power
which few have equalled, during the whole period in
which it was effected, and Henry may well have begun to
think that it was time for his removal.

Whether Wolsey was now anxious to repair his blunder
by siding with Francis against Charles, or to snatch
some profit from the Emperor's victory by completing
the ruin of France, the refusal of Englishmen to find
more money for the war left him no option but peace.
In April, 1525, Tunstall and Sir Richard Wingfield were
sent to Spain with proposals for the exclusion of Francis
and his children from the French throne and the dis-
memberment of his kingdom.[4] It is doubtful if Wolsey
himself desired the fulfilment of so preposterous and
iniquitous a scheme. It is certain that Charles was in
no mood to abet it. He had no wish to extract profit
for England out of the abasement of Francis, to see
Henry King of France, or lord of any French provinces.
He had no intention of even performing his part of the
Treaty of Windsor. He had pledged himself to marry
the Princess Mary, and the splendour of that match may
have contributed to Henry's desire for an alliance with
Charles. But another matrimonial project offered the
Emperor more substantial advantages. Ever since 1517
his Spanish subjects had been pressing him to marry
the daughter of Emmanuel, King of Portugal. The
Portuguese royal family had claims to the throne of

[1] Hall, *Chronicle*, ed. 1809, p. 698.
[2] *L. and P.* iii. 3076.   [3] *Ibid.* iii. 3082.
[4] *Ibid.* iv. 1212, 1249, 1255, 1264, 1296 ; *Stowe MS.* 147 ff. 67, 86
(Brit. Mus.).

Castile which would be quieted by Charles's marriage with a Portuguese princess. Her dowry of a million crowns was also an argument not to be lightly disregarded in Charles's financial embarrassments ; and in March, 1526, the Emperor's wedding with Isabella of Portugal was solemnised.

Wolsey, on his part, was secretly negotiating with Louise of Savoy during her son's imprisonment in Spain. In August, 1525, a treaty of amity was signed, by which England gave up all its claims to French territory in return for the promise of large sums of money to Henry and his minister.[1] The impracticability of enforcing Henry's pretensions to the French crown or to French provinces, which had been urged as excuses for squandering English blood and treasure, was admitted, even when the French King was in prison and his kingdom defenceless. But what good could the treaty do Henry or Francis ? Charles had complete control over his captive, and could dictate his own terms. Neither the English nor the French King was in a position to continue the war ; and the English alliance with France could abate no iota of the concessions which Charles extorted from Francis in January, 1526, by the Treaty of Madrid.[2] Francis surrendered Burgundy ; gave up his claims to Milan, Genoa and Naples ; abandoned his allies, the King of Navarre, the Duke of Guelders and Robert de la Marck ; engaged to marry Charles's sister Eleanor, the widowed Queen of Portugal ; and handed over his two sons to the Emperor as hostages for the fulfilment of the treaty. But he had no intention of keeping his promises. No sooner was he free than he protested that the treaty had been extracted by force, and that his oath to keep it was not binding. The Estates of France readily refused their assent, and the Pope was, as usual, willing, for political reasons, to absolve Francis from his oath. For the time being, consideration for the safety of his sons and the hope of obtaining their release prevented him from openly breaking with Charles, or listening to the proposals for a marriage with the Princess Mary, held out

[1] L. and P. iv. 1525, 1531, 1600, 1633.   [2] Ibid. iv. 1891.

as a bait by Wolsey.[1] The Cardinal's object was merely to injure the Emperor as much as he could without involving England in war ; and by negotiations for Mary's marriage, first with Francis, and then with his second son, the Duke of Orléans, he was endeavouring to draw England and France into a closer alliance. For similar reasons he was extending his patronage to the Holy League, formed by Clement VII between the princes of Italy to liberate that distressful country from the grip of the Spanish forces.

The policy of Clement, of Venice, and of other Italian States had been characterised by as much blindness as that of England. Almost without exception they had united, in 1523, to expel the French from Italy. The result was to destroy the balance of power south of the Alps, and to deliver themselves over to a bondage more galling than that from which they sought to escape. Clement himself had been elected Pope by imperial influence, and the Duke of Sessa, Charles's representative in Rome, described him as entirely the Emperor's creature.[2] He was, wrote Sessa, " very reserved, irresolute, and decides few things himself. He loves money and prefers persons who know where to find it to any other kind of men. He likes to give himself the appearance of being independent, but the result shows that he is generally governed by others."[3] Clement, however, after his election, tried to assume an attitude more becoming the head of Christendom than slavish dependence on Charles. His love for the Emperor, he told Charles, had not diminished, but his hatred for others had disappeared ;[4] and throughout 1524 he was seeking to promote concord between Christian princes. His methods were unfortunate ; the failure of the imperial invasion of Provence and Francis's passage of the Alps, convinced the Pope that Charles's star was waning, and that of France was in the ascendant. " The Pope," wrote Sessa to Charles V, " is at the disposal of the conqueror ".[5] So

[1] *L. and P.* iv. 2039, 2148, 2320, 2325.   [2] *Sp. Cal.* ii. 610.
[3] *Ibid.* ii. 619.   [4] *Ibid.* ii. 707
[5] *Ibid.* ii. 699, 30th Nov., 1524.

on 19th January, 1525, a Holy League between Clement and Francis was publicly proclaimed at Rome, and joined by most of the Italian States.[1] It was almost the eve of Pavia.

Charles received the news of that victory with astonishing humility. But he was not likely to forget that at the critical moment he had been deserted by most of his Italian allies; and it was with fear and trembling that the Venetian ambassador besought him to use his victory with moderation.[2] Their conduct could hardly lead them to expect much from the Emperor's clemency. Distrust of his intentions induced the Holy League to carry on desultory war with the imperial troops; but mutual jealousies, the absence of effective aid from England or France, and vacillation caused by the feeling that after all it might be safer to accept the best terms they could obtain, prevented the war from being waged with any effect. In September, 1526, Hugo de Moncada, the imperial commander, concerted with Clement's bitter foes, the Colonnas, a means of overawing the Pope. A truce was concluded, wrote Moncada, "that the Pope, having laid down his arms, may be taken unawares".[3] On the 19th he marched on Rome. Clement, taken unawares, fled to the castle of St. Angelo; his palace was sacked, St. Peter's rifled, and the host profaned. "Never," says Casale, "was so much cruelty and sacrilege".[4]

It was soon thrown into the shade by an outrage at which the whole world stood aghast. Charles's object was merely to render the Pope his obedient slave; neither God nor man, said Moncada, could resist with impunity the Emperor's victorious arms.[5] But he had little control over his own irresistible forces. With no enemy to check them, with no pay to content them, the

[1] *Sp. Cal.* ii. 702-11.   [2] *Ven. Cal.* iii. 413.
[3] *Sp. Cal.* ii. 898.   [4] *L. and P.* iv. 2510.
[5] Buonaparte's *Narrative*, ed. Buchon, p. 190, ed. Milanesi, p. 279; cf. Gregorovius, *Gesch. der Stadt Rom.* viii. 568 n., and Alberini's *Diary*, ed. Drano 1901 (extracts are printed in Creighton, *Papacy*, ed. 1901, vi. 419-37).

imperial troops were ravaging, pillaging, sacking cities and churches throughout Northern Italy without let or hindrance. At length a sudden frenzy seized them to march upon Rome. Moncada had shown them the way, and on 6th May, 1527, the Holy City was taken by storm. Bourbon was killed at the first assault ; and the richest city in Christendom was given over to a motley, leaderless horde of German, Spanish and Italian soldiery. The Pope again fled to the castle of St. Angelo ; and for weeks Rome endured an orgy of sacrilege, blasphemy, robbery, murder and lust, the horrors of which no brush could depict nor tongue recite. " All the churches and the monasteries," says a cardinal who was present, " both of friars and nuns, were sacked. Many friars were beheaded, even priests at the altar ; many old nuns beaten with sticks ; many young ones violated, robbed and made prisoners ; all the vestments, chalices, silver, were taken from the churches. . . . Cardinals, bishops, friars, priests, old nuns, infants, pages and servants—the very poorest— were tormented with unheard-of cruelties—the son in the presence of his father, the babe in the sight of its mother. All the registers and documents of the Camera Apostolica were sacked, torn in pieces, and partly burnt."[1] " Having entered," writes an imperialist to Charles, " our men sacked the whole Borgo and killed almost every one they found. . . . All the monasteries were rifled, and the ladies who had taken refuge in them carried off. Every person was compelled by torture to pay a ransom. . . . The ornaments of all the churches were pillaged and the relics and other things thrown into the sinks and cess-pools. Even the holy places were sacked. The Church of St. Peter and the papal palace, from the basement to the top, were turned into stables for horses. . . . Every one considers that it has taken place by the just judgment of God, because the Court of Rome was so ill-ruled. . . . We are expecting to hear from your Majesty how the city is to be governed and whether the Holy See is to be retained or not. Some are of opinion it should not continue in Rome, *lest the French King should make a*

[1] Cardinal Como in *Il Sacco di Roma*, ed. C. Milanesi, 1867, p. 471.

*patriarch in his kingdom, and deny obedience to the said
See, and the King of England and all other Christian
princes do the same.*"[1]

So low was brought the proud city of the Seven Hills,
the holy place, watered with the blood of the martyrs
and hallowed by the steps of the saints, the goal of the
earthly pilgrim, the seat of the throne of the Vicar of
God. No Jew saw the abomination of desolation standing
where it ought not with keener anguish than the devout
sons of the Church heard of the desecration of Rome.
If a Roman Catholic and an imperialist could term it the
just judgment of God, heretics and schismatics, preparing
to burst the bonds of Rome and " deny obedience to
the said See," saw in it the fulfilment of the woes pronounced by St. John the Divine on the Rome of Nero,
and by Daniel the Prophet on Belshazzar's Babylon.
Babylon the great was fallen, and become the habitation
of devils, and the hold of every foul spirit ; her ruler was
weighed in the balances and found wanting ; his kingdom
was divided and given to kings and peoples who came,
like the Medes and the Persians, from the hardier realms
of the North.

[1] *Il Sacco di Roma*, ed. Milanesi, pp. 499, 517.

CHAPTER VII

THE ORIGIN OF THE DIVORCE[1]

MATRIMONIAL discords have, from the days of Helen of Troy, been the fruitful source of public calamities ; and one of the most decisive events in English history, the breach with the Church of Rome, found its occasion in the divorce of Catherine of Aragon. Its origin has been traced to various circumstances. On one hand, it is attributed to Henry's passion for Anne Boleyn, on the other, to doubts of the validity of Henry's marriage, raised by the Bishop of Tarbes in 1527, while negotiating a matrimonial alliance between the Princess Mary and Francis I. These are the two most popular theories, and both are demonstrably false.[2] Doubts of the legality of Henry's marriage had existed long before the Bishop of Tarbes paid his visit to England, and even before Anne Boleyn was born. They were urged, not only on the eve of the completion of the marriage, but when it was first suggested. In 1503, when Henry VII applied to Julius II for a dispensation to enable his second son to marry his brother's widow, the Pope replied that " the dispensation was a great matter ; nor did he well know, *prima facie*, if it were competent for the Pope to dispense in such a case ".[3] He granted the dispensation, but the doubts were not entirely removed. Catherine's confessor instilled them into her mind, and was recalled by Ferdinand on that account. The Spanish King himself felt it necessary to dispel certain " scruples of conscience " Henry might entertain as to the " sin " of marrying his

[1] It is impossible to avoid the term " divorce," although neither from Henry VIII's nor from the Pope's point of view was there any such thing (see the present writer's *Cranmer* p. 24 *n.*).

[2] See, besides the original authorities cited in this chapter, Busch, *Der Ursprung der Ehescheidung König Heinrichs VIII* (Hist. Taschenbuch, Leipzig, VI. viii. 271-327).

[3] *L. and P.* iv. 5773 ; Pocock, *Records of the Reformation* i. 1.

brother's widow.[1] Warham and Fox debated the matter,
and Warham apparently opposed the marriage.[2] A
general council had pronounced against the Pope's dispensing power ;[3] and, though the Popes had, in effect,
established their superiority over general councils, those
who still maintained the contrary view can hardly have
failed to doubt the legality of Henry's marriage.

So good a papalist as the young King, however, would
hardly allow theoretical doubts of the general powers of
the Pope to outweigh the practical advantages of a
marriage in his own particular case ; and it is safe to
assume that his confidence in its validity would have
remained unshaken, but for extraneous circumstances of a
definite and urgent nature. On the 31st of January, 1510,
seven months after his marriage with Catherine, she gave
birth to her first child ; it was a daughter, and was still-
born.[4] On the 27th of May following she told her father
that the event was considered in England to be of evil
omen, but that Henry took it cheerfully, and she thanked
God for having given her such a husband. " The King,"
wrote Catherine's confessor, " adores her, and her highness him ". Less than eight months later, on the 1st of
January, 1511, she was delivered of her first-born son.[5]
A tourney was held to celebrate the joyous event, and
the heralds received a handsome largess at the christening.
The child was named Henry, styled Prince of Wales, and
given a serjeant-at-arms on the 14th, and a clerk of the
signet on the 19th of February. Three days later he was
dead ; he was buried at the cost of some ten thousand
pounds in Westminster Abbey. The rejoicings were
turned to grief, which, aggravated by successive dis-
appointments, bore with cumulative force on the mind

[1] Sp. Cal. vol. ii. Pref. p. xiv. No. 8.
[2] L. and P. iv. 5774 [6].   [3] Ibid. iv. 5376.
[4] D.N.B. ix. 292, gives this date. Catherine herself, writing on 27th
May, 1510, says that " some days before she had been delivered of a
still-born daughter " (Sp. Cal. ii. 43). On 1st November, 1509, Henry
informed Ferdinand that Catherine was pregnant, and the child had
quickened (ibid. ii. 23).
[5] Ven. Cal. ii. 95-96 ; L. and P. vol. i. 1491, 1495, 1513, Pref. p. lxxiii. ;
ii. 4692.

of the King and his people. In September, 1513, the Venetian ambassador announced the birth of another son,[1] who was either still-born, or died immediately afterwards. In June, 1514, there is again a reference to the christening of the " King's new son,"[2] but he, too, was no sooner christened than dead.

Domestic griefs were now embittered by political resentments. Ferdinand valued his daughter mainly as a political emissary ; he had formally accredited her as his ambassador at Henry's Court, and she naturally used her influence to maintain the political union between her father and her husband. The arrangement had serious drawbacks ; when relations between sovereigns grew strained, their ambassadors could be recalled, but Catherine had to stay. In 1514 Henry was boiling over with indignation at his double betrayal by the Catholic king ; and it is not surprising that he vented some of his rage on the wife who was Ferdinand's representative. He reproached her, writes Peter Martyr from Ferdinand's Court, with her father's ill-faith, and taunted her with his own conquests. To this brutality Martyr attributes the premature birth of Catherine's fourth son towards the end of 1514.[3] Henry, in fact, was preparing to cast off, not merely the Spanish alliance, but his Spanish wife. He was negotiating for a joint attack on Castile with Louis XII and threatening the divorce of Catherine.[4] " It is said," writes a Venetian from Rome in August, 1514, " that the King of England means to repudiate his present wife, the daughter of the King of Spain and his brother's widow, because he is unable to have children by her, and intends to marry a daughter of the French Duke of Bourbon. . . . He intends to annul his own marriage, and will obtain what he wants from the Pope as France did from Pope Julius II."[5]

But the death of Louis XII (January, 1515) and the consequent loosening of the Anglo-French alliance made Henry and Ferdinand again political allies ; while, as the

---

[1] *Ven. Cal.* ii. 329.   [2] *L. and P.* i. 5192.
[3] *Ibid.* i. 5718.   [4] See above p. 60.
[5] *Ven. Cal.* ii. 479. The Pope was really Alexander VI.

F

year wore on, Catherine was known to be once more
pregnant, and Henry's hopes of issue revived. This time
they were not disappointed; the Princess Mary was
born on the 18th of February, 1516.[1] Ferdinand had
died on the 23rd of January, but the news was kept from
Catherine, lest it might add to the risks of her confinement.[2] The young princess seemed likely to live, and
Henry was delighted. When Giustinian, amid his
congratulations, said he would have been better pleased
had it been a son, the King replied : " We are both
young ; if it was a daughter this time, by the grace of God
the sons will follow ".[3] All thoughts of a divorce passed
away for the time, but the desired sons did not arrive.
In August, 1517, Catherine was reported to be again
expecting issue, but nothing more is heard of the matter,
and it is probable that about this time the Queen had
various miscarriages. In July, 1518, Henry wrote to
Wolsey from Woodstock that Catherine was once more
pregnant, and that he could not move the Court to
London, as it was one of the Queen's " dangerous
times ".[4] His precautions were unavailing, and, on the
10th of November, his child arrived still-born. Giustinian notes the great vexation with which the people
heard the news, and expresses the opinion that, had it
occurred a month or two earlier, the Princess Mary would
not have been betrothed to the French dauphin, " as the
one fear of England was lest it should pass into subjection
to France through that marriage ".[5]

The child was the last born of Catherine. For some
years Henry went on hoping against every probability
that he might still have male issue by his Queen ; and
in 1519 he undertook to lead a crusade against the Turk
in person if he should have an heir.[6] But physicians
summoned from Spain were no more successful than
their English colleagues. By 1525 the last ray of hope
had flickered out. Catherine was then forty years old ;

---

[1] *L. and P.* ii. 1505, 1573.   [2] *Ibid.* ii. 1563, 1610.
[3] *Ven. Cal.* ii. 691.
[4] *Cotton MS.*, Vespasian, F iii. fol. 34, *b ;* cf. *L. and P.* ii. 4074, 4288.
[5] *Ven. Cal.* ii. 1103.   [6] *L. and P.* iii. 432.

and Henry, at the age of thirty-four, in the full vigour of youthful manhood, seemed doomed by the irony of fate and by his union with Catherine to leave a disputed inheritance. Never did England's interests more imperatively demand a secure and peaceful succession. Never before had there been such mortality among the children of an English king ; never before had an English king married his brother's widow. So striking a coincidence could be only explained by the relation of cause and effect. Men who saw the judgment of God in the sack of Rome, might surely discern in the fatality that attended the children of Henry VIII a fulfilment of the doom of childlessness pronounced in the Book of the Law against him who should marry his brother's wife. " God," wrote the French ambassador in 1528, " has long ago Himself passed sentence on it " ; [1] and there is no reason to doubt Henry's assertion, that he had come to regard the death of his children as a Divine judgment, and that he was impelled to question his marriage by the dictates of conscience. The " scruples of conscience," which Henry VII had urged as an excuse for delaying the marriage, were merely a cloak for political reasons ; but scruples of conscience are dangerous playthings, and the pretence of Henry VII became, through the death of his children, a terrible reality to Henry VIII.

Queen Catherine, too, had scruples of conscience about the marriage, though of a different sort. When she first heard of Henry's intention to seek a divorce, she is reported to have said that " she had not offended, but it was a judgment of God, for that her former marriage was made in blood " ; the price of it had been the head of the innocent Earl of Warwick, demanded by Ferdinand of Aragon. [2] Nor was she alone in this feeling. " He had heard," witnessed Buckingham's chancellor in 1521, " the Duke grudge that the Earl of Warwick was put to death, and say that God would punish it, by not suffering

---

[1] Du Bellay to Montmorenci, 1st Nov., 1528, *L. and P.* iv. 4899.
[2] *Sp. Cal.* i. 249 ; *L. and P. of Richard III and Henry VII*, vol. i. pp. xxxiii. 113 ; Hall, *Chron.* p. 491 ; Bacon, *Henry VII*, ed. 1870, p. 376 ; *Transactions of the Royal Hist. Soc.* N.S. xviii. 187.

the King's issue to prosper, as appeared by the death of
his sons ; and that his daughters prosper not, and that
he had no issue male ".[1]

Conscience, however, often moves men in directions
indicated by other than conscientious motives, and, of
the other motives which influenced Henry's mind, some
were respectable and some the reverse. The most
legitimate was his desire to provide for the succession to
the throne. It was obvious to him and his council that, if
he died with no children but Mary, England ran the
risk of being plunged into an anarchy worse than that
of the civil wars. "By English law," wrote Falier, the
Venetian ambassador, in 1531, "females are excluded from
the throne " ; [2] that was not true, but it was undoubtedly
a widespread impression, based upon the past history
of England. No Queen-Regnant had asserted a right
to the English throne but one, and that one precedent
provided the most effective argument for avoiding a
repetition of the experiment. Matilda was never crowned,
though she had the same claim to the throne as Mary,
and her attempt to enforce her title involved England in
nineteen years of anarchy and civil war. Stephen stood
to Matilda in precisely the same relation as James V of
Scotland stood to the Princess Mary ; and in 1532, as
soon as he came of age, James was urged to style himself
"Prince of England " and Duke of York, in manifest
derogation of Mary's title.[3] At that time Charles V
was discussing alternative plans for deposing Henry VIII.
One was to set up James V, the other to marry Mary
to some great English noble and proclaim them King
and Queen ;[4] Mary by herself was thought to have no
chance of success. John of Gaunt had maintained in
Parliament that the succession descended only through
males ;[5] the Lancastrian case was that Henry IV, the
son of Edward III's fourth son, had a better title to the

[1] L. and P. iii. 1284.   [2] Ven. Cal. iv. 300.
[3] L. and P. v. 609, 817.   [4] Ibid. vi. 446.
[5] Chronicon Angliae, Rolls Ser. p. 92, s.a. 1376 ; D.N.B. xxix. 421.
This became the orthodox Lancastrian theory (cf. Fortescue, Governance
of England, ed. Plummer, pp. 352-55).

throne than Philippa, the daughter of the third ; an Act limiting the succession to the male line was passed in 1406 ;[1] and Henry VII himself only reigned through a tacit denial of the right of women to sit on the English throne.

The objection to female sovereigns was grounded not so much on male disbelief in their personal qualifications, as upon the inevitable consequence of matrimonial and dynastic problems.[2] If the Princess Mary succeeded, was she to marry ? If not, her death would leave the kingdom no better provided with heirs than before ; and in her weak state of health, her death seemed no distant prospect. If, on the other hand, she married, her husband must be either a subject or a foreign prince. To marry a subject would at once create discords like those from which the Wars of the Roses had sprung ; to marry a foreign prince was to threaten Englishmen, then more jealous than ever of foreign influence, with the fear of alien domination. They had before their eyes numerous instances in which matrimonial alliances had involved the union of states so heterogeneous as Spain and the Netherlands ; and they had no mind to see England absorbed in some continental empire. In the matrimonial schemes arranged for the princess, it was generally stipulated that she should, in default of male heirs, succeed to the throne of England ; her succession was obviously a matter of doubt, and it is quite certain that her marriage in France or in Spain would have proved a bar in the way of her succession to the English throne, or at least have given rise to conflicting claims.

These rival pretensions began to be heard as soon as it became evident that Henry VIII would have no male heirs by Catherine of Aragon. In 1519, a year after the birth of the Queen's last child, Giustinian reported to

[1] Stubbs, *Const. Hist.* iii. 58. This Act was, however, repealed before the end of the same year.

[2] Professor Maitland has spoken of the " Byzantinism " of Henry's reign, and possibly the objection to female sovereigns was strengthened by the prevalent respect for Roman imperial and Byzantine custom (cf. Hodgkin, *Charles the Great* p. 180).

the Venetian signiory on the various nobles who had hopes of the crown. The Duke of Norfolk had expectations in right of his wife, a daughter of Edward IV, and the Duke of Suffolk in right of his Duchess, the sister of Henry VIII. But the Duke of Buckingham was the most formidable : " It was thought that, were the King to die without male heirs, that Duke might easily obtain the crown ".[1] His claims had been canvassed in 1503, when the issue of Henry VII seemed likely to fail,[2] and now that the issue of Henry VIII was in even worse plight, Buckingham's claims to the crown became again a matter of comment. His hopes of the crown cost him his head ; he had always been discontented with Tudor rule, especially under Wolsey ; he allowed himself to be encouraged with hopes of succeeding the King, and possibly spoke of asserting his claim in case of Henry's death. This was to touch Henry on his tenderest spot, and in 1521 the Duke was tried by his peers, found guilty of high treason, and sent to the block.[3] In this, as in all the great trials of Henry's reign, and indeed in most state trials of all ages, considerations of justice were subordinated to the real or supposed dictates of political expediency. Buckingham was executed, not because he was a criminal, but because he was, or might become, dangerous ; his crime was not treason, but descent from Edward III. Henry VIII, like Henry VII, showed his grasp of the truth that nothing makes a government so secure as the absence of all alternatives.

Buckingham's execution is one of the symptoms that, as early as 1521, the failure of his issue had made Henry nervous and susceptible about the succession. Even in

[1] *Ven. Cal.* ii. 1287. Buckingham's end was undoubtedly hastened by Wolsey's jealousy ; before the end of 1518 the Cardinal had been instilling into Henry's ear suspicions of Buckingham (*L. and P.* iii. 1 ; cf. *ibid.* ii. 3973, 4057). Brewer regards the hostility of Wolsey to Buckingham as one of Polydore Vergil's " calumnies " (*ibid.* vol. iii. Introd. p. lxvi.).

[2] *L. and P. of Richard III and Henry VII.* i. 233.

[3] See detailed accounts in *L. and P.* iii. 1284, 1356. Shakespeare's account in " Henry VIII " is remarkably accurate, except in matters of date.

1519, when Charles V's minister, Chièvres, was proposing
to marry his niece to the Earl of Devonshire, a grandson
of Edward IV, Henry was suspicious, and Wolsey inquired
whether Chièvres was "looking to any chance of the
Earl's succession to the throne of England ".[1] If further
proof were needed that Henry's anxiety about the
succession was not, as has been represented, a mere
afterthought intended to justify his divorce from
Catherine, it might be found in the extraordinary
measures taken with regard to his one and only illegitimate
son. The boy was born in 1519. His mother was Elizabeth
Blount, sister of Erasmus's friend, Lord Mountjoy ; and
she is noticed as taking part in the Court revels during the
early years of Henry's reign.[2] Outwardly, at any rate,
Henry's Court was long a model of decorum ; there was
no parade of vice as in the days of Charles II, and the
existence of this royal bastard was so effectually concealed
that no reference to him occurs in the correspondence of
the time until 1525, when it was thought expedient to
give him a position of public importance. The necessity
of providing some male successor to Henry was considered
so urgent that, two years before the divorce is said to have
occurred to him, he and his council were meditating a
scheme for entailing the succession on the King's illegitimate son. In 1525 the child was created Duke of Richmond and Somerset. These titles were significant ; Earl
of Richmond had been Henry VII's title before he came
to the throne ; Duke of Somerset had been that of his
grandfather and of his youngest son. Shortly afterwards
the boy was made Lord High Admiral of England, Lord
Warden of the Marches, and Lord Lieutenant of Ireland,[3]
the two latter being offices which Henry VIII himself
had held in his early youth. In January, 1527, the
Spanish ambassador reported that there was a scheme
on foot to make the Duke King of Ireland ;[4] it was
obviously a design to prepare the way for his succession
to the kingdom of England. The English envoys in

---

[1] L. and P. iii. 386.   [2] Ibid. ii. p. 1461.
[3] See G. E. C[okayne]'s and Doyle's Peerages, s.v. " Richmond ".
[4] Sp. Cal. iii. 109 ; L. and P. iv. 2988, 3028, 3140.

Spain were directed to tell the Emperor that Henry
proposed to demand some noble princess of near blood
to the Emperor as a wife for the Duke of Richmond.
The Duke, they were to say, " is near of the King's blood
and of excellent qualities, and is already furnished to
keep the state of a great prince, and yet may be easily,
by the King's means, exalted to higher things ".[1] The
lady suggested was Charles's niece, a daughter of the
Queen of Portugal ; she was already promised to the
Dauphin of France, but the envoys remarked that, if that
match were broken off, she might find " another dauphin "
in the Duke of Richmond. Another plan for settling the
succession was that the Duke should, by papal dispensation, marry his half-sister Mary ! Cardinal Campeggio
saw no moral objection to this. " At first I myself," he
writes on his arrival in England in October, 1528, " had
thought of this as a means of establishing the succession,
but I do not believe that this design would suffice to
satisfy the King's desires ".[2] The Pope was equally
willing to facilitate the scheme, on condition that Henry
abandoned his divorce from Catherine.[3] Possibly Henry
saw more objections than Pope or Cardinal to a marriage
between brother and sister. At all events Mary was
soon betrothed to the French prince, and the Emperor
recorded his impression that the French marriage was
designed to remove the Princess from the Duke of
Richmond's path to the throne.[4]

The conception of this violent expedient is mainly of
interest as illustrating the supreme importance attached
to the question of providing for a male successor to
Henry. He wanted an heir to the throne, and he wanted
a fresh wife for that reason. A mistress would not satisfy
him, because his children by a mistress would hardly

[1] L. and P. iv. 3051. In ibid. iv. 3135, Richmond is styled " The
Prince ".

[2] Laemmer, Monumenta Vaticana p. 29 ; L. and P. vi. 4881. It
was claimed that the Pope's dispensing power was unlimited, extending
even to marriages between brothers and sisters (ibid. v. 468). Campeggio
told Du Bellay in 1528 that the Pope's power was " infinite " (ibid. iv.
4942)

[3] L. and P. iv. 5072.   [4] Sp. Cal. iii. 482.

succeed without dispute to the throne, not because he
laboured under any moral scruples on the point. He had
already had two mistresses, Elizabeth Blount, the mother
of the Duke of Richmond, and Anne's sister, Mary Boleyn.
Possibly, even probably, there were other lapses from
conjugal fidelity, for, in 1533, the Duke of Norfolk told
Chapuys that Henry was always inclined to amours ;[1]
but none are capable of definite proof, and if Henry had
other illegitimate children besides the Duke of Richmond
it is difficult to understand why their existence should
have been so effectually concealed when such publicity
was given their brother. The King is said to have had
ten mistresses in 1528, but the statement is based on
a misrepresentation of the only document adduced in its
support.[2] It is a list of New Year's presents,[3] which
runs " To thirty-three noble ladies " such and such gifts,
then " to ten mistresses " other gifts ; it is doubtful if the
word then bore its modern sinister signification ; in this
particular instance it merely means " gentlewomen," and
differentiates them from the noble ladies. Henry's morals,
indeed, compare not unfavourably with those of other
sovereigns. His standard was neither higher nor lower
than that of Charles V, who was at this time negotiating
a marriage between his natural daughter and the Pope's
nephew ; it was not lower than those of James II, of
William III, or of the first two Georges ; it was infinitely
higher than the standard of Francis I, of Charles II, or
even of Henry of Navarre and Louis XIV.

The gross immorality so freely imputed to Henry seems
to have as little foundation as the theory that his sole
object in seeking the divorce from Catherine and separation from Rome was the gratification of his passion for
Anne Boleyn. If that had been the case, there would be
no adequate explanation of the persistence with which he
pursued the divorce. He was " studying the matter so

[1] *L. and P.* vi. 241.
[2] E. L. Taunton, *Wolsey* 1902, p. 173, where the words are erroneously
given as " To the King's ten mistresses " ; " the King's " is an inter-
polation.
[3] *L. and P.* iv. 3748

diligently," Campeggio says, " that I believe in this case
he knows more than a great theologian and jurist " ; he
was so convinced of the justice of his cause " that an
angel descending from heaven would be unable to persuade him otherwise ".[1] He sent embassy after embassy
to Rome ; he risked the enmity of Catholic Europe ; he
defied the authority of the vicar of Christ ; and lavished
vast sums to obtain verdicts in his favour from most of
the universities in Christendom. It is not credible that
all this energy was expended merely to satisfy a sensual
passion, which could be satisfied without a murmur from
Pope or Emperor, if he was content with Anne Boleyn
as a mistress, and is believed to have been already satisfied
in 1529, four years before the divorce was obtained.[2]
So, too, the actual sentence of divorce in 1533 was precipitated not by Henry's passion for Anne, but by the
desire that her child should be legitimate. She was
pregnant before Henry was married to her or divorced
from Catherine. But, though the representation of
Henry's passion for Anne Boleyn as the sole *fons et origo*
of the divorce is far from convincing, that passion introduced various complications into the question ; it was
not merely an additional incentive to Henry's desires ; it
also brought Wolsey and Henry into conflict ; and the
unpopularity of the divorce was increased by the feeling
that Henry was losing caste by seeking to marry a lady
of the rank and character of Anne Boleyn.

The Boleyns were wealthy merchants of London, of
which one of them had been Lord-Mayor, but Anne's
mother was of noble blood, being daughter and co-heir of
the Earl of Ormonde,[3] and it is a curious fact that all of

[1] *L. and P.* iv. 4858.

[2] No conclusive evidence on this point is possible ; the French
ambassador, Clement VII and others believed that Henry VIII and
Anne Boleyn had been cohabiting since 1529. On the other hand, if such
was the case, it is singular that no child should have been born before 1533 ;
for after that date Anne seems to have had a miscarriage nearly every
year. Ortiz, indeed, reports from Rome that she had a miscarriage in
1531 (*L. and P.* v. 594), but the evidence is not good.

[3] See Friedmann's *Anne Boleyn*, 2 vols., 1884, and articles on the
Boleyn family in *D.N.B.* vol. v.

Henry's wives could trace their descent from Edward I.[1]
Anne's age is uncertain, but she is generally believed to
have been born in 1507.[2] Attempts have been made to
date her influence over the King by the royal favours
bestowed on her father, Sir Thomas, afterwards Viscount
Rochford and Earl of Wiltshire, but, as these favours
flowed in a fairly regular stream from the beginning of
the reign, as Sir Thomas's services were at least a colourable excuse for them, and as his other daughter Mary
was Henry's mistress before he fell in love with Anne,
these grants are not a very substantial ground upon
which to build. Of Anne herself little is known except
that, about 1519, she was sent as maid of honour to the
French Queen, Claude ; five years before, her sister Mary
had accompanied Mary Tudor in a similar capacity on
her marriage with Louis XII.[3] In 1522, when war with
France was on the eve of breaking out, Anne was recalled
to the English Court,[4] where she took part in revels and
love-intrigues. Sir Thomas Wyatt, the poet, although a
married man, sued for her favours ;[5] Henry, Lord Percy
made her more honest proposals, but was compelled to
desist by the King himself, who had arranged for her
marriage with Piers Butler, son of the Earl of Ormonde,
as a means to end the feud between the Butler and the
Boleyn families.

None of these projects advanced any farther, possibly

[1] See George Fisher, *Key to the History of England*, Table xvii. ;
Gentleman's Magazine, May, 1829.

[2] Henry would then be fifteen, yet a fable was invented and often
repeated that Henry VIII was Anne Boleyn's father. Nicholas Sanders,
whose *De Origine ac Progressu Schismatis Anglicani* became the basis of
Roman Catholic histories of the English Reformation, gave currency to
the story ; and some modern writers prefer Sanders' veracity to Foxe's.

[3] The error that it was Anne who accompanied Mary Tudor in 1514
was exposed by Brewer more than forty years ago, but it still lingers
and was repeated with innumerable others in the Catalogue of the New
Gallery Portrait Exhibition of 1902.

[4] *L. and P.* iii. 1994.

[5] In Harpsfield's *Pretended Divorce* there is a very improbable story
that Wyatt told Henry VIII his relations with Anne were far from
innocent and warned the King against marrying a woman of Anne's
character.

because they conflicted with the relations developing between Anne and the King himself. As Wyatt complained in a sonnet,[1]

> There is written her fair neck round about
> *Noli me tangere ;* for Cæsar's I am
> And wild for to hold, though I seem tame.

But, for any definite documentary evidence to the contrary, it might be urged that Henry's passion for Anne was subsequent to the commencement of his proceedings for a divorce from Catherine. Those proceedings began at least as early as March, 1527, while the first allusion to the connection between the King and Anne Boleyn occurs in the instructions to Dr. William Knight, sent in the following autumn to procure a dispensation for her marriage with Henry.[2] The King's famous love-letters, the earliest of which are conjecturally assigned to July, 1527,[3] are without date and with but slight internal indications of the time at which they were written ; they may be earlier than 1527, they may be as late as the following winter. It is unlikely that Henry would have sought for the Pope's dispensation to marry Anne until he was assured of her consent, of which in some of the letters he appears to be doubtful ; on the other hand, it is difficult to see how a lady of the Court could refuse an offer of marriage made by her sovereign. Her reluctance was to fill a less honourable position, into which Henry was not so wicked as to think of forcing her. " I trust," he writes in one of his letters, " your absence is not wilful on your part ; for if so, I can but lament my ill-fortune, and by degrees abate my great folly ".[4] His love for Anne Boleyn was certainly his " great folly," the one overmastering passion of his life. There is,

---

[1] Wyatt, *Works*, ed. G. F. Nott, 1816, p. 143.

[2] *L. and P.* iv. 3422.

[3] *Ibid.* iv. 3218-20, 3325-26, 3990, 4383, 4403, 4410, 4477, 4537, 4539, 4597, 4648, 4742, 4894. They have also been printed by Hearne at the end of his edition of *Robert of Avesbury*, in the *Pamphleteer*, vol. xxi., and in the *Harleian Miscellany*, vol. iii. The originals in Henry's hand are in the Vatican Library.

[4] *L. and P.* iv. 3326.

however, nothing very extraordinary in the letters themselves ; in one he says he has for more than a year been
"wounded with the dart of love," and is uncertain
whether Anne returns his affection. In others he bewails
her briefest absence as though it were an eternity ;
desires her father to hasten his return to Court ; is torn
with anxiety lest Anne should take the plague, comforts
her with the assurance that few women have had it, and
sends her a hart killed by his own hand, making the
inevitable play on the word. Later on, he alludes to the
progress of the divorce case ; excuses the shortness of a
letter on the ground that he has spent four hours over
the book he was writing in his own defence[1] and has a
pain in his head. The series ends with an announcement
that he has been fitting up apartments for her, and with
congratulations to himself and to her that the " well-
wishing " Legate, Campeggio, who has been sent from
Rome to try the case, has told him he was not so
" imperial " in his sympathies as had been alleged.

The secret of her fascination over Henry was a puzzle
to observers. " Madame Anne," wrote a Venetian, " is
not one of the handsomest women in the world. She is
of middling stature, swarthy complexion, long neck, wide
mouth, bosom not much raised, and in fact has nothing
but the King's great appetite, and her eyes, which are
black and beautiful ".[2] She had probably learnt in France
the art of using her beautiful eyes to the best advantage ;
her hair, which was long and black, she wore loose, and
on her way to her coronation Cranmer describes her as
" sitting *in* her hair ".[3] Possibly this was one of the
French customs, which somewhat scandalised the staider
ladies of the English Court. She is said to have had a
slight defect on one of her nails, which she endeavoured
to conceal behind her other fingers.[4] Of her mental
accomplishments there is not much evidence ; she

[1] In 1531 he was said to have written " many books " on the divorce
question (*L. and P.* v. 251).
[2] *Ven. Cal.* iv. 365.
[3] Cranmer, *Works* (Parker Soc.) ii. 245 ; cf. *Ven. Cal.* iv. 351, 418.
[4] *L. and P.* iv. Introd. p. ccxxxvii.

naturally, after some years' residence at the Court of France, spoke French, though she wrote it in an orthography that was quite her own. Her devotion to the Gospel is the one great virtue with which Foxe and other Elizabethans strove to invest the mother of the Good Queen Bess. But it had no nobler foundation than the facts that Anne's position drove her into hostility to the Roman jurisdiction, and that her family shared the envy of church goods, common to the nobility and the gentry of the time.[1] Her place in English history is due solely to the circumstance that she appealed to the less refined part of Henry's nature ; she was pre-eminent neither in beauty nor in intellect, and her virtue was not of a character to command or deserve the respect of her own or subsequent ages.

It is otherwise with her rival, Queen Catherine, the third of the principal characters involved in the divorce. If Henry's motives were not so entirely bad as they have often been represented, neither they nor Anne Boleyn's can stand a moment's comparison with the unsullied purity of Catherine's life or the lofty courage with which she defended the cause she believed to be right. There is no more pathetic figure in English history, nor one condemned to a crueller fate. No breath of scandal touched her fair name, or impugned her devotion to Henry. If she had the misfortune to be identified with a particular policy, the alliance with the House of Burgundy, the fault was not hers ; she had been married to Henry in consideration of the advantages which that alliance was supposed to confer ; and, if she used her influence to further Spanish interest, it was a natural feeling as near akin to virtue as to vice, and Carroz at least complained, in 1514, that she had completely identified

---

[1] There is not much historical truth in Gray's phrase about " the Gospel light which dawned from Bullen's eyes " ; but Brewer goes too far in minimising the " Lutheran " proclivities of the Boleyns. In 1531 Chapuys described Anne and her father as being " more Lutheran than Luther himself " (*L. and P.* v. 148), in 1532 as " true apostles of the new sect " (*ibid.* v. 850), and in 1533 as " perfect Lutherans " (*ibid.* vi. 142).

herself with her husband and her husband's subjects.[1]
If her miscarriages and the death of her children were a
grief to Henry, the pain and the sorrow were hers in far
greater measure ; if they had made her old and deformed,
as Francis brutally described her in 1519,[2] the fact must
have been far more bitter to her than it was unpleasant
to Henry. There may have been some hardship to
Henry in the circumstance that, for political motives, he
had been induced by his council to marry a wife who was
six years his senior ; but to Catherine herself a divorce
was the height of injustice. The question was in fact
one of justice against a real or supposed political necessity,
and in such cases justice commonly goes to the wall.
In politics, men seek to colour with justice actions based
upon considerations of expediency. They first convince
themselves, and then they endeavour with less success
to persuade mankind.

So Henry VIII convinced himself that the dispensation granted by Julius II was null and void, that he had
never been married to Catherine, and that to continue to
live with his brother's wife was sin. " The King," he
instructed his ambassador to tell Charles V in 1533,
" taketh himself to be in the right, not because so many
say it, but because he, being learned, knoweth the matter
to be right. . . . The justice of our cause is so rooted in
our breast that nothing can remove it, and even the
canons say that a man should rather endure all the
censures of the Church than offend his conscience."[3] No
man was less tolerant of heresy than Henry, but no man
set greater store on his own private judgment. To that
extent he was a Protestant ; " though," he instructed
Paget in 1534 to tell the Lutheran princes, " the law of
every man's conscience be but a private court, yet it is
the highest and supreme court for judgment or justice ".
God and his conscience, he told Chapuys in 1533, were

---

[1] *Sp. Cal.* ii. 201. [2] *Ven. Cal.* ii. 1230.
[3] *L. and P.* vi. 775. *Hoc volo, sic jubeo ; stet pro ratione voluntas.* Luther
quoted this line *à propos* of Henry ; see his preface to Robert Barnes'
Bekenntniss des Glaubens, Wittemberg, 1540.

on very good terms.[1] On another occasion he wrote to
Charles *Ubi Spiritus Domini, ibi libertas*,[2] with the
obvious implication that he possessed the spirit of the
Lord, and therefore he might do as he liked. To him,
as to St. Paul, all things were lawful ; and Henry's
appeals to the Pope, to learned divines, to universities at
home and abroad, were not for his own satisfaction, but
were merely concessions to the profane herd, unskilled
in royal learning and unblessed with a kingly conscience.
Against that conviction, so firmly rooted in the royal
breast, appeals to pity were vain, and attempts to shake
it were perilous. It was his conscience that made Henry
so dangerous. Men are tolerant of differences about
things indifferent, but conscience makes bigots of us all ;
theological hatreds are proverbially bitter, and religious
wars are cruel. Conscience made Sir Thomas More
persecute, and glory in the persecution of heretics,[3]
and conscience earned Mary her epithet " Bloody ".
They were moved by conscientious belief in the Catholic
faith, Henry by conscientious belief in himself ; and
conscientious scruples are none the less exigent for being
reached by crooked paths.

[1] *L. and P.* vi. 351 ; vii. 148.   [2] *Ibid.* iv. 6111.
[3] It has been denied that More either persecuted or gloried in the
persecution of heretics ; but he admits himself that he recommended
corporal punishment in two cases and " it is clear that he underestimated
his activity " (*D.N.B.* xxxviii. 436, and instances and authorities there
cited).

CHAPTER VIII

THE POPE'S DILEMMA

In February, 1527, in pursuance of the alliance with France, which Wolsey, recognising too late the fatal effects of the union with Charles, was seeking to make the basis of English policy, a French embassy arrived in England to conclude a marriage between Francis I and the Princess Mary. At its head was Gabriel de Grammont, Bishop of Tarbes ; and in the course of his negotiations he is alleged to have first suggested those doubts of the validity of Henry's marriage, which ended in the divorce. The allegation was made by Wolsey three months later, and from that time down to our own day it has done duty with Henry's apologists as a sufficient vindication of his conduct. It is now denounced as an impudent fiction, mainly on the ground that no hint of these doubts occurs in the extant records of the negotiations. But unfortunately we have only one or two letters relating to this diplomatic mission.[1] There exists, indeed, a detailed narrative, drawn up some time afterwards by Claude Dodieu, the French secretary ; but the silence, on so confidential a matter, of a third party who was not present when the doubts were presumably suggested, proves little or nothing. Du Bellay, in 1528, reported to the French Government Henry's public assertion that Tarbes had mentioned these doubts ;[2] the

[1] Dr. Gairdner (*Engl. Hist. Rev.* xi. 675) speaks of the " full diplomatic correspondence which we possess " ; the documents are these : (1) an undated letter (*L. and P.* iv. App. 105) announcing the ambassador's arrival in England ; (2) a letter of 21st March (*ibid.* iv. 2974) ; (3) a brief note of no importance to Dr. Brienne, dated 2nd April (*ibid.* 3012) ; (4) the formal commission of Francis I, dated 13th April (*ibid.* 3059) ; (5) the treaty of 30th April (3080) ; and (6) three brief notes from Turenne to Montmorenci, dated 6th, 7th and 24th April. From Tarbes himself there are absolutely no letters relating to his negotiations, and it would almost seem as though they had been deliberately destroyed. Our knowledge depends solely upon Dodieu's narrative.

[2] *L. and P.* iv. 4942.

statement was not repudiated ; Tarbes himself believed
in the validity of Henry's case and was frequently
employed in efforts to win from the Pope an assent to
Henry's divorce. It is rather a strong assumption to
suppose in the entire absence of positive evidence that
Henry and Wolsey were deliberately lying. There is
nothing impossible in the supposition that some such
doubts were expressed ; indeed, Francis I had every
reason to encourage doubts of Henry's marriage as a
means of creating a breach between him and Charles V.
In return for Mary's hand, Henry was endeavouring to
obtain various advantages from Francis in the way of
pensions, tribute and territory. Tarbes represented that
the French King was so good a match for the English
princess, that there was little need for further concession ;
to which Henry replied that Francis was no doubt an
excellent match for his daughter, but was he free to
marry ? His precontract with Charles V's sister, Eleanor,
was a complication which seriously diminished the value
of Francis's offer ; and the papal dispensation, which he
hoped to obtain, might not be forthcoming or valid.[1] As
a counter to this stroke, Tarbes may well have hinted that
the Princess Mary was not such a prize as Henry made
out. Was the dispensation for Henry's own marriage
beyond cavil ? Was Mary's legitimacy beyond question ?
Was her succession to the English throne, a prospect
Henry dangled before the Frenchman's eyes, so secure ?
These questions were not very new, even at the time of
Tarbes's mission. The divorce had been talked about in
1514, and now, in 1527, the position of importance given
to the Duke of Richmond was a matter of public comment, and inevitably suggested doubts of Mary's succession. There is no documentary evidence that this
argument was ever employed, beyond the fact that,
within three months of Tarbes's mission, both Henry

---

[1] " There will be great difficulty," wrote Clerk, " *circa istud bene-
dictum divortium* ". Brewer interpreted this as the earliest reference to
Henry's divorce ; it was really, as Dr. Ehses shows, in reference to the
dissolution of the precontract between Francis I and Charles V's sister
Eleanor (*Engl. Hist. Rev.* xi. 676).

and Wolsey asserted that the Bishop had suggested doubts of the validity of Henry's marriage.[1] Henry, however, does not say that Tarbes *first* suggested the doubts, nor does Wolsey. The Cardinal declares that the Bishop objected to the marriage with the Princess Mary on the ground of these doubts; and some time later, when Henry explained his position to the Lord Mayor and aldermen of London, he said, according to Du Bellay, that the scruple of conscience, which he had *long* entertained, had terribly increased upon him since Tarbes had spoken of it.[2]

However that may be, before the Bishop's negotiations were completed the first steps had been taken towards the divorce, or, as Wolsey and Henry pretended, towards satisfying the King's scruples as to the validity of his marriage. Early in April, 1527, Dr. Richard Wolman was sent down to Winchester to examine old Bishop Fox on the subject.[3] The greatest secrecy was observed and none of the Bishop's councillors were allowed to be

[1] *L. and P.* iv. 3231.

[2] *Ibid.* iv. 4231, 4942. Henry's own account of the matter was as follows: "For some years past he had noticed in reading the Bible the severe penalty inflicted by God on those who married the relicts of their brothers"; he at length "began to be troubled in his conscience, and to regard the sudden deaths of his male children as a Divine judgment. The more he studied the matter, the more clearly it appeared to him that he had broken a Divine law. He then called to counsel men learned in pontifical law, to ascertain their opinion of the dispensation. Some pronounced it invalid. So far he had proceeded as secretly as possible that he might do nothing rashly" (*L and P.* iv. 5156; cf. iv. 3641). Shakespeare, following Cavendish (p. 221), makes Henry reveal his doubts first to his confessor, Bishop Longland of Lincoln: "First I began in private with you, my Lord of Lincoln" ("Henry VIII," Act II, sc. iv.); and there is contemporary authority for this belief. In 1532 Longland was said to have suggested a divorce to Henry ten years previously (*L. and P.* v. 1114), and Chapuys termed him "the principal promoter of these practices" (*ibid.* v. 1046); and in 1536 the northern rebels thought that he was the beginning of all the trouble (*ibid.* xi. 705); the same assertion is made in the anonymous "Life and Death of Cranmer" (*Narr. of the Reformation,* Camden Soc. p. 219). Other persons to whom the doubtful honour was ascribed are Wolsey and Stafileo, Dean of the Rota at Rome (*L. and P.* iv. 3400; *Sp. Cal.* iv. 159).

[3] *L. and P.* iv. 5291. This examination took place on 5th and 6th April.

present. Other evidence was doubtless collected from
various sources, and on 17th May, a week after Tarbes's
departure, Wolsey summoned Henry to appear before
him to explain his conduct in living with his brother's
widow.[1] Wolman was appointed promoter of the suit;
Henry put in a justification, and on 31st May Wolman
replied. With that the proceedings terminated. In
instituting them Henry was following a precedent set by
his brother-in-law, the Duke of Suffolk.[2] In very early
days that nobleman had contracted to marry Sir Anthony
Browne's daughter, but for some reason the match was
broken off, and he sought the hand of one Margaret
Mortimer, to whom he was related in the second and third
degrees of consanguinity; he obtained a dispensation,
completed the marriage, and cohabited with Margaret
Mortimer. But, like Henry VIII, his conscience or other
considerations moved him to regard his marriage as sin,
and the dispensation as invalid. He caused a declaration
to that effect to be made by " the official of the Arch-
deacon of London, to whom the cognisance of such causes
of old belongs," married Anne Browne, and, after her
death, Henry's sister Mary. A marriage, the validity of
which depended, like Henry's, upon a papal dispensation,
and which, like Henry's, had been consummated, was
declared null and void on exactly the same grounds as
those upon which Henry himself sought a divorce, namely,
the invalidity of the previous dispensation. On 12th May,
1528, Clement VII issued a bull confirming Suffolk's
divorce and pronouncing ecclesiastical censures on all
who called in question the Duke's subsequent marriages.
That is precisely the course Henry wished to be followed.
Wolsey was to declare the marriage invalid on the ground
of the insufficiency of the papal dispensation; Henry
might then marry whom he pleased; the Pope was to
confirm the sentence, and censure all who should dispute
the second marriage or the legitimacy of its possible issue.

Another precedent was also forced on Henry's mind.
On 11th March, 1527, two months before Wolsey opened

---

[1] *L. and P.* iv. 3140.　　　　[2] *Ibid.* iv. 5859; cf. iv. 737.

his court, a divorce was granted at Rome to Henry's sister Margaret, Queen of Scotland.[1] Her pretexts were infinitely more flimsy than Henry's own. She alleged a precontract on the part of her husband, Angus, which was never proved. She professed to believe that James IV had survived Flodden three years, and was alive when she married Angus. Angus had been unfaithful, but that was no ground for divorce by canon law ; and she herself was living in shameless adultery with Henry Stewart, who had also procured a divorce to be free to marry his Queen. No objection was found at Rome to either of these divorces ; but neither Angus nor Margaret Mortimer had an Emperor for a nephew ; no imperial armies would march on Rome to vindicate the validity of their marriages, and Clement could issue his bulls without any fear that their justice would be challenged by the arms of powerful princes. Not so with Henry ; while the secret proceedings before Wolsey were in progress, the world was shocked by the sack of Rome, and Clement was a prisoner in the hands of the Emperor's troops. There was no hope that a Pope in such a plight would confirm a sentence to the detriment of his master's aunt. " If the Pope," wrote Wolsey to Henry on receipt of the news, " be slain or taken, it will hinder the King's affairs not a little, which have hitherto been going on so well ".[2] A little later he declared that, if Catherine repudiated his authority, it would be necessary to have the assent of the Pope or of the cardinals to the divorce. To obtain the former the Pope must be liberated ; to secure the latter the cardinals must be assembled in France.[3]

To effect the Pope's liberation, or rather to call an assembly of cardinals in France during Clement's captivity, was the real object of the mission to France, on which Wolsey started in July. Such a body, acting under Wolsey's presidency and in the territories of the French King, was as likely to favour an attack upon the Emperor's aunt as the Pope in the hands of Charles's armies was

---

[1] L. and P. iv. 4130.   [2] Ibid. iv. 3147.
[3] Ibid. iv. 3311.

certain to oppose it. Wolsey went in unparalleled splendour, not as Henry's ambassador but as his lieutenant ; and projects for his own advancement were, as usual, part of the programme. Louise of Savoy, the queen-mother of France, suggested to him that all Christian princes should repudiate the Pope's authority so long as he remained in captivity, and the Cardinal replied that, had the overture not been made by her, it would have been started by himself and by Henry.[1] It was rumoured in Spain that Wolsey " had gone into France to separate the Church of England and of France from the Roman, not merely during the captivity of the Pope and to effect his liberation, but for a perpetual division,"[2] and that Francis was offering Wolsey the patriarchate of the two schismatic churches. To win over the Cardinal to the interest of Spain, it was even suggested that Charles should depose Clement and offer the Papacy to Wolsey.[3] The project of a schism was not found feasible ; the cardinals at Rome were too numerous, and Wolsey only succeeded in gaining four, three French and one Italian, to join him in signing a protest repudiating Clement's authority so long as he remained in the Emperor's power. It was necessary to fall back after all on the Pope for assent to Henry's divorce, and the news that Charles had already got wind of the proceedings against Catherine made it advisable that no time should be lost. The Emperor, indeed, had long been aware of Henry's intentions ; every care had been taken to prevent communication between Catherine and her nephew, and a plot had been laid to kidnap a messenger she was sending in August to convey her appeal for protection. All was in vain, for the very day after Wolsey's court had opened in May, Mendoza wrote to Charles that Wolsey " as the finishing stroke to all his iniquities, had been scheming to bring about the Queen's divorce " ; and on the 29th of July, some days before Wolsey had any suspicion that a hint was abroad, Charles informed Mendoza that he had despatched Cardinal Quignon to Rome, to act on

[1] *L. and P.* iv. 3247, 3263. [2] *Ibid.* iv. 3291.
[3] *Sp Cal.* iii. 273.

the Queen's behalf and to persuade Clement to revoke Wolsey's legatine powers.[1]

In ignorance of all this, Wolsey urged Henry to send Ghinucci, the Bishop of Worcester, and others to Rome with certain demands, among which was a request for Clement's assent to the abortive proposal for a council in France.[2] But now a divergence became apparent between the policy of Wolsey and that of his king. Both were working for a divorce, but Wolsey wanted Henry to marry as his second wife Renée, the daughter of Louis XII, and thus bind more closely the two kings, upon whose union the Cardinal's personal and political schemes were now exclusively based. Henry, however, had determined that his second wife was to be Anne Boleyn, and of this determination Wolsey was as yet uninformed. The Cardinal had good reason to dread that lady's ascendancy over Henry's mind ; for she was the hope and the tool of the anti-clerical party, which had hitherto been kept in check by Wolsey's supremacy. The Duke of Norfolk was her uncle, and he was hostile to Wolsey for both private and public reasons ; her father, Viscount Rochford, her cousins, Sir William Fitzwilliam and Sir Francis Brian, and many more distant connections, were anxious at the first opportunity to lead an attack on the Church and Cardinal. Before the divorce case began Wolsey's position had grown precarious ; taxes at home and failure abroad had turned the loyalty of the people to sullen discontent, and Wolsey was mainly responsible. "Disaffection to the King," wrote Mendoza in March, 1527, " and hatred of the Legate are visible everywhere. . . . The King would soon be obliged to change his councillors, were only a leader to present himself and head the malcontents ; " and in May he reported a general rumour to the effect that Henry intended to relieve the Legate of his share in the administration.[3] The Cardinal had incurred the dislike of nearly every section of the

[1] *Sp. Cal.* iii. 193, 276, 300 ; *L. and P.* iv. 3312.
[2] *Ibid.* iv. 3400.
[3] *Sp. Cal.* iii. 109, 190, 192, 193 ; cf. iv. 3951, Du Bellay to Montmorenci, " those who desire to catch him tripping are very glad the people cry out ' Murder ' ".

community ; the King was his sole support and the King
was beginning to waver. In May there were high words
between Wolsey and Norfolk in Henry's presence ;[1] in
July King and Cardinal were quarrelling over ecclesiastical patronage at Calais,[2] and long before the failure of
the divorce suit, there were other indications that Henry
and his minister had ceased to work together in harmony.

It is, indeed, quite a mistake to represent Wolsey's
failure to obtain a sentence in Henry's favour as the sole
or main cause of his fall. Had he succeeded, he might
have deferred for a time his otherwise unavoidable
ruin, but it was his last and only chance. He was driven
to playing a desperate game, in which the dice were
loaded against him. If his plan failed, he told Clement
over and over again, it would mean for him irretrievable
ruin, and in his fall he would drag down the Church.
If it succeeded, he would be hardly more secure, for
success meant the predominance of Anne Boleyn and of
her anti-ecclesiastical kin. Under the circumstances, it
is possible to attach too much weight to the opinion of
the French and Spanish ambassadors, and of Charles V
himself, that Wolsey suggested the divorce as the means
of breaking for ever the alliance between England and
the House of Burgundy, and substituting for it a union
with France.[3] The divorce fitted in so well with Wolsey's
French policy that the suspicion was natural ; but the
same observers also recorded the impression that Wolsey
was secretly opposing the divorce from fear of the
ascendancy of Anne Boleyn.[4] That suspicion had been
brought to Henry's mind as early as June, 1527. It
was probably due to the fact that Wolsey was not
blinded by passion, as Henry was, to the difficulties in
the way, and that it was he who persuaded Henry to have
recourse to the Pope in the first instance,[5] when the

---

[1] L. and P. iv. 1411.   [2] Ibid. iv. 3304.   [3] Ibid. iv. 4112, 4865, 5512.
[4] Sp. Cal. iii. 432, 790 ; Ven. Cal. 1529, 212.
[5] " He showed me," writes Campeggio, " that in order to maintain
and increase here the authority of the Holy See and the Pope he had
done his utmost to persuade the King to apply for a legate . . . although
many of these prelates declared it was possible to do without one "
(iv. 4857 ; cf. iv. 5072, 5177).

King desired to follow Suffolk's precedent, obtain a sentence in England, marry again, and trust to the Pope to confirm his proceedings.

It is not, however, impossible to trace Wolsey's real designs behind these conflicting reports. He knew that Henry was determined to have a divorce and that this was one of those occasions upon which " he would be obeyed, whosoever spoke to the contrary ". As minister he must therefore either resign—a difficult thing in the sixteenth century—or carry out the King's policy. For his own part he had no objection to the divorce in itself ; he was no more touched by the pathos of Catherine's fate than was her nephew Charles V, he wished to see the succession strengthened, he thought that he might restore his tottering influence by obtaining gratification for the King, and he was straining every nerve to weaken Charles V, either because the Emperor's power was really too great, or out of revenge for his betrayal over the papal election. But he was strenuously hostile to Henry's marriage with Anne Boleyn for two excellent reasons : firstly she and her kin belonged to the anti-ecclesiastical party which Wolsey had dreaded since 1515, and secondly he desired Henry to marry the French Princess Renée in order to strengthen his anti-imperial policy. Further, he was anxious that the divorce problem should be solved by means of the Papacy, because its solution by merely national action would create a breach between England and Rome, would ruin Wolsey's chances of election as Pope, would threaten his ecclesiastical supremacy in England, which was merely a legatine authority dependent on the Pope,[1] and would throw Clement into the arms of Charles V, whereas Wolsey desired him to be an effective member of the anti-imperial alliance. Thus Wolsey was prepared to go part of the way with Henry VIII, but he clearly saw the point at which their paths would diverge ; and his efforts on Henry's behalf were hampered by his

---

[1] Wolsey " certainly proves himself very zealous for the preservation of the authority of the See Apostolic in this kingdom *because all his grandeur is connected with it* " (Campeggio to Sanga, 28th Oct., 1528, *L. and P.* iv. 4881).

endeavours to keep the King on the track which he had
marked out.

Henry's suspicions, and his knowledge that Wolsey
would be hostile to his marriage with Anne Boleyn,
induced him to act for the time independently of the
Cardinal ; and while Wolsey was in France hinting at
a marriage between Henry and Renée, the King himself
was secretly endeavouring to remove the obstacles to his
union with Anne Boleyn. Instead of adopting Wolsey's
suggestion that Ghinucci should be sent to Rome as an
Italian versed in the ways of the Papal Curia, he despatched
his secretary, Dr. William Knight, with two extraordinary
commissions, the second of which he thought would not
be revealed " for any craft the Cardinal or any other can
find ".[1] The first was to obtain from the Pope a dispensation to marry a second wife, without being divorced
from Catherine, the issue from both marriages to be
legitimate. This " licence to commit bigamy " has
naturally been the subject of much righteous indignation.
But marriage-laws were lax in those days, when Popes
could play fast and loose with them for political purposes ;
and besides the " great reasons and precedents, especially
in the Old Testament," to which Henry referred,[2] he
might have produced a precedent more pertinent, more
recent, and better calculated to appeal to Clement VII.
In 1521 Charles V's Spanish council drew up a memorial
on the subject of his marriage, in which they pointed out
that his ancestor, Henry IV of Castile, had, in 1437,
married Dona Blanca, by whom he had no children ; and
that the Pope thereupon granted him a dispensation to
marry a second wife on condition that, if within a fixed
time he had no issue by her, he should return to his
first.[3] A licence for bigamy, modelled after this precedent,
would have suited Henry admirably, but apparently he
was unaware of this useful example, and was induced to
countermand Knight's commission before it had been
communicated to Clement. The demand would not,

[1] Henry VIII to Knight in Corpus Christi College, Oxford, MS. 318,
f. 3, printed in the *Academy* xv. 239, and *Engl. Hist. Rev.* xi. 685.
[2] *L. and P.* iv. 4977.   [3] *Sp. Cal.* ii. 379.

however, have shocked the Pope so much as his modern defenders, for on 18th September, 1530, Casale writes to Henry : " A few days since the Pope secretly proposed to me that your Majesty might be allowed two wives. I told him I could not undertake to make any such proposition, because I did not know whether it would satisfy your Majesty's conscience. I made this answer because I know that the Imperialists have this in view, and are urging it ; but why, I know not."[1] Ghinucci and Benet were equally cautious, and thought the Pope's suggestion was only a ruse ; whether a ruse or not, it is a curious illustration of the moral influence Popes were then likely to exert on their flock.

The second commission, with which Knight was entrusted, was hardly less strange than the first. By his illicit relations with Mary Boleyn, Henry had already contracted affinity in the first degree with her sister Anne, in fact precisely the same affinity (except that it was illicit) as that which Catherine was alleged to have contracted with him before their marriage. The inconsistency of Henry's conduct, in seeking to remove by the same method from his second marriage the disability which was held to invalidate his first, helps us to define the precise position which Henry took up and the nature of his peculiar conscience. Obviously he did not at this stage deny the Pope's dispensing power ; for he was invoking its aid to enable him to marry Anne Boleyn. He asserted, and he denied, no principle whatever, though it must be remembered that his own dispensation was an almost, if not quite, unprecedented stretch of papal power. To dispense with the " divine " law against marrying the brother's wife, and to dispense with the merely canonical obstacle to his marriage with Anne arising out of his relations with Mary Boleyn, were very different matters ; and in this light the breach between England and Rome might be represented as caused by a novel extension of papal claims. Henry, however, was a casuist concerned exclusively with his own case. He maintained merely that the particular dispensation,

[1] *L. and P.* iv. 6627, 6705, App. 261.

granted for his marriage with Catherine, was null and
void. As a concession to others, he condescended to
give a number of reasons, none of them affecting any
principle, but only the legal technicalities of the case—
the causes for which the dispensation was granted, such
as his own desire, and the political necessity for the
marriage were fictitious ; he had himself protested against
the marriage, and so forth. For himself, his own conviction was ample sanction ; he knew he was living in
sin with Catherine because his children had all died but
one, and that was a manifest token of the wrath of
Providence. The capacity for convincing himself of his
own righteousness is the most effective weapon in the
egotist's armoury, and Henry's egotism touched the
sublime. His conscience was clear, whatever other people
might think of the maze of apparent inconsistencies in
which he was involved. In 1528 he was in some fear
of death from the plague ; fear of death is fatal to the
peace of a guilty conscience, and it might well have made
Henry pause in his pursuit after the divorce and Anne
Boleyn. But Henry never wavered ; he went on in
serene assurance, writing his love letters to Anne, as a
conscientiously unmarried man might do, making his
will,[1] " confessing every day and receiving his Maker at
every feast,"[2] paying great attention to the morals of
monasteries, and to charges of malversation against
Wolsey, and severely lecturing his sister Margaret on
the sinfulness of her life.[3] He hopes she will turn " to
God's word, the vively doctrine of Jesu Christ, the only
ground of salvation—1 COR. 3, etc." ; he reminds her
of " the divine ordinance of inseparable matrimony first
instituted in Paradise," and urges her to avoid " the
inevitable damnation threatened against advoutrers ".
Henry's conscience was convenient and skilful. He
believed in the " ordinance of inseparable matrimony,"

---

[1] *L. and P.* iv. 4404.   [2] *Ibid.* iv. 4542.
[3] *Ibid.* iv. 4131. Wolsey writes the letter, but he is only giving Henry's
" message ". The letter is undated, but it refers to the " shameless
sentence sent from Rome," i.e. sentence of divorce which is dated 11th
March, 1527.

so, when he wished to divorce a wife, his conscience warned him that he had never really been married to her. Hence his nullity suits with Catherine of Aragon, with Anne Boleyn and with Anne of Cleves. Moreover, if he had never been married to Catherine, his relations with Mary Boleyn and Elizabeth Blount were obviously not adultery, and he was free to denounce that sin in Margaret with a clear conscience.

Dr. Knight had comparatively little difficulty in obtaining the dispensation for Henry's marriage with Anne Boleyn ; but it was only to be effective after sentence had been given decreeing the nullity of his marriage with Catherine of Aragon ; and, as Wolsey saw, that was the real crux of the question.[1] Knight had scarcely turned his steps homeward, when he was met by a courier with fresh instructions from Wolsey to obtain a further concession from Clement ; the Pope was to empower the Cardinal himself, or some other safe person, to examine the original dispensation, and, if it were found invalid, to annul Henry's marriage with Catherine. So Knight returned to the Papal Court ; and then began that struggle between English and Spanish influence at Rome which ended in the victory of Charles V and the repudiation by England of the Roman jurisdiction. Never did two parties enter upon a contest with a clearer perception of the issues involved, or carry it on with their eyes more open to the magnitude of the results. Wolsey himself, Gardiner, Foxe, Casale, and every English envoy employed in the case, warned and threatened Clement that, if he refused Henry's demands, he would involve Wolsey and the Papal cause in England in a common ruin. " He alleged," said Campeggio of Wolsey, " that if the King's

---

[1] For these intricate negotiations see Stephan Ehses, *Römische Dokumente zur Geschichte der Ehescheidung Heinrichs VIII von England*, 1893 ; these documents had all, I think, been previously printed by Laemmer or Theiner, but only from imperfect copies often incorrectly deciphered. Ehses has printed the originals with the utmost care, and thrown much new light on the subject. The story of the divorce is retold in this new light by Dr. Gairdner in the *English Historical Review*, vols. xi. and xii. ; the documents in *L. and P.* must be corrected from these sources.

desire were not complied with . . . there would follow
the speedy and total ruin of the kingdom, of his Lordship
and of the Church's influence in this kingdom ".[1] " I cannot reflect upon it," wrote Wolsey himself, " and close my
eyes, for I see ruin, infamy and subversion of the whole
dignity and estimation of the See Apostolic if this course
is persisted in. You see in what dangerous times we are.
If the Pope will consider the gravity of this cause, and
how much the safety of the nation depends upon it, he
will see that the course he now pursues will drive the
King to adopt remedies which are injurious to the Pope,
and are frequently instilled into the King's mind."[2] On
one occasion Clement confessed that, though the Pope
was supposed to carry the papal laws locked up in his
breast, Providence had not vouchsafed him the key
wherewith to unlock them ; and Gardiner roughly asked
in retort whether in that case the papal laws should not
be committed to the flames.[3] He told how the Lutherans
were instigating Henry to do away with the temporal possessions of the Church.[4] But Clement could only bewail
his misfortune, and protest that, if heresies and schisms
arose, it was not his fault. He could not afford to offend
the all-powerful Emperor ; the sack of Rome and Charles's
intimation conveyed in plain and set terms that it was the
judgment of God[5] had cowed Clement for the rest of his
life, and made him resolve never again to incur the
Emperor's enmity.

From the point of view of justice, the Pope had an
excellent case ; even the Lutherans, who denied his dispensing power, denounced the divorce. *Quod non fieri
debuit*, was their just and common-sense point, *factum
valet*. But the Pope's case had been hopelessly weakened
by the evil practice of his predecessors and of himself.
Alexander VI had divorced Louis XII from his Queen
for no other reasons than that Louis XII wanted to unite
Brittany with France by marrying its duchess, and that

[1] *L. and P.* iv. 4881.   [2] *Ibid.* iv. 4897.
[3] *Ibid.* iv. 4167 ; cf. iv. 5156, and Ehses, *Römische Dokumente*, No. 20,
where Cardinal Pucci gives a somewhat different account of the interviews.
[4] *L. and P.* iv. 5038, 5417, 5476.   [5] *Sp. Cal.* iii. 309.

Alexander, the Borgia Pope, required Louis' assistance in
promoting the interests of the iniquitous Borgia family.[1]
The injustice to Catherine was no greater than that to
Louis' Queen. Henry's sister Margaret, and both the
husbands of his other sister, Mary, had procured divorces
from Popes, and why not Henry himself ? Clement was
ready enough to grant Margaret's divorce ;[2] he was
willing to give a dispensation for a marriage between
the Princess Mary and her half-brother, the Duke of
Richmond ; the more insuperable the obstacle, the more
its removal enhanced his power. It was all very well to
dispense with canons and divine laws, but to annul papal
dispensations—was that not to cheapen his own wares ?
Why, wrote Henry to Clement, could he not dispense
with human laws, if he was able to dispense with divine
at pleasure ?[3] Obviously because divine authority could
take care of itself, but papal prerogatives needed a careful
shepherd. Even this principle, such as it was, was not
consistently followed, for he had annulled a dispensation
in Suffolk's case. Clement's real anxiety was to avoid
responsibility. More than once he urged Henry to settle
the matter himself,[4] as Suffolk had done, obtain a sentence
from the courts in England, and marry his second wife.
The case could then only come before him as a suit
against the validity of the second marriage, and the
accomplished fact was always a powerful argument. Moreover, all this would take time, and delay was as dear to
Clement as irresponsibility. But Henry was determined
to have such a sentence as would preclude all doubts of
the legitimacy of his children by the second marriage, and
was as anxious to shift the responsibility to Clement's
shoulders as the Pope was to avoid it. Clement next
urged Catherine to go into a nunnery, for that would

[1] *L. and P.* iv. 5152, where Henry's ambassadors quote this precedent
to the Pope. Cf. *ibid.* v. 45, for other precedents.

[2] The sentence was actually pronounced by the Cardinal of Ancona,
and the date was 11th March, 1527, just before Henry commenced
proceedings against Catherine. Henry called it a " shameless sentence " ;
but it may nevertheless have suggested to his mind the possibility of
obtaining one like it.

[3] *L. and P.* iv. 5966.   [4] *Ibid.* iv. 3802, 6290.

only entail injustice on herself, and would involve the
Church and its head in no temporal perils.[1] When
Catherine refused, he wished her in the grave, and
lamented that he seemed doomed through her to lose the
spiritualties of his Church, as he had lost its temporalties
through her nephew, Charles V.[2]

It was thus with the utmost reluctance that he granted
the commission brought by Knight. It was a draft, drawn
up by Wolsey, apparently declaring the law on the matter
and empowering Wolsey, if the facts were found to be
such as were alleged, to pronounce the nullity of Catherine's marriage.[3] Wolsey desired that it should be granted
in the form in which he had drawn it up. But the Pope's
advisers declared that such a commission would disgrace
Henry, Wolsey and Clement himself. The draft was
therefore amended so as to be unobjectionable, or, in
other words, useless for practical purposes ; and, with
this commission, Knight returned to England, rejoicing
in the confidence of complete success. But, as soon as
Wolsey had seen it, he pronounced the commission " as
good as none at all ".[4] The discovery did not improve
his or Henry's opinion of the Pope's good faith ; but, dis-
sembling their resentment, they despatched, in February,
1528, Stephen Gardiner and Edward Foxe to obtain fresh
and more effective powers. Eventually, on 8th June a
commission was issued to Wolsey and Campeggio to try
the case and pronounce sentence ;[5] even if one was
unwilling, the other might act by himself ; and all appeals
from their jurisdiction were forbidden. This was not a
decretal commission ; it did not bind the Pope or prevent

---

[1] L. and P. iv. 5072. "It would greatly please the Pope," writes his
secretary Sanga, "if the Queen could be induced to enter some religion,
because, although this course would be portentous and unusual, he could
more readily entertain the idea, *as it would involve the injury of only one
person*".   [2] *Ibid.* iv. 5518.

[3] It was called a " decretal commission," and it was a legislative as well
as an administrative act ; the Pope being an absolute monarch, his decrees
were the laws of the Church ; the difficulties of Clement VII and indeed
the whole divorce question could never have arisen had the Church been
a constitutional monarchy.

[4] L. and P. iv. 3913.   [5] *Ibid.* iv. 4345.

him from revoking the case. Such a commission was,
however, granted on condition that it should be shown to
no one but the King and Wolsey, and that it should not
be used in the procedure. The Pope also gave a written
promise, in spite of a protest lodged on Catherine's behalf
by the Spanish ambassador, Muxetula,[1] that he would not
revoke, or do anything to invalidate, the commission, but
would confirm the cardinals' decision.[2] If, Clement had
said in the previous December, Lautrec, the French commander in Italy, came nearer Rome, he might excuse
himself to the Emperor as having acted under pressure.[3]
He would send the commission as soon as Lautrec
arrived. Lautrec had now arrived ; he had marched
down through Italy ; he had captured Melfi ; the
Spanish commander, Moncada, had been killed ; Naples
was thought to be on the eve of surrender.[4] The Spanish
dominion in Italy was waning, the Emperor's thunderbolts were less terrifying, and the justice of the cause
of his aunt less apparent.

On 25th July Campeggio embarked at Corneto,[5] and
proceeded by slow stages through France towards
England. Henry congratulated himself that his hopes
were on the eve of fulfilment. But, unfortunately for
him, the basis on which they were built was as unstable
as water. The decision of his case still depended upon
Clement, and Clement wavered with every fluctuation in
the success or the failure of the Spanish arms in Italy.
Campeggio had scarcely set out, when Doria, the famous
Genoese admiral, deserted Francis for Charles ;[6] on the
17th of August Lautrec died before Naples ;[7] and on
10th September an English agent sent Wolsey news of
a French disaster, which he thought more serious than the
battle of Pavia or the sack of Rome.[8] On the following
day Sanga, the Pope's secretary, wrote to Campeggio

[1] *Engl. Hist. Rev.* xii. 110-14.
[2] Ehses, *Römische Dok.*, No. 23 ; *Engl. Hist. Rev.* xii. 8.
[3] *L. and P.* iv. 3682, 3750.   [4] *Ibid.* iv. 3934, 3949, 4224.
[5] *Ibid.* iv. 4605.   [6] *Ibid.* iv. 4626.
[7] *Ibid.* iv. 4663.   [8] *Ibid.* iv. 4713.

G

that, " as the Emperor is victorious, the Pope must not give him any pretext for a fresh rupture, lest the Church should be utterly annihilated. . . . Proceed on your journey to England, and there do your utmost to restore mutual affection between the King and Queen. You are not to pronounce any opinion without a new and express commission hence."[1] Sanga repeated the injunction a few days later. " Every day," he wrote, " stronger reasons are discovered ; " to satisfy Henry " involves the certain ruin of the Apostolic See and the Church, owing to recent events. . . . If so great an injury be done to the Emperor . . . the Church cannot escape utter ruin, as it is entirely in the power of the Emperor's servants. You will not, therefore, be surprised at my repeating that you are not to proceed to sentence, under any pretext, without express commission ; but to protract the matter as long as possible."[2] Clement himself wrote to Charles that nothing would be done to Catherine's detriment, that Campeggio had gone merely to urge Henry to do his duty, and that the whole case would eventually be referred to Rome.[3] Such were the secret instructions with which Campeggio arrived in England in October.[4] He readily promised not to proceed to sentence, but protested against the interpretation which he put upon the Pope's command, namely, that he was not to begin the trial. The English, he said, " would think that I had come to hoodwink them, and might resent it. You know how much that would involve."[5] He did not seem to realise that the refusal to pass sentence was equally hoodwinking the English, and that the trial would only defer the moment of their penetrating the deception ; a trial was of no use without sentence.

In accordance with his instructions, Campeggio first sought to dissuade Henry from persisting in his suit for the divorce. Finding the King immovable, he endeavoured to induce Catherine to go into a nunnery, as the divorced wife of Louis XII had done, " who still

[1] *L. and P.* iv. 4721.　　　　　[2] *Ibid.* iv. 4736-37.
[3] *Sp. Cal.* iii. 779.　　　　　　[4] *L. and P.* iv. 4857.
[5] *Ibid.* iv. 4736.

lived in the greatest honour and reputation with God and all that kingdom ".[1] He represented to her that she had nothing to lose by such a step; she could never regain Henry's affections or obtain restitution of her conjugal rights. Her consent might have deferred the separation of the English Church from Rome; it would certainly have relieved the Supreme Pontiff from a humiliating and intolerable position. But these considerations of expediency weighed nothing with Catherine. She was as immovable as Henry, and deaf to all Campeggio's solicitations. Her conscience was, perhaps, of a rigid, Spanish type, but it was as clear as Henry's and a great deal more comprehensible. She was convinced that her marriage was valid; to admit a doubt of it would imply that she had been living in sin and imperil her immortal soul. Henry did not in the least mind admitting that he had lived for twenty years with a woman who was not his wife; the sin, to his mind, was continuing to live with her after he had become convinced that she was really not his wife. Catherine appears, however, to have been willing to take the monastic vows, if Henry would do the same. Henry was equally willing, if Clement would immediately dispense with the vows in his case, but not in Catherine's.[2] But there were objections to this course, and doubts of Clement's power to authorise Henry's re-marriage, even if Catherine did go into a nunnery.

Meanwhile, Campeggio found help from an unexpected quarter in his efforts to waste the time. Quite unknown to Henry, Wolsey, or Clement, there existed in Spain a brief of Julius II fuller than the original bull of dispensation which he had granted for the marriage of Henry and Catherine, and supplying any defects that might be found in it. Indeed, so conveniently did the brief meet the criticisms urged against the bull, that Henry and Wolsey at once pronounced it an obvious forgery, concocted after the doubts about the bull had been raised. No copy of the brief could be found in the English archives, nor could any trace be discovered of its having been registered

[1] *L. and P.* iv. 4858.   [2] *Ibid.* iv. 4977.

at Rome ; while Ghinucci and Lee, who examined the original in Spain, professed to see in it such flagrant inaccuracies as to deprive it of all claim to be genuine.[1] Still, if it were genuine, it shattered the whole of Henry's case. That had been built up, not on the denial of the Pope's power to dispense, but on the technical defects of a particular dispensation. Now it appeared that the validity of the marriage did not depend upon this dispensation at all. Nor did it depend upon the brief, for Catherine was prepared to deny on oath that the marriage with Arthur had been anything more than a form ;[2] in that case the affinity with Henry had not been contracted, and there was no need of either dispensation or brief. This assertion seems to have shaken Henry ; certainly he began to shift his position, and, early in 1529, he was wishing for some noted divine, friar or other, who would maintain that the Pope could not dispense at all.[3] This was his first doubt as to the plenitude of papal power ; his marriage with Catherine must be invalid, because his conscience told him so ; if it was not invalid through defects in the dispensation, it must be invalid because the Pope could not dispense. Wolsey met the objection with a legal point, perfectly good in itself, but trivial. There were two canonical disabilities which the dispensation must meet for Henry's marriage to be valid ; first, the consummation of Catherine's marriage with Arthur ; secondly, the marriage, even though it was not consummated, was yet celebrated *in facie ecclesiæ*, and generally reputed complete. There was thus an *impedimentum publicæ honestatis* to the marriage of Henry and Catherine, and this impediment was not mentioned in, and therefore not removed by, the dispensation.[4]

[1] *L. and P.* iv. 5376-77, 5470-71, 5486-87. For the arguments as to its validity see Busch, *England under the Tudors*, Eng. trs. i. 376-8 ; Friedmann, *Anne Boleyn* ii. 329 ; and Lord Acton in the *Quarterly Rev.* cxliii. 1-51.

[2] She made this statement to Campeggio in the confessional (*L. and P.* v. 4875).

[3] *Ibid.* iv. 5377, 5438 ; *Sp. Cal.* iii. 276, 327.

[4] *L. and P.* iv. 3217. See this point discussed in Taunton's *Cardinal Wolsey*, chap. x.

But all this legal argument might be invalidated by the brief. It was useless to proceed with the trial until the promoters of the suit knew what the brief contained. According to Mendoza, Catherine's " whole right " depended upon the brief, a statement indicating a general suspicion that the bull was really insufficient.[1] So the winter of 1528-29 and the following spring were spent in efforts to get hold of the original brief, or to induce Clement to declare it a forgery. The Queen was made to write to Charles that it was absolutely essential to her case that the brief should be produced before the legatine Court in England.[2] The Emperor was not likely to be caught by so transparent an artifice. Moreover, the emissary, sent with Catherine's letter, wrote as soon as he got to France, warning Charles that his aunt's letter was written under compulsion and expressed the reverse of her real desires.[3] In the spring of 1529 several English envoys, ending with Gardiner, were sent to Rome to obtain a papal declaration of the falsity of the brief. Clement, however, naturally refused to declare the brief a forgery, without hearing the arguments on the other side,[4] and more important developments soon supervened. Gardiner wrote from Rome, early in May, that there was imminent danger of the Pope revoking the case, and the news determined Henry and Wolsey to relinquish their suit about the brief, and push on the proceedings of the legatine Court, so as to get some decision before the case was called to Rome. Once the legates had pronounced in favour of the divorce, Clement was informed, the English cared little what further fortunes befel it elsewhere.

So, on the 31st of May, 1529, in the great hall of the Black Friars, in London, the famous Court was formally

[1] *Sp. Cal.* iii. 882.   [2] *L. and P.* iv. 4841.
[3] *Ibid.* iv. 5154, 5177, 5211 (ii.) ; *Sp. Cal.* iii. 877, 882.
[4] *L. and P.* iv. 5474. Yet there is a letter from Clement to Campeggio (*Cotton MS.*, Vitellius, B xii. 164 ; *L. and P.* iv. 5181) authorising him " to reject whatever evidence is tendered in behalf of this brief as an evident forgery ". Clement was no believer in the maxim *qui facit per alium facit per se ;* he did not mind what his legates did, so long as he was free to repudiate their action when convenient.

opened, and the King and Queen were cited to appear before it on the 18th of June.[1] Henry was then represented by two proxies, but Catherine came in person to protest against the competence of the tribunal.[2] Three days later both the King and the Queen attended in person to hear the Court's decision on this point. Catherine threw herself on her knees before Henry ; she begged him to consider her honour, her daughter's and his. Twice Henry raised her up ; he protested that he desired nothing so much as that their marriage should be found valid, in spite of the " perpetual scruple " he had felt about it, and declared that only his love for her had kept him silent so long ; her request for the removal of the cause to Rome was unreasonable, considering the Emperor's power there. Again protesting against the jurisdiction of the Court and appealing to Rome, Catherine withdrew. Touched by her appeal, Henry burst out in her praise. " She is, my Lords," he said, " as true, as obedient, and as conformable a wife, as I could, in my phantasy, wish or desire. She hath all the virtuous qualities that ought to be in a woman of her dignity, or in any other of baser estate."[3] But these qualities had nothing to do with the pitiless forms of law. The legate overruled her protest, refused her appeal, and summoned her back. She took no notice, and was declared contumacious.

The proceedings then went on without her ; Fisher, Bishop of Rochester, made a courageous defence of the validity of the marriage, to which Henry drew up a bitter reply in the form of a speech addressed to the legates.[4] The speed with which the procedure was hurried on was little to Campeggio's taste. He had not prejudged the case ; he was still in doubt as to which way the sentence would go ; and he entered a dignified protest against the orders he received from Rome to give sentence, if it came to that point, against Henry.[5] He would pronounce what judgment seemed to him just, but

---

[1] *L. and P.* iv. 5611, 5612.   [2] *Ibid.* iv. 5685, 5694, 5695, 5702.
[3] *Ibid.* iv. Introd. p. ccclxxv.   [4] *Ibid.* iv. Introd. p. ccclxxix.
[5] *Ibid.* iv. 5732, 5734.

he shrank from the ordeal, and he did his best to follow out Clement's injunctions to procrastinate.[1] In this he succeeded completely. It seemed that judgment could no longer be deferred ; it was to be delivered on the 23rd of July.[2] On that day the King himself, and the chief men of his Court, were present ; his proctor demanded sentence. Campeggio stood up, and instead of giving sentence, adjourned the Court till October.[3] " By the mass ! " burst out Suffolk, giving the table a great blow with his hand, " now I see that the old-said saw is true, that there was never a legate nor cardinal that did good in England." The Court never met again ; and except during the transient reaction, under Mary, it was the last legatine Court ever held in England. They might assure the Pope, Wolsey had written to the English envoys at Rome a month before, that if he granted the revocation he would lose the devotion of the King and of England to the See Apostolic, and utterly destroy Wolsey for ever.[4]

Long before the vacation was ended, news reached Henry that the case had been called to Rome ; the revocation was, indeed, decreed a week before Campeggio adjourned his court. Charles's star, once more in the ascendant, had cast its baleful influence over Henry's fortunes. The close alliance between England and France had led to a joint declaration of war on the Emperor in January, 1528, into which the English ambassadors in Spain had been inveigled by their French colleagues, against Henry's wishes.[5] It was received with a storm of opposition in England, and Wolsey had some difficulty in justifying himself to the King. " You may be sure," wrote Du Bellay, " that he is playing a

---

[1] L. and P. iv. 3604.   [2] Ibid. iv. 5789.

[3] It was alleged that this adjournment was only the usual practice of the curia ; but it is worth noting that in 1530 Charles V asserted that it was usual to carry on matters so important as the divorce during vacation (ibid. iv. 6452), and that Clement had repeatedly ordered Campeggio to prolong the suit as much as possible and above all to pronounce no sentence.

[4] L. and P. iv. 5703, 5715, 5780.

[5] Ibid. iv. 4564 ; Sp. Cal. iii. 729.

terrible game, for I believe he is the only Englishman who wishes a war with Flanders."[1] If that was his wish, he was doomed to disappointment. Popular hatred of the war was too strong; a project was mooted by the clothiers in Kent for seizing the Cardinal and turning him adrift in a boat, with holes bored in it.[2] The clothiers in Wiltshire were reported to be rising; in Norfolk employers dismissed their workmen.[3] War with Flanders meant ruin to the most prosperous industry in both countries, and the attempt to divert the Flanders trade to Calais had failed.[4] So Henry and Charles were soon discussing peace; no hostilities took place; an agreement that trade should go on as usual with Flanders[5] was followed by a truce in June,[6] and the truce by the Peace of Cambrai in the following year. That peace affords the measure of England's decline since 1521. Wolsey was carefully excluded from all share in the negotiations. England was, indeed, admitted as a participator, but only after Louise and Margaret of Savoy had practically settled the terms, and after Du Bellay had told Francis that, if England were not admitted, it would mean Wolsey's immediate ruin.[7]

By the Treaty of Cambrai Francis abandoned Italy to Charles. His affairs beyond the Alps had been going from bad to worse since the death of Lautrec; and the suggested guard of French and English soldiers which was to relieve the Pope from fear of Charles was never formed.[8] That failure was not the only circumstance which made Clement imperialist. Venice, the ally of England and France, seized Ravenna and Cervia, two papal towns.[9] "The conduct of the Venetians," wrote John Casale from Rome, "moves the Pope more than anything else, and he would use the assistance of any one, except the Devil, to avenge their injury."[10] "The King and the Cardinal," repeated Sanga to Campeggio, "must

[1] L. and P. iv. 3930.   [2] Ibid. iv. 4310.
[3] Ibid. iv. 4012, 4040, 4043, 4044, 4239.
[4] Ibid. iv. 3262.   [5] Ibid. iv. 4147.
[6] Ibid. iv. 4376.   [7] Ibid. iv. 5679, 5701, 5702, 5713.
[8] Ibid. iv. 5179.   [9] Ibid. iv. 4680-84.   [10] Ibid. iv. 4900.

not expect him to execute his intentions, until they have
used their utmost efforts to compel the Venetians to
restore the Pope's territories."[1] Henry did his best, but
he was not sincerely helped by Francis ; his efforts proved
vain, and Clement thought he could get more effective
assistance from Charles. " Every one is persuaded," said
one of the Emperor's agents in Italy on 10th January,
1529, " that the Pope is now sincerely attached to his
Imperial Majesty."[2] " I suspect," wrote Du Bellay from
London, in the same month, " that the Pope has commanded Campeggio to meddle no further, seeing things
are taking quite a different turn from what he had been
assured, and that the Emperor's affairs in Naples are in
such a state that Clement dare not displease him."[3] The
Pope had already informed Charles that his aunt's petition
for the revocation of the suit would be granted.[4] The
Italian League was practically dissolved. " I have quite
made up my mind," said Clement to the Archbishop of
Capua on 7th June, " to become an Imperialist, and to
live and die as such. . . . I am only waiting for the
return of my nuncio."[5]

That nuncio had gone to Barcelona to negotiate an
alliance between the Pope and the Emperor ; and the
success of his mission completed Clement's conversion.
The revocation was only delayed, thought Charles's
representative at Rome, to secure better terms for the
Pope.[6] On 21st June, the French commander, St. Pol,
was utterly defeated at Landriano ; " not a vestige of the
army is left," reported Casale.[7] A few days later the
Treaty of Barcelona between Clement and Charles was
signed.[8] Clement's nephew was to marry the Emperor's
natural daughter ; the Medici tyranny was to be re-
established in Florence ; Ravenna, Cervia and other
towns were to be restored to the Pope ; His Holiness was
to crown Charles with the imperial crown, and to absolve

[1] L. and P. iv. 5447.   [2] Sp. Cal. iii. 875.
[3] L. and P. iv. 5209.   [4] Sp. Cal. iii. 890.
[5] Ibid. iv. 72.   [6] Ibid. iv. 154.
[7] L. and P. iv. 5705, 5767 ; cf. Sp. Cal. iv. 150.
[8] L. and P. iv. 5779 ; Sp. Cal. iv. 117, 161.

from ecclesiastical censures all those who were present at, or consented to, the sack of Rome. It was, in effect, a family compact ; and part of it was the quashing of the legates' proceedings against the Emperor's aunt, with whom the Pope was now to be allied by family ties. " We found out secretly," write the English envoys at Rome, on the 16th of July, " that the Pope signed the revocation yesterday morning, as it would have been dishonourable to have signed it after the publication of the new treaty with the Emperor, which will be published here on Sunday."[1] Clement knew that his motives would not bear scrutiny, and he tried to avoid public odium by a characteristic subterfuge. Catherine could hope for no justice in England, Henry could expect no justice at Rome. Political expediency would dictate a verdict in Henry's favour in England ; political expediency would dictate a verdict for Catherine at Rome. Henry's ambassadors were instructed to appeal from Clement to the " true Vicar of Christ," but where was the true Vicar of Christ to be found on earth ?[2] There was no higher tribunal. It was intolerable that English suits should be decided by the chances and changes of French or Habsburg influence in Italy, by the hopes and the fears of an Italian prince for the safety of his temporal power. The natural and inevitable result was the separation of England from Rome.

[1] *L. and P.* iv. 5780 ; *Sp. Cal.* iv. 156. Another detail was the excommunication of Zapolya, the rival of the Habsburgs in Hungary—a step which Henry VIII denounced as " letting the Turk into Hungary " (*L. and P.* v. 274).

[2] *Ibid.* iv. 5650, 5715.

CHAPTER IX

THE CARDINAL'S FALL [1]

THE loss of their spiritual jurisdiction in England was part of the price paid by the Popes for their temporal possessions in Italy. The papal domains were either too great or too small. If the Pope was to rely on his temporal power, it should have been extensive enough to protect him from the dictation and resentment of secular princes; and from this point of view there was no little justification for the aims of Julius II. Had he succeeded in driving the barbarians across the Alps or into the sea, he and his successors might in safety have judged the world, and the breach with Henry might never have taken place. If the Pope was to rely on his spiritual weapons, there was no need of temporal states at all. In their existing extent and position, they were simply the heel of Achilles, the vulnerable spot, through which secular foes might wound the Vicar of Christ. France threatened him from the north and Spain from the south; he was ever between the upper and the nether mill-stone. Italy was the cockpit of Europe in the sixteenth century, and the eyes of the Popes were perpetually bent on the worldly fray, seeking to save or extend their dominions. Through the Pope's temporal power, France and Spain exerted their pressure. He could only defend himself by playing off one against the other, and in this game his spiritual powers were his only effective pieces. More and more the spiritual authority, with which he was entrusted, was made to serve political ends. Temporal princes were branded as "sons of iniquity and children of perdition," not because their beliefs or their morals were worse than other men's, but because they stood in the way of the family ambitions of various popes. Their frequent use

[1] See, besides the documents cited, Busch, *Der Sturz des Cardinal Wolsey* (Hist. Taschenbuch, VI. ix. 39-114).

and abuse brought ecclesiastical censures into public contempt, and princes soon ceased to be frightened with false fires. James IV, when excommunicated, said he would appeal to Prester John, and that he would side with any council against the Pope, even if it contained only three bishops.[1] The Vicar of Christ was lost in the petty Italian prince. *Corruptio optimi pessima.* The lower dragged the higher nature down. If the Papal Court was distinguished from the courts of other Italian sovereigns, it was not by exceptional purity. " In this Court as in others," wrote Silvester de Giglis from Rome, " nothing can be effected without gifts."[2] The election of Leo X was said to be free from bribery ; a cardinal himself was amazed, and described the event as *Phœnix et rara avis.*[3] If poison was not a frequent weapon at Rome, popes and cardinals at least believed it to be. Alexander VI was said to have been poisoned ; one cardinal was accused of poisoning his fellow-cardinal, Bainbridge ; and others were charged with an attempt on the life of Leo X.[4] In 1517, Pace described the state of affairs at Rome as *plane monstra, omni dedecore et infamia plena ; omnis fides, omnis honestas, una cum religione, a mundo abvolasse videntur.*[5] Ten years later, the Emperor himself declared that the sack of Rome was the just judgment of God, and one of his ambassadors said that the Pope ought to be deprived of his temporal states, as they had been at the bottom of all the dissensions.[6] Clement himself claimed to have been the originator of that war which brought upon him so terrible and so just a punishment.

Another result of the merging of the Pope in the

---

[1] *L. and P.* i. 3838, 3876.

[2] *Ibid.* ii. 3781 ; cf. i. 4283, " all here have regard only to their own honour and profit ".

[3] *Ibid.* ii. 2362.   [4] *Ibid.* ii. 3277, 3352.   [5] *Ibid.* ii. 3523.

[6] *Sp. Cal.* iii. 209, 210, 309 ; cf. *L. and P.* iv. 3051, 3352. Clement had given away Sicily and Naples to one of Charles's vassals " which dealing may make me not take him as Pope, no, not for all the excommunications that he can make ; for I stand under appellation to the next general council ". Every one—Charles V, Henry VIII, Cranmer—played an appeal to the next general council against the Pope's excommunication.

Italian prince was the practical exclusion of the English and other Northern nations from the supreme council of Christendom. There was no apparent reason why an Englishman should not be the head of the Christian Church just as well as an Italian ; but there was some incongruity in the idea of an Englishman ruling over Italian States, and no Englishman had attained the Papacy for nearly four centuries. The double failure of Wolsey made it clear that the door of the Papacy was sealed to Englishmen, whatever their claims might be. The roll of cardinals tells a similar tale ; the Roman curia graciously conceded that there should generally be one English cardinal in the sacred college, but one in a body of forty or fifty was thought as much as England could fairly demand. It is not so very surprising that England repudiated the authority of a tribunal in which its influence was measured on such a contemptible scale. The other nations of Europe thought much the same, and it is only necessary to add up the number of cardinals belonging to each nationality to arrive at a fairly accurate indication of the peoples who rejected papal pretensions. The nations most inadequately represented in the college of cardinals broke away from Rome ; those which remained faithful were the nations which controlled in the present, or might hope to control in the future, the supreme ecclesiastical power. Spain and France had little temptation to abolish an authority which they themselves wielded in turn ; for if the Pope was a Spaniard to-day, he might well be a Frenchman to-morrow. There was no absurdity in Frenchmen or Spaniards ruling over the papal States ; for France and Spain already held under their sway more Italian territory than Italian natives themselves. It was the subjection of the Pope to French and Spanish domination that prejudiced his claims in English eyes. His authority was tolerable so long as the old ideal of the unity of Christendom under a single monarch retained its force, or even so long as the Pope was Italian pure and simple. But when Italy was either Spanish or French, and the Pope the chaplain of one or the other monarch, the growing spirit of nationality could bear it no longer ; it responded at once to Henry's appeals against the claims of a foreign jurisdiction.

It was a mere accident that the breach with Rome grew out of Spanish control of the Pope. The separation was nearly effected more than a century earlier, as a result of the Pope's Babylonish captivity in France ; and the wonder is, not that the breach took place when it did, but that it was deferred for so long. At the beginning of the fifteenth century all the elements were present but one for the ecclesiastical revolution which was reserved for Henry VIII to effect. The Papacy had been discredited in English eyes by subservience to France, just as it had in 1529 by subservience to Charles. Lollardy was more powerful in England in the reign of Henry IV than heresy was in the middle of that of Henry VIII. There was as strong a demand for the secularisation of Church property on the part of the lay peers and gentry ; and Wycliffe himself had anticipated the cardinal point of the later movement by appealing to the State to reform the Church. But great revolutions depend on a number of causes working together, and often fail for the lack of one. The element lacking in the reign of Henry IV was the King himself. The Lancastrians were orthodox from conviction and from the necessities of their position ; they needed the support of the Church to bolster up a weak title to the crown. The civil wars followed ; and Henry VII was too much absorbed in securing his throne to pursue any quarrels with Rome. But when his son began to rule as well as to reign, it was inevitable that not merely questions of Church property and of the relations with the Papacy should come up for revision, but also those issues between Church and State which had remained in abeyance during the fifteenth century. The divorce was the spark which ignited the flame, but the combustible materials had been long existent. If the divorce had been all, there would have been no Reformation in England. After the death of Anne Boleyn, Henry might have done some trifling penance at his subjects' expense, made the Pope a present, or waged war on one of Clement's orthodox foes, and that would have been the end. Much had happened since the days of Hildebrand, and Popes were no longer able to exact heroic repentance. The divorce, in fact, was the occasion, and not the cause, of the Reformation.

That movement, so far as Henry VIII was concerned, was not in essence doctrinal; neither was it primarily a schism between the English and Roman communions. It was rather an episode in the eternal dispute between Church and State. Throughout the quarrel, Henry and Elizabeth maintained that they were merely reasserting their ancient royal prerogative over the Church, which the Pope of Rome had usurped. English revolutions have always been based on specious conservative pleas, and the only method of inducing Englishmen to change has been by persuasions that the change is not a change at all, or is a change to an older and better order. The Parliaments of the seventeenth century regarded the Stuart pretensions, as Henry and Elizabeth did those of the Pope, in the light of usurpations upon their own imprescriptible rights; and more recently, movements to make the Church Catholic have been based on the ground that it has never been anything else. The Tudor contention that the State was always supreme over the Church has been transformed into a theory that the Church was always at least semi-independent of Rome. But it is not so clear that the Church has always been anti-papal, as that the English laity have always been anti-clerical.

The English people were certainly very anti-sacerdotal from the very beginning of Henry VIII's reign. In 1512 James IV complained to Henry that Englishmen seized Scots merchants, ill-treated them, and abused them as " the Pope's men ".[1] At the end of the same year Parliament deprived of their benefit of clergy all clerks under the rank of sub-deacon who committed murder or felony.[2]

---

[1] *L. and P.* i. 3320. In 1516 one Humphrey Bonner preached a sermon ridiculing the Holy See (*ibid.* ii. 2692).

[2] In this, as in many other reforms, the English Parliament only anticipated the action of the Church; for on 12th February, 1516, Leo X issued a bull prohibiting any one from being admitted, for the next

This measure at once provoked a cry of " the Church in danger ". The Abbot of Winchcombe preached that the act was contrary to the law of God and to the liberties of the Church, and that the lords, who consented thereto, had incurred a liability to spiritual censures. Standish, warden of the Mendicant Friars of London, defended the action of Parliament, while the temporal peers requested the bishops to make the Abbot of Winchcombe recant.[1] They refused, and, at the Convocation of 1515, Standish was summoned before it to explain his conduct. He appealed to the King; the judges pronounced that all who had taken part in the proceedings against Standish had incurred the penalties of *præmunire*. They also declared that the King could hold a Parliament without the spiritual lords, who only sat in virtue of their temporalties. This opinion seems to have nothing to do with the dispute, but it is remarkable that, in one list of the peers attending the Parliament of 1515, there is not a single abbot.[2]

With regard to the Abbot of Winchcombe and Friar Standish, the prelates claimed the same liberty of speech for Convocation as was enjoyed by Parliament; so that they could, without offence, have maintained certain acts of Parliament to be against the laws of the Church.[3] Wolsey interceded on their behalf, and begged that the matter might be left to the Pope's decision, while Henry contented himself with a declaration that he would maintain intact his royal jurisdiction. This was not all that passed during that session of Parliament and Convocation. At the end of his summary of the proceedings, Dr. John Taylor, who was both clerk of Parliament and prolocutor of Convocation, remarks : " In this Parliament and

five years, into minor orders unless he were simultaneously promoted to be sub-deacon ; as many persons, to avoid appearing before the civil courts and to enjoy immunity, received the tonsure and minor orders without proceeding to the superior (*L. and P.* ii. 1532).

[1] *L. and P.* ii. 1313. Brewer impugns the authority of Keilway's report of this incident on the ground that he lived in Elizabeth's reign ; that is true, but according to the *D.N.B.* he was born in 1497, which makes him a strictly contemporary authority.

[2] *L. and P.* ii. 1131.   [3] *Ibid.* ii. 1314.

HENRY VIII

(Reproduced by gracious permission of H.M. the Queen)

CATHERINE OF ARAGON

HENRY VIII WITH PRINCE EDWARD
AND CATHERINE PARR (?)

(*Reproduced by gracious permission of H.M. the Queen*)

Convocation the most dangerous quarrels broke out between the clergy and the secular power, respecting the Church's liberties " ;[1] and there exists a remarkable petition presented to this Parliament against clerical exactions ; it complained that the clergy refused burial until after the gift of the deceased's best jewel, best garment or the like, and demanded that every curate should administer the sacrament when required to do so.[2] It was no wonder that Wolsey advised " the more speedy dissolution " of this Parliament,[3] and that, except in 1523, when financial straits compelled him, he did not call another while he remained in power. His fall was the sign for the revival of Parliament, and it immediately took up the work where it was left in 1515.

These significant proceedings did not stand alone. In 1515 the Bishop of London's chancellor was indicted for the murder of a citizen who had been found dead in the Bishop's prison.[4] The Bishop interceded with Wolsey to prevent the trial ; any London jury would, he said, convict any clerk, " be he innocent as Abel ; they be so maliciously set *in favorem hæreticæ pravitatis*".[5] The heresy was no matter of belief, but hatred of clerical immunities. The *Epistolæ Obscurorum Virorum*, wrote More to Erasmus in 1516, was " popular everywhere " ;[6] and no more bitter a satire had yet been penned on the clergy. In this matter Henry and his lay subjects were at one. Standish, whom Taylor describes as the promoter and instigator of all these evils, was a favourite preacher at Henry's Court. The King, said Pace, had " often praised his doctrine ".[7] But what was it ? It was no advocacy of Henry's loved " new learning," for Standish

[1] *L. and P.* ii. 1312.

[2] *Ibid.* ii. 1315 ; cf. another petition to the same effect from the inhabitants of London (*ibid.* i. 5725 (i.)).

[3] *Ibid.* ii. 1223.

[4] See Dr. Gairdner, *History of English Church in Sixteenth Century*, ch. iii., where the story of Richard Hunne is critically examined in detail. Its importance consists, however, not in the question whether Hunne was or was not murdered by the Bishop's chancellor Horsey, but in the popular hostility to the clergy revealed by the incident.

[5] *L. and P.* ii. 2.   [6] *Ibid.* ii. 2492.   [7] *Ibid.* ii. 4074.

denounced the Greek Testament of Erasmus, and is held
up to ridicule by the great Dutch humanist ;[1] Standish,
too, was afterwards a stout defender of the Pope's
dispensing power, and followed Fisher in his protest
against the divorce before the legatine Court. The
doctrine, which pleased the King so much, was Standish's
denial of clerical immunity from State control, and his
assertion of royal prerogatives over the Church. In 1518
the Bishopric of St. Asaph's fell vacant. Wolsey, who was
then at the height of his power, recommended Bolton,[2]
prior of St. Bartholomew's, a learned man ; but Henry
was resolved to reward his favourite divine, and Standish
obtained the see. Pace, a good churchman, expressed
himself to Wolsey as " mortified " at the result, but said
it was inevitable, as besides the King's good graces,
Standish enjoyed " the favour of all the courtiers for the
singular assistance he has rendered towards subverting
the Church of England ".[3]

Eleven more years were to roll before the Church was
subverted. They were years of Wolsey's supremacy ; he
alone stood between the Church and its subjection. It was
owing, wrote Campeggio in 1528, to Wolsey's vigilance
and solicitude that the Holy See retained its rank and
dignity.[4] His ruin would drag down the Church, and the
fact was known to Anne Boleyn and her faction, to
Campeggio and Clement VII, as well as to Henry VIII.[5]
" These Lords intend," wrote Du Bellay, on the eve of
Wolsey's fall, " after he is dead or ruined, to impeach the
State of the Church, and take all its goods ; which it is
hardly needful for me to write in cipher, for they proclaim
it openly. I expect they will do fine miracles."[6] A few
days later he says, " I expect the priests will never have
the great seal again ; and that in this Parliament they
will have terrible alarms. I think Dr. Stephen (Gardiner)
will have a good deal to do with the management of
affairs, *especially if he will abandon his order*."[7] At
Easter, 1529, Lutheran books were circulating in Henry's

[1] L. and P. 929.   [2] L. and P. ii. 4082.   [3] Ibid. ii. 4074.
[4] Ibid. iv. 4898.   [5] Ibid. iv. 5210, 5255, 5581, 5582.
[6] Ibid. iv. 6011.   [7] Ibid. 6019.

Court, advocating the confiscation of ecclesiastical property and the restoration of his Church to its primitive simplicity. Campeggio warned the King against them and maintained that it had been determined by councils and theologians that the Church justly held her temporalties. Henry retorted that according to the Lutherans " those decisions were arrived at by ecclesiastics and now it was necessary for the laity to interpose ".[1] In his last interview with Henry, Campeggio " alluded to this Parliament, which is about to be holden, and I earnestly pressed upon him the liberty of the Church. He certainly seemed to me very well disposed to exert his power to the utmost."[2] " Down with the Church " was going to be the Parliament cry. Whether Henry would really " exert his power " to maintain her liberties remained to be seen, but there never was a flimsier theory than that the divorce of Catherine was the sole cause of the break with Rome. The centrifugal forces were quite independent of the divorce ; its historical importance lies in the fact that it alienated from Rome the only power in England which might have kept them in check. So long as Wolsey and the clerical statesmen, with whom he surrounded the King, remained supreme, the Church was comparatively safe. But Wolsey depended entirely on Henry's support ; when that was withdrawn, Church and Cardinal fell together.

Wolsey's ruin was, however, due to more causes than his failure to get a divorce for the King. It was at bottom the result of the natural development of Henry's character. Egotism was from the first his most prominent trait ; it was inevitably fostered by the extravagant adulation paid to Tudor sovereigns, and was further encouraged by his realisation, first of his own mental

---

[1] *L. and P.* iv. 5416.

[2] *Ibid.* iv. 5995. Henry VIII no doubt also had his eye on Gustavus in Sweden where the Vesterås Recess of 1427 had provided that all episcopal, capitular and monastic property which was not absolutely required should be handed over to the King, and conferred upon him an ecclesiastical jurisdiction as extensive as that afterwards conferred upon Henry VIII (*Cambridge Modern Hist.* ii. 626).

powers, and then of the extent to which he could force his will upon others. He could never brook a rival in whatever sphere he wished to excel. In the days of his youth he was absorbed in physical sports, in gorgeous pageantry and ceremonial; he was content with such exhibitions as prancing before the ladies between every course in a tourney, or acting as pilot on board ship, blowing a whistle as loud as a trumpet, and arrayed in trousers of cloth of gold. Gradually, as time wore on, the athletic mania wore off, and pursuits, such as architecture, took the place of physical sports. A generation later, a writer describes Henry as " the only Phœnix of his time for fine and curious masonry ".[1] From his own original designs York House was transformed into Whitehall Palace, Nonsuch Palace was built, and extensive alterations were made at Greenwich and Hampton Court.

But architecture was only a trifle ; Henry's uncontrollable activity also broke out in political spheres, and the eruption was fatal to Wolsey's predominance. The King was still in the full vigour of manhood ; he had not reached his fortieth year, and his physical graces were the marvel of those who saw him for the first time. Falier, the new Venetian ambassador, who arrived in England in 1529, is as rapturous over the King's personal attractions as Giustinian or Pasqualigo had been. " In this Eighth Henry," he writes, " God has combined such corporeal and intellectual beauty as not merely to surprise but astound all men. . . . His face is angelic (nine years before a Frenchman had called it " feminine ") rather than handsome ; his head imperial and bold ; and he wears a beard, contrary to the English custom. Who would not be amazed, when contemplating such singular beauty of person, coupled with such bold address, adapting itself with the greatest ease to every manly exercise ? "[2] But Henry's physique was no longer proof against every ailment ; frequent mention is made

[1] Harrison, *Description of England*, in Holinshed, ed. 1577, bk. ii. chap. ix.

[2] *Ven. Cal.* iv. 184, 185, 293.

about this time of headaches[1] which incapacitated him
from business, and it was not long before there appeared
on his leg the fistula which racked him with pain till the
end of his life, and eventually caused his death.

The divorce and the insuperable obstacles which he
discovered in attaining the end he thought easy at first,
did more to harden Henry's temper than any bodily ills.
He became a really serious man, and developed that
extraordinary power of self-control which stood him in
good stead in his later years. Naturally a man of violent
passions, he could never have steered clear of the dangers
that beset him without unusual capacity for curbing his
temper, concealing his intentions, and keeping his own
counsel. Ministers might flatter themselves that they
could read his mind and calculate his actions, but it is
quite certain that henceforth no minister read so clearly
his master's mind as the master did his minister's.
" Three may keep counsel," said the King in 1530,[2] " if
two be away ; and if I thought that my cap knew my
counsel, I would cast it into the fire and burn it."
" Never," comments a modern writer,[3] " had the King
spoken a truer word, or described himself more accurately.
Few would have thought that, under so careless and
splendid an exterior—the very ideal of bluff, open-hearted
good-humour and frankness—there lay a watchful and
secret eye, that marked what was going on, without
appearing to mark it ; kept its own counsel until it was
time to strike, and then struck, as suddenly and remorse-
lessly as a beast of prey. It was strange to witness so
much subtlety, combined with so much strength."

In spite of his remorseless blows and arbitrary temper,
Henry was too shrewd and too great a man to despise the
counsel of others, or think any worse of an adviser because
his advice differed from his own. He loved to meet
argument with argument, even when he might command.
To the end of his days he valued a councillor who would

[1] *L. and P.* iv. 4546. Henry had had small-pox in February, 1514
(*ibid.* i. 4831), without any serious consequences, but apart from that
he had had no great illness.   [2] Cavendish, *Life of Wolsey*, p. 397.
[3] Brewer, Introd. to *L. and P.* iv. p. dcxxi.

honestly maintain the opposite of what the King desired.
These councillors to whom he gave his confidence were
never minions or servile flatterers. Henry had his Court
favourites with whom he hunted and shot and diced ;
with whom he played—always for money—tennis,
primero and bowls, and the more mysterious games of
Pope July, Imperial and Shovelboard ;[1] and to whom he
threw many an acre of choice monastic land. But they
never influenced his policy. No man was ever advanced
to political power in Henry's reign merely because he
pandered to the King's vanity or to his vices. No one
was a better judge of conduct in the case of others, or a
sterner champion of moral probity, when it did not
conflict with his own desires or conscience. In 1528
Anne Boleyn and her friends were anxious to make a
relative abbess of Wilton.[2] But she had been notoriously
unchaste. "Wherefore," wrote Henry to Anne herself,
" I would not, for all the gold in the world, cloak your
conscience nor mine to make her ruler of a house which
is of so ungodly demeanour ; nor I trust you would not
that neither for brother nor sister I should so distain
mine honour or conscience." He objected, on similar
grounds, to the prioress whom Wolsey wished to nominate ; the Cardinal neglected Henry's wishes, and thereby
called down upon himself a rebuke remarkable for dignity
and delicacy. " The great affection and love I bear you,"
wrote the King, " causeth me, using the doctrine of my
Master, saying *Quem diligo, castigo*, thus plainly, as
ensueth, to break to you my mind. . . . Methink it is not
the right train of a trusty loving friend and servant, when
the matter is put by the master's consent into his arbitre
and judgment (specially in a matter wherein his master
hath both royalty and interest), to elect and choose a
person which was by him defended [forbidden]. And
yet another thing, which much displeaseth me more,—
that is, to cloak your offence made by ignorance of my
pleasure, saying that you expressly knew not my deter-
minate mind in that behalf." Then, after showing how

[1] See various entries in Privy Purse Expenses, *L. and P.* v. 747-62.
[2] *Ibid*. iv. 4477, 4488, 4507, 4509.

empty were Wolsey's excuses, he continues : " Ah ! my
Lord, it is a double offence, both to do ill and colour it
too ; but with men that have wit it cannot be accepted so.
Wherefore, good my Lord, use no more that way with me,
for there is no man living that more hateth it." He then
proceeds to warn the Cardinal against sinister reports with
regard to his methods of raising money for his college at
Oxford. " They say the college is a cloak for all mischief.
I perceive by your letter that you have received money
of the exempts for having their old visitors. If your
legacy [legatine authority] is a cloak *apud homines*, it is
not *apud Deum*. I doubt not, therefore, you will desist."
Wolsey had used his legatine authority to extort money
from monasteries as the price of their immunity from his
visitatorial powers. The monasteries, too, had strenuously
opposed the late Amicable Loan to the King ; by
Wolsey's means they had been released from that obligation ; and Henry strongly suspected that they had
purchased their exemption from relieving his necessities
by lavish contributions to the Cardinal's colleges. " I
pray you, my Lord," he concludes, " think not that it is
upon any displeasure that I write this unto you. For
surely it is for my discharge afore God, being in the room
that I am in ; and secondly for the great zeal I bear unto
you." Henry possessed in the highest degree not a few
of the best kingly attributes. His words are not the words
of a hypocrite without conscience, devoid of the fear of
God and man. For all the strange and violent things
that he did, he obtained the sanction of his conscience,
but his imperious egotism made conscience his humble
slave, and blinded to his own sins a judgment so keen to
detect and chastise the failings of others.

These incidents, of more than a year before the
Cardinal's fall, illustrate the change in the respective
positions of monarch and minister. There was no doubt
now which was the master ; there was no king but one.
Henry was already taking, as Du Bellay said, " the
management of everything ".[1] Wolsey himself knew

---

[1] *L. and P.* iv. 5983 ; cf. iv. 3992, where Henry has an interview
(March, 1528) with a Scots ambassador and tells no one about it.

that he had lost the King's confidence. He began to talk of retirement. He told Du Bellay, in or before August, 1528, that when he had established a firm amity between France and England, extinguished the hatred between the two nations, reformed the laws and customs of England, and settled the succession, he would retire and serve God to the end of his days.[1] The Frenchman thought this was merely to represent as voluntary a loss of power which he saw would soon be inevitable; but the conversation is a striking illustration of the difference between Henry and Wolsey, and helps to explain why Wolsey accomplished so little that lasted, while Henry accomplished so much. The Cardinal seems to have been entirely devoid of that keen perception of the distinction between what was, and what was not, practicable, which was Henry's saving characteristic. In the evening of his days, after sixteen years of almost unlimited power, he was speaking of plans, which might have taxed the energies of a life-time, as preliminaries to a speedy withdrawal from the cares of State. He had enjoyed an unequalled opportunity of effecting these reforms, but what were the results of his administration? The real greatness and splendour of Henry's reign are said to have departed with Wolsey's fall.[2] The gilt and the tinsel were indeed stripped off, but the permanent results of Henry's reign were due to its later course. Had he died when Wolsey fell, what would have been his place in history? A brilliant figure, no doubt, who might have been thought capable of much, had he not failed to achieve anything. He had made wars from which England derived no visible profit; not an acre of territory had been acquired; the wealth, amassed by Henry VII, had been squandered, and Henry VIII, in 1529, was reduced to searching for gold mines in England.[3] The loss of his subjects' blood and treasure had been followed by the loss of their affections. The exuberant loyalty of 1509 had been turned

---

[1] *L. and P.* iv. 4649.   [2] Brewer, *ibid.* iv. Introd. p. dcxxii.

[3] *Ibid.* iv. 5209. One Hochstetter was imported from Germany in connection with "the gold mines that the King was seeking for" (Du Bellay to Montmorenci, 25th January, 1529).

into the wintry discontent of 1527. England had been raised to a high place in the councils of Europe by 1521, but her fall was quite as rapid, and in 1525 she counted for less than she had done in 1513. At home the results were equally barren ; the English hold on Ireland was said, in 1528, to be weaker than it had been since the conquest ;[1] and the English statute-book between 1509 and 1529 may be searched in vain for an act of importance, while the statute-book between 1529 and 1547 contains a list of acts which have never been equalled for their supreme importance in the subsequent history of England.

Wolsey's policy was, indeed, a brilliant fiasco ; with a pre-eminent genius for diplomacy, he thought he could make England, by diplomacy alone, arbiter of Europe. Its position in 1521 was artificial ; it had not the means to support a grandeur which was only built on the wealth left by Henry VII and on Wolsey's skill. England owed her advance in repute to the fact that Wolsey made her the paymaster of Europe. " The reputation of England for wealth," said an English diplomatist in 1522, " is a great cause of the esteem in which it is held."[2] But, by 1523, that wealth had failed ; Parliament refused to levy more taxes, and Wolsey's pretensions collapsed like a pack of cards. He played no part in the peace of Cambrai, which settled for the time the conditions of Europe. When rumours of the clandestine negotiations between France and Spain reached England, Wolsey staked his head to the King that they were pure invention.[3] He could not believe that peace was possible, unless it were made by him. But the rumours were true, and Henry exacted the penalty. The positive results of the Cardinal's policy were nil ; the chief negative result was that he had staved off for many years the ruin of the Church, but he only did it by plunging England in the maëlstrom of foreign intrigue and of futile wars.

The end was not long delayed. " I see clearly," writes Du Bellay on 4th October, 1529, " that by this Parliament Wolsey will completely lose his influence ; I see no

---

[1] *L. and P.* iv. 4933.   [2] *Ibid.* iii. 1978.   [3] *Ibid.* iv. 5231.

chance to the contrary."[1] Henry anticipated the temper
of Parliament. A bill of indictment was preferred against
him in the Court of King's Bench, and on the 22nd of
October he acknowledged his liability to the penalties of
præmunire.[2] The Great Seal was taken from him by
the Dukes of Norfolk and Suffolk. In November the
House of Lords passed a bill of attainder against him,
but the Commons were persuaded by Cromwell, acting
with Henry's connivance, to throw it out. "The King,"
wrote Chapuys, "is thought to bear the Cardinal no
ill-will;" and Campeggio thought that he would "not
go to extremes, but act considerately in this matter, as he
is accustomed to do in all his actions."[3] Wolsey was
allowed to retain the Archbishopric of York, a sum in
money and goods equivalent to at least £70,000, and a
pension of 1,000 marks from the See of Winchester.[4] In
the following spring he set out to spend his last days in
his northern see; six months he devoted to his archi-
episcopal duties, confirming thousands of children,
arranging disputes among neighbours, and winning such
hold on the hearts of the people as he had never known in
the days of his pride. Crowds in London had flocked to
gloat over the sight of the broken man; now crowds in
Yorkshire came to implore his blessing.

He prepared for his installation at York on 7th November, 1530; on the 4th he was arrested for treason. His
Italian physician, Agostini, had betrayed him; he was
accused of having asked Francis I to intercede with Henry
on his behalf, which was true;[5] and he seems also to have
sought the mediation of Charles V. But Agostini further
declared that Wolsey had written to Clement, urging
him to excommunicate Henry and raise an insurrection,
by which the Cardinal might recover his power.[6] By

[1] *L. and P.* iv. 5983.   [2] *Ibid.* iv. 6017.
[3] *Ibid.* iv. 6199, 6050; cf. iv. 6295, where Henry orders Dacre to
treat Wolsey as became his rank; *Ven. Cal.* 1529, p. 237.
[4] *L. and P.* iv. 6220.   [5] *Ibid.* iv. 6018, 6199, 6273, 6738.
[6] De Vaux writes on 8th November, 1530, to Montmorenci, that the
King had told him "where and how" Wolsey had intrigued against
him, but he does not repeat the information (*ibid.* iv. 6720), though

Pontefract, Doncaster, Nottingham, with feeble steps and slow, the once-proud prelate, broken in spirit and shattered in health, returned to meet his doom. His gaol was to be the cell in the Tower, which had served for the Duke of Buckingham.[1] But a kindlier fate than a traitor's death was in store. "I am come," he said to the monks of Leicester Abbey, "I am come to leave my bones among you." He died there at eight o'clock on St. Andrew's morning, and there, on the following day, he was simply and quietly buried. "If," he exclaimed in his last hour, "I had served God as diligently as I have done the King, He would not have given me over in my grey hairs." That cry, wrung from Wolsey, echoed throughout the Tudor times.[2] Men paid *le nouveau Messie* a devotion they owed to the old; they rendered unto Cæsar the things that were God's. They reaped their reward in riches and pomp and power, but they won no peace of mind. The favour of princes is fickle, and "the wrath of the King is death". So thought Wolsey and Warham and Norfolk. "Is that all?" said More, with prophetic soul, to Norfolk; "then in good faith between your grace and me is but this, that I shall die to-day and you shall die to-morrow."[3]

Bryan's remark (*ibid.* iv. 6733) that "De Vaux has done well in disclosing the misdemeanour of the Cardinal" suggests that De Vaux knew more than he says.

[1] So Chapuys reports (iv. 6738); that Wolsey had used Agostini to sound Chapuys is obvious from the latter's remark, "were the physician to say all that passed between us, he could not do anything to impugn me".

[2] Cf. Buckingham's remark in *L. and P.* iii. 1356: "An he had not offended no more unto God than he had done to the Crown, he should die as true a man as ever was in the world".

[3] *D.N.B.* xxxviii. 437.

CHAPTER X

THE KING AND HIS PARLIAMENT

In the closing days of July, 1529, a courier came posting
from Rome with despatches announcing the alliance
of Clement and Charles, and the revocation to the Papal
Court of the suit between Henry VIII and the Emperor's
aunt. Henry replied with no idle threats or empty
reproaches, but his retort was none the less effective. On
the 9th of August[1] writs were issued from Chancery
summoning that Parliament which met on the 3rd of
November and did not separate till the last link in the
chain which bound England to Rome was sundered, and
the country was fairly launched on that sixty years'
struggle which the defeat of the Spanish Armada concluded.[2] The step might well seem a desperate hazard.
The last Parliament had broken up in discontent ; it had
been followed by open revolt in various shires ; while
from others there had since then come demands for the
repayment of the loan, which Henry was in no position

[1] Rymer, *Fœdera* xiv. 302.

[2] It has been alleged that the immediate object of this Parliament
was to relieve the King from the necessity of repaying the loan (*D.N.B.*
xxvi. 83) ; and much scorn has been poured on the notion that it had
any important purpose (*L. and P.* iv. Introd. p. dcxlvii.). Brewer even
denies its hostility to the Church on the ground that it was composed
largely of lawyers, and " lawyers are not in general enemies to things
established ; they are not inimical to the clergy ". Yet the law element
was certainly stronger in the Parliaments of Charles I than in that of
1529 ; were they not hostile to " things established " and " inimical to
the clergy " ? Contemporaries had a different opinion of the purpose
of the Parliament of 1529. " It is intended," wrote Du Bellay on the
23rd of August, three months before Parliament met, " to hold a Parliament here this winter and act by their own absolute power, in default of
justice being administered by the Pope in this divorce " (*ibid*. iv. 5862 ;
cf. iv. 6011, 6019, 6307) ; " nothing else," wrote a Florentine in December, 1530, " is thought of in that island every day except of arranging
affairs in such a way that they do no longer be in want of the Pope,
neither for filling vacancies in the Church, nor for any other purpose "
(*ibid*. iv. 6774).

to grant. Francis and Charles, on whose mutual enmity England's safety largely depended, had made their peace at Cambrai ; and the Emperor was free to foment disaffection in Ireland and to instigate Scotland to war. His chancellor was boasting that the imperialists could, if they would, drive Henry from his kingdom within three months,[1] and he based his hopes on revolt among Henry's own subjects. The divorce had been from the beginning, and remained to the end, a stumbling-block to the people. Catherine received ovations wherever she went, while the utmost efforts of the King could scarcely protect Anne Boleyn from popular insult. The people were moved, not only by a creditable feeling that Henry's first wife was an injured woman, but by the fear lest a breach with Charles should destroy their trade in wool, on which, said the imperial ambassador, half the realm depended for sustenance.[2]

To summon a Parliament at such a conjuncture seemed to be courting certain ruin. In reality, it was the first and most striking instance of the audacity and insight which were to enable Henry to guide the whirlwind and direct the storm of the last eighteen years of his reign. Clement had put in his hands the weapon with which he secured his divorce and broke the bonds of Rome. " If," wrote Wolsey a day or two before the news of the revocation arrived, " the King be cited to appear at Rome in person or by proxy, and his prerogative be interfered with, none of his subjects will tolerate it. If he appears in Italy, it will be at the head of a formidable army."[3] A sympathiser with Catherine expressed his resentment at his King being summoned to plead as a party in his own realm before the legatine Court ;[4] and it has even been suggested that those proceedings were designed to irritate popular feeling against the Roman jurisdiction. Far more offensive was it to national prejudice, that England's king should be cited to appear before a court in a distant land, dominated by the arms of a foreign prince. Nothing did more to

---

[1] L. and P. iv. 4909, 4911 ; cf. 5177, 5501.
[2] Ibid. vi. 1528.   [3] Ibid. iv. 5797.
[4] Cavendish p. 210 ; L. and P. iv. Introd. p. dv.

alienate men's minds from the Papacy. Henry would
never have been able to obtain his divorce on its merits
as they appeared to his people. But now the divorce
became closely interwoven with another and a wider
question, the papal jurisdiction in England ; and on that
question Henry carried with him the good wishes of the
vast bulk of the laity. There were few Englishmen who
would not resent the petition presented to the Pope in
1529 by Charles V and Ferdinand that the English
Parliament should be forbidden to discuss the question
of divorce.[1] By summoning Parliament, Henry opened
the floodgates of anti-papal and anti-sacerdotal feelings
which Wolsey had long kept shut ; and the unpopular
divorce became merely a cross-current in the main stream
which flowed in Henry's favour.

It was thus with some confidence that Henry appealed
from the Pope to his people. He could do so all the
more surely, if, as is alleged, there was no freedom of
election, and if the House of Commons was packed with
royal nominees.[2] But these assertions may be dismissed
as gross exaggerations. The election of county members
was marked by unmistakable signs of genuine popular
liberty. There was often a riot, and sometimes a secret
canvass among freeholders to promote or defeat a particular candidate.[3] In 1547 the council ventured to
recommend a minister to the freeholders of Kent. The
electors objected ; the council reprimanded the sheriff for
representing its recommendation as a command ; it
protested that it never dreamt of depriving the shire of
its " liberty of election," but " would take it thankfully "
if the electors would give their voices to the ministerial
candidate. The electors were not to be soothed by soft

[1] *Sp. Cal.* iii. 979.

[2] " The choice of the electors," says Brewer (*L. and P.* iv. Introd.
p. dcxlv.), " was still determined by the King or his powerful ministers
with as much certainty and assurance as that of the sheriffs."

[3] *L. and P.* i. 792, vii. 1178, where mention is made of " secret labour "
among the freeholders of Warwickshire for the bye-election on Sir E.
Ferrers' death in 1534 ; and x. 1063, where there is described a hotly
contested election between the candidate of the gentry of Shropshire and
the candidate of the townsfolk of Shrewsbury.

words, and that Government candidate had to find another seat.[1] In the boroughs there was every variety of franchise. In some it was almost democratic ; in others elections were in the hands of one or two voters. In the city of London the election for the Parliament of 1529 was held on 5th October, *immensa communitate tunc presente*, in the Guildhall ; there is no hint of royal interference, the election being conducted in the customary way, namely, two candidates were nominated by the mayor and aldermen, and two by the citizens.[2] The general tendency had for more than a century, however, been towards close corporations in whose hands the parliamentary franchise was generally vested, and consequently towards restricting the basis of popular representation. The narrower that basis became, the greater the facilities it afforded for external influence. In many boroughs elections were largely determined by recommendations from neighbouring magnates, territorial or official.[3] At Gatton the lords of the manor nominated the members for Parliament, and the formal election was merely a matter of drawing up an indenture between Sir Roger Copley and the sheriff,[4] and the Bishop of Winchester was wont to select representatives for more than one borough within the bounds of his diocese.[5] The Duke of Norfolk claimed to be able to return ten members in Sussex and Surrey alone.[6]

But these nominations were not royal, and there is no reason to suppose that the nominees were any more

[1] *Acts of the Privy Council* 1547-50, pp. 516, 518, 519 ; *England under Protector Somerset* pp. 71, 72.

[2] *Narratives of the Reformation*, Camden Soc. pp. 295, 296.

[3] Cf. Duchess of Norfolk's letter to John Paston, 8th June, 1455 (*Paston Letters*, ed. 1900, i. 337), and in 1586 Sir Henry Bagnal asked the Earl of Rutland if he had a seat to spare in Parliament as Bagnal was anxious " for his learning's sake to be made a Parliament man " (*D.N.B.* Suppl. i. 96).

[4] *L. and P.* xiv. 645 ; cf. Hallam, 1884, iii. 44-45.

[5] Foxe, ed. Townsend vi. 54. There are some illustrations and general remarks on Henry's relations with Parliament in Porritt's *Unreformed House of Commons*, 2 vols., 1903.

[6] At Reigate, says the Duke, " I doubt whether any burgesses be there or not " (*L. and P.* x. 816) ; and apparently there were none at Gatton.

likely to be subservient to the Crown than freely elected
members unless the local magnate happened to be a royal
minister. Their views depended on those of their patrons,
who might be opposed to the Court; and in 1539
Cromwell's agents were considering the advisability of
setting up Crown candidates against those of Gardiner,
Bishop of Winchester.[1] The curious letter to Cromwell
in 1529,[2] upon which is based the theory that the House of
Commons consisted of royal nominees, is singularly
inconclusive. Cromwell sought Henry's permission to
serve in Parliament for two reasons; firstly, he was still
a servant of the obnoxious and fallen Cardinal; secondly,
he was seeking to transfer himself to Henry's service,
and thought he might be useful to the King in the House
of Commons. If Henry accepted his offer, Cromwell
was to be nominated for Oxford; if he were not elected
there, he was to be put up for one of the boroughs in the
diocese of Winchester, then vacant through Wolsey's
resignation. Even with the King's assent, his election
at Oxford was not regarded as certain; and, as a matter
of fact, Cromwell sat neither for Oxford, nor for any
constituency in the diocese of Winchester, but for the
borough of Taunton.[3] Crown influence could only make
itself effectively felt in the limited number of royal
boroughs; and the attempts to increase that influence
by the creation of constituencies susceptible to royal
influence were all subsequent in date to 1529. The returns
of members of Parliament are not extant from 1477 to

[1] This seems to have been the object of Southampton's tour through
the constituencies of Surrey and Hampshire in March, 1539; with one
of Gardiner's pocket-boroughs he did not meddle, because the lord
chamberlain was the Bishop's steward there (*L. and P.* xiv. i. 520). There
were some royal nominees in the House of Commons. In 1523 the
members for Cumberland were nominated by the Crown (*ibid.* iii. 2931);
at Calais the lord-deputy and council elected one of the two burgesses
and the mayor and burgesses the other (*ibid.* x. 736). Calais and the
Scottish Borders were of course exceptionally under Crown influence,
but this curious practice may have been observed in some other cities
and boroughs; in 1534, for instance, the King was to nominate to one
of the two vacancies at Worcester (*ibid.* vii. 56).

[2] *Ibid.* iv. App. 238.

[3] *Official Return of Members of Parliament* i. 370.

1529, but a comparison of the respective number of constituencies in those two years reveals only six in 1529 which had not sent members to a previous Parliament ; and almost if not all of these six owed their representation to their increasing population and importance, and not to any desire to pack the House of Commons. Indeed, as a method of enforcing the royal will upon Parliament, the creation of half a dozen boroughs was both futile and unnecessary. So small a number of votes was useless, except in the case of a close division of well-drilled parties, of which there is no trace in the Parliaments of Henry VIII.[1] The House of Commons acted as a whole, and not in two sections. " The sense of the House " was more apparent in its decisions then than it is to-day. Actual divisions were rare ; either a proposal commended itself to the House, or it did not ; and in both cases the question was usually determined without a vote.

The creation of boroughs was also unnecessary. Parliaments packed themselves quite well enough to suit Henry's purpose, without any interference on his part. The limiting of the county franchise to forty-shilling (*i.e.*, thirty pounds in modern currency) freeholders, and the dying away of democratic feeling in the towns, left parliamentary representation mainly in the hands of the landed gentry and of the prosperous commercial classes ; and from them the Tudors derived their most effective support, There was discontent in abundance during Tudor times, but it was social and economic, and not as a rule political. It was directed against the enclosers of common lands ; against the agricultural capitalists, who bought up farms, evicted the tenants, and converted their holdings to pasture ; against the large traders in towns who monopolised commerce at the expense of their poorer competitors. It was concerned, not with the one tyrant on the throne, but with the thousand petty tyrants of the villages and towns, against whom the poorer commons

---

[1] Occasionally there were divisions, e.g. in 1523 when the court party voted a subsidy of 2*s*. in the pound ; but this was only half the sum demanded by Wolsey (Hall pp. 656, 657, Ellis, *Orig. Letters*, I. i. 220, 221).

H

looked to their King for protection. Of this discontent Parliament could not be the focus, for members of Parliament were themselves the offenders. " It is hard," wrote a contemporary radical, " to have these ills redressed by Parliament, because it pricketh them chiefly which be chosen to be burgesses. . . . Would to God they would leave their old accustomed choosing of burgesses ! For whom do they choose but such as be rich or bear some office in the country, many times such as be boasters and braggers ? Such have they ever hitherto chosen ; be he never so very a fool, drunkard, extortioner, adulterer, never so covetous and crafty a person, yet, if he be rich, bear any office, if he be a jolly cracker and bragger in the country, he must be a burgess of Parliament. Alas, how can any such study, or give any godly counsel for the commonwealth ? "[1] This passage gives no support to the theory that members of Parliament were nothing but royal nominees. If the constituencies themselves were bent on electing " such as bare office in the country," there was no call for the King's intervention ; and the rich merchants and others, of whom complaint is made, were almost as much to the royal taste as were the officials themselves.

For the time being, in fact, the interests of the King and of the lay middle classes coincided, both in secular and ecclesiastical affairs. Commercial classes are generally averse from war, at least from war waged within their own borders, from which they can extract no profit. They had every inducement to support Henry's Government against the only alternative, anarchy. In ecclesiastical politics they, as well as the King, had their grievances against the Church. Both thought the clergy too rich, and that ecclesiastical revenues could be put to better uses in secular hands. Community of interests produced harmony of action ; and a century and a half was to pass

[1] Brinkelow, *Complaynt of Roderik Mors* (Early English Text Society) pp. 12, 13 ; for other evidence of the attitude of Parliament towards social grievances, see John Hales's letter to Somerset in *Lansdowne MS.* 238 ; Crowley's *Works* (Early English Text Society), *passim ;* Latimer, *Sermons* p. 247.

before Parliament again met so often, or sat so long, as it did during the latter half of Henry's reign. From 1509 to 1515 there had been on an average a parliamentary session once a year,[1] and in February, 1512, Warham, as Lord Chancellor, had in opening the session discoursed on the necessity of frequent Parliaments.[2] Then there supervened the ecclesiastical despotism of Wolsey, who tried, like Charles I, to rule without Parliament, and with the same fatal result to himself; but, from Wolsey's fall till Henry's death, there was seldom a year without a parliamentary session. Tyrants have often gone about to break Parliaments, and in the end Parliaments have generally broken them. Henry was not of the number; he never went about to break Parliament. He found it far too useful, and he used it. He would have been as reluctant to break Parliament as Ulysses the bow which he alone could bend.

No monarch, in fact, was ever a more zealous champion of parliamentary privileges, a more scrupulous observer of parliamentary forms, or a more original pioneer of sound constitutional doctrine. In 1543 he first enunciated the constitutional principle that sovereignty is vested in the " King in Parliament ". " We," he declared to the Commons, " at no time stand so highly in our estate royal as in the time of Parliament, wherein we as head and you as members are conjoined and knit together in one body politic, so as whatsoever offence or injury during that time is offered to the meanest member of the House, is to be judged as done against our person and the whole Court of Parliament."[3] He was careful to observe himself the

---

[1] The first Parliament of the reign met in January, 1510, the second in February, 1512. It had a second session, November-December of the same year (L. and P. i. 3502). A third Parliament met for its first session on 23rd January, 1514, for its second on 5th February, 1515, and for its third on 12th November, 1515 (ibid. i. 5616, 5725, ii. 1130). It was this last of which Wolsey urged " the more speedy dissolution "; then for fourteen years there was only one Parliament, that of 1523. These dates illustrate the antagonism between Wolsey and Parliament and show how natural it was that Wolsey should fall in 1529, and that his fall should coincide with the revival of Parliament.

[2] L. and P. i. 2082.   [3] Holinshed, Chronicles iii. 956.

deference to parliamentary privilege which he exacted
from others. It is no strange aberration from the general
tenor of his rule that in 1512 by Strode's case[1] the freedom
of speech of members of Parliament was established, and
their freedom from arrest by Ferrers' case in 1543. In
1515 Convocation had enviously petitioned for the same
liberty of speech as was enjoyed in Parliament, where
members might even attack the law of the land and not
be called in question therefor.[2] " I am," writes Bishop
Gardiner, in 1547, apologising for the length of a letter,
" like one of the Commons' house, that, when I am in my
tale, think I should have liberty to make an end ; "[3] and
again he refers to a speech he made during Henry's reign
" in the Parliament house, *where was free speech without
danger* ".[4] Wolsey had raised a storm in 1523 by trying
to browbeat the House of Commons. Henry never erred
in that respect. In 1532 a member moved that Henry
should take back Catherine to wife.[5] Nothing could
have touched the King on a tenderer spot. Charles I,
for a less offence, would have gone to the House to
arrest the offender. All Henry did was to argue the
point of his marriage with the Speaker and a deputation
from the Commons ; no proceedings whatever were taken
against the member himself. In 1529 John Petit, one of
the members for London, opposed the bill releasing Henry
from his obligation to repay the loan ; the only result

---

[1] Hallam, *Const. Hist.* ii. 4.

[2] *L. and P.* ii 1314. In some respects the House of Commons appears
to have exercised unconstitutional powers, e.g. in 1529 one Thomas
Bradshaw, a cleric, was indicted for having conspired to poison members
of Sir James Worsley's household, and on 27th February, 1531, Henry
VIII orders Lady Worsley not to trouble Bradshaw any more, " as the
House of Commons has decided that he is not culpable " (*ibid.* iv. 6293 ;
v. 117 ; cf. the case of John Wolf and his wife, *ibid.* vi. 742 ; vii. *passim*).
The claim to criminal jurisdiction which the House of Commons asserted
in Floyd's case (1621) seems in fact to have been admitted by Henry VIII ;
compare the frequent use of acts of attainder.

[3] Foxe, ed. Townsend vi. 33.

[4] *Ibid.* vi. 43.

[5] In the House of Lords in 1531 the Bishops of St. Asaph and of Bath
with a similar immunity attacked the defence of Henry's divorce policy
made by the Bishops of Lincoln and London (*L. and P.* v. 171).

apparently was to increase Petit's repute in the eyes of
the King, who " would ask in Parliament time if Petit
were on his side ".[1] There is, in fact, nothing to show
that Henry VIII intimidated his Commons at any time,
or that he packed the Parliament of 1529. Systematic
interference in elections was a later expedient devised by
Thomas Cromwell. It was apparently tried during the
bye-elections of 1534, and at the general elections of
1536[2] and 1539. Cromwell then endeavoured to secure
a majority in favour of himself and his own particular
policy against the reactionary party in the council. His
schemes had created a division among the laity, and
rendered necessary recourse to political methods of which
there was no need, so long as the laity remained united
against the Church. Nor is it without significance that
its adoption was shortly followed by Cromwell's fall.
Henry did not approve of ministers who sought to make
a party for themselves. The packing of Parliaments has
in fact been generally the death-bed expedient of a mori-
bund Government. The Stuarts had their " Under-
takers," and the only Parliament of Tudor times which

[1] *Narratives of the Reformation* (Camden Soc.) p. 25.

[2] Hence the complaints of the northern rebels late in that year (*L. and
P.* xi. 1143, 1182 [15], 1244, 1246) ; these are so to speak the election
petitions of the defeated party ; the chief complaint is that non-residents
were chosen who knew little about the needs of their constituents, and
they made the advanced demand that all King's servants or pensioners
be excluded.

The most striking instance of interference in elections is Cromwell's
letter to the citizens of Canterbury, written on 18th May, 1536, and
first printed in Merriman's *Cromwell*, 1902 ii. 13 ; he there requires the
electors to annul an election they had made in defiance of previous letters,
and return as members Robert Derknall (a member of the royal household,
L. and P. xv. pp. 563-5) and John Brydges, M.P. for Canterbury in
1529-36, instead of the two who had been unanimously chosen by eighty
electors on 11th May (*L. and P.* x. 852). The Mayor thereupon assembled
ninety-seven citizens who " freely with one voice and without any
contradiction elected the aforesaid " (*ibid.* x. 929). These very letters
show that electors did exercise a vote, and the fact that from 1534 to
1539 we find traces of pressure being put upon them, affords some presumption that before the rise of Cromwell, when we find no such traces
no such pressure was exerted. The most striking exception must not be
taken as the rule. See p. 254 *n.*

consisted mainly of Government nominees was that gathered by Northumberland on the eve of his fall in March, 1553; and that that body was exceptionally constituted is obvious from Renard's inquiry in August, 1553, as to whether Charles V would advise his cousin, Queen Mary, to summon a general Parliament or merely an assembly of " notables " after the manner introduced by Northumberland.

But, while Parliament was neither packed nor terrorised to any great extent, the harmony which prevailed between it and the King has naturally led to the charge of servility. Insomuch as it was servile at all, Parliament faithfully represented its constituents ; but the mere coincidence between the wishes of Henry and those of Parliament is no proof of servility.[1] That accusation can only be substantiated by showing that Parliament did, not what it wanted, but what it did not want, out of deference to Henry. And that has never been proved. It has never been shown that the nation resented the statutes giving Henry's proclamations the force of laws, enabling him to settle the succession by will, or any of the other acts usually adduced to prove the subservience of Parliament. When Henry was dead, Protector Somerset secured the repeal of most of these laws, but he lost his head for his pains. There is, indeed, no escape from the conclusion that the English people then approved of a dictatorship, and that Parliament was acting deliberately and voluntarily when it made Henry dictator. It made him dictator because it felt that he would do what it wanted, and better with, than without, extraordinary powers. The fact that Parliament rejected some of Henry's measures is strong presumption that it could have rejected more, had it been so minded. No projects were more dear to Henry's heart than the statutes of

---

[1] " Parliament," says Brewer, " faithfully reflected the King's wishes." It is equally true to say that the King reflected the wishes of Parliament ; and the accusation of servility is based on the assumption that Parliament must either be in chronic opposition to the Crown or servile. One of Brewer's reasons for Henry's power is that he " required no grants of money " (*L. and P.* iv. Introd. p. dcxlv.).

Wills and of Uses, yet both were rejected twice at least in the Parliament of 1529-36.[1]

The general harmony between King and Parliament was based on a fundamental similarity of interests; the harmony in detail was worked out, not by the forcible exertion of Henry's will, but by his careful and skilful manipulation of both Houses. No one was ever a greater adept in the management of the House of Commons, which is easy to humour but hard to drive. Parliaments are jealous bodies, but they are generally pleased with attentions; and Henry VIII was very assiduous in the attentions he paid to his lay Lords and Commons. From 1529 he suffered no intermediary to come between Parliament and himself. Cromwell was more and more employed by the King,[2] but only in subordinate matters, and when important questions were at issue Henry managed the business himself. He constantly visited both Houses and remained within their precincts for hours at a time,[3] watching every move in the game and taking note of every symptom of parliamentary feeling. He sent no

---

[1] "Henry," writes Chapuys in 1532, "has been trying to obtain from Parliament the grant of a third of the feudal property of deceased lords, but as yet has got nothing" (*L. and P.* v. 805). Various other instances are mentioned in the following pages, and they could doubtless be multiplied if the Journals of the House of Commons were extant for this period.

[2] Cromwell used to report to the King on the feeling of Parliament; thus in 1534 (*L. and P.* vii. 51) he tells Henry how far members were willing to go in the creation of fresh treasons, "they be contented that deed and writing shall be treason," but words were to be only misprision; they refused to include an heir's rebellion or disobedience in the bill, "as rebellion is already treason and disobedience is no cause of forfeiture of inheritance," and they thought "that the King of Scots should in no wise be named" (there is in the Record Office a draft of the Treasons Bill of 1534 materially differing from the Act as passed. Therefore either the bill did not originate with the Government and was modified under Government pressure, or it did originate with the Government and was modified under parliamentary pressure). This is how Henry's legislation was evolved; there is no foundation for the assertion that Parliament merely registered the King's edicts.

[3] E.g. *L. and P.* v. 120. At other times Parliament visited him. "On Thursday last," writes one on 8th March, 1534, "the whole Parliament were with the King at York Place for three hours" (*ibid.* vii. 304).

royal commands to his faithful Commons ; in this respect he was less arbitrary than his daughter, Queen Elizabeth. He submitted points for their consideration, argued with them, and frankly gave his reasons. It was always done, of course, with a magnificent air of royal condescension, but with such grace as to carry the conviction that he was really pleased to condescend and to take counsel with his subjects, and that he did so because he trusted his Parliament, and expected his Parliament to place an equal confidence in him. Henry VIII acted more as the leader of both Houses than as a King ; and, like modern parliamentary leaders, he demanded the bulk of their time for measures which he himself proposed.

The fact that the legislation of Henry's reign was initiated almost entirely by Government is not, however, a conclusive proof of the servility of Parliament. For, though it may have been the theory that Parliament existed to pass laws of its own conception, such has never been the practice, except when there has been chronic opposition between the executive and the legis-lature. Parliament has generally been the instrument of Government, a condition essential to strong and successful administration ; and it is still summoned mainly to discuss such measures as the executive thinks fit to lay before it. Certainly the proportion of Govern-ment bills to other measures passed in Henry's reign was less than it is to-day. A private member's bill then stood more chance of becoming law, and a Government bill ran greater risks of being rejected. That, of course, is not the whole truth. One of the reasons why Henry's House of Commons felt at liberty to reject bills proposed by the King, was that such rejection did not involve the fall of a Government which on other grounds the House wished to support. It did not even entail a dissolution. Not that general elections possessed any terrors for sixteenth-century Parliaments. A seat in the House of Commons was not considered a very great prize. The classes from which its members were drawn were much more bent on the pursuit of their own private fortunes than on participation in public affairs. Their membership was not seldom a burden,[1] and the long sessions of the Reformation Parliament constituted an especial grievance. One member complained that those sessions cost him equivalent to about five hundred pounds over and above the wages paid him by his constituents.[2] Leave to go home was often requested, and the imperial ambassador records that Henry, with characteristic craft, granted such licences to hostile members, but refused them to his own supporters.[3] That was a legitimate parliamentary stratagem. It was not Henry's fault if members preferred their private concerns to the interests of Catherine of Aragon or to the liberties of the Catholic Church.

Henry's greatest advantage lay, however, in a circumstance which constitutes the chief real difference between the Parliaments of the sixteenth century and those of to-day. His members of Parliament were representatives rather than delegates. They were elected as fit and proper persons to decide upon such questions as should be submitted to them in the Parliament House, and not merely as fit and proper persons to register decisions already reached by their constituents. Although they were in the habit of rendering to their constituents an account of their proceedings at the close of each session,[4] and although the fact that they depended upon their constituencies for their wages prevented their acting in opposition to their constituents' wishes, they received no precise instructions. They went to Parliament unfettered by definite pledges. They were thus more susceptible, not only to pressure, but also to argument ; and it is possible that in those days votes were sometimes affected by speeches. The action of members was determined, not by previous engagements or party discipline, but by their view of the merits and necessities of the case before them. Into that view extraneous circumstances, such as fear of the King, might to a certain extent intrude ; but such evidence as is available points decisively to the

---

[1] Some at least of the royal nominations to Parliament were due to the fact that nothing less than a royal command could produce a representative at all.

[2] *L. and P.* vii. 302.   [3] *Ibid.* v. 120.   [4] Cf. *ibid.* iv. App. 1.

conclusion that co-operation between the King and
Parliament was secured, partly by Parliament doing
what Henry wanted, and partly by Henry doing what
Parliament wanted. Parliament did not always do as
the King desired, nor did the King's actions always commend themselves to Parliament. Most of the measures
of the Reformation Parliament were matters of give and
take. It was due to Henry's skill, and to the circumstances of the time that the King's taking was always to
his own profit, and his giving at the expense of the clergy.
He secured the support of the Commons for his own
particular ends by promising the redress of their grievances against the bishops and priests. It is said that he
instituted the famous petitions urged against the clergy
in 1532, and it is hinted that the abuses, of which those
petitions complained, had no real existence. No doubt
Henry encouraged the Commons' complaints; he had
every reason to do so, but he did not invent the abuses.
If the Commons did not feel the grievances, the King's
promise to redress them would be no inducement to
Parliament to comply with the royal demands. The
hostility of the laity to the clergy, arising out of these
grievances, was in fact the lever with which Henry
overthrew the papal authority, and the basis upon which
he built his own supremacy over the Church.

This anti-ecclesiastical bias on the part of the laity was
the dominant factor in the Reformation under Henry
VIII. But the word in its modern sense is scarcely
applicable to the ecclesiastical policy of that King. Its
common acceptation implies a purification of doctrine;
but it is doubtful whether any idea of interfering with
dogma ever crossed the minds of the monarchs, who, for
more than a generation, had been proclaiming the need
for a reformation. Their proposal was to reform the
practice of the clergy; and the method they favoured
most was the abolition of clerical privileges and the
appropriation of ecclesiastical property. The Reformation
in England, so far as it was carried by Henry VIII, was,
indeed, neither more nor less than a violent self-assertion
of the laity against the immunities which the Church had

herself enjoyed, and the restraints which she imposed upon others.   It was not primarily a breach between the Church of England and the Roman communion, a repudiation on the part of English ecclesiastics of a harassing papal yoke ; for it is fairly obvious that under Henry VIII the Church took no measures against Rome that were not forced on it by the State.   It was not till the reigns of Edward VI and Elizabeth that the Church accorded a consent, based on conviction, to a settlement originally extorted by force.   The Reformation was rather a final assertion by the State of its authority over the Church in England. The breach with the Roman Church, the repudiation of papal influence in English ecclesiastical affairs, was not a spontaneous clerical movement ; it was the effect of the subjection of the Church to the national temporal power. The Church in England had hitherto been a semi-independent part of the political community.   It was semi-national, semi-universal ; it owed one sort of fealty to the universal Pope, and another to the national King. The rising spirit of nationality could brook no divided allegiance ; and the universal gave way to the national idea.   There was to be no *imperium in imperio*, but " one body politic,"[1] with one Supreme Head.   Henry VIII is reported by Chapuys as saying that he was King, Emperor and Pope, all in one, so far as England was concerned.[2]   The Church was to be nationalised ; it was to compromise its universal character, and to become the Church *of* England, rather than a branch of the Church universal *in* England.

The revolution was inevitably effected through the action of the State rather than that of the Church.   The Church, which, like religion itself, is in essence universal and not national, regarded with abhorrence the prospect of being narrowed and debased to serve political ends. The Church in England had moreover no means and no

---

[1] The phrase occurs in Cromwell's draft bill for the submission of Convocation (*L. and P.* v. 721).

[2] *Ibid.* v. 361.   This was in reference to Henry's refusal to allow a visitation of the Cistercian monasteries, of which Chapuys thought they stood in great need (31st July, 1531).

weapons wherewith to effect an internal reformation independent of the Papacy ; as well might the Court of King's Bench endeavour to reform itself without the authority of King and Parliament. The whole jurisdiction of the Church was derived in theory from the Pope ; when Wolsey wished to reform the monasteries he had to seek authority from Leo X ; the Archbishop of Canterbury held a court at Lambeth and exercised juridical powers, but he did so as *legatus natus* of the Apostolic See, and not as archbishop, and this authority could at any time be superseded by that of a legate *a latere*, as Warham's was by Wolsey's. It was not his own but the delegated jurisdiction of another.[1] Bishops and archbishops were only the channels of a jurisdiction flowing from a papal fountain. Henry charged Warham in 1532 with *præmunire* because he had consecrated the Bishop of St. Asaph before the Bishop's temporalties had been restored.[2] The Archbishop in reply stated that he merely acted as commissary of the Pope, " the act was the Pope's act," and he had no discretion of his own. He was bound to consecrate as soon as the Bishop had been declared such in consistory at Rome. Chapters might elect, the Archbishop might consecrate, and the King might restore the temporalties ; but none of these things gave a bishop jurisdiction. There were in fact two and only two sources of power and jurisdiction, the temporal sovereign and the Pope ; reformation must be effected by the one or the other. Wolsey had ideas of a national ecclesiastical reformation, but he could have gone no farther than the Pope, who gave him his authority, permitted. Had the Church in England transgressed that limit, it would have

[1] Cf. Maitland, *Roman Canon Law ;* Pollock and Maitland, *History of English Law* i. 90 (Bracton regards the Pope as the Englishman's " Ordinary ") ; and Leadam, *Select Cases from the Star Chamber* Introd. pp. lxxxvi.-viii.

[2] *L. and P.* v. 1247. A curious point about this document, unnoticed by the editor, is that the Bishop of St. Asaph had been consecrated as far back as 1518, and that he was the Standish who had played so conspicuous a part in the early Church and State disputes of Henry's reign. This is an echo of the " Investiture " controversy (Luchaire, *Manuel* pp. 509, 510).

become dead in schism, and Wolsey's jurisdiction would have *ipso facto* ceased. Hence the fundamental impossibility of Wolsey's scheme; hence the ultimate resort to the only alternative, a reformation by the temporal sovereign, which Wycliffe had advocated and which the Anglicans of the sixteenth century justified by deriving the royal supremacy from the authority conceded by the early Fathers to the Roman Emperor—an authority prior to the Pope's.

Hence, too, the agency employed was Parliament and not Convocation.[1] The representatives of the clergy met of course as frequently as those of the laity, but their activity was purely defensive. They suggested no changes themselves, and endeavoured without much success to resist the innovations forced upon them by King and by Parliament. They had every reason to fear both Henry and the Commons. They were conscious that the Church had lost its hold upon the nation. Its impotence was due in part to its own corruption, in part to the fact that thriving commercial and industrial classes, like those which elected Tudor Parliaments, are as a rule impatient of religious or at least sacerdotal dictation. God and Mammon, in spite of all efforts at compromise, do not really agree. In 1529, before the meeting of Parliament, Campeggio had appealed to Henry to prevent the ruin of the Church; he felt that without State protection the Church could hardly stand. In 1531 Warham, the successor of Becket and Langton, excused his compliance with Henry's demands by pleading *Ira principis mors est*.[2] In the draft of a speech he drew up just before his

---

[1] "It was not from Parliament," says Brewer (*L. and P.* iv. Introd. p. dcxlvii.), "but from Convocation that the King had to anticipate any show of independence or opposition." True, to some extent; but the fact does not prove, as Brewer alleges, that Convocation was more independent than Parliament, but that Henry was doing what Parliament liked and Convocation disliked.

[2] "The Queen replied that they were all fine councillors, for when she asked advice of the Archbishop of Canterbury, he replied that he would not meddle in these affairs, saying frequently, *Ira principis mors est*" (Chapuys to Charles V, 6th June, 1531). Warham was one of the counsel assigned to the Queen for the divorce question.

death,[1] the Archbishop referred to the case of St. Thomas, hinted that Henry VIII was going the way of Henry II, and compared his policy with the constitutions of Clarendon. The comparison was extraordinarily apt; Henry VIII was doing what Henry II had failed to do, and the fate that attended the Angevin king might have befallen the Tudor had Warham been Becket and the Church of the sixteenth been the same as the Church of the twelfth century. But they were not, and Warham appealed in vain to the liberties of the Church granted by Magna Carta, and to the " ill end " of " several kings who violated them ". Laymen, he complained, now ' advanced " their own laws rather than those of the Church. The people, admitted so staunch a churchman as Pole, were beginning to hate the priests.[2] " There were," wrote Norfolk, " infinite clamours of the temporalty here in Parliament against the misuse of the spiritual jurisdiction. . . . This realm did never grudge the tenth part against the abuses of the Church at no Parliament in my days, as they do now."[3]

These infinite clamours and grudging were not the result of the conscientious rejection of any Catholic or papal doctrine. Englishmen are singularly free from the bondage of abstract ideas, and they began their Reformation not with the enunciation of some new truth, but with an attack on clerical fees. Reform was stimulated by a practical grievance, closely connected with money, and not by a sense of wrong done to the conscience. No dogma plays such a part in the English Reformation as Justification by Faith did in Germany, or Predestination in Switzerland. Parliament in 1530 had not been appreciably affected by Tyndale's translation of the Bible or by any of Luther's works. Tyndale was still an exile in the

---

[1] L. and P. v. 1247. Warham also made a formal protest against the legislation of 1529-32 (ibid. v. 818). The likeness between Henry VIII and Henry II extended beyond their policy to their personal characteristics, and the great Angevin was much in the Tudor's mind at this period. Chapuys also called Henry VIII's attention to the fate of Henry II (ibid. vii. 94).

[2] L. and P. v. App. 10.

[3] Ibid. v. 831 ; cf. v. 898, 989, App. 28.

Netherlands, pleading in vain for the same toleration in England as Charles V permitted across the sea. Frith was in the Tower—a man, wrote the lieutenant, Walsingham, whom it would be a great pity to lose, if only he could be reconciled[1]—and Bilney was martyred in 1531. A parliamentary inquiry was threatened in the latter case, not because Parliament sympathised with Bilney's doctrine, but because it was said that the clergy had procured his burning before obtaining the State's consent.[2] Parliament was as zealous as Convocation against heresy, but wanted the punishment of heretics left in secular hands.

In this, as in other respects, the King and his Parliament were in the fullest agreement. Henry had already given proof of his anti-clerical bias by substituting laymen for churchmen in those great offices of State which churchmen had usually held. From time immemorial the Lord Chancellor had been a Bishop,[3] but in 1529 Wolsey was succeeded by More, and, later on, More by Audley. Similarly, the privy seal had been held in Henry's reign by three bishops successively, Fox, Ruthal and Tunstall: now it was entrusted to the hands of Anne Boleyn's father, the Earl of Wiltshire. Gardiner remained secretary for the time, but Du Bellay thought his power would have increased had he abandoned his clerical vows,[4] and he, too, was soon superseded by Cromwell. Even the clerkship of Parliament was now given up to a layman. During the first half of Henry's reign clerical influence had been supreme in Henry's councils; during the second it was almost entirely excluded. Like his Parliament, he was now impugning the jurisdiction of the clergy in the matter of heresy; they were doctors, he said, of the soul, and had nothing to do with the body.[5] He was even inclining to the very modern theory that marriage is a civil contract, and that matrimonial suits should therefore

---

[1] *L. and P.* v. 1458. [2] *Ibid.* v. 522; vii. 171.
[3] Thomas Beaufort, afterwards Duke of Exeter, who was Chancellor in 1410-12, and Richard, Earl of Salisbury, who was Chancellor in 1454-5, are exceptions.
[4] *L. and P.* iv. 6019. [5] *Ibid.* v. 1013.

be removed from clerical cognisance.[1] As early as 1529
he ordered Wolsey to release the Prior of Reading, who
had been imprisoned for Lutheranism, " unless the
matter is very heinous ".[2] In 1530 he was praising
Latimer's sermons ;[3] and in the same year the Bishop
of Norwich complained of a general report in his diocese
that Henry favoured heretical books.[4] " They say that,
wherever they go, they hear that the King's pleasure is
that the New Testament in English shall go forth."
There seems little reason to doubt Hall's statement that
Henry now commanded the bishops, who, however,
did nothing, to prepare an English translation of the
Bible to counteract the errors of Tyndale's version.[5] He
wrote to the German princes extolling their efforts
towards the reformation of the Church ;[6] and many
advisers were urging him to begin a similar movement
in England. Anne Boleyn and her father were, said
Chapuys, more Lutheran than Luther himself ; they
were the true apostles of the new sect in England.[7]

But, however Lutheran Anne Boleyn may have been,
Henry was still true to the orthodox faith. If he dallied
with German princes, and held out hopes to his heretic
subjects, it was not because he believed in the doctrines
of either, but because both might be made to serve his
own ends. He rescued Crome from the flames, not
because he doubted or favoured Crome's heresy, but
because Crome appealed from the Church to the King,
and denied the papal supremacy ; that, said Henry, is not
heresy, but truth.[8] When he sent to Oxford for the

---

[1] L. and P. v. 805 ; vii. 232. Chapuys had told him that " all the
Parliament could not make the Princess Mary a bastard, for the cognisance of cases concerning legitimacy belonged to ecclesiastical judges " ;
to which Henry replied that " he did not care for all the canons which
might be alleged, as he preferred his laws according to which he should
have illegitimacy judged by lay judges who could also take cognisance
of matrimonial causes ".

[2] Ibid. iv. 5925.   [3] Ibid. iv. 6325.   [4] Ibid. iv. 6385.
[5] The net result at the time was a royal proclamation promising an
authorised version of the Scriptures in English " if the people would
come to a better mind " (Ibid. iv. 6487).

[6] Ibid. v. App. 7.   [7] Ibid. v. 148, 850.   [8] Ibid. v. 129, 148.

HENRY VIII WITH HENRY VII IN
THE BACKGROUND

ANNE BOLEYN

JANE SEYMOUR

ANNE OF CLEVES

articles on which Wycliffe had been condemned,[1] it was not to study the great Reformer's doctrine of the mass, but to discover Wycliffe's reasons for calling upon the State to purify a corrupt Church, and to digest his arguments against the temporal wealth of the clergy. When he lauded the reforms effected by the German princes he was thinking of their secularisation of ecclesiastical revenues. The spoliation of the Church was consistent with the most fervent devotion to its tenets. In 1531 Henry warned the Pope that the Emperor would probably allow the laity " to appropriate the possessions of the Church, which is a matter which does not touch the foundations of the faith ; and what an example this will afford to others it is easy to see ".[2] Henry managed to improve upon Charles's example in this respect. " He meant," he told Chapuys in 1533, " to repair the errors of Henry II and John, who, being in difficulties, had made England and Ireland tributary to the Pope ; he was determined also to reunite to the Crown the goods which churchmen held of it, which his predecessors could not alienate to his prejudice ; and he was bound to do this by the oath he had taken at his coronation."[3] Probably it was about this time, or a little later, that he drew up his suggestions for altering the coronation oath, and making the royal obligations binding, only so far as the royal conscience thought fit. The German princes had a further claim to his consideration beyond the example they set him in dealing with the temporalties of the Church. They might be very useful if his difference with Charles over Catherine of Aragon came to an open breach ; and the English envoys, who congratulated them on their zeal for reform, also endeavoured to persuade them that Henry's friendship might be no little safeguard against a despotic Emperor.

All these phenomena, the Reformation in Germany, heresy at home, and the anti-sacerdotal prejudices of his subjects, were regarded by Henry merely as circumstances which might be made subservient to his own particular purpose ; and the skill with which he used

[1] *L. and P.* iv. 6546.　　　[2] *Ibid.* v. 326.　　　[3] *Ibid.* vi. 235.

them is a monument of farsighted statecraft.[1] He did
not act on the impulse of rash caprice. His passions
were strong, but his self-control was stronger ; and the
breach with Rome was effected with a cold and calculated
cunning, which the most adept disciple of Machiavelli
could not have excelled. He did not create the factors he
used ; hostility to the Church had a real objective
existence. Henry was a great man ; but the burdens his
people felt were not the product of Henry's hypnotic
suggestion. He could only divert those grievances to his
own use. He had no personal dislike to probate dues or
annates ; he did not pay them, but the threat of their
abolition might compel the Pope to grant his divorce.
Heresy in itself was abominable, but if heretics would
maintain the royal against the papal supremacy, might
not their sins be forgiven ? The strength of Henry's
position lay in the fact that he stood between two evenly
balanced parties. It is obvious that by favouring the anti-
clericals he could destroy the power of the Church. It is
not so certain, but it is probable that, by supporting the
Church, he could have staved off its ruin so long as he
lived. Parliament might have been urgent, but there
was no necessity to call it together. The Reformation
Parliament, which sat for seven years, would probably
have been dissolved after a few weeks had Clement
granted the divorce. It met session after session, to
pass one measure after another, each of which was
designed to put fresh pressure on the Pope. It began with
the outworks of the papal fortress ; as soon as one was
dismantled, Henry cried " Halt," to see if the citadel
would surrender. When it refused, the attack recom-
menced. First one, then another of the Church's privileges and the Pope's prerogatives disappeared, till there
remained not one stone upon another of the imposing
edifice of ecclesiastical liberty and papal authority in
England.

[1] Cf. A. Zimmermann, " Zur kirchlichen Politik Heinrichs VIII, nach
den Trennung vom Rom," in *Römische Quartalschrift* xiii. 263, 283.

CHAPTER XI

" DOWN WITH THE CHURCH "

THE Reformation Parliament met for its first session on the 3rd of November, 1529, at the Black Friars' Hall in London.[1] No careful observer was in any doubt as to what its temper would be with regard to the Church. It was opened by the King in person, and the new Lord Chancellor, Sir Thomas More, delivered an address in which he denounced his predecessor, Wolsey, in scathing terms.[2] Parliament had been summoned, he said, to reform such things as had been used or permitted in England by inadvertence. On the following day both Houses adjourned to Westminster on account of the plague, and the Commons chose as their Speaker, Sir Thomas Audley, the future Lord Chancellor. One of their first duties was to consider a bill of attainder against Wolsey,[3] and the fate of that measure seems to be destructive of one or the other of two favourite theories respecting Henry VIII's Parliaments. The bill was opposed in the Commons by Cromwell and thrown out; either it was not a mere expression of the royal will, or Parliament was something more than the tool of the Court. For it is hardly credible that Henry first caused the bill to be introduced, and then ordered its rejection. The next business was Henry's request for release from the obligation to repay the loan which Wolsey had raised; that, too, the Commons refused, except on conditions.[4] But no such opposition greeted the measures

---

[1] *L. and P.* iv. 6043-44. [2] Hall, *Chronicle* p. 764.
[3] *L. and P.* iv. 6075.
[4] That it passed at all is often considered proof of parliamentary servility; it is rather an illustration of the typical Tudor policy of burdening the wealthy few in order to spare the general public. If repayment of the loan were exacted, fresh taxation would be necessary, which would fall on many more than had lent the King money. It was very irregular, but the burden was thus placed on the shoulders of those individuals who benefited most by Henry's ecclesiastical and

for reforming the clergy.[1] Bills were passed in the
Commons putting a limit on the fees exacted by bishops
for probate, and for the performance of other duties then
regarded as spiritual functions. The clergy were prohibited from holding pluralities, except in certain cases,
but the act was drawn with astonishing moderation ; it
did not apply to benefices acquired before 1530, unless
they exceeded the number of four. Penalties against non-
residents were enacted, and an attempt was made to check
the addiction of spiritual persons to commercial pursuits.

These reforms seem reasonable enough, but the idea of
placing a bound to the spiritual exaction of probate
seemed sacrilege to Bishop Fisher. " My lords," he
cried, " you see daily what bills come hither from the
Common House, and all is to the destruction of the
Church. For God's sake, see what a realm the kingdom
of Bohemia was ; and when the Church went down, then
fell the glory of the kingdom. Now with the Commons
is nothing but ' Down with the Church ! ' And all this,
meseemeth, is for lack of faith only."[2] The Commons
thought a limitation of fees an insufficient ground for a
charge of heresy, and complained of Fisher to the King
through the mouth of their Speaker. The Bishop
explained away the offensive phrase, but the spiritual
peers succeeded in rejecting the Commons' bills. The
way out of the deadlock was suggested by the King ; he
proposed a conference between eight members of either
House. The Lords' delegates were half spiritual, half
temporal, peers.[3] Henry knew well enough that the
Commons would vote solidly for the measures, and that
the temporal peers would support them. They did so ;

general policy and were rapidly accumulating wealth. Taxation on the
whole was remarkably light during Tudor times ; the tenths, fifteenths
and subsidies had become fixed sums which did not increase with the
national wealth, and indeed brought in less and less to the royal exchequer
(see *L. and P.* vii. 344, " considerations why subsidies in diverse shires
were not so good in Henry's seventh year as in his fifth " ; cf. vii. 1490,
and xix. ii. 689, where Paget says that benevolences did not " grieve the
common people ").

[1] *L. and P.* iv. 6083.   [2] Hall, *Chronicle* p. 766.
[3] Cf. Stubbs, *Lectures* 1887 p. 317.

the bills were passed; and on 17th December Parliament was prorogued. We may call it a trick or skilful parliamentary strategy; the same trick, played by the *Tiers État* in 1789, ensured the success of the French Revolution, and it was equally effective in England in 1529.

These mutterings of the storm fell on deaf ears at Rome. Clement was deaf, not because he had not ears to hear, but because the clash of imperial arms drowned more distant sounds. " If any one," wrote the Bishop of Auxerre in 1531, " was ever in prison or in the power of his enemies, the Pope is now."[1] He was as anxious as ever to escape responsibility. " He has told me," writes the Bishop of Tarbes to Francis I on the 27th of March, 1530, " more than three times in secret that he would be glad if the marriage (with Anne Boleyn) was already made, either by a dispensation of the English legate or otherwise, provided it was not by his authority, or in diminution of his power as to dispensation and limitation of Divine law."[2] Later in the year he made his suggestion that Henry should have two wives without prejudice to the legitimacy of the children of either. Henry, however, would listen to neither suggestion.[3] He would be satisfied with nothing less than the sanction of the highest authority recognised in England. When it became imperative that his marriage with Anne should be legally sanctioned, and evident that no such sanction would be forthcoming from Rome, he arranged that the highest ecclesiastical authority recognised by law in England should be that of the Archbishop of Canterbury.

Meanwhile, the exigencies of the struggle drove Clement into assertions of papal prerogative which would at any time have provoked an outburst of national anger. On 7th March, 1530, he promulgated a bull to be affixed to the church doors at Bruges, Tournay and Dunkirk, inhibiting Henry, under pain of the greater excommunication, from proceeding to that second marriage, which he was telling the Bishop of Tarbes he wished

---

[1] *L. and P.* v. 562.   [2] *Ibid.* iv. 6290.
[3] See above, p. 207.

Henry would complete.[1] A fortnight later he issued a second bull forbidding all ecclesiastical judges, doctors, advocates and others to speak or write against the validity of Henry's marriage with Catherine.[2] If he had merely desired to prohibit discussion of a matter under judicial consideration, he should have imposed silence also on the advocates of the marriage, and not left Fisher free to write books against the King and secretly send them to Spain to be printed.[3] On the 23rd of December following it was decreed in Consistory at Rome that briefs should be granted prohibiting the Archbishop of Canterbury from taking cognisance of the suit, and forbidding Henry to cohabit with any other woman than Catherine, and " all women in general to contract marriage with the King of England ".[4] On the 5th of January, 1531, the Pope inhibited laity as well as clergy, universities, parliaments and courts of law from coming to any decision in the case.[5]

To these fulminations the ancient laws of England provided Henry with sufficient means of reply. " Let not the Pope suppose," wrote Henry to Clement, " that either the King or his nobles will allow the fixed laws of his kingdom to be set aside."[6] A proclamation, based on the Statutes of Provisors, was issued on 12th September, 1530, forbidding the purchasing from the Court of Rome or the publishing of any thing prejudicial to the realm, or to the King's intended purposes ;[7] and Norfolk was sent to remind the papal nuncio of the penalties attaching to the importation of bulls into England without the King's consent. But the most notorious expedient of Henry's was the appeal to the universities of Europe, first suggested by Cranmer.[8] Throughout 1530 English agents were busy abroad

---

[1] L. and P. iv. 6256.   [2] Ibid. iv. 6279.
[3] Ibid. iv. 6199, 6596, 6738 ; v. 460.   [4] Ibid. iv. 6772.
[5] Ibid. v. 27.   [6] Ibid. iv. 6759.   [7] Ibid. iv. 6615 ; v. 45.
[8] See the present writer's Cranmer pp. 39-41. Cranmer's suggestion was made early in August, 1529, and on the 23rd Du Bellay writes that Wolsey and the King " appeared to desire very much that I should go over to France to get the opinions of the learned men there about the divorce " (L. and P. iv. 5862). In October Stokesley was sent to France and Croke to Italy (ibid. p. 2684) ; Cranmer did not start till 1530.

obtaining decisions from the universities on the question
of the Pope's power to dispense with the law against
marrying a deceased brother's wife. Their success was
considerable. Paris and Orleans, Bourges and Toulouse,
Bologna and Ferrara, Pavia and Padua, all decided against
the Pope.[1] Similar verdicts, given by Oxford and Cambridge, may be as naturally ascribed to intimidation by
Henry, as may the decisions of Spanish universities in
the Pope's favour to pressure from Charles; but the
theory that all the French and Italian universities were
bribed is not very credible. The cajolery, the threats
and the bribes were not all on one side; and in Italy at
least the imperial agents would seem to have enjoyed
greater facilities than Henry's. In some individual cases
there was, no doubt, resort to improper inducements;
but if the majority in the most famous seats of learning
in Europe could be induced by filthy lucre to vote against
their conscience, it implies a greater need for drastic
reformation than the believers in the theory of corruption
are usually disposed to admit. Their decisions were,
however, given on general grounds; the question of the
consummation of Catherine's marriage with Arthur seems
to have been carefully excluded. How far that consideration would have affected the votes of the universities can
only be assumed; but it does not appear to have materially influenced the view taken by Catherine's advocates.
They allowed that Catherine's oath would not be considered sufficient evidence in a court of law; they
admitted the necessity of proving that urgent reasons
existed for the grant of the dispensation, and the only
urgent reason they put forward was an entirely imaginary
imminence of war between Henry VII and Ferdinand in
1503. Cardinal Du Bellay, in 1534, asserted that no one
would be so bold as to maintain in Consistory that the
dispensation ever was valid;[2] and the papalists were
driven to the extreme contention, which was certainly
not then admitted by Catholic Europe, that, whether the
marriage with Arthur was merely a form or not, whether

---

[1] *L. and P.* iv. 6332, 6448, 6491, 6632, 6636.
[2] *Ibid.* vii. App. 12.

it was or was not against Divine law, the Pope could, of
his absolute power, dispense.[1]

Pending the result of Henry's appeal to the universities,
little was done in the matter in England. The lords
spiritual and temporal signed in June, 1530, a letter to
the Pope urging him to comply with their King's request
for a divorce.[2] Parliament did not meet until 16th
January, 1531, and even then Chapuys reports that it was
employed on nothing more important than cross-bows
and hand-guns, the act against which was not, however,
passed till 1534. The previous session had shown that,
although the Commons might demur to fiscal exactions,
they were willing enough to join Henry in any attack on
the Church, and the question was how to bring the clergy
to a similar state of acquiescence. It was naturally a
more difficult task, but Henry's ingenuity provided a
sufficient inducement. His use of the statutes of *præmunire* was very characteristic. It was conservative, it
was legal, and it was unjust. Those statutes were no
innovation designed to meet his particular case ; they
had been for centuries the law of the land ; and there
was no denying the fact that the clergy had broken the
law by recognising Wolsey as legate. Henry, of course,
had licensed Wolsey to act as legate, and to punish the
clergy for an offence, at which he had connived, was
scarcely consistent with justice ; but no King ever showed
so clearly how the soundest constitutional maxims could
be used to defeat the pleas of equity ; it was frequently
laid down during his reign that no licence from the King
could be pleaded against penalties imposed by statute,
and not a few parliamentary privileges were first asserted
by Henry VIII.[3] So the clergy were cunningly caught
in the meshes of the law. Chapuys declares that no one
could understand the mysteries of *præmunire* ; " its
interpretation lies solely in the King's head, who amplifies

---

[1] *L. and P.* v. 468.   [2] *Ibid.* iv. 6513.

[3] Cf. *ibid.* iv. 6199. Chapuys writes on 6th February, 1530, " I am
told the King did not wish the Cardinal's case to be tried by Parliament, as, if it had been decided against him, the King could not have
pardoned him ".

it and declares it at his pleasure, making it apply to any case he pleases". He at least saw how *præmunire* could be made to serve his purposes.[1]

These, at the moment, were two. He wanted to extract from the clergy a recognition of his supremacy over the Church, and he wanted money. He was always in need of supplies, but especially now, in case war should arise from the Pope's refusal to grant his divorce ; and Henry made it a matter of principle that the Church should pay for wars due to the Pope.[2] The penalty for *præmunire* was forfeiture of goods and imprisonment, and the King probably thought he was unduly lenient in granting a pardon for a hundred thousand pounds, when he might have taken the whole of the clergy's goods and put them in gaol as well. The clergy objected strongly ; in the old days of the Church's influence they would all have preferred to go to prison, and a unanimous refusal of the King's demands would even now have baulked his purpose. But the spirit was gone out of them. Chapuys instigated the papal nuncio to go down to Convocation and stiffen the backs of the clergy.[3] They were horrified at his appearance, and besought him to depart in haste, fearing lest this fresh constitutional breach should be visited on their heads. Warham frightened them with the terrors of royal displeasure ; and the clerics had to content their conscience with an Irish bull and a subter- fuge. "Silence gives consent," said the Archbishop when putting the question ; "Then are we all silent," cried the clergy. To their recognition of Henry as

---

[1] *L. and P.* iv. 6488, 6699.

[2] Cf. *ibid*. vi. 1381 [3], " that if the Pope attempts war, the King shall have a moiety of the temporal lands of the Church for his defence ".

[3] *Ibid*. v. 62. Dr. Stubbs (*Lectures*, 1887, p. 318) represents the nuncio as being pressed into the King's service, and the clergy as resisting him as the Commons had done Wolsey in 1523. But this independence is imaginary ; " it was agreed," writes Chapuys, " between the nuncio and me that he should go to the said ecclesiastics in their congregation and recommend them to support the immunity of the Church. . . . They were all utterly astonished and scandalised, and without allowing him to open his mouth they begged him to leave them in peace, for they had not the King's leave to speak with him."

Supreme Head of the Church, they added the salvo " so far as the law of Christ allows ". It was an empty phrase, thought Chapuys, for no one would venture to dispute with the King the point where his supremacy ended and that of Christ began ;[1] there was in fact " a new Papacy made here ".[2] The clergy repented of the concession as soon as it was granted ; they were " more conscious every day," wrote Chapuys, " of the great error they committed in acknowledging the King as sovereign of the Church"; and they made a vain, and not very creditable, effort to get rejected by spiritual votes in the House of Lords the measures to which they had given their assent in Convocation.[3] The Church had surrendered with scarcely a show of fight ; henceforth Henry might feel sure that, whatever opposition he might encounter in other quarters, the Church in England would offer no real resistance.

In Parliament, notwithstanding Chapuys' remark on the triviality of its business, more than a score of acts were passed, some limiting such abuses as the right of sanctuary, some dealing in the familiar way with social evils like the increase of beggars and vagabonds. The act depriving sanctuary-men, who committed felony, of any further protection from their sanctuary was recommended to Parliament by the King in person. So was a curious act making poisoning treason.[4] There had recently been an attempt to poison Fisher, which the King brought before the House of Lords. However familiar poisoning might be at Rome, it was a novel method in England, and was considered so heinous a crime that the ordinary penalties for murder were thought to be insufficient. Then the King's pardon to the clergy was embodied in a parliamentary bill. The Commons perceived that they were not included, took alarm, and refused to pass the bill. Henry at first assumed a superior tone ; he pointed out that the Commons could not prevent his pardoning the clergy ; he could do it as well under the Great Seal as by statute. The Commons, however, were not satisfied. " There was great murmur-

---

[1] *L. and P.* v. 105. [2] *Ibid.* v. 112.
[3] *Ibid.* v. 124. [4] *Ibid.* v. 120.

ing among them," says Chapuys, "in the House of Commons, where it was publicly said in the presence of some of the Privy Council that the King had burdened and oppressed his kingdom with more imposts and exactions than any three or four of his predecessors, and that he ought to consider that the strength of the King lay in the affections of his people. And many instances were alleged of the inconveniences which had happened to princes through the ill-treatment of their subjects."[1] Henry was too shrewd to attempt to punish this very plain speaking. He knew that his faithful Commons were his one support, and he yielded at once. "On learning this," continues Chapuys, "the King granted the exemption which was published in Parliament on Wednesday last without any reservation." The two acts for the pardon of the spiritualty and temporalty were passed concurrently. But, whereas the clergy had paid for their pardon with a heavy fine and the loss of their independence, the laity paid nothing at all. The last business of the session was the reading of the sentences in Henry's favour obtained from the universities.[2] Parliament was then prorogued, and its members were enjoined to relate to their constituents that which they had seen and heard.

Primed by communion with their neighbours, members of Parliament assembled once more on 15th January, 1532, for more important business than they had yet transacted. Every effort was made to secure a full attendance of Peers and Commons; almost all the lords would be present, thought Chapuys, except Tunstall, who had not been summoned; Fisher came without a summons, and apparently no effort was made to exclude him.[3] The readiness of the Commons to pass measures against the Church, and their reluctance to consent to

---

[1] *L. and P.* v. 171. This and other incidents (see p. 232) form a singular comment on Brewer's assertion (*ibid.* iv. Introd. p. dcxlvii.) that "there is scarcely an instance on record, in this or any succeeding Parliament throughout the reign, of a parliamentary patriot protesting against a single act of the Crown, however unjust and tyrannical it might be".

[2] *Ibid.* v. 171.   [3] *Ibid.* v. 737.

taxation, were even more marked than before. Their
critical spirit was shown by their repeated rejection of
the Statutes of Wills and Uses designed by Henry to
protect from evasion his feudal rights, such as reliefs and
primer seisins.[1] This demand, writes Chapuys,[2] " has
been the occasion of strange words against the King and
the Council, and in spite of all the efforts of the King's
friends, it was rejected ".[3] In the matter of supplies they
were equally outspoken ; they would only grant one-tenth
and one-fifteenth, a trifling sum which Henry refused
to accept.[4] It was during this debate on the question of
supplies that two members moved that the King be asked
to take back Catherine as his wife.[5] They would then,
they urged, need no fresh armaments and their words are
reported to have been well received by the House. The
Commons were not more enthusiastic about the bill
restraining the payment of annates to the Court at Rome.[6]
They did not pay them ; their grievance was against
bishops in England, and they saw no particular reason
for relieving those prelates of their financial burdens.
Cromwell wrote to Gardiner that he did not know how
the annates bill would succeed ;[7] and the King had
apparently to use all his persuasion to get the bill through
the Lords and the Commons. Only temporal lords voted
for it in the Upper House, and in the Lower recourse
was had to the rare expedient of a division.[8] In both
Houses the votes were taken in the King's presence.
But it is almost certain that his influence was brought
to bear, not so much in favour of the principle of the

[1] Henry had ordered Cromwell to have a bill with this object ready
for the 1531 session (L. and P. v. 394), and another for the " augmentation
of treasons " ; apparently neither then proved acceptable to Parliament.
  [2] L. and P. v. 805.   [3] Ibid. v. 989.   [4] Ibid. v. 1046.
  [5] Ibid. v. 989. This was in May during the second part of the session,
after the other business had been finished ; redress of grievances con-
stitutionally preceded supply.
  [6] Annates were attacked first, partly because they were the weakest
as well as the most sensitive part in the papal armour ; there was no law
in the Corpus Juris Canonici requiring the payment of annates (Maitland
in Engl. Hist. Rev. xvi. 43).
  [7] L. and P. v. 723.   [8] Ibid. v. 898.

bill, as of the extremely ingenious clause which left the execution of the Act in Henry's discretion, and provided him with a powerful means of putting pressure on the Pope. That was Henry's statement of the matter. He told Chapuys, before the bill was passed, that the attack on annates was being made without his consent ;[1] and after it had been passed he instructed his representatives at Rome to say that he had taken care to stop the mouth of Parliament and to have the question of annates referred to his decision.[2] " The King," writes the French envoy in England at the end of March, " has been very cunning, for he has caused the nobles and people to remit all to his will, so that the Pope may know that, if he does nothing for him, the King has the means of punishing him."[3] The execution of the clauses providing for the confirmation and consecration of bishops without recourse to Rome was also left at Henry's option.

But no pressure was needed to induce the Commons to attack abuses, the weight of which they felt themselves. Early in the session they were discussing the famous petition against the clergy, and, on 28th February, Norfolk referred to the " infinite clamours " in Parliament against the Church.[4] The fact that four corrected drafts of this petition are extant in the Record Office, is taken as conclusive proof that it really emanated from the Court.[5] But the drafts do not appear to be in the known hand of any of the Government clerks. The corrections in Cromwell's hand doubtless represent the wishes of the King ; but even were the whole in Cromwell's hand it would be no bar to the hypothesis that Cromwell reduced to writing, for the King's consideration, complaints which he heard from independent members in his

[1] *L. and P.* v. 832.   [2] *Ibid.* v. 886.
[3] *Ibid.* v. 150. This letter is misplaced in *L. and P.* ; it should be under 23rd March, 1532, instead of 1531. The French envoy, Giles de la Pommeraye, did not arrive in England till late in 1531, and his letter obviously refers to the proceedings in Parliament in March, 1532 ; cf. v. 879.   [4] *Ibid.* v. 831.
[5] *Ibid.* v. 1017-23. If the Court was responsible for all the documents complaining of the clergy drawn up at this time, it must have been very active. See others in *L. and P.* v. 49, App. 28 ; vi. 122.

place in Parliament. The fact that nine-tenths of our modern legislation is drawn up by Government draughtsmen cannot be accepted as proof that that legislation represents no popular feeling. On the face of them, these petitions bear little evidence of Court dictation; the grievances are not such as were felt by Henry, whose own demands of the clergy were laid directly before Convocation, without any pretence that they really came from the Commons. Some are similar to those presented to the Parliament of 1515; others are directed against abuses which recent statutes had sought, but failed, to remedy. Such were the citation of laymen out of their dioceses, the excessive fees taken in spiritual courts, the delay and trouble in obtaining probates. Others complained that the clergy in Convocation made laws inconsistent with the laws of the realm; that the ordinaries delayed instituting parsons to their benefices; that benefices were given to minors; that the number of holy-days, especially in harvest-time, was excessive; and that spiritual men occupied temporal offices. The chief grievance seems to have been that the ordinaries cited poor men before the spiritual courts without any accuser being produced, and then condemned them to abjure or be burnt. Henry, reported Chapuys, was "in a most gracious manner" promising to support the Commons against the Church "and to mitigate the rigours of the inquisition which they have here, and which is said to be more severe than in Spain".[1]

After debating these points in Parliament, the Commons agreed that "all the griefs, which the temporal men should be grieved with, should be put in writing and delivered to the King"; hence the drafts in the Record Office. The deputation, with the Speaker at its head, presented the complaints to Henry on 18th March. Its reception is quite unintelligible on the theory that the grievances existed only in the King's imagination. Henry was willing, he said, to consider the Commons' petition. But, if they expected him to comply with their wishes, they must make some concession to his; and he

[1] *L. and P.* v. 989.

recommended them to forgo their opposition to the bills of Uses and Wills, to which the Lords had already agreed. After Easter he sent the Commons' petition to Convocation ; the clergy appealed to the King for protection. Henry had thus manœuvred himself into the position of mediator, in which he hoped, but in vain, to extract profit for himself from both sides.[1] From Convocation he demanded submission to three important claims ; the clergy were to consent to a reform of ecclesiastical law, to abdicate their right of independent legislation, and to recognise the necessity of the King's approval for existing canons. These demands were granted. As usual, Henry was able to get what he wanted from the clergy ; but from the Commons he could get no more than they were willing to give. They again rejected the bills of Uses and Wills, and would only concede the most paltry supplies. But they passed with alacrity the bills embodying the submission of the clergy. These were the Church's concessions to Henry, but it must bend the knee to the Commons as well, and other measures were passed reforming some of the points in their petition. Ordinaries were prohibited from citing men out of their proper dioceses, and benefit of clergy was denied to clerks under the order of sub-deacon who committed murder, felony, or petty treason ; the latter was a slight extension of a statute passed in 1512. The bishops, however, led by Gardiner and aided by More,[2] secured in the House of Lords the rejection of the concessions made by the Church to the King, though they passed those made to the Commons. Parliament, which had sat for the unusual space of four months, was prorogued on the 14th of May ; two days later, More resigned the chancellorship and Gardiner retired in disfavour to Winchester.

[1] Stubbs, *Lectures*, 1887, pp. 320-24 ; Hall pp. 784, 785 ; see also *Lords' Journals*, 1532.

[2] *L. and P.* v. 1013. More had, as Henry knew, been all along opposed to the divorce, but as More gratefully acknowledged, the King only employed those whose consciences approved of the divorce on business connected with it (vii. 289).

Meanwhile the divorce case at Rome made little progress. In the highest court in Christendom the facilities afforded for the law's delays were naturally more extended than before inferior tribunals ; and two years had been spent in discussing whether Henry's " excusator," sent merely to maintain that the King of England could not be cited to plead before the Papal Court, should be heard or not. Clement was in suspense between two political forces. In December, 1532, Charles was again to interview the Pope, and imperialists in Italy predicted that his presence would be as decisive in Catherine's favour as it had been three years before. But Henry and Francis had, in October, exhibited to the world the closeness of their friendship by a personal interview at Boulogne.[1] No pomp or ceremony, like that of the Field of Cloth of Gold, dazzled men's eyes ; but the union between the two Kings was never more real. Neither Queen was present ; Henry would not take Catherine, and he objected so strongly to Spanish dress that he could not endure the sight of Francis's Spanish Queen.[2] Anne Boleyn, recently created Marquis (so she was styled, to indicate the possession of the peerage in her own right) of Pembroke,[3] took Catherine's place ; and plans for the promotion of the divorce formed the staple of the royal discussions. Respect for the power of the two Kings robbed the subsequent interview between Emperor and Pope of much of its effect ; and before Charles and Clement parted, the Pope had secretly agreed to accord a similar favour to Francis ; he was to meet him at Nice in the following summer. Long before then the divorce had been brought to a crisis. By the end of January Henry knew that Anne Boleyn was pregnant. Her issue must at any cost be made legitimate. That could only be done by Henry's divorce from Catherine, and by his marriage with Anne Boleyn.[4] There was little hope of

[1] See P. A. Hamy, *Entrevue de François I avec Henri VIII, à Boulogne en* 1532. Paris, 1898.

[2] *L. and P.* v. 1187.   [3] *L. and P.* v. 1274.

[4] In 1529 Du Bellay had written *si le ventre croist, tout sera gasté* (*L. and P.* iv. 5679).

obtaining these favours from Rome. Therefore it must
be done by means of the Archbishop of Canterbury ; and
to remove all chance of disputing his sentence, the Court
of the Archbishop of Canterbury must, before his decision
was given, be recognised as the supreme tribunal for
English ecclesiastical cases.

These circumstances, of which not a hint was suffered
to transpire in public, dictated Henry's policy during the
early months of 1533. Never was his skill more clearly
displayed ; he was, wrote Chapuys in December, 1532,
practising more than ever with his Parliament,[1] though
he received the Spanish ambassador " as courteously as
ever ".[2] The difficulties with which he was surrounded
might have tried the nerve of any man, but they only
seemed to render Henry's course more daring and steady.
The date of his marriage with Anne Boleyn is even now
a matter of conjecture.[3] Cranmer repudiated the report
that he performed the ceremony.[4] He declares he did
not know of it until a fortnight after the event, and says
it took place about St. Paul's Day (25th January). A
more important question was the individuality of the
archbishop who was to pronounce the nullity of Henry's
marriage with Catherine of Aragon. He must obviously
be one on whom the King could rely. Fortunately for
Henry, Archbishop Warham had died in August, 1532.
His successor was to be Thomas Cranmer, who had first
suggested to Henry the plan of seeking the opinions of
the universities on the divorce, and was now on an
embassy at the Emperor's Court. No time was to be
lost. Henry usually gathered a rich harvest during the
vacancy of great bishoprics, but now Canterbury was to
be filled up without any delay, and the King even lent
Cranmer 1,000 marks to meet his expenses.[5] But would
the Pope be so accommodating as to expedite the bulls,

[1] *L. and P.* v. 1633.   [2] *Ibid.* v. 1579.
[3] Cranmer, *Works* ii. 246. The antedating of the marriage to 14th
November, 1532, by Hall and Holinshed was doubtless due to a desire
to shield Anne's character ; Stow gives the correct date.
[4] See the present writer's *Cranmer* p. 60 n.
[5] *L. and P.* vi. 131.

I

suspecting, as he must have done, the object for which
they were wanted ?

For this contingency also Henry had provided ; and he
was actually using the Pope as a means for securing the
divorce. An appearance of friendship with Clement was
the weapon he now employed with the greatest effect.
The Pope was discussing with the French ambassadors
a proposal to remit the divorce case to some neutral spot,
such as Cambrai, and delaying that definite sentence in
Catherine's favour which imperialists had hoped that
his interview with Charles would precipitate ;[1] the papal
nuncio was being feasted in England, and was having
suspiciously amicable conferences with members of Henry's
council. Henry himself was writing to Clement in the
most cordial terms ; he had instructed his ambassadors
in 1531 to " use all gentleness towards him,"[2] and
Clement was saying that Henry was of a better nature
and more wise than Francis I.[3] Henry was now willing to
suspend his consent to the general council, where the
Pope feared that a scheme would be mooted for restoring
the papal States to the Emperor ;[4] and he told the papal
nuncio in England that, though he had studied the
question of the Pope's authority and retracted his defence
of the Holy See,[5] yet possibly Clement might give him
occasion to probe the matter further still, and to reconfirm
what he had originally written.[6] Was he not, moreover,
withholding his assent from the Act of Annates, which
would deprive the Pope of large revenues ? Backed by
this gentle hint, Henry's request not merely for Cranmer's
bulls, but for their expedition without the payment of
the usual 10,000 marks, reached Rome. The cardinals
were loth to forgo their perquisites for the bulls, but the

[1] *L. and P.* vi. 26. The interview took place at Bologna in December,
1532.

[2] *Ibid.* v. 326.   [3] *Ibid.* v. 555.   [4] *Ibid.* vi. 89, 212.

[5] E.g. *ibid.* v. 820, where Henry tells Tunstall that to follow the Pope
is to forsake Christ, that it was no schism to separate from Rome, and that
" God willing, we shall never separate from the universal body of Christian
men," and admits that he was misled in his youth to make war upon
Louis XII by those who sought only their own pomp, wealth and glory.

[6] *Ibid.* vi. 296.

annates of all England were more precious still, and, on 22nd February, Consistory decided to do what Henry desired.

The same deceptive appearance of concord between King and Pope was employed to lull both Parliament and Convocation. The delays in the divorce suit disheartened Catherine's adherents. The Pope, wrote Chapuys, would lose his authority little by little, unless the case were decided at once ;[1] every one, he said, cried out " au murdre " on Clement for his procrastination on the divorce, and for the speed with which he granted Cranmer's bulls.[2] There was a general impression that " he would betray the Emperor," and " many think that there is a secret agreement between Henry and the Pope ".[3] That idea was sedulously fostered by Henry. Twice he took the Pope's nuncio down in state to Parliament to advertise the excellent terms upon which he stood with the Holy See.[4] In the face of such evidence, what motive was there for prelates and others to reject the demands which Henry was pressing upon them ? The Convocations of Canterbury and York repeated the submission of 1532, and approved, by overwhelming majorities, of two propositions : firstly, that, as a matter of law, the Pope was not competent to dispense with the obstacle to a marriage between a man and his deceased brother's wife, when the previous marriage had been consummated ; and secondly, that, as a matter of fact, the marriage between Catherine and Prince Arthur had been so consummated.[5] In Parliament, the Act forbidding Appeals to Rome,[6] and providing for the confirmation and consecration of bishops, without recourse to the Papal Court, was discussed. It was, like the rest of Henry's

---

[1] *L. and P.* vi. 142.   [2] *Ibid*. vi. 296.   [3] *Ibid*. vi. 89.

[4] *Ibid*. vi. 142, 160. The nuncio sat on Henry's right and the French ambassador on his left, this trinity illustrating the league existing between Pope, Henry and Francis.

[5] *Ibid*. vi. 276, 311, 317, 491.

[6] The germ of this Act may be found in a despatch from Henry dated 7th October, 1530; that the system of appeals had been subject to gross abuse is obvious from the fact that the Council of Trent prohibited it (*Cambridge Modern Hist*. ii. 671).

measures, based on a specious conservative plea. General councils had, the King said, decreed that suits should be determined in the place in which they originated ;[1] so there was no need for appeals to go out of England. Such opposition as it encountered was based on no religious principle. Commercial interests were the most powerful impulse of the age, and the Commons were afraid that the Act of Appeals might be followed by a papal interdict. They did not mind the interdict as depriving them of religious consolations, but they dreaded lest it might ruin their trade with the Netherlands.[2] Henry, however, persuaded them that the wool trade was as necessary to Flemings as it was to Englishmen, and that an interdict would prove no more than an empty threat. He was careful to make no other demands upon the Commons. No subsidies were required ; no extension of royal prerogative was sought ; and eventually the Act of Appeals was passed with a facility that seems to have created general surprise.[3]

Henry's path was now clear. Cranmer was archbishop and *legatus natus* with a title which none could dispute. By Act of Parliament his Court was the final resort for all ecclesiastical cases. No appeals from his decision could be lawfully made. So, on 11th April, before he was yet consecrated, he besought the King's gracious permission to determine his " great cause of matrimony, because much bruit exists among the common people on the subject ".[4] No doubt there did ; but that was not the cause for the haste. Henry was pleased to accede to this request of the " principal minister of our spiritual jurisdiction " ; and, on the 10th of May, the Archbishop opened his Court at Dunstable. Catherine, of course, could recognise no authority in Cranmer to try a cause that was before the papal curia. She was declared contumacious, and on the 23rd the Archbishop gave his sentence. Following the line of Convocation, he pronounced that the Pope had no power to license marriages such as Henry's, and that the King and Catherine had never been husband and

[1] *L. and P.* vi. 1489.   [2] *Ibid.* vi. 296.
[3] *Ibid.* XII. ii. 952.   [4] Cranmer, *Works* ii. 237.

wife.[1] Five days later, after a secret investigation, he declared that Henry and Anne Boleyn were lawfully married, and on Whitsunday, the 1st of June, he crowned Anne as Queen in Westminster Abbey.[2] Three months later, on Sunday, the 7th of September, between three and four in the afternoon, Queen Anne gave birth to a daughter at Greenwich.[3] The child was christened on the following Wednesday by Stokesley, Bishop of London, and Cranmer stood godfather. Chapuys scarcely considered the matter worth mention. The King's *amie* had given birth to a bastard, a detail of little importance to anyone, and least of all to a monarch like Charles V.[4] Yet the "bastard" was Queen Elizabeth, and the child, thus ushered into a contemptuous world, lived to humble the pride of Spain, and to bear to a final triumph the banner which Henry had raised.

[1] Cranmer, *Works* ii. 241, 244 ; *L. and P.* vi. 332, 469, 470, 525. This sentence did not bastardise the Princess Mary according to Chapuys, for "even if the marriage were null, the Princess was legitimate owing to the lawful ignorance of her parents. The Archbishop of Canterbury had foreseen this and had not dared to be so shameless as to declare her a bastard " (*ibid*. vii. 94).

[2] See *Tudor Tracts* edited by the present writer, 1903, pp. 10-28, and *L. and P.* vi. 561, 563, 584, 601.

[3] *Ibid*. vi. 1089, 1111.   [4] *Ibid*. vi. 1112.

CHAPTER XII

"THE PREVAILING OF THE GATES OF HELL"

THAT victorious issue of the Tudor struggle with the power, against which Popes proclaimed that the gates of hell should not prevail, was distant enough in 1533. Then the Tudor monarch seemed rushing headlong to irretrievable ruin. Sure of himself and his people, and feeling no longer the need of Clement's favour, Henry threw off the mask of friendship, and on the 9th of July confirmed, by letters patent, the Act of Annates.[1] Cranmer's proceedings at Dunstable, Henry's marriage, and Anne's coronation, constituted a still more flagrant defiance of Catholic Europe. The Pope's authority was challenged with every parade of contempt. He could do no less than gather round him the relics of his dignity and prepare to launch against Henry the final ban of the Church.[2] So, on the 11th of July, the sentence of the greater excommunication was drawn up. Clement did not yet, nor did he ever, venture to assert his claims to temporal supremacy in Christendom, by depriving the English King of his kingdom ; he thought it prudent to rely on his own undisputed prerogative. His spiritual powers seemed ample ; and he applied to himself the words addressed to the Prophet Jeremiah, " Behold, I

---

[1] *L. and P.* vi. 793.

[2] *Ibid.* vi. 807, App. 3 ; vii. 185. The declaration of it was at the same time suspended until September, and the delicate question of entrusting the *executoriales* to princes who repudiated the honour caused further delays. The bull of excommunication was eventually dated 30th August, 1535 (ix. 207) ; and a bull depriving Henry of his kingdom was sanctioned, printed and prepared for publication (x. Introd. p. xv. Nos. 82, 107), but first Francis and then Charles put difficulties in the way. In December, 1538, Paul III, now that he, Charles and Francis were united in the bond of friendship, published with additions the bull of August, 1535 (XIII. ii. 1087, Introd. p. xli.). Even then no bull of deprivation was published. Apparently that was an honour reserved for Henry's daughter.

have set thee above nations and kingdoms that thou mayest root up and destroy, build and plant, a lord over all kings of the whole earth and over all peoples bearing rule ".[1] In virtue of this prerogative Henry was cut off from the Church while he lived, removed from the pale of Christian society, and deprived of the solace of the rites of religion ; when he died, he must lie without burial, and in hell suffer torment for ever.[2]

What would be the effect of this terrific anathema ? The omens looked ill for the English King. If he had flouted the Holy See, he had also offended the temporal head of Christendom. The Emperor's aunt had been divorced, his cousin's legitimacy had been impugned, and the despatches of his envoy, Chapuys, were filled with indignant lamentations over the treatment meted out to Catherine and to her daughter. Both proud and stubborn women, they resolutely refused to admit in any way the validity of Henry's acts and recent legislation. Catherine would rather starve as Queen, than be sumptuously clothed and fed as Princess Dowager. Henry would give her anything she asked, if she would acknowledge that she was not the Queen, nor her daughter the Princess ; but her bold resistance to his commands and wishes brought out all the worst features of his character.[3] His anger was not the worst the Queen and her daughter had to fear ; he still preserved a feeling of respect for Catherine and of affection for Mary. " The King himself," writes Chapuys, " is not ill-natured ; it is this Anne who has put him in this perverse and wicked temper, and alienates him from his former humanity." [4] The new Queen's

---

[1] Jeremiah i. 10. The Vulgate text adopted in Papal bulls differs materially from that in the English Authorised Version.

[2] See the text in Burnet, ed. Pocock iv. 318-31.

[3] *L. and P*. vi. 805, 1186.

[4] *Ibid*. vi. 351 ; vii. 171, 871 ; cf. v. 216, where Chapuys says Anne hated the Princess Mary more than she did Queen Catherine because she saw that Henry had some affection for Mary, and praised her in Anne's presence. At the worst Henry's manners were generally polite ; on one occasion, writes Chapuys, " when the King was going to mount his horse, the Princess went on to a terrace at the top of the house to see him. The King, either being told of it or by chance, turned round, and

jealous malignity passed all bounds. She caused her
aunt to be made governess to Mary, and urged her to
box her charge's ears ; and she used every effort to force
the Princess to serve as a maid upon her little half-sister
Elizabeth.[1]

This humiliation was deeply resented by the people,
who, says Chapuys, though forbidden, on pain of their
lives, to call Catherine Queen, shouted it at the top of
their voices.[2] "You cannot imagine," he writes a few
weeks later to Charles, " the great desire of all this people
that your Majesty should send men. Every day I have
been applied to about it by Englishmen of rank, wit and
learning, who give me to understand that the last King
Richard was never so much hated by his people as this
King."[3] The Emperor, he went on, had a better chance
of success than Henry VII, and Ortiz at Rome was
cherishing the belief that England would rise against the
King for his contumacy and schismatic disobedience.[4]
Fisher was urgent that Charles should prepare an invasion
of England ; the young Marquis of Exeter, a possible
claimant to the throne, was giving the same advice.[5]
Abergavenny, Darcy and other peers brooded in sullen
discontent. They were all listening to the hysterical
ravings of Elizabeth Barton,[6] the Nun of Kent, who
prophesied that Henry had not a year to live. Charles's
emissaries were busy in Ireland, where Kildare was about
to revolt. James V of Scotland was hinting at his claims
to the English crown should Henry be deprived by the
Pope ;[7] and Chapuys was divided in mind whether it
would be better to make James the executor of the
papal sentence, or marry Mary to some great English

seeing her on her knees with her hands joined, bowed to her and put his
hand to his hat. Then all those present who had not dared to raise their
heads to look at her [surely they may not have seen her] rejoiced at what
the King had done, and saluted her reverently with signs of good-will
and compassion " (L. and P. vii. 83).

[1] L. and P. vii. 171.   [2] Ibid. vi. 918.
[3] Ibid. vi. 508 ; vii. 121.   [4] Ibid. v. 1324.   [5] Ibid. v. 416.
[6] See Transactions of the Royal Hist. Soc., N.S. xviii. ; L. and P. vi. 1419,
1445, 1464, 1467, 1468.
[7] L. and P. v. 609, 807 ; vi. 815, 821.

noble, and raise an internal rebellion.[1] At Catherine's suggestion he recommended to the Emperor Reginald Pole, a grandson of George, Duke of Clarence, as a suitor for Mary's hand ; and he urged, on his own account, Pole's claims to the English throne.[2] Catherine's scruples, not about deposing her husband, or passing over the claims of Henry's sisters, but on the score of Edward IV's grandson, the Marquis of Exeter, might, thought Chapuys, be removed by appealing to the notorious sentence of Bishop Stillington, who, on the demand of Richard III, had pronounced Edward IV's marriage void and his children illegitimate.[3] Those who had been the King's firm supporters when the divorce first came up were some of them wavering, and others turning back.[4] Archbishop Lee, Bishops Tunstall and Gardiner, and Benet,[5] were now all in secret or open opposition, and even Longland was expressing to Chapuys regrets that he had ever been Henry's confessor ;[6] like other half-hearted revolutionists, they would never have started at all had they known how far they would have to go, and now they were setting their sails for an adverse breeze. It was the King, and the King alone, who kept England on the course which he had mapped out. Pope and Emperor were defied ; Europe was shocked ; Francis himself disapproved of the breach with the Church ; Ireland was in revolt ; Scotland, as ever, was hostile ; legislation had been thrust down the throats of a recalcitrant Church, and, we are asked to believe, of a no less unwilling House of Commons, while the people at large were seething with indignation at the insults heaped upon the injured Queen and her daughter. By all the laws of nature, of morals, and of politics, it would seem, Henry was doomed to the fate of the monarch in the Book of Daniel the Prophet,[7] who did according to his will and exalted and magnified himself above every

[1] *L. and P.* vi. 446, 541 ; vii. 114.   [2] *Ibid.* vi. 1164.
[3] *Ibid.* vii. 1368.
[4] Even Norfolk, and Suffolk and his wife wanted to dissuade Henry in 1531 from persisting in the divorce (*ibid.* v. 287).
[5] *Ibid.* v. 696.   [6] *Ibid.* vii. 14.   [7] Daniel xi. 36-45.

god ; who divided the land for gain, and had power over
the treasures of gold and silver ; who was troubled by
tidings from the east and from the north ; who went
forth with great fury to destroy and utterly make away
many, and yet came to his end, and none helped him.

All these circumstances, real and alleged, would be
quite convincing as reasons for Henry's failure ; but they
are singularly inconclusive as explanations of his success,
of the facts that his people did not rise and depose him,
that no Spanish Armada disgorged its host on English
shores, and that, for all the papal thunderbolts, Henry
died quietly in his bed fourteen years later, and was
buried with a pomp and respect to which Popes themselves were little accustomed. He may have stood alone
in his confidence of success, and in his penetration
through these appearances into the real truth of the
situation behind. That, from a purely political or non-
moral point of view, is his chief title to greatness. He
knew from the beginning what he could do ; he had
counted the cost and calculated the risks ; and, writes
Russell in August, 1533, " I never saw the King merrier
than he is now ".[1] As early as March, 1531, he told
Chapuys that if the Pope issued 10,000 excommunications he would not care a straw for them.[2] When
the papal nuncio first hinted at excommunication and a
papal appeal to the secular arm, Henry declared that he
cared nothing for either.[3] He would open the eyes of
princes, he said, and show them how small was really
the power of the Pope ;[4] and " when the Pope had done
what he liked on his side, Henry would do what he liked
here ".[5] That threat, at least, he fulfilled with a vengeance. He did not fear the Spaniards ; they might come,
he said (as they did in 1588), but perhaps they might not
return.[6] England, he told his subjects, was not conquer-
able, so long as she remained united ;[7] and the patriotic
outburst with which Shakespeare closes " King John " is
but an echo and an expansion of the words of Henry VIII.

[1] L. and P. vi. 948.   [2] Ibid. v. 148.   [3] Ibid. v. 738.
[4] Ibid. v. 1292.   [5] Ibid. v. 287.
[6] Ibid. vi. 1479.   [7] Ibid. vi. 324.

This England never did, nor never shall,
Lie at the proud foot of a conqueror,
But when it first did help to wound itself. . . .
Come the three corners of the world in arms,
And we shall shock them. Nought shall make us rue,
If England to itself do rest but true.

The great fear of Englishmen was lest Charles should ruin them by prohibiting the trade with Flanders. "Their only comfort," wrote Chapuys, "is that the King persuades the people that it is not in your Majesty's power to do so."[1] Henry had put the matter to a practical test in the autumn of 1533 by closing the Staple at Calais.[2] It is possible that the dispute between him and the merchants, alleged as the cause for this step, was real; but the King could have provided his subjects with no more forcible object-lesson. Distress was felt at once in Flanders; complaints grew so clamorous that the Regent sent an embassy post-haste to Henry to remonstrate, and to represent the closing of the Staple as an infraction of commercial treaties. Henry coldly replied that he had broken no treaties at all; it was merely a private dispute between his merchants and himself, in which foreign powers had no ground for intervention. The envoys had to return, convinced against their will. The Staple at Calais was soon reopened, but the English King was able to demonstrate to his people that the Flemings "could not do without England's trade, considering the outcry they made when the Staple of Calais was closed for only three months".

Henry, indeed, might almost be credited with second-sight into the Emperor's mind. On 31st May, 1533, Charles's council discussed the situation.[3] After considering Henry's enormities, the councillors proceeded to deliberate on the possible remedies. There were three: justice, force and a combination of both. The objections to relying on methods of justice, that is, on the papal sentence, were, firstly, that Henry would not obey, and secondly, that the Pope was not to be trusted. The

[1] L. and P. vi. 1460.   [2] Ibid. vi. 1510, 1523, 1571.
[3] Ibid. vi. 568.

objections to the employment of force were, that war would imperil the whole of Europe, and especially the Emperor's dominions, and that Henry had neither used violence towards Catherine nor given Charles any excuse for breaking the Treaty of Cambrai. Eventually, it was decided to leave the matter to Clement. He was to be urged to give sentence against Henry, but on no account to lay England under an interdict, as that " would disturb her intercourse with Spain and Flanders. If, therefore, an interdict be resorted to, it should be limited to one diocese, or to the place where Henry dwells."[1] Such an interdict might put a premium on assassination, but otherwise neither Henry nor his people were likely to care much about it. The Pope should, however, be exhorted to depose the English King ; that might pave the way for Mary's accession and for the predominance in England of the Emperor's influence ; but the execution of the sentence must not be entrusted to Charles.[2] It would be excellent if James V or the Irish would undertake to beard the lion in his den, but the Emperor did not see his way clear to accepting the risk himself.

Charles was, indeed, afraid, not merely of Henry, but of Francis, who was meditating fresh Italian schemes ; and various expedients were suggested to divert his attention in other directions. He might be assisted in an attack upon Calais. " Calais," was Charles's cautious comment, " is better as it is, for the security of Flanders."[3] The Pope hinted that the grant of Milan would win over Francis. It probably would ; but Charles would have abandoned half a dozen aunts rather than see Milan in French possession. His real concern in the matter was not the injustice to Catherine, but the destruction of the prospect of Mary's succession. That was a tangible political interest, and Charles was much less anxious to

[1] L. and P. vi. 570.

[2] In January, 1534, Charles's ambassador at Rome repudiated the Pope's statement that the Emperor had ever offered to assist in the execution of the Pope's sentence (Ibid. vii. 96).

[3] Ibid. vi. 774. The sense of this passage is spoilt in L. and P. by the comma being placed after " better " instead of after " is ".

have Henry censured than to have Mary's legitimate claim to the throne established.[1] He was a great politician, absolutely impervious to personal wrong when its remedy conflicted with political interests. "Though the Emperor," he said, "is bound to the Queen, this is a private matter, and public considerations must be taken into account." And public considerations, as he admitted a year later, "compelled him to conciliate Henry ".[2] So he refused Chapuys' request to be recalled lest his presence in England should lead people to believe that Charles had condoned Henry's marriage with Anne Boleyn,[3] and dissuaded Catherine from leaving England.[4] The least hint to Francis of any hostile intent towards Henry would, thought Charles, be at once revealed to the English King, and the two would join in making war on himself. War he was determined to avoid, for, apart from the ruin of Flanders, which it would involve, Henry and Francis had long been intriguing with the Lutherans in Germany. A breach might easily precipitate civil strife in the Empire ; and, indeed, in June, 1534, Würtemberg was wrested from the Habsburgs by Philip of Hesse with the connivance of France. Francis, too, was always believed to have a working agreement with the Turk ; Barbarossa was giving no little cause for alarm in the Mediterranean ; while Henry on his part had established close relations

[1] Control over England was the great objective of Habsburg policy. In 1513 Margaret of Savoy was pressing Henry to have the succession settled on his sister Mary, then betrothed to Charles himself (*L. and P.* i. 4833).

[2] *Ibid.* vii. 229. All that Charles thought practicable was to "embarrass Henry in his own kingdom, and to execute what the Emperor wrote to the Irish chiefs " (cf. vii. 342, 353).

[3] *Ibid.* vi. 351. Charles's conduct is a striking vindication of Wolsey's foresight in 1528, when he told Campeggio that the Emperor would not wage war over the divorce of Catherine, and said there would be a thousand ways of keeping on good terms with him (Ehses, *Römische Dokumente* p. 69 ; *L. and P.* iv. 4881). Dr. Gairdner thinks Wolsey was insincere in this remark (*English Hist. Rev.* xii. 242), but he seems to have gauged Charles V's character and embarrassments accurately.

[4] *L. and P.* vi. 863. Her departure would have prejudiced Mary's claim to the throne, but Charles's advice was particularly callous in view of the reports which Chapuys was sending Charles of her treatment.

with Lübeck and Hamburg, and was fomenting dissensions in Denmark, the crown of which he was offered but cautiously declined.[1]

This incurable jealousy between Francis and Charles made the French King loth to weaken his friendship with Henry. The English King was careful to impress upon the French ambassador that he could, in the last resort, make his peace with Charles by taking back Catherine and by restoring Mary to her place in the line of succession.[2] Francis had too poignant a recollection of the results of the union between Henry and Charles from 1521 to 1525 ever to risk its renewal. The age of the crusades and chivalry was gone, commercial and national rivalries were as potent in the sixteenth century as they are to-day. Then, as in subsequent times, mutual suspicions made impossible an effective concert of Europe against the Turk. The fall of Rhodes and the death of one of Charles's brothers-in-law at Mohacz and the expulsion of another from the throne of Denmark had never been avenged, and in 1534 the Emperor was compelled to evacuate Coron.[3] If Europe could not combine against the common enemy of the Faith, was it likely to combine against one who, in spite of all his enormities, was still an orthodox Christian ? And, without a combination of princes to execute them, papal censures, excommunications, interdicts, and all the spiritual paraphernalia, served only to probe the hollowness of papal pretensions, and to demonstrate the deafness of Europe to the calls of religious enthusiasm. In Spain, at least, it might have been thought that every sword would leap from its scabbard at a summons from Charles on behalf of the Spanish Queen. "Henry," wrote Chapuys, " has always fortified himself by the consent of Parliament."[4] It would be well, he thought, if Charles would follow suit, and induce the Cortes of Aragon and Castile, " or at least the

---

[1] *L. and P.* vii. 737, 871, 957-58, and vol. viii. *passim ;* cf. C. F. Wurm, *Die politischen Beziehungen Heinrichs VIII zu Marcus Meyer und Jürgen Wullenwever,* Hamburg, 1852.

[2] *L. and P.* vi. 1572.   [3] *Ibid.* vii. 670.   [4] *Ibid.* vi. 720.

grandees," to offer their persons and goods in Catherine's cause. Such an offer, if published in England, " will be of inestimable service ". But here comes the proof of Charles's pitiful impotence ; in order to obtain this public offer, the Emperor was " to give them privately an exemption from such offer and promise of persons and goods ". It was to be one more pretence like the others, and unfortunately for the Pope and for the Emperor, Henry had an inconvenient habit of piercing disguises.

The strength of Henry's position at home was due to a similar lack of unity among his domestic enemies. If the English people had wished to depose him, they could have effected their object without much difficulty. In estimating the chances of a possible invasion, it was pointed out how entirely dependent Henry was upon his people : he had only one castle in London, and only a hundred yeomen of the guard to defend him:[1] He would, in fact, have been powerless against a united people or even against a partial revolt, if well organised and really popular. There was chronic discontent throughout the Tudor period, but it was sectional. The remnants of the old nobility always hated Tudor methods of government, and the poorer commons were sullen at their ill-treatment by the lords of the land ; but there was no concerted basis of action between the two. The dominant class was commercial, and it had no grievance against Henry, while it feared alike the lords and the lower orders. In the spoliation of the Church temporal lords and commercial men, both of whom could profit thereby, were agreed ; and nowhere was there much sympathy with the Church as an institution apart from its doctrine. Chapuys himself admits that the act, depriving the clergy of their profits from leases, was passed " to please the people " ;[2] and another conservative declared that, if the Church were deprived of all its temporal goods, many would be glad and few would bemoan.[3] Sympathy with Catherine and hatred of Anne were general, but people thought, like Charles, that these were private griefs, and

[1] *L. and P.* vi. App. 7.   [2] *Ibid.* vii. 114.   [3] *Ibid.* vii. 24.

that public considerations must be taken into account. Englishmen are at all times reluctant to turn out one Government until they see at least the possibility of another to take its place, and the only alternative to Henry VIII was anarchy. The opposition could not agree on a policy, and they could not agree on a leader. There were various grandchildren of Edward IV and of Clarence, who might put forward distant claims to the throne ; and there were other candidates in whose multitude lay Henry's safety. It was quite certain that the pushing of any one of these claimants would throw the rest on Henry's side. James V, whom at one time Chapuys favoured, knew that a Scots invasion would unite the whole of England against him ; and Charles was probably wise in rebuking his ambassador's zeal, and in thinking that any attempt on his own part would be more disastrous to himself than to Henry.[1] For all this, the English King was, as Chapuys remarks, keeping a very watchful eye on the countenance of his people,[2] seeing how far he could go and where he must stop, and neglecting no precaution for the peace and security of himself and his kingdom. Acts were passed to strengthen the navy, improvements in arms and armament were being continually tested, and the fortifications at Calais, on the Scots Borders and elsewhere were strengthened. Wales was reduced to law and order, and, through the intermediation of Francis, a satisfactory peace was made with Scotland.[3]

Convinced of his security from attack at home and abroad, Henry proceeded to accomplish what remained for the subjugation of the Church in England and the final breach with Rome. Clement had no sooner excommunicated Henry than he began to repent ; he was

[1] Chapuys is quite plaintive when he hints at the advantages which might follow if only " your Majesty were ever so little angry " with Henry VIII (L. and P. vii. 114). A few days later he " apologises for his previous letters advocating severity " (ibid. vii. 171).

[2] Ibid. vi. 351.

[3] Ibid. vi. 729, 1161. One of Henry's baits to James V. was a suggestion that he would get Parliament to entail the succession on James if his issue by Anne Boleyn failed (ibid. vii. 114).

much more alarmed than the English King at the probable effects of his sentence. Henry at once recalled his ambassadors from Rome, and drew up an appeal to a General Council.[1] The Pope feared he would lose England for ever. Even the Imperialists proved but Job's comforters, and told him that, after all, it was only " an unprofitable island,"[2] the loss of which was not to be compared with the renewed devotion of Spain and the Emperor's other dominions ; possibly they assured him that there would never again be a sack of Rome. Clement delayed for a time the publication of the sentence against Henry, and in November he went to his interview with Francis I at Marseilles.[3] While he was there, Bonner intimated to him Henry's appeal to a General Council. Clement angrily rejected the appeal as frivolous, and Francis regarded this defiance of the Pope as an affront to himself in the person of his guest, and as the ruin of his attempts to reconcile the two parties. " Ye have clearly marred all," he said to Gardiner ; " as fast as I study to win the Pope, you study to lose him,"[4] and he declared that, had he known of the intimation beforehand, it should never have been made. Henry, however, had no desire that the Pope should be won.[5] He was, he told the French ambassador, determined to separate from Rome ; " he will not, in consequence of this, be less Christian, but more so, for in everything and in every place he desires to cause Jesus Christ to be recognised, who alone is the patron of Christians ; and he will cause the Word to be preached, and not the canons and decrees of the Pope."[6]

Parliament was to meet to effect this purpose in

---

[1] L. and P. vi. 721, 979, 980, 998.   [2] Ibid. vi. 997.

[3] He is said, while there, to have privately admitted to Francis that the dispensation of Julius II was invalid (ibid. vii. 1348, App. 8).

[4] Ibid. vi. 1425, 1426, 1427.

[5] On his side he was angry with Francis for telling the Pope that Henry would side against the Lutherans ; he was afraid it might spoil his practices with them (ibid. vi. 614, 707) ; the Lübeckers had already suggested to Henry VIII that he should seize the disputed throne of Denmark (ibid. vi. 428 ; cf. the present writer in Cambridge Modern History ii. 229).

[6] L. and P. vi. 1435, 1479.

January, 1534, and during the previous autumn there
are the first indications, traceable to Cromwell's hand,
of an attempt to pack it. He drew up a memorandum
of such seats as were vacant from death or from other
causes ; most of the new members appear to have been
freely elected, but four vacancies were filled by " the
King's pleasure."[1] More extensive and less doubtful was
the royal interference in the election of abbots. Many
abbeys fell vacant in 1533, and in every case commissioners were sent down to secure the election of the
King's nominee ; in many others, abbots were induced
to resign, and fresh ones put in their place.[2] It is not
clear that the main object was to pack the clerical
representation in the House of Lords, because only a few

---

[1] *L. and P.* vi. 1382 ; vii. 56. A whole essay might be written on this
latter brief document ; it is not what it purports to be, a list of knights
of the shires who had died since the beginning of Parliament, for the
names are those of living men. Against most of the constituencies two
or three names are placed ; Dr. Gardiner suggests that these are the
possible candidates suggested by Cromwell and to be nominated by the
King. But why is " the King's pleasure " placed opposite only three
vacancies, if the whole twenty-eight were to be filled on his nomination ?
The names are probably those of influential magnates in the neighbour-
hood who would naturally have the chief voice in the election ; and thus
they would correspond with the vacancies, e.g. Hastings, opposite which
is placed " Not for the Warden of the Cinque Ports," and Southwark,
for which there is a similar note for the Duke of Suffolk. It is obvious
that the King could not fill up all the vacancies by nomination ; for
opposite Worcester town, where *both* members, Dee and Brenning, had
died, is noted, " the King to name *one* ". It is curious to find " the King's
pleasure " after Winchester city, as that was one of the constituencies for
which Gardiner as bishop afterwards said he was wont to nominate
burgesses (Foxe, ed. Townsend vi. 54). It must also be remembered that
these were bye-elections and possibly a novelty. In 1536 the rebels
demand that " if a knight or burgess died during Parliament his room
should continue void to the end of the same " (*L. and P.* xi. 1182 [17]).
In the seventeenth century supplementary members were chosen for
the Long Parliament to fill possible vacancies ; there were no bye-
elections.

[2] *L. and P.* vi. 716, 816, 847, 1007, 1056, 1057, 1109 (where by the
Bishopric of " Chester " is meant Coventry and Lichfield, and not
Chichester, as suggested by the editor ; the See of Coventry and Lichfield
was often called Chester before the creation of the latter see), 1239, 1304,
1376, 1408, 1513 ; vii. 108, 257, 297, 344, 376.

of these abbots had seats there, the abbots gave much
less trouble than the bishops in Parliament, and Convocation, where they largely outnumbered the bishops,
was much more amenable than the House of Peers,
where the bishops' votes preponderated. It is more
probable that the end in view was already the dissolution
of the monasteries by means of surrender. Cromwell,
who was now said to "rule everything,"[1] was boasting
that he would make his King the richest monarch in
Christendom, and his methods may be guessed from his
praise of the Sultan as a model to other princes for the
authority he wielded over his subjects.[2] Henry, however,
was fortunate in 1533, even in the matter of episcopal
representation. He had, since the fall of Wolsey, had
occasion to fill up the Sees of York, Winchester, London,
Durham and Canterbury; and in this year five more
became vacant: Bangor, Ely, Coventry and Lichfield by
death, and Salisbury and Worcester through the deprivation by Act of Parliament of their foreign and absentee
pastors, Campeggio and Ghinucci.[3] Of the other
bishops, Clerk of Bath and Wells, and Longland of
Lincoln, had been active in the divorce, which, indeed,
Longland, the King's confessor, was said to have originally
suggested about the year 1523; the Bishops of Norwich
and of Chichester were both over ninety years of age.[4]
Llandaff was Catherine's confessor, a Spaniard who could
not speak a word of English. On the whole bench there
was no one but Fisher of Rochester who had the will or
the courage to make any effective stand on behalf of the
Church's liberty.

Before Parliament met Francis sent Du Bellay, Bishop
of Paris, to London to make one last effort to keep the
peace between England and Rome. Du Bellay could get
no concessions of any value from Henry. All the King
would promise was that, if Clement would before Easter
declare his marriage with Catherine null and that with
Anne valid, he would not complete the extirpation of the
papal authority.[5] Little enough of that remained, and

---

[1] L. and P. vi. 1445.   [2] Ibid. vii. 1554.
[3] Ibid. vii. 48. 54, 634.   [4] Ibid. vii. 171.   [5] Ibid. vii. App. 13.

Henry himself had probably no expectation and no wish that his terms should be accepted. Long before Du Bellay had reached Rome, Parliament was discussing measures designed to effect the final severance. Opposition was of the feeblest character alike in Convocation and in both Houses of Parliament. Chapuys himself gloomily prophesied that there would be no difficulty in getting the principal measures, abolishing the Pope's authority and arranging for the election of bishops, through the House of Lords.[1] The second Act of Appeals embodied the concessions made by Convocation in 1532 and rejected that year in the House of Lords. Convocation was neither to meet nor to legislate without the King's assent ; Henry might appoint a royal commission to reform the canon law ;[2] appeals were to be permitted to Chancery from the Archbishop's Court ;[3] abbeys and other religious houses, which had been exempt from episcopal authority, were placed immediately under the jurisdiction of Chancery. A fresh Act of Annates defined more precisely the new method of electing bishops, and provided that, if the Chapter did not elect the royal nominee within twelve days, the King might appoint him by letters patent. A third act forbade the payment of Peter-pence and other impositions to the Court of Rome, and handed over the business of dispensations and licences to the Archbishop of Canterbury ; at the same time it declared that neither King nor realm meant to vary from the articles of the Catholic Faith of Christendom.

Another act provided that charges of heresy must be supported by two lay witnesses, and that indictments for that offence could only be made by lay authorities. This, like the rest of Henry's anti-ecclesiastical legislation, was based on popular clamour. On the 5th of March the

---

[1] *L. and P.* vii. 171 ; cf. XII. ii. 952.

[2] This commission was not appointed till 1551 : see the present writer's *Cranmer* pp. 280-4.

[3] 25 Henry VIII, c. 19. The first suggestion appears to have been "to give the Archbishop of Canterbury the seal of Chancery, and pass bulls, dispensations and other provisions under it" (*L. and P.* vii. 14 ; cf. vii. 57) ; his title was changed from *Apostolicæ Sedis legatus* to *Metropolitanus (ibid.* vii. 1555).

whole House of Commons, with the Speaker at their head, had waited on the King at York Place and expatiated for three hours on the oppressiveness of clerical jurisdiction. At length it was agreed that eight temporal peers, eight representatives of the Lower House and sixteen bishops " should discuss the matter and the King be umpire "[1]— a repetition of the plan of 1529 and a very exact reflection of Henry's methods and of the Church-and-State situation during the Reformation Parliament.

The final act of the session, which ended on 30th March, was a constitutional innovation of the utmost importance. From the earliest ages the succession to the crown had in theory been determined, first by election, and then by hereditary right. In practice it had often been decided by the barbarous arbitrament of war. For right is vague, it may be disputed, and there was endless variety of opinion as to the proper claimant to the throne if Henry should die. So vague right was to be replaced by definite law, which could not be disputed, but which, unlike right, could easily be changed. The succession was no longer to be regulated by an unalterable principle, but by the popular (or royal) will expressed in Acts of Parliament.[2] The first of a long series of Acts of Succession was now passed to vest the succession to the crown in the heirs of the King by Anne Boleyn ; clauses were added declaring that persons who impugned that marriage by writing, printing, or other deed were guilty of treason, and those who impugned it by words, of misprision. The Government proposal that both classes of offenders should be held guilty of treason was modified by the House of Commons.[3]

On 23rd March, a week before the prorogation of Parliament, and seven years after the divorce case had first begun, Clement gave sentence at Rome pronouncing valid the marriage between Catherine and Henry.[4] The

---

[1] *L. and P.* vii. 304, 393, 399 ; the provision about two witnesses was in 1547 extended to treason.

[2] The succession to the crown was one of the last matters affected by the process of substituting written law for unwritten right which began with the laws of Ethelbert of Kent. There had of course been *ex post facto* acts recognising that the crown was vested in the successful competitor.

[3] *L. and P.* vii. 51.   [4] *Ibid.* vii. 362.

decision produced not a ripple on the surface of English
affairs ; Henry, writes Chapuys, took no account of it and
was making as good cheer as ever.[1] There was no reason
why he should not. While the imperialist mob at Rome
after its kind paraded the streets in crowds, shouting
" Imperio et Espagne," and firing *feux-de-joie* over the
news, the imperialist agent was writing to Charles that
the judgment would not be of much profit, except for
the Emperor's honour and the Queen's justification, and
was congratulating his master that he was not bound to
execute the sentence.[2] Flemings were tearing down the
papal censures from the doors of their churches,[3] and
Charles was as convinced as ever of the necessity of
Henry's friendship. He proposed to the Pope that some
one should be sent from Rome to join Chapuys in " trying
to move the King from his error " ; and Clement could
only reply that " he thought the embassy would have no
effect on the King, but that nothing would be lost by it,
and it would be a good compliment ! "[4] Henry, however,
was less likely to be influenced by compliments, good or
bad, than by the circumstance that neither Pope nor
Emperor was in a position to employ any ruder persuasive.
There was none so poor as to reverence a Pope, and, when
Clement died six months later, the Roman populace
broke into the chamber where he lay and stabbed his
corpse ; they were with difficulty prevented from dragging
it in degradation through the streets.[5] Such was the
respect paid to the Supreme Pontiff in the Holy City, and
deference to his sentence was not to be expected in more
distant parts.

Henry's political education was now complete ; the
events of the last five years had proved to him the truth
of the assertion, with which he had started, that the Pope
might do what he liked at Rome, but that he also could
do what he liked in England, so long as he avoided the
active hostility of the majority of his lay subjects. The
Church had, by its actions, shown him that it was powerless ; the Pope had proved the impotence of his spiritual

[1] *L. and P.* vii. 469.   [2] *Ibid.* vii. 368.   [3] *Ibid.* vii. 184.
[4] *Ibid.* vii. 804.   [5] *Ibid.* vii. 1262.

weapons; and the Emperor had admitted that he was both unable and unwilling to interfere. Henry had realised the extent of his power, and the opening of his eyes had an evil effect upon his character. Nothing makes men or Governments so careless or so arbitrary as the knowledge that there will be no effective opposition to their desires. Henry, at least, never grew careless; his watchful eye was always wide open. His ear was always strained to catch the faintest rumbling of a coming storm, and his subtle intellect was ever on the alert to take advantage of every turn in the diplomatic game. He was always efficient, and he took good care that his ministers should be so as well. But he grew very arbitrary; the knowledge that he could do so much became with him an irresistible reason for doing it. Despotic power is twice cursed; it debases the ruler and degrades the subject; and Henry's progress to despotism may be connected with the rise of Thomas Cromwell, who looked to the Great Turk as a model for Christian princes.[1] Cromwell became secretary in May, 1534; in that month Henry's security was enhanced by the definitive peace with Scotland,[2] and he set to work to enforce his authority with the weapons which Parliament had placed in his hands. Elizabeth Barton, and her accomplices, two Friars Observants, two monks, and one secular priest, all attainted of treason by Act of Parliament, were sent to the block.[3] Commissioners were sent round, as Parliament had ordained, to enforce the oath of succession throughout the land.[4] A general refusal would have stopped Henry's career, but the general consent left Henry free to deal as he liked with the exceptions. Fisher and More were sent to the Tower. They were willing to swear to the succession, regarding

---

[1] "The Lord Cromwell," says Bishop Gardiner, "had once put in the King our late sovereign lord's head, to take upon him to have his will and pleasure regarded for a law; for that, he said, was to be a very King," and he quoted the *quod principi placuit* of Roman civil law. Gardiner replied to the King that "to make the laws his will was more sure and quiet" and "agreeable with the nature of your people". Henry preferred Gardiner's advice (Foxe, ed. Townsend, vi. 46).

[2] *L. and P.* vii. 483, 647.　　　[3] *Ibid.* vii. 522.

[4] *Ibid.* vii. 665.

that as a matter within the competence of Parliament, but they refused to take the oath required by the commissioners ;[1] it contained, they alleged, a repudiation of the Pope not justified by the terms of the statute. Two cartloads of friars followed them to the Tower in June, and the Order of Observants, in whose church at Greenwich Henry had been baptised and married, and of whom in his earlier years he had written in terms of warm admiration, was suppressed altogether.[2]

In November Parliament[3] reinforced the Act of Succession by laying down the precise terms of the oath, and providing that a certificate of refusal signed by two commissioners was as effective as the indictment of twelve jurors. Other acts empowered the King to repeal by royal proclamation certain statutes regulating imports and exports. The first-fruits and tenths, of which the Pope had been already deprived, were now conferred on the King as a fitting ecclesiastical endowment for the Supreme Head of the Church. That title, granted him four years before by both Convocations, was confirmed by Act of Parliament ; its object was to enable the King as Supreme Head to effect the " increase of virtue in Christ's Religion within this Realm of England, and to repress and extirp all Errors, Heresies and other Enormities, and Abuses heretofore used in the same ". The Defender of the Faith was to be armed with more than a delegate power ; he was to be supreme in himself, the champion not of the Faith of any one else, but of his own ; and the qualifying clause, " as far as the law of Christ allows," was omitted. His orthodoxy must be above suspicion, or at least beyond the reach of open cavil in England. So new treasons were enacted, and any one who called the King a heretic, schismatic, tyrant, infidel, or usurper, was rendered liable to the heaviest penalty which the law could inflict. As an earnest of the royal and parliamentary desire for an increase of virtue in

[1] *L. and P.* vii. 499.
[2] *Ibid.* vii. 841, 856. The order had been particularly active in opposition to the divorce (*ibid.* iv. 6156 ; v. 266).
[3] *Ibid.* vii. 1377.

religion, an act was concurrently passed providing for the creation of a number of suffragan bishops.[1]

Henry was now Pope in England with powers no Pope had possessed.[2] The Reformation is variously regarded as the liberation of the English Church from the Roman yoke it had long impatiently borne, as its subjection to an Erastian yoke which it was henceforth, with more or less patience, long to bear, or as a comparatively unimportant assertion of a supremacy which Kings of England had always enjoyed. The Church is the same Church, we are told, before and after the change; if anything, it was Protestant before the Reformation, and Catholic after. It is, of course, the same Church. A man may be described as the same man before and after death, and the business of a coroner's jury is to establish the identity; but it does not ignore the vital difference. Even Saul and Paul were the same man. And the identity of the Church before and after the legislation of Henry VIII covers a considerable number of not unimportant changes. It does not, however, seem strictly accurate to say that Henry either liberated or enslaved the Church. Rather, he substituted one form of despotism for another, a sole for a dual control; the change, complained a reformer, was merely a *translatio imperii*.[3] The democratic movement within the Church had died away, like the democratic movements in national and municipal politics, before the end of the fifteenth century. It was never merry with the Church,[4] complained a Catholic in 1533,

[1] These were not actually created till 1540; the way in which Henry VIII sought statutory authority for every conceivable thing is very extraordinary. There seems no reason why he could not have created these bishoprics without parliamentary authority.

[2] With limitations, of course. Henry's was only a *potestas jurisdictionis* not a *potestas ordinis* (see Makower, *Const. Hist. of the Church of England*, and the present writer's *Cranmer* pp. 83, 84, 95, 232, 233). Cranmer acknowledged in the King also a *potestatem ordinis*, just as Cromwell would have made him the sole legislator in temporal affairs; Henry's unrivalled capacity for judging what he could and could not do saved him from adopting either suggestion.   [3] *L. and P.* XIV. ii. p. 141.

[4] *Ibid.* vi. 797 [2]; a Venetian declared that Huguenotism was "due to the abolition of the election of the clergy" (Armstrong, *Wars of Religion* p. 11).

since the time when bishops were wont to be chosen by the Holy Ghost and by their Chapters.

Since then the Church had been governed by a partnership between King and Pope, without much regard for the votes of the shareholders. It was not Henry who first deprived them of influence; neither did he restore it. What he did was to eject his foreign partner, appropriate his share of the profits, and put his part of the business into the hands of a manager. First-fruits and tenths were described as an intolerable burden; but they were not abolished; they were merely transferred from the Pope to the King. Bishops became royal nominees, pure and simple, instead of the joint nominees of King and Pope. The supreme appellate jurisdiction in ecclesiastical causes was taken away from Rome, but it was not granted the English Church to which in truth it had never belonged.[1] Chancery, and not the Archbishop's Court, was made the final resort for ecclesiastical appeals. The authority, divided erstwhile between two, was concentrated in the hands of one; and that one was thus placed in a far different position from that which either had held before.

The change was analogous to that in Republican Rome from two consuls to one dictator. In both cases the dictatorship was due to exceptional circumstances. There had long been a demand for reform in the Church in England as well as elsewhere, but the Church was powerless to reform itself. The dual control was in effect, as dual controls often are, a practical anarchy. The condition of the Church before the Reformation may be compared with that of France before the Revolution. In purely spiritual matters the Pope was supreme: the conciliar movement of the fifteenth century had failed. The Pope had gathered all powers to himself, in much the same way as the French monarch in the eighteenth century had done; and the result was the same, a formal despot-

---

[1] For one year, indeed, Cranmer remained *legatus natus*, and by a strange anomaly exercised a jurisdiction the source of which had been cut off. Stokesley objected to Cranmer's use of that style in order to escape a visitation of his see, and Gardiner thought it an infringement of the royal prerogative. It was abolished in the following year.

ism and a real anarchy. Pope and Monarch were crushed
by the weight of their own authority; they could not
reform, even when they wanted to. From 1500 to 1530
almost every scheme, peaceful or bellicose, started in
Europe was based on the plea that its ultimate aim was
the reform of the Church; and so it would have continued, *vox et præterea nihil*, had not the Church been
galvanised into action by the loss of half its inheritance.

In England the change from a dual to a sole control
at once made that control effective, and reform became
possible. But it was a reform imposed on the Church
from without and by means of the exceptional powers
bestowed on the Supreme Head. Hence the burden of
modern clerical criticism of the Reformation. Objection
is raised not so much to the things that were done, as to
the means by which they were brought to pass, to the
fact that the Church was forcibly reformed by the State,
and not freed from the trammels of Rome, and then left
to work out its own salvation. But such a solution
occurred to few at that time; the best and the worst of
Henry's opponents opposed him on the ground that he
was divorcing the Church in England from the Church
universal. Their objection was to what was done more
than to the way in which it was done; and Sir Thomas
More would have fought the Reformation quite as
strenuously had it been effected by the Convocations
of Canterbury and York. On the other side there was
equally little thought of a Reformation by clerical hands.
Henry and Cromwell carried on and developed the
tradition of the Emperor Frederick II and Peter de
Vinea,[1] of Philippe le Bel and Pierre Dubois, or Lewis the
Bavarian and Marsiglio of Padua[2] who maintained the
supremacy of the temporal over the spiritual power and

---

[1] The comparison has been drawn by Huillard-Bréholles in his *Vie
et Correspondance de Pierre de la Vigne*, Paris, 1865.

[2] Marsiglio's *Defensor Pacis* was a favourite book with Cromwell who
lent a printer £20 to bring out an English edition of it in 1535 (see the
present writer in *D.N.B.*, *s.v.* Marshall, William). Marshall distributed
twenty-four copies among the monks of Charterhouse to show them
how the Christian commonwealth had been " unjustly molested, vexed
and troubled by the spiritual and ecclesiastical tyrant ". See also Maitland,
English Law and the Renaissance pp. 14, 60, 61.

asserted that the clergy wielded no jurisdiction and only bore the keys of heaven in the capacity of turnkeys.[1] It was a question of the national State against the universal Church. The idea of a National Church was a later development, the result and not the cause of the Reformation.

Henry's dictatorship was also temporary in character. His supremacy over the Church was royal, and not parliamentary. It was he, and not Parliament, who had been invested with a semi-ecclesiastical nature. In one capacity he was head of the State, in another, head of the Church. Parliament and Convocation were co-ordinate one with another, and subordinate both to the King. The Tudors, and especially Elizabeth, vehemently denied to their Parliaments any share in their ecclesiastical powers. Their supremacy over the Church was their own, and, as a really effective control, it died with them. As the authority of the Crown declined, its secular powers were seized by Parliament; its ecclesiastical powers fell into abeyance between Parliament and Convocation. Neither has been able to vindicate an exclusive claim to the inheritance; and the result of this dual claim to control has been a state of helplessness, similar in some respects to that from which the Church was rescued by the violent methods of Henry VIII.[2]

[1] *Defensor Pacis* ii. 6.

[2] A much neglected but very important constitutional question is whether the King *quâ* Supreme Head of the Church was limited by the same statute and common law restrictions as he was *quâ* temporal sovereign. Gardiner raised the question in a most interesting letter to Protector Somerset in 1547 (Foxe vi. 42). It had been provided, as Lord Chancellor Audley told Gardiner, that no spiritual law and no exercise of the royal supremacy should abate the common law or Acts of Parliament; but within the ecclesiastical sphere there were no limits on the King's authority. The Popes had not been fettered, *habent omnia jura in suo scrinio;* and their jurisdiction in England had been transferred whole and entire to the King. Henry was in fact an absolute monarch in the Church, a constitutional monarch in the State; he could reform the Church by injunction when he could not reform the State by proclamation. There was naturally a tendency to confuse the two capacities not merely in the King's mind but in his opponents'; and some of the objections to the Stuarts' dispensing practice, which was exercised chiefly in the ecclesiastical sphere, seem due to this confusion. Parliament in fact, as soon as the Tudors were gone, began to apply common law and statute law limitations to the Crown's ecclesiastical prerogative.

CHAPTER XIII

THE CRISIS

HENRY's title as Supreme Head of the Church was incorporated in the royal style by letters patent of 15th January, 1535,[1] and that year was mainly employed in compelling its recognition by all sorts and conditions of men. In April, Houghton, the Prior of the Charterhouse, a monk of Sion, and the Vicar of Isleworth, were the first victims offered to the Supreme Head. But the machinery supplied by Parliament was barely sufficient to bring the penalties of the statute to bear on the two most illustrious of Henry's opponents, Fisher and More. Both had been attainted of misprision of treason by Acts of Parliament in the previous autumn ; but those penalties extended no further than to lifelong imprisonment and forfeiture of goods. Their lives could only be exacted by proving that they had maliciously attempted to deprive Henry of his title of Supreme Head ;[2] their opportunities in the Tower for compassing that end were limited ; and it is possible that they would not have been further molested, but for the thoughtlessness of Clement's successor, Paul III. Impotent to effect anything against the King, the Pope did his best to sting Henry to fury by creating Fisher a cardinal on 20th May. He afterwards explained that he meant no harm, but the harm was done, and it involved Fisher's friend and ally, Sir Thomas More. Henry declared that he would send the new cardinal's head to Rome for the hat ; and he immediately despatched commissioners to the Tower to inform Fisher and More

[1] *L. and P.* viii. 52 ; Rymer xiv. 549.

[2] The general idea that Fisher and More were executed for refusing to take an oath prescribed in the Act of Supremacy is technically inaccurate. No oath is there prescribed, and not till 1536 was it made high treason to refuse to take the oath of supremacy ; even then the oath was to be administered only to civil and ecclesiastical officers. The Act under which they were executed was 26 Henry VIII, c. 13, and the common mistake arises from a confusion between the oath to the succession and the oath of supremacy.

that, unless they acknowledged the royal supremacy, they
would be put to death as traitors.[1] Fisher apparently
denied the King's supremacy, More refused to answer ;
he was, however, entrapped during a conversation with
the Solicitor-General, Rich, into an admission that
Englishmen could not be bound to acknowledge a
supremacy over the Church in which other countries did
not concur. In neither case was it clear that they came
within the clutches of the law. Fisher, indeed, had really
been guilty of treason. More than once he had urged
Chapuys to press upon Charles the invasion of England,
a fact unknown, perhaps, to the English Government.[2]
The evidence it had collected was, however, considered
sufficient by the juries which tried the prisoners ; Fisher
went to the scaffold on 22nd June, and More on 6th July.
Condemned justly or not by the law, both sought their
death in a quarrel which is as old as the hills and will
last till the crack of doom. Where shall we place the
limits of conscience, and where those of the national will ?
Is conscience a luxury which only a king may enjoy in
peace ? Fisher and More refused to accommodate theirs
to Acts of Parliament, but neither believed conscience to
be the supreme tribunal.[3] More admitted that in

[1] L. and P. viii. 876.

[2] Ibid. iv. 6199 ; vi. 1164, 1249. He told Chapuys that if Charles
invaded England he would be doing " a work as agreeable to God as
going against the Turk," and suggested that the Emperor should make
use of Reginald Pole " to whom, according to many, the kingdom would
belong " (Chapuys to Charles, 27th September, 1533). Again, says
Chapuys, " the holy Bishop of Rochester would like you to take active
measures immediately, as I wrote in my last ; which advice he has sent
to me again lately to repeat " (10th October, 1533). Canon Whitney, in
criticising Froude (Engl. Hist. Rev. xii. 353), asserts that " nothing
Chapuys says justifies the charge against Fisher ! "

[3] This statement has been denounced as " astounding " in a Roman
Catholic periodical ; yet if More believed individual conscience (i.e.
private judgment) to be superior to the voice of the Church, how did he
differ from a Protestant ? The statement in the text is merely a paraphrase
of More's own, where he says that men are " not bound on pain of God's
displeasure to change their conscience for any particular law made anywhere except by a general council or a general faith growing by the working
of God universally through all Christian nations " (More's English Works
p. 1434 ; L. and P. vii. 432).

temporal matters his conscience was bound by the laws of England ; in spiritual matters the conscience of all was bound by the will of Christendom ; and on that ground both Fisher and he rejected the plea of conscience when urged by heretics condemned to the flames. The dispute, indeed, passes the wit of man to decide. If conscience must reign supreme, all government is a *pis aller*, and in anarchy the true millennium must be found. If conscience is deposed, man sinks to the level of the lower creation. Human society can only be based on compromise, and compromise itself is a matter of conscience. Fisher and More protested by their death against a principle which they had practised in life ; both they and the heretics whom they persecuted proclaimed, as Antigone had done thousands of years before,[1] that they could not obey laws which they could not believe God had made.

It was the personal eminence of the victims rather than the merits of their case that made Europe thrill with horror at the news of their death ; for thousands of others were sacrificing their lives in a similar cause in most of the countries of Christendom. For the first and last time in English history a cardinal's head had rolled from an English scaffold ; and Paul III made an effort to bring into play the artillery of his temporal powers. As supreme lord over all the princes of the earth, he arrogated to himself the right to deprive Henry VIII of his kingdom ; and he sent couriers to the various courts to seek their co-operation in executing his judgment. But the weapons of Innocent III were rusty with age. Francis denounced the Pope's claim as a most impudent attack on monarchial dignity ; and Charles was engaged in the conquest of Tunis. Thus Henry was able to take a high tone in reply to the remonstrances addressed to him, and to proceed undisturbed with the work of enforcing his royal supremacy. The autumn was occupied mainly by a visitation of the monasteries and of the universities of Oxford and Cambridge ; the schoolmen,

[1] Οὐ γάρ τί μοι Ζεὺς ἦν ὁ κηρύξας τάδε
οὐδ᾽ ἡ ξύνοικος τῶν κάτω θεῶν Δίκη.
Sophocles, *Antigone*, 450.

Thomas Aquinas, Duns Scotus and others were deposed from the seat of authority they had held for so many centuries, and efforts were made to substitute studies like that of the civil law, more in harmony with the King's doctrine and with his views of royal authority.

The more boldly Henry defied the Fates, the more he was favoured by Fortune. "Besides his trust in his subjects," wrote Chapuys in 1534, "he has great hope in the Queen's death ; "[1] and the year 1536 was but eight days old when the unhappy Catherine was released from her trials, resolutely refusing to the last to acknowledge in any way the invalidity of her marriage with Henry. She had derived some comfort from the papal sentence in her favour, but that was not calculated to soften the harshness with which she was treated. Her pious soul, too, was troubled with the thought that she had been the occasion, innocent though she was, of the heresies that had arisen in England, and of the enormities which had been practised against the Church. Her last days were cheered by a visit from Chapuys,[2] who went down to Kimbolton on New Year's Day and stayed until the 5th of January, when the Queen seemed well on the road to recovery. Three days later she passed away, and on the 29th she was buried with the state of a princess dowager in the church of the Benedictine abbey at Peterborough. Her physician told Chapuys that he suspected poison, but the symptoms are now declared, on high medical authority, to have been those of cancer of the heart.[3] The suspicion was the natural result of the circumstance that her death relieved the King of a pressing anxiety. "God be praised ! " he exclaimed, " we are free from all suspicion of war ; "[4] and on the following day he proclaimed his joy by appearing at a ball, clad in yellow from head to foot.[5] Every inch a King, Henry VIII never attained to the stature of a gentleman, but even Bishop

---

[1] L. and P. vii. 83.   [2] Ibid. x. 28, 59, 60, 141.

[3] Dr. Norman Moore in Athenæum 1885 i. 152, 215, 281.

[4] L. and P. x. 51.

[5] Ibid. Hall only tells his readers that Anne Boleyn wore yellow for the mourning (Chronicle p. 818).

Gardiner wrote that by Queen Catherine's death " God had given sentence " in the divorce suit between her and the King.[1]

A week later, the Reformation Parliament met for its seventh and last session. It sat from 4th February to 14th April, and in those ten weeks succeeded in passing no fewer than sixty-two Acts. Some were local and some were private, but the residue contained not a few of public importance. The fact that the King obtained at last his Statute of Uses[2] may indicate that Henry's skill and success had so impressed Parliament that it was more willing to acquiesce in his demands than it had been in its earlier sessions. But if the drafts in the Record Office are to be taken as indicating the proposals of Government, and the Acts themselves are those proposals as modified in one or other House, Parliament must have been able to enforce views of its own to a certain extent ; for those drafts differ materially from the Acts as finally passed.[3] Not a few of the bills were welcome, if unusual, concessions to the clergy. They were relieved from paying tenths in the year they paid their first-fruits. The payment of tithes, possibly rendered doubtful in the wreck of canon law, was enjoined by Act of Parliament. An attempt was made to deal with the poor, and another, if not to check enclosures, at least to extract some profit for the King from the process. It was made high treason to counterfeit the King's sign-manual, privy signet, or privy seal ; and Henry was empowered by Parliament, as he had before been by Convocation, to appoint a commission to reform the canon law. But the chief acts of the session were for the dissolution of the lesser monasteries and for the erection of a Court of Augmentations in order to deal with the revenues which were thus to accrue to the King.

The way for this great revolution had been carefully

---

[1] *L. and P.* x. 256.

[2] This Act has generally been considered a failure, but recent research does not confirm this view (see Joshua Williams, *Principles of the Law of Real Property*, 18th ed., 1896).

[3] *L. and P.* x. 246.

prepared during the previous autumn and winter. In virtue of his new and effective supremacy, Henry had ordered a general visitation of the monasteries throughout the greater part of the kingdom ; and the reports of these visitors were made the basis of parliamentary action. On the face of them they represent a condition of human depravity which has rarely been equalled ;[1] and the extent to which those reports are worthy of credit will always remain a point of contention. The visitors themselves were men of doubtful character ; indeed, respectable men could hardly have been persuaded to do the work. Their methods were certainly harsh ; the object of their mission was to get up a case for the Crown, and they probably used every means in their power to induce the monks and the nuns to incriminate themselves. Perhaps, too, an entirely false impression may be created by the fact that in most cases only the guilty are mentioned ; the innocent are often passed over in silence, and the proportion between the two is not recorded. Some of the terms employed in the reports are also open to dispute ; it is possible that in many instances the stigma of unchastity attached to a nun merely meant that she had been unchaste before entering religion,[2] and it is known that nunneries were considered the proper resort for ladies who had not been careful enough of their honour.

On the other hand, the lax state of monastic morality does not depend only upon the visitors' reports ; apart from satires like those of Skelton, from ballads and from other mirrors of popular opinion or prejudice, the correspondence of Henry VIII's reign is, from its commencement, full of references, by bishops and other unimpeachable witnesses, to the necessity of drastic reform. In 1516, for instance, Bishop West of Ely visited that

---

[1] See the documents in *L. and P.* vols. ix, x. The most elaborate criticism of the Dissolution is contained in Gasquet's *Henry VIII and the Monasteries*, 2 vols., 4th ed. 1893 ; some additional details and an excellent monastic map will be found in Gairdner's *Church History*, 1902.

[2] " Religion " of course in the middle ages and sixteenth century was a term almost exclusively applied to the monastic system, and the most ludicrous mistakes are often made from ignorance of this fact ; " religiosi " are sharply distinguished from " clerici ".

house, and found such disorder that he declared its continuance would have been impossible but for his visitation.[1] In 1518 the Italian Bishop of Worcester writes from Rome that he had often been struck by the necessity of reforming the monasteries.[2] In 1521 Henry VIII, then at the height of his zeal for the Church, thanks the Bishop of Salisbury for dissolving the nunnery of Bromehall because of the " enormities " practised there.[3] Wolsey felt that the time for reform had passed, and began the process of suppression, with a view to increasing the number of cathedrals and devoting other proceeds to educational endowments. Friar Peto, afterwards a cardinal, who had fled abroad to escape Henry's anger for his bold denunciation of the divorce, and who had no possible motive for cloaking his conscientious opinion, admitted that there were grave abuses, and approved of the dissolution of monasteries, if their endowments were used for proper ends.[4] There is no need to multiply instances, because a commission of cardinals, appointed by Paul III himself, reported in 1537 that scandals were frequent in religious houses.[5] The reports of the visitors, too, can hardly be entirely false, though they may not be entirely true. The charges they make are not vague, but very precise. They specify names of the offenders, and the nature of their offences ; and an air of verisimilitude, if nothing more, is imparted to the condemnations they pronounce against the many, by the commendations they bestow on the few.[6]

[1] L. and P. ii. 1733.   [2] Ibid. ii. 4399.

[3] Ibid. iii. 1863 ; see also iii. 77, 533, 567, 569, 600, 693, 1690 ; iv. 4900.

[4] D.N.B. xlv. 89. Chapuys had stated in 1532 that the Cistercian monasteries were greatly in need of dissolution (L. and P. iii. 361).

[5] Cambridge Modern History ii. 643.

[6] Nor, of course, were the symptoms peculiar to England ; it is absurd to attribute the dissolution of the monasteries solely to Henry VIII and Cromwell, because monasteries were dissolved in many countries of Europe, Catholic as well as Protestant. So, too, the charges are not naturally incredible, because the kind of vice alleged against the monks has unfortunately been far from unknown wherever and whenever numbers of men, young or middle-aged, have lived together in enforced celibacy.

Probably the staunchest champion of monasticism would acknowledge that in the reign of Henry VIII there was at least a plausible case for mending monastic morals. But that was not then the desire of the Government of Henry VIII ; and the case for mending their morals was tacitly assumed to be the same as a case for ending the monasteries. It would be unjust to Henry to deny that he had always shown himself careful of the appearance, at least, of morality in the Church ; but it requires a robust faith in the King's disinterestedness to believe that dissolution was not the real object of the visitation, and that it was merely forced upon him by the reports of the visitors. The moral question afforded a good excuse, but the monasteries fell, not so much because their morals were lax, as because their position was weak. Moral laxity contributed no doubt to the general result, but there were other causes at work. The monasteries themselves had long been conscious that their possession of wealth was not, in the eyes of the middle-class laity, justified by the use to which it was put ; and, for some generations at least, they had been seeking to make friends with Mammon by giving up part of their revenues, in the form of pensions and corrodies to courtiers, in the hope of being allowed to retain the remainder.[1] It had also become the custom to entrust the stewardship of their possessions to secular hands ; and, possibly as a result, the monasteries were soon so deeply in debt to the neighbouring gentry that their lay creditors saw no hope of recovering their claims except by extensive foreclosures.[2] There had certainly been a good deal of private spoliation before the King gave the practice a national character. The very privileges of the monasteries were now turned to their ruin. Their immunity from episcopal jurisdiction deprived them of episcopal aid ; their exemption from all authority, save that of the Pope, left them without support when the papal jurisdiction

[1] See Fortescue, *Governance of England*, ed. Plummer, cap. xviii., and notes pp. 337-40.
[2] E.g. Christ Church, London, which surrendered to Henry in 1532, was deeply in debt to him (*L. and P.* v. 823).

was abolished. Monastic orders knew no distinction of nationality. The national character claimed for the mediæval Church in England could scarcely cover the monasteries, and no place was found for them in the Church when it was given a really national garb.

Their dissolution is probably to be connected with Cromwell's boast that he would make his king the richest prince in Christendom. That was not its effect, because Henry was compelled to distribute the greater part of the spoils among his nobles and gentry. One rash reformer suggested that monastic lands should be devoted to educational purposes;[1] had that plan been followed, education in England would have been more magnificently endowed than in any other country of the world, and England might have become a democracy in the seventeenth century. From this point of view Henry spoilt one of the greatest opportunities in English history; from another, he saved England from a most serious danger. Had the Crown retained the wealth of the monasteries, the Stuarts might have made themselves independent of Parliament. But this service to liberty was not voluntary on Henry's part. The dissolution of the monasteries was, in effect and probably in intention, a gigantic bribe to the laity to induce them to acquiesce in the revolution effected by Henry VIII. When he was gone, his successors might desire, or fail to prevent, a reaction; something more permanent than Henry's iron hand was required to support the fabric he had raised. That support was sought in the wealth of the Church. The prospect had, from the very opening of the Reformation Parliament, been dangled before the eyes of the new nobles, the members of Parliament, the justices of the peace, the rich merchants who thirsted for lands wherewith to make themselves gentlemen. Chapuys

[1] *The Complaynt of Roderick Mors* (Early Eng. Text Soc.) pp. 47-52. The author, Henry Brinkelow (see *D.N.B.* vi. 346), also suggested that both Houses of Parliament should sit together as one assembly " for it is not rytches or autoryte that bringeth wisdome " (*Complaynt* p. 8). Some of the political literature of the later part of Henry's reign is curiously modern in its ideas.

again and again mentions a scheme for distributing the lands of the Church among the laity as a project for the ensuing session ; but their time was not yet ; not until their work was done were the labourers to reap their reward.[1] The dissolution of the monasteries harmonised well with the secular principles of these predominant classes. The monastic ideal of going out of the world to seek something, which cannot be valued in terms of pounds, shillings and pence, is abhorrent to a busy, industrial age ; and every principle is hated most at the time when it most is needed.

Intimately associated as they were in their lives, Catherine of Aragon and Anne Boleyn were not long divided by death ; and piteous as is the story of the last years of Catherine, it pales before the hideous tragedy of the ruin of Anne Boleyn. " If I have a son, as I hope shortly, I know what will become of her," wrote Anne of the Princess Mary.[2] On 29th January, 1536, the day of her rival's funeral, Anne Boleyn was prematurely delivered of a dead child, and the result was fatal to Anne herself. This was not her first miscarriage,[3] and Henry's old conscience began to work again. In Catherine's case the path of his conscience was that of a slow and laborious pioneer ; now it moved easily on its royal road to divorce. On 29th January, Chapuys, ignorant of Anne's miscarriage, was retailing to his master a court rumour that Henry intended to marry again. The King was reported to have said that he had been seduced by witchcraft when he married his second queen, and that the marriage was null for this reason, and because God would not permit them to have male issue.[4] There was no peace for her who supplanted her mistress. Within six months of her marriage Henry's roving fancy had

[1] " The King," says Chapuys in September, 1534, " will distribute among the gentlemen of the kingdom the greater part of the ecclesiastical revenues to gain their good-will " (*L. and P.* vii. 1141).

[2] *Ibid.* x. 307.

[3] Anne was pregnant in Feb., 1534, when Henry told Chapuys he thought he should have a son soon (*L. and P.* vii. 232 ; cf. vii. 958).

[4] *Ibid.* x. 199.

given her cause for jealousy, and, when she complained, he is said to have brutally told her she must put up with it as her betters had done before.[1] These disagreements, however, were described by Chapuys as mere lovers' quarrels, and they were generally followed by reconciliations, after which Anne's influence seemed as secure as ever. But by January, 1536, the imperial ambassador and others were counting on a fresh divorce. The rumour grew as spring advanced, when suddenly, on 2nd May, Anne was arrested and sent to the Tower. She was accused of incest with her brother, Lord Rochford, and of less criminal intercourse with Sir Francis Weston, Henry Norris, William Brereton, and Mark Smeaton. All were condemned by juries to death for high treason on 12th May. Three days later Anne herself was put on her trial by a panel of twenty-six peers, over which her uncle, the Duke of Norfolk, presided.[2] They returned a unanimous verdict of guilty, and on the 19th the Queen's head was struck off with the sword of an executioner brought for the purpose from St. Omer.[3]

[1] *L. and P.* vi. 1054, 1069. As early as April, 1531, Chapuys reports that Anne " was becoming more arrogant every day, using words and authority towards the King of which he has several times complained to the Duke of Norfolk, saying that she was not like the Queen [Catherine] who never in her life used ill words to him " (*ibid.* v. 216). In Sept., 1534, Henry was reported to be in love with another lady (*ibid*. vii. 1193, 1257). Probably this was Jane Seymour, as the lady's kindness to the Princess Mary—a marked characteristic of Queen Jane—is noted by Chapuys. This intrigue, we are told, was furthered by many lords with the object of separating the King from Anne Boleyn, who was disliked by the lords on account of her pride and that of her kinsmen and brothers (*ibid*. vii. 1279). Henry's behaviour to the Princess was becoming quite benevolent, and Chapuys begins to speak of his " amiable and cordial nature " (*ibid*. vii. 1297).

[2] In 1533 Anne had accused her uncle of having too much intercourse with Chapuys and of maintaining the Princess Mary's title to the throne (*Ibid*. vi. 1125).

[3] *Ibid*. x. 902, 910, 919. The Regent Mary of the Netherlands writes : " That the vengeance might be executed by the Emperor's subjects, he sent for the executioner of St. Omer, as there were none in England good enough " (*ibid*. x. 965). It is perhaps well to be reminded that even at this date there were more practised executioners in the Netherlands than in England.

Two days before Anne's death her marriage with Henry
had been declared invalid by a court of ecclesiastical
lawyers with Cranmer at its head. The grounds of the
sentence are not stated, but there may have been two—
the alleged precontract with the Earl of Northumberland,
which the Earl denied on oath and on the sacrament, and
the previous affinity between Anne and Henry arising
from the King's relations with Mary Boleyn. The latter
seems the more probable. Henry had obtained of Clement
VII a dispensation from this disability ; but the Pope's
power to dispense had since been repudiated, while the
canonical objection remained and was given statutory
authority in this very year.[1] The effects of this piece of
wanton injustice were among the troubles which Henry
bequeathed to Queen Elizabeth ; the sole advantage to
Henry was that his infidelities to Anne ceased to be
breaches of the seventh commandment. The justice of
her sentence to death is also open to doubt. Anne herself
went to the block boldly proclaiming her innocence.[2]
Death she regarded as a relief from an intolerable situation, and she " laughed heartily," writes the Lieutenant
of the Tower as she put her hands round her " little
neck," and thought how easy the executioner's task would
be.[3] She complained when the day of her release from
this world was deferred, and regretted that so many
innocent persons should suffer through her. Of her
accomplices, none confessed but Smeaton, though Henry
is said, before Anne's arrest, to have offered Norris a
pardon if he would admit his crime. On the other hand,
her conduct must have made the charges plausible. Even
in those days, when justice to individuals was regarded
as dust if weighed in the balance against the real or
supposed interests of the State, it is not credible that

[1] This Act indirectly made Elizabeth a bastard and Henry's marriage
with Anne invalid (cf. Chapuys to Granvelle, L. and P. x. 909). The
Antinomian theory of marital relations, which Chapuys ascribes to Anne,
was an Anabaptist doctrine of the time. Chapuys calls Anne a Messalina,
but he of course was not an impartial witness.

[2] According to some accounts, but a Spaniard who writes as an eye-
witness says she cried " mercy to God and the King for the offence she
had done " (Ibid. x. 911).   [3] Ibid. x. 910.

the juries should have found her accomplices guilty, that
twenty-six peers, including her uncle, should have
condemned Anne herself, without some colourable
justification. If the charges were merely invented to ruin
the Queen, one culprit besides herself would have been
enough. To assume that Henry sent four needless victims
to the block is to accuse him of a lust for superfluous
butchery, of which even he, in his most bloodthirsty
moments, was not capable.[1]

On the day that his second queen was beheaded, Henry
obtained from Cranmer a special licence to marry a third.[2]
He was betrothed on the morrow and privately married
" in the Queen's closet at York Place " on the 30th of
May. The lady of his choice was Jane, daughter of Sir
John Seymour of Wolf Hall in Wiltshire.[3] She was
descended on her mother's side from Edward III, and
Cranmer had to dispense with a canonical bar to the
marriage arising from her consanguinity to the King in
the third and fourth degrees. She had been lady-in-
waiting to the two previous queens, and her brother, Sir
Edward Seymour, the future Protector, had for years
been steadily rising in Henry's favour. In October, 1535,
the King had paid a visit to Wolf Hall, and from that time
his attentions to Jane became marked. She seems to have
received them with real reluctance ; she refused a purse
of gold and returned the King's letters unopened.[4] She
even obtained a promise from Henry that he would not
speak with her except in the presence of others, and the
King ejected Cromwell from his rooms in the Palace in
order to bestow them on Sir Edward Seymour, and thus
to provide a place where he and Jane could converse

[1] The execution of Anne was welcomed by the Imperialists and
Catholics, and it is possible that it was hastened on by rumours of disquiet
in the North. A few days later the nobles and gentry who were in London
were ordered to return home to put the country in a state of defence
(L. and P. x. 1016).

[2] Ibid. x. 915, 926, 993, 1000. There is a persistent fable that they
were married on the day or the day after Anne's execution ; Dr. Gairdner
says it is repeated " in all histories ".

[3] See Wilts Archæol. Mag. vols. xv. xvi., documents printed from the
Longleat MSS.   [4] L. and P. x. 245.

without scandal. All this modesty has, of course, been attributed to prudential and ambitious motives, which were as wise as they were successful. But Jane seems to have had no enemies, except Alexander Aless, who denounced her to Luther as an enemy to the Gospel, probably because she extinguished the shining light of Anne Boleyn.[1] Cardinal Pole described her as "full of goodness,"[2] and she certainly did her best to reconcile Henry with his daughter the Princess Mary, whose treatment began to improve from the fall of Anne Boleyn. "She is," writes Chapuys, "of middle stature, and no great beauty ; so fair that one would call her rather pale than otherwise."[3] But all agreed in praising her intelligence. She had neither Catherine's force of character nor the temper of Anne Boleyn ; she was a woman of gentle spirit, striving always to mitigate the rigour of others ; her brief married life was probably happier than that of any other of Henry's Queens ; and her importance is mainly due to the fact that she bore to Henry his only legitimate son.

The disgrace of Anne Boleyn necessitated the summons of a fresh Parliament to put the succession to the crown on yet another basis. The Long Parliament had been dissolved on 14th April ; another was called to meet on the 8th of June. The eighteen acts passed during its six weeks' session illustrate the parallel development of the Reformation and of the royal autocracy. The Act of Succession made Anne's daughter, Elizabeth, a bastard, without declaring Catherine's daughter, Mary, legitimate, and settled the crown on Henry's prospective issue by Jane. A unique clause empowered the King to dispose of the crown at will, should he have no issue by his present Queen.[4] Probably he intended it, in that case, for the

---

[1] Luther, *Briefe* v. 22 ; *L. and P.* xi. 475.

[2] Strype, *Eccl. Memorials* I. ii. 304.   [3] *L. and P.* x. 901.

[4] Parliament preferred to risk the results of Henry's nomination to the risk of civil war, which would inevitably have broken out had Henry died in 1536. Hobbes, it may be noted, made this power of nomination an indispensable attribute of the sovereign, and if the sovereign be interpreted as the "King in Parliament" the theory is sound constitu-

Duke of Richmond ; but the Duke's days were numbered, and four days after the dissolution of Parliament he breathed his last. The royal prerogative was extended by a statute enabling a king, when he reached the age of twenty-four, to repeal by proclamation any act passed during his minority ; and the royal caste was further exalted by a statute making it high treason for any one to marry a king's daughter, legitimate or not, his sister, his niece, or his aunt on the father's side, without royal licence. The reform of clerical abuses was advanced by an act to prevent non-residence, and by another to obviate the delay in instituting to benefices practised by bishops with a view to keeping the tithes of the vacant benefice in their own hands. The breach with Rome was widened still further by a statute, declaring all who extolled the Pope's authority to be guilty of *præmunire*, imposing an oath of renunciation on all lay and clerical officers, and making the refusal of that oath high treason. Thus the hopes of a reaction built on the fall of those " apostles of the new sect," Anne Boleyn and her relatives, were promptly and roughly destroyed.

Henry's position had been immensely strengthened alike by the death of Catherine of Aragon and by the fall of Anne Boleyn ; and on both occasions he had expressed his appreciation of the fact in the most indecent and heartless manner. He was now free to marry whom he liked, and no objection based on canon or on any other law could be raised to the legitimacy of his future issue ; whether the Pope could dispense or not, it made no difference to

tionalism and was put in practice in 1701 as well as in 1536. But the limitations on Henry's power of bequeathing the crown have generally been forgotten ; he never had power to leave the crown away from Edward VI, that is, away from the only heir whose legitimacy was undisputed. The later acts went further, and entailed the succession upon Mary and Elizabeth unless Henry wished otherwise—which he did not. The preference of the Suffolk to the Stuart line may have been due to (1) the common law forbidding aliens to inherit English land (cf. *L. and P.* vii. 337) ; (2) the national dislike of the Scots ; (3) a desire to intimate to the Scots that if they would not unite the two realms by the marriage of Edward and Mary, they should not obtain the English crown by inheritance.

Edward VI's claim to the throne. The fall of Anne
Boleyn, in spite of some few rumours that she might have
been condemned on insufficient evidence, was generally
popular ; for her arrogance and that of her family made
them hated, and they were regarded as the cause of the
King's persecution of Catherine, of Mary, and of those
who maintained their cause. Abroad the effect was still
more striking. The moment Henry heard of Catherine's
death, he added a postscript to Cromwell's despatch to the
English ambassadors in France, bidding them to take a
higher tone with Francis, for all cause of difference had
been removed between him and Charles V.[1] The
Emperor secretly believed that his aunt had been
poisoned,[2] but that private grief was not to affect his
public policy ; and Charles, Francis, and even the Pope,
became more or less eager competitors for Henry's
favour. The bull of deprivation, which had been drawn
up and signed, became a dead letter, and every one was
anxious to disavow his share in its promotion. Charles
obtained the suspension of its publication, made a merit
of that service to Henry, and tried to represent that it
was Francis who, with his eyes on the English crown,
had extorted the bull from the Pope.[3] Paul III himself
used words to the English envoy at Rome, which might
be interpreted as an apology for having made Fisher
a cardinal and having denounced his and More's
execution.[4]

Henry had been driven by fear of Charles in the
previous year to make further advances than he relished
towards union with the German princes ; but the
Lutherans could not be persuaded to adopt Henry's
views of the mass and of his marriage with Catherine ;
and now he was glad to substitute an understanding with
the Emperor for intrigues with the Emperor's subjects.[5]
Cromwell and the council were, indeed, a little too eager
to welcome Chapuys' professions of friendship and to

[1] L. and P. x. 54.   [2] Ibid. x. 230.
[3] Ibid. x. 887.   [4] Ibid. x. 977.
[5] Cf. Stern, Heinrich VIII und der Schmalkaldische Bund, and P.
Singer, Beziehung des Schmalkald, Bundes zu England. Greifswald, 1901

entertain his demands for help against Francis. Henry allowed them to go on for a time ; but Cromwell was never in Wolsey's position, and the King was not inclined to repeat his own and the Cardinal's errors of 1521. He had suffered enough from the prostration of France and the predominance of Charles ; and he was anxious now that neither should be supreme. So, when the imperial ambassador came expecting Henry's assent, he, Cromwell and the rest of the council were amazed to hear the King break out into an uncompromising defence of the French King's conduct in invading Savoy and Piedmont.[1] That invasion was the third stroke of good fortune which befel Henry in 1536. As Henry and Ferdinand had, in 1512, diverted their arms from the Moors in order to make war on the Most Christian King, so, in 1536, the Most Christian King and the sovereign, who was at once King Catholic and the temporal head of Christendom, instead of turning their arms against the monarch who had outraged and defied the Church, turned them against one another. Francis had never lost sight of Milan ; he had now recovered from the effects of Pavia ; and in the spring of 1536 he overran Savoy and Piedmont. In April the Emperor once more visited Rome, and on the 17th he delivered a famous oration in the papal Consistory.[2] In that speech he denounced neither Luther nor Henry VIII ; he reserved his invectives for Francis I. Unconsciously he demonstrated once and for all that unity of faith was impotent against diversity of national interests, and that, whatever deference princes might profess to the counsels of the Vicar of Christ, the counsels they would follow would be those of secular impulse.

Henry was thus left to deal with the great domestic crisis of his reign without intervention from abroad. The dissolution of the monasteries inevitably inflicted considerable hardship on a numerous body of men. It had been arranged that the inmates of the dissolved religious houses should either be pensioned or transferred to other monasteries ; but, although the pensions were adequate

---

[1] *L. and P.* x. 699.   [2] *Ibid.* x. 678, 684, 968.

and sometimes even generous in scale,[1] and although the commissioners themselves showed a desire to prevent unnecessary trouble by obtaining licences for many houses to continue for a time,[2] the monks found some difficulty in obtaining their pensions, and Chapuys draws a moving picture of their sufferings as they wandered about the country, seeking employment in a market that was already overstocked with labour, and endeavouring to earn a livelihood by means to which they had never been accustomed.[3] They met with no little sympathy from the commons, who were oppressed with a like scarcity of work, and who had looked to the monasteries for such relief as charity could afford. Nowhere were these feelings so strong as in the north of England, and there the commissioners for dissolving the monasteries were often met with open resistance. Religious discontent was one of the motives for revolt, but probably the rebels were drawn mainly[4] from evicted tenants, deprived of their holdings by enclosures or by the conversion of land from tillage to pasture, men who had nothing to lose and everything to gain by a general turmoil. In these men the wandering monks found ready listeners to their complaints, and there were others, besides the monks, who eagerly turned to account the prevailing dissatisfaction. The northern lords, Darcy and Hussey, had for years been representing to Chapuys the certainty of success if the Emperor invaded England, and promising to do their part when he came. Darcy had, at Christmas 1534, sent the imperial

---

[1] *E.g.*, the Prioress of Tarent received £100 a year, the Abbot of Evesham £240 (Gasquet, ii. 230, 310); these sums must be multiplied by ten to bring them to their present value. Most of these lavish pensions were doubtless given as bribes or rewards for the surrender of monasteries.

[2] *L. and P.*, xi., 385, 519.   [3] *Ibid.*, xi. 42.

[4] The exact proportion is of course difficult to determine; Mr. E. F. Gay in an admirable paper (*Trans. Royal Hist. Soc.*, N.S., xviii. 208, 209) thinks that I have exaggerated the part played by the property-less class in the rebellion. They were undoubtedly present in large numbers; but my remark is intended to guard against the theory that the grievances were entirely religious, not to exclude those grievances; and the northern lords were of course notable examples of the discontent of the propertied class.

ambassador a sword as an intimation that the time had
come for an appeal to its arbitrament ; and he was seeking
Henry's licence to return to his house in Yorkshire in
order to raise " the crucifix " as the standard of revolt.[1]
The King, however, was doubtful of Darcy's loyalty, and
kept him in London till early in 1536. It would have
been well had he kept him longer.

Towards the end of the summer rumours[2] were spread
among the commons of the North that heavy taxes would
be levied on every burial, wedding and christening, that
all cattle would be marked and pay a fine to the King, and
that all unmarked beasts would be forfeit ; churches
within five miles of each other were to be taken down as
superfluous, jewels and church plate confiscated ; taxes
were to be paid for eating white bread, goose, or capon ;
there was to be a rigid inquisition into every man's
property ; and a score of other absurdities gained
currency, obviously invented by malicious and lying
tongues. The outbreak began at Caistor, in Lincolnshire,
on the 3rd of October, with resistance, not to the commissioners for dissolving the monasteries, but to those
appointed to collect the subsidy granted by Parliament.
The rebels entered Lincoln on the 6th ; they could, they
said, pay no more money ; they demanded the repeal of
religious changes, the restoration of the monasteries, the
banishment of heretics like Cranmer and Latimer, and
the removal of low-born advisers such as Cromwell
and Rich from the council.[3] The mustering of an army
under Suffolk and the denial by heralds and others that
the King had any such intentions as were imputed to him,
induced the commons to go home ; the reserves which
Henry was collecting at Ampthill were disbanded ; and
the commotion was over in less than a fortnight.

The Lincolnshire rebels, however, had not dispersed
when news arrived of a much more serious rising which
affected nearly the whole of Yorkshire. It was here that
Darcy and his friends were most powerful ; but, though
there is little doubt that they were the movers, the

---

[1] *L. and P.* vii. 1206 ; viii. 48.   [2] *Ibid*. xi. 768, 826[2].
[3] *Ibid*. xi. 786, 1182, 1244, 1246.

ostensible leader was Robert Aske, a lawyer. Even here
the rebellion was little more than a magnified riot, which
a few regiments of soldiers could soon have suppressed.
The rebels professed complete loyalty to Henry's person ;
they suggested no rival candidate for the throne ; they
merely demanded a change of policy, which they could
not enforce without a change of government. They had
no means of effecting that change without deposing Henry,
which they never proposed to do, and which, had they
done it, could only have resulted in anarchy. The
rebellion was formidable mainly because Henry had no
standing army ; he had to rely almost entirely on the
goodwill or at least acquiescence of his people. Outside
Yorkshire the gentry were willing enough ; possibly they
had their eyes on monastic rewards ; and they sent to
Cambridge double[1] or treble the forces Henry demanded,
which they could hardly have done had their tenants
shown any great sympathy with the rebellion. But
transport in those days was more difficult even than now ;
and before the musters could reach the Trent, Darcy,
after a show of reluctance, yielded Pomfret Castle to
the rebels and swore to maintain their cause. Henry
was forced, much against his will, to temporise. To
pardon or parley with rebels he thought would distain his honour.[2] If Norfolk was driven to offer a
pardon, he must on no account involve the King in his
promise.

Norfolk apparently had no option. An armistice was
accordingly arranged on the 27th of October, and a
deputation came up to lay the rebels' grievances before
the King. It was received graciously, and Henry's reply
was a masterly piece of statecraft.[3] He drew it up " with
his own hand, and made no creature privy thereto until it
was finished ". Their complaints about the Faith were,
he said, " so general that hard they be to be answered,"
but he intended always to live and to die in the faith of
Christ. They must specify what they meant by the
liberties of the Church, whether they were lawful or un-

[1] Surrey to Norfolk, 15th Oct. xi. 727, 738.
[2] L. and P. xi. 864.   [3] Ibid. xi. 957.

lawful liberties; but he had done nothing inconsistent with the laws of God and man. With regard to the Commonwealth, what King had kept his subjects so long in wealth and peace, ministering indifferent justice, and defending them from outward enemies? There were more low-born councillors when he came to the throne than now; then there were " but two worth calling noble.[1] Others, as the Lords Marny and Darcy, were scant well-born gentlemen, and yet of no great lands till they were promoted by us. The rest were lawyers and priests. . . . How came you to think that there were more noble men in our Privy Council then than now? " It did not become them to dictate to their sovereign whom he should call to his Council; yet, if they could prove, as they alleged, that certain of the Council were subverters of God's law and the laws of the realm, he would proceed against them. Then, after denouncing their rebellion and referring to their request for pardon, he says: " To show our pity, we are content, if we find you penitent, to grant you all letters of pardon on your delivering to us ten such ringleaders of this rebellion as we shall assign to you. Now note the benignity of your Prince, and how easily bloodshed may be eschewed. Thus I, as your head, pray for you, my members, that God may enlighten you for your benefit."

A conference was held at Doncaster in December,[2] and towards the end of the year Aske came at Henry's invitation to discuss the complaints with him.[3] No one could be more gracious than the King, when he chose; no one could mask his resentment more completely, when he had an object to gain. It was important to win over Aske, and convince him that Henry had the

[1] The records of the Privy Council for the greater part of Henry's reign have disappeared, and only a rough list of his privy Councillors can be gathered from the *Letters and Papers*. Surrey, of course, was one of the two nobles, and probably Shrewsbury was the other, though Oxford, whose peerage was older than theirs, seems also to have been a member of the Privy Council (*L. and P.* i. 51). The complaint of the rebels applied to the whole Tudor period; at Henry's death no member of his Privy Council held a peerage twelve years old.

[2] *Ibid*. xi. 1244-46.   [3] *Ibid*. xi. 1306.

interests of the rebels at heart. So on Aske were lavished
all the royal arts. They were amply rewarded. In
January, 1537, the rebel leader went down to Yorkshire
fully convinced of the King's goodwill, and anxious
only that the commons should observe his conditions.[1]
But there were wilder spirits at work over which he had
little control. They declared that they were betrayed.
Plots were formed to seize Hull and Scarborough ; both
were discovered.[2] Aske, Constable, and other leaders of
the original Pilgrimage of Grace exerted themselves to
stay this outbreak of their more violent followers ; and
between moderates and extremists the whole movement
quickly collapsed. The second revolt gave Henry an
excuse for recalling his pardon, and for exacting revenge
from all who had been implicated in either movement.
Darcy deserved little pity ; the earliest in his treason, he
continued the game to the end ; but Aske was an honest
man, and his execution, condemned though he was by a
jury, was a violent act of injustice.[3] Norfolk was sent to
the North on a Bloody Assize,[4] and if neither he nor the
King was a Jeffreys, the rebellion was stamped out with
a good deal of superfluous cruelty. Henry was resolved
to do the work once and for all, and he based his system
on terror. His measures for the future government of
the North, now threatened by James V, were, however,
wise on the whole. He would put no more nobles in
places of trust ; the office of Warden of the Marches he
took into his own hands, appointing three deputies of
somewhat humble rank for the east, middle and west
marches.[5] A strong Council of the North was appointed to sit at York, under the presidency of Tunstall,
Bishop of Durham, and with powers almost as extensive
as those of the Privy Council at London ; and hence-

[1] L. and P. XII. i. 20, 23, 43, 44, 46.

[2] Ibid. XII. i. 46, 64, 102, 104, 141, 142.

[3] Henry, says Dr. Gairdner, examined " the evidence sent up to him
in the spirit of a detective policeman " (XII. i. p. xxix.).

[4] L. and P. XII. i. 227, 228, 401, 402, 416, 457, 458, 468, 478, 498.

[5] Ibid. XII. i. 594, 595, 636, 667. Norfolk thought Henry's plan was
to govern the North by the aid of thieves and murderers.

forth Henry had little trouble from disaffection in England.[1]

With one aftermath of the Pilgrimage of Grace he had yet to deal. The opportunity had been too good for Paul III to neglect; and early in 1537 he had sent a legate *a latere* to Flanders to do what he could to abet the rebellion.[2] His choice fell on Reginald Pole, the son of the Countess of Salisbury and grandson of George, Duke of Clarence. Pole had been one of Henry's great favourites; the King had paid for his education, given him, while yet a layman, rich church preferments, and contributed the equivalent of about twelve hundred pounds a year to enable him to complete his studies in Italy.[3] In 1530 Pole was employed to obtain opinions at Paris favourable to Henry's divorce,[4] and was offered the Archbishopric of York. He refused from conscientious scruples,[5] sought in vain to turn the King from his evil ways, and in 1532 left England; they parted friends, and Henry continued Pole's pensions. While Pole was regarding with increasing disgust the King's actions, Henry still hoped that Pole was on his side, and in 1536, in answer to Henry's request for his views, Pole sent his famous treatise *De Unitate Ecclesiæ*. His heart was better than his head; he thought Henry had been treated too gently, and that the fulmination of a bull of excommunication earlier in his course would have stopped his headlong career. To repair the Pope's omissions, Pole now proceeded to administer the necessary castigation; " flattery," he said, " had been the cause of all the evil ". Even his friend, Cardinal Contarini, thought the book too bitter, and among his family in England it produced consternation.[6] Some of them were hand in glove with

---

[1] Much of the correspondence of this Council found its way to Hamilton Palace in Scotland, and thence to Germany; it was purchased for the British Museum in 1889 and now comprises *Addit. MSS.* 32091, 32647-48, 32654 and 32657 (printed as *Hamilton Papers*, 2 vols., 1890-92).

[2] *L. and P.* XII. i. 367, 368, 779.

[3] *Ibid.* ii. 3943 (reference misprinted in *D.N.B.* xlvi. 35, as 3493); iii. 1544.

[4] *Ibid.* iv. 6003, 6252, 6383, 6394, 6505.   [5] *Ibid.* v. 737.

[6] *Ibid.* x. 420, 426; xi. 72, 93, 156.

Chapuys, who had suggested Pole to Charles as a candidate for the throne; and his book might well have broken the thin ice on which they stood. Henry, however, suppressed his anger and invited Pole to England; he, perhaps wisely, refused, but immediately afterwards he accepted the Pope's call to Rome, where he was made cardinal,[1] and sent to Flanders as legate to foment the northern rebellion.

He came too late to do anything except exhibit his own and the papal impotence. The rebellion was crushed before his commission was signed. As Pole journeyed through France, Henry sent to demand his extradition as a traitor.[2] With that request Francis could hardly comply, but he ordered the legate to quit his dominions. Pole sought refuge in Flanders, but was stopped on the frontier. Charles could no more than Francis afford to offend the English King, and the cardinal-legate was informed that he might visit the Bishop of Liége, but only if he went in disguise.[3] Never, wrote Pole to the Regent, had a papal legate been so treated before. Truly Henry had fulfilled his boast that he would show the princes of Europe how small was the power of a Pope. He had obliterated every vestige of papal authority in England and defied the Pope to do his worst; and now, when the Pope attempted to do it, his legate was chased out of the dominions of the faithful sons of the Church at the demand of the excommunicate King. Henry had come triumphant out of perils which every one else believed would destroy him. He had carried England through the greatest revolution in her history. He had crushed the only revolt which that revolution evoked at home; and abroad the greatest princes of Europe had shown that they valued as nothing the goodwill of the Pope against that of Henry VIII.

The culminating point in his good fortune was reached in the following autumn. On the 12th of October, 1537, Queen Jane gave birth to a son. Henry had determined

---

[1] On 22nd December, 1536 (*L. and P.* xi. 1353).
[2] *Ibid.* XII. i. 760, 939, 987, 988, 996.
[3] *Ibid.* XII. i. 997, 1061, 1135, 1167, 1174.

that, had he a son by Anne Boleyn, the child should be named Henry after himself, or Edward after his grandfather, Edward IV. Queen Jane's son was born on the eve of the feast of St. Edward, and that fact decided the choice of his name. Twelve days later the mother, who had never been crowned, passed away.[1] She, alone of Henry's wives, was buried with royal pomp in St. George's Chapel at Windsor; and to her alone the King paid the compliment of mourning. His grief was sincere, and for the unusual space of more than two years he remained without a wife. But Queen Jane's death was not to be compared in importance with the birth of Edward VI. The legitimate male heir, the object of so many desires and the cause of so many tragedies, had come at last to fill to the brim the cup of Henry's triumph. The greatest storm and stress of his reign was passed. There were crises to come, which might have been deemed serious in a less troubled reign, and they still needed all Henry's wary cunning to meet; Francis and Charles were even now preparing to end a struggle from which only Henry drew profit; and Paul was hoping to join them in war upon England. Yet Henry had weathered the worst of the gale, and he now felt free to devote his energies to the extension abroad of the authority which he had established so firmly at home.

[1] The fable that the Cæsarean operation was performed on her, invented or propagated by Nicholas Sanders, rests upon the further error repeated by most historians that Queen Jane died on the 14th of October, instead of the 24th (see Nichols, *Literary Remains of Edward VI* pp. xxiv. xxv.).

CHAPTER XIV

REX ET IMPERATOR

NOTWITHSTANDING the absence of "Empire" and "Emperor" from the various titles which Henry VIII possessed or assumed, he has more than one claim to be reputed the father of modern imperialism. It is not till a year after his death that we have any documentary evidence of an intention on the part of the English Government to unite England and Scotland into one Empire, and to proclaim their sovereign the Emperor of Great Britain.[1] But a marriage between Edward VI and Mary, Queen of Scots, by which it was sought to effect that union, had been the main object of Henry's efforts during the closing years of his reign, and the imperial idea was a dominant note in Henry's mind. No king was more fond of protesting that he wore an imperial crown and ruled an imperial realm. When, in 1536, Convocation declared England to be "an imperial See of itself," it only clothed in decent and formal language Henry's own boast that he was not merely King, but Pope and Emperor, in his own domains. The rest of Western Europe was under the temporal sway of Cæsar, as it was under the spiritual sway of the Pope ; but neither to one nor to the other did Henry owe any allegiance.[2]

---

[1] Odet de Selve, *Corresp. Pol.* p. 268.

[2] This was part of the revived influence of the Roman Civil Law in England which Professor Maitland has sketched in his *English Law and the Renaissance*, 1901. But the influence of these ideas extended into every sphere, and not least of all into the ecclesiastical. Englishmen, said Chapuys, were fond of tracing the King's imperial authority back to a grant from the Emperor Constantine—giving it thus an antiquity as great and an origin as authoritative as that claimed for the Pope by the false *Donation of Constantine* (*L. and P.* v. 45 ; vii. 232). This is the meaning of Henry's assertion that the Pope's authority in England was "usurped," not that it was usurped at the expense of the English national Church, but at the expense of his prerogative. So, too, we find instructive complaints from a different sort of reformers that the reformation as effected by Henry VIII was merely a *translatio imperii* (*ibid.* XIV. ii. 141).

For the word " imperial " itself he had shown a marked predilection from his earliest days. *Henry Imperial* was the name of the ship in which his admiral hoisted his flag in 1513, and " Imperial " was the name given to one of his favourite games. But, as his reign wore on, the word was translated into action, and received a more definite meaning. To mark his claim to supreme dignity, he assumed the style of " His Majesty " instead of that of " His Grace," which he had hitherto shared with mere dukes and archbishops ; and possibly " His Majesty " banished " His Grace " from Henry's mind no less than it did from his title. The story of his life is one of consistent, and more or less orderly, evolution. For many years he had been kept in leading-strings by Wolsey's and other clerical influences. The first step in his self-assertion was to emancipate himself from this control, and to vindicate his authority within the precincts of his Court. His next was to establish his personal supremacy over Church and State in England ; this was the work of the Reformation Parliament between 1529 and 1536. The final stage in the evolution was to make his rule more effective in the outlying parts of England, on the borders of Scotland, in Wales and its Marches, and then to extend it over the rest of the British Isles.

The initial steps in the process of expanding the sphere of royal authority had already been taken. The condition of Wales exercised the mind of King and Parliament, even in the throes of the struggle with Rome.[1] The " manifold robberies, murders, thefts, trespasses, riots, routs, embraceries, maintenances, oppressions, ruptures of the peace, and many other malefacts, which be there daily practised, perpetrated, committed and done," obviously demanded prompt and swift redress, unless the redundant eloquence of parliamentary statutes protested

Henry VIII's encouragement of the civil law was the natural counterpart of the prohibition of its study by Pope Honorius in 1219 and Innocent IV in 1254 (Pollock and Maitland i. 102, 103).

[1] Cromwell has a note in 1533, " for the establishing of a Council in the Marches of Wales " (*L. and P.* vi. 386), and there had been numerous complaints in Parliament about their condition (*ibid.* vii. 781). Henry was a great Unionist, though Separatist as regards his wives and the Pope.

too much ; and in 1534 several acts were passed restraining local jurisdictions, and extending the authority
of the President and Council of the Marches.[1] Chapuys
declared that the effect of these acts was to rob the
Welsh of their freedom, and he thought that the probable
discontent might be turned to account by stirring an
insurrection in favour of Catherine of Aragon and of the
Catholic faith.[2] If, however, there was discontent, it
did not make itself effectively felt, and in 1536 Henry
proceeded to complete the union of England and Wales.
First, he adapted to Wales the institution of justices of
the peace, which had proved the most efficient instrument
for the maintenance of his authority in England. A
more important statute followed. Recalling the facts
that " the rights, usages, laws and customs " in Wales
" be far discrepant from the laws and customs of this
realm," that its people " do daily use a speech nothing
like, nor consonant to, the natural mother-tongue used
within this realm," and that " some rude and ignorant
people have made distinction and diversity between the
King's subjects of this realm " and those of Wales, " His
Highness, of a singular zeal, love and favour " which he
bore to the Welsh, minded to reduce them " to the perfect
order, notice and knowledge of his laws of this realm,
and utterly to extirp, all and singular, the sinister usages
and customs differing from the same ". The Principality
was divided into shires, and the shires into hundreds ;
justice in every court, from the highest to the lowest, was
to be administered in English, and in no other tongue ;
and no one who spoke Welsh was to " have or enjoy any
manner of Office or Fees " whatsoever. On the other
hand, a royal commission was appointed to inquire into
Welsh laws, and such as the King thought necessary

[1] See an admirable study by Miss C. A. J. Skeel, *The Council in the
Marches of Wales*, 1904. Cromwell's great constitutional idea was
government by council rather than by Parliament ; in 1534 he had a
scheme for including in the King's Ordinary Council (not of course the
Privy Council) " the most assured and substantial gentlemen in every
shire " (*L. and P.* vii. 420 ; cf. his draft bill for a new court of conservators
of the commonwealth and the more rigid execution of statutes, vii. 1611).

[2] *L. and P.* vii. 1554.

might still be observed ; while the Welsh shires and boroughs were to send members to the English Parliament. This statute was, to all effects and purposes, the first Act of Union in English history. Six years later a further act reorganised and developed the jurisdiction of the Council of Wales and the Marches. Its functions were to be similar to those of the Privy Council in London, of which the Council of Wales, like that of the already established Council of the North, was an offshoot. Its object was to maintain peace with a firm hand in a specially disorderly district ; and the powers, with which it was furnished, often conflicted with the common law of England,[1] and rendered the Council's jurisdiction, like that of other Tudor courts, a grievance to Stuart Parliaments.

But Ireland demanded even more than Wales the application of Henry's doctrines of union and empire ; for if Wales was thought by Chapuys to be receptive soil for the seeds of rebellion, sedition across St. George's Channel was ripe unto the harvest. Irish affairs, among other domestic problems, had been sacrificed to Wolsey's passion for playing a part in Europe, and on the eve of his fall English rule in Ireland was reported to be weaker than it had been since the Conquest. The outbreak of war with Charles V in 1528, was followed by the first appearance of Spanish emissaries at the courts of Irish chiefs, and from Spanish intrigue in Ireland Tudor monarchs were never again to be free. In the autumn of 1534 the whole of Ireland outside the pale blazed up in revolt. Sir William Skeffington succeeded in crushing the rebellion ; but Skeffington died in the following year, and his successor, Lord Leonard Grey, failed to overcome the difficulties caused by Irish disaffection and by jealousies

---

[1] Cf. Maitland, *English Law and the Renaissance* p. 70 ; Lee to Cromwell : " if we should do nothing but as the common law will, these things so far out of order will never be redressed " (*D.N.B.* xxxii. 375 ; the letter is dated 18th July, 1538, by the *D.N.B.* and Maitland, but there is no letter of that date from Roland Lee in *L. and P.* ; probably the sentence occurs in Lee's letter of 18th July, 1534, or that of 18th July, 1535 (*L. and P.* vii. 988, viii. 1058), though the phrase is not given in *L. and P.*).

in his council. His sister was wife of Fitzgerald, the Earl of Kildare, and the revolt of the Geraldines brought Grey himself under suspicion. He was accused by his council of treason ; he returned to England in 1540, declaring the country at peace. But, before he had audience with Henry, a fresh insurrection broke out, and Grey was sent to the Tower ; thence, having pleaded guilty to charges of treason, he trod the usual path to the block.

Henry now adopted fresh methods ; he determined to treat Ireland in much the same way as Wales. A commission, appointed in 1537, had made a thorough survey of the land, and supplied him with the outlines of his policy. As in Wales, the English system of land tenure, of justice and the English language were to supersede indigenous growths ; the King's supremacy in temporal and ecclesiastical affairs was to be enforced, and the whole of the land was to be gradually won by a judicious admixture of force and conciliation.[1] The new deputy, Sir Anthony St. Leger, was an able man, who had presided over the commission of 1537. He landed at Dublin in 1541, and his work was thoroughly done. Henry, no longer so lavish with his money as in Wolsey's days, did not stint for this purpose.[2] The Irish Parliament passed an act that Henry should be henceforth styled King, instead of Lord, of Ireland ; and many of the chiefs were induced to relinquish their tribal independence in return for glittering coronets. By 1542 Ireland had not merely peace within her own borders, but was able to send two thousand kernes to assist the English on the borders of Scotland ; and English rule in Ireland was more widely and more firmly established than it had ever been before.

Besides Ireland and Wales, there were other spheres in which Henry sought to consolidate and extend the Tudor methods of government. The erection, in 1542, of the Courts of Wards and Liveries, of First-fruits and Tenths, and the development of the jurisdiction of the Star

[1] See R. Dunlop in *Owens College Studies*, 1901, and the *Calendar of Carew MSS.* and *Calendar of Irish State Papers* vol. i.
[2] *L. and P.* xvi. 43, 77.

Chamber and of the Court of Requests,[1] were all designed
to further two objects dear to Henry's heart, the efficiency
of his administration and the exaltation of his prerogative.
It was thoroughly in keeping with his policy that the
parliamentary system expanded concurrently with the
sphere of the King's activity. Berwick had first been
represented in the Parliament of 1529,[2] and a step, which
would have led to momentous consequences, had the idea
on which it was based been carried out, was taken in
1536, when two members were summoned from Calais.
There was now only one district under English rule which
was not represented in Parliament, and that was the
county of Durham, known as *the* bishopric, which still
remained detached from the national system. It was left
for Oliver Cromwell to complete England's parliamentary
representation by summoning members to sit for that
palatine county.[3] This was not the only respect in which
the Commonwealth followed in the footsteps of Henry
VIII, for the Parliament of 1542, in which members from
Wales and from Calais are first recorded as sitting,[4] passed
an " Act for the Navy," which provided that goods could
only be imported in English ships. It was, however, in
his dealings with Scotland that Henry's schemes for the
expansion of England became most marked ; but, before
he could develop his plans in that direction, he had to
ward off a recrudescence of the danger from a coalition
of Catholic Europe.

In spite of Henry's efforts to fan the flames of strife [5]
between the Emperor and the King of France, the war,
which had prevented either monarch from countenancing
the mission of Cardinal Pole or from profitting by the

[1] *L. and P.* xvi. 28 ; cf. Leadam, *Court of Requests*, Selden Soc. Introd.

[2] *Official Return of Members of Parliament* i. 369.

[3] See G. T. Lapsley, *The County Palatine of Durham*, in *Harvard Historical Series.*

[4] There are no records in the *Official Return* for 1536 and 1539, but Calais had been granted Parliamentary representation by an Act of the previous Parliament (27 Hen. VIII, Private Acts, No. 9 ; cf. *L. and P.* x. 1086).

[5] Vols. xii. and xiii. of the *L. and P.* are full of these attempts.

Pilgrimage of Grace, was gradually dying down in the autumn of 1537 ; and, in order to check the growing and dangerous intimacy between the two rivals, Henry was secretly hinting to both that the death of his Queen had left him free to contract a marriage which might bind him for ever to one or the other.[1] To Francis he sent a request for the hand of Mary of Guise, who had already been promised to James V of Scotland. He refused to believe that the Scots negotiations had proceeded so far that they could not be set aside for so great a king as himself, and he succeeded in convincing the lady's relatives that the position of a Queen of England provided greater attractions than any James could hold out.[2] Francis, however, took matters into his own hands, and compelled the Guises to fulfil their compact with the Scottish King. Nothing daunted, Henry asked for a list of other French ladies eligible for the matrimonial prize. He even suggested that the handsomest of them might be sent, in the train of Margaret of Navarre, to Calais, where he could inspect them in person.[3] " I trust to no one," he told Castillon, the French ambassador, " but myself. The thing touches me too near. I wish to see them and know them some time before deciding."[4] This idea of " trotting out the young ladies like hackneys "[5] was not much relished at the French Court ; and Castillon, to shame Henry out of the indelicacy of his proposal, made an ironical suggestion for testing the ladies' charms, the grossness of which brought the only recorded blush to Henry's cheeks.[6] No more was said of the beauty-show ; and Henry declared that he did not intend to marry in France or in Spain at all, unless his

[1] For the negotiations with France from 1537 onwards see Kaulek, *Corresp. de MM. Castillon et Marillac*, Paris, 1885.

[2] *L. and P.* XIII. i. 165, 273.

[3] Is this another trace of " Byzantinism " ? It was a regular custom at the Byzantine and other Oriental Courts to have a " concourse of beauty " for the Emperor's benefit when he wished to choose a wife (*Histoire Générale* i. 381 n. v. 728) ; and the story of Theophilus and Theodora is familiar (Finlay ii. 146-47).

[4] *L. and P.* XIII. ii. 77 ; Kaulek p. 80.

[5] *Ibid.* XII. ii. 1125 ; XIII. ii. p. xxxi.   [6] *Ibid.* XIII. ii. 77.

marriage brought him a closer alliance with Francis or
Charles than the rivals had formed with each other.

While these negotiations for obtaining the hand of a
French princess were in progress, Henry set on foot a
similar quest in the Netherlands. Before the end of 1537
he had instructed Hutton, his agent, to report on the
ladies of the Regent Mary's Court ;[1] and Hutton replied
that Christina of Milan was said to be " a goodly person-
age and of excellent beauty ". She was daughter of the
deposed King of Denmark and of his wife, Isabella,
sister of Charles V ; at the age of thirteen she had been
married to the Duke of Milan, but she was now a virgin
widow of sixteen, " very tall and competent of beauty, of
favour excellent and very gentle in countenance ".[2] On
10th March, 1538, Holbein arrived at Brussels for the
purpose of painting the lady's portrait, which he finished
in a three hours' sitting.[3] Christina's fascinations do
not seem to have made much impression on Henry ; indeed, his taste in feminine beauty cannot be commended.
There is no good authority for the alleged reply of the
young duchess herself, that, if she had two heads, she
would willingly place one of them at His Majesty's
disposal.[4] Henry had, as yet, beheaded only one of his
wives, and even if the precedent had been more firmly
established, Christina was too wary and too polite to refer
to it in such uncourtly terms. She knew that the disposal
of her hand did not rest with herself, and though the
Emperor sent powers for the conclusion of the match,
neither he nor Henry had any desire to see it concluded.

[1] *L. and P.* XII. ii. 1172.

[2] *Ibid.* XII. ii. Pref. p. xxviii. No. 1187.

[3] *Ibid.* XIII. i. 380, 507. The magnificent portrait of Christina
belonging to the Duke of Norfolk, and now on loan at the National
Gallery, must have been painted by Holbein afterwards.

[4] It may have crystallised from some such rumour as is reported in
L. and P. XIV. ii. 141. " Marry," says George Constantyne, " she
sayeth that the King's Majesty was in so little space rid of the Queens
that she dare not trust his Council, though she durst trust his Majesty ;
for her council suspecteth that her great-aunt was poisoned, that the
second was innocently put to death, and the third lost for lack of keeping
in her childbed." Constantyne added that he was not sure whether this
was Christina's answer or Anne of Cleves'.

The cementing of his friendship with Francis freed Charles from the need of Henry's goodwill, and impelled the English King to seek elsewhere for means to counter-balance the hostile alliance.

The Emperor and the French King had not been deluded by English intrigues, nor prevented from coming together by Henry's desire to keep them apart. Charles, Francis, and Paul III met at Nice in June, 1538, and there the Pope negotiated a ten years' truce. Henceforth they were to consider their interests identical, and their ambassadors in England compared notes in order to defeat more effectively Henry's skilful diplomacy.[1] The moment seemed ripe for the execution of the long-cherished project for a descent upon England. Its King had just added to his long list of offences against the Church by despoiling the shrine of St. Thomas at Canterbury and burning the bones of the saint. The saint was even said to have been put on his trial in mockery, declared con-tumacious, and condemned as a traitor.[2] If the canonised bones of martyrs could be treated thus, who would, for the future, pay respect to the Church or tribute at its shrines ? At Rome a party, of which Pole was the most zealous, proclaimed that the real Turk was Henry, and that all Christian princes should unite to sweep him from the face of God's earth, which his presence had too long defiled. Considering the effect of Christian leagues against the Ottoman, the English Turk was probably not dismayed. But Paul III and Pole were determined to do their worst. The Pope resolved to publish the bull of depriva-tion, which had been drawn up in August, 1535, though its execution had hitherto been suspended owing to papal hopes of Henry's amendment and to the request of various princes. Now the bull was to be published in France, in

---

[1] L. and P. XIII. ii. 232, 277, 914, 915.

[2] The burning of the bones is stated as a fact in the Papal Bull of December, 1538 (L. and P. XIII. ii. 1087 ; see Pref. p. xvi. n.) ; but the documents printed in Wilkins's Concilia iii. 835, giving an account of an alleged trial of the body of St. Thomas are forgeries (L. and P. XIII. ii. pp. xli., xlii., 49). A precedent might have been found in Pope Stephen VI's treatment of his predecessor, Formosus (Hist. Générale i. 536).

Flanders, in Scotland and in Ireland. Beton was made
a cardinal and sent home to exhort James V to invade
his uncle's kingdom,[1] while Pole again set out on his
travels to promote the conquest of his native land.[2]

It was on Pole's unfortunate relatives that the effects
of the threatened bull were to fall. Besides the Cardinal's
treason, there was another motive for proscribing his
family. He and his brothers were grandchildren of
George, Duke of Clarence ; years before, Chapuys had
urged Charles V to put forward Pole as a candidate for
the throne ; and Henry was as convinced as his father
had been that the real way to render his Government
secure was to put away all the possible alternatives.
Now that he was threatened with deprivation by papal
sentence, the need became more urgent than ever. But,
while the proscription of the Poles was undoubtedly
dictated by political reasons, their conduct enabled Henry
to effect it by legal means. There was no doubt of the
Cardinal's treason ; his brother, Sir Geoffrey, had often
taken counsel with Charles's ambassador, and discussed
plans for the invasion of England ;[3] and even their mother,
the aged Countess of Salisbury, although she had denounced the Cardinal as a traitor and had lamented the
fact that she had given him birth, had brought herself
within the toils by receiving papal bulls and corresponding
with traitors.[4] The least guilty of the family appears
to have been the Countess's eldest son, Lord Montague ;[5]
but he, too, was involved in the common ruin. Plots
were hatched for kidnapping the Cardinal and bringing
him home to stand his trial for treason. Sir Geoffrey
was arrested in August, 1538, was induced, or forced,
to turn King's evidence, and as a reward was granted
his miserable, conscience-struck life.[6] The Countess was

---

[1] L. and P. XIII. ii. 1108-9, 1114-16, 1130, 1135-36.
[2] Ibid. XIII. ii. 950, 1110.   [3] Ibid. vii. 1368 ; viii. 750.
[4] Ibid. XIII. ii. 835, 838, 855.
[5] He had, however, been sending information to Chapuys as early
as 1534 (L. and P. vii. 957), when Charles V was urged to make use of
him and of Reginald Pole (ibid. vii. 1040 ; cf. ibid. XIII. ii. 702, 830, 954).
[6] Ibid. XIII. pt. ii. passim. He attempted to commit suicide (ibid. 703).

spared for a while, but Montague mounted the scaffold in December.

With Montague perished his cousin, the Marquis of Exeter, whose descent from Edward IV was as fatal to him as their descent from Clarence was to the Poles. The Marquis was the White Rose, the next heir to the throne if the line of the Tudors failed. His father, the Earl of Devonshire, had been attainted in the reign of Henry VII; but Henry VIII had reversed the attainder, had treated the young Earl with kindness, had made him Knight of the Garter and Marquis of Exeter, and had sought in various ways to win his support. But his dynastic position and dislike of Henry's policy drove the Marquis into the ranks of the discontented. He had been put in the Tower in 1531 on suspicion of treason; after his release he listened to the hysterics of Elizabeth Barton, intrigued with Chapuys, and corresponded with Reginald Pole;[1] and in Cornwall in 1538, men conspired to make him King.[2] Less evidence than this would have convinced a jury of peers in Tudor times of the expediency of Exeter's death; and on the 9th of December his head paid the price of his royal descent.

These executions do not seem to have produced the faintest symptoms of disgust in the popular mind. The threat of invasion evoked a national enthusiasm for defence. In August, 1538, Henry went down to inspect the fortifications he had been for years erecting at Dover; masonry from the demolished monasteries was employed in dotting the coast with castles, such as Calshot and Hurst, which were built with materials from the neighbouring abbey of Beaulieu. Commissioners were sent to repair the defences at Calais and Guisnes, on the Scottish Borders, along the coasts from Berwick to the mouth of the Thames, and from the Thames to Lizard Point.[3] Beacons were repaired, ordnance was supplied wherever it was needed, lists of ships and of mariners were drawn up in every port, and musters were taken throughout the kingdom. Everywhere the people pressed forward to

---

[1] *L. and P.* v. 416; vi. 1419, 1464.   [2] *Ibid.* XIII. ii. 802, 961.
[3] *Ibid.* XIV. i. 478, 533, 630, 671, 762, 899.

help ; in the Isle of Wight they were lining the shores
with palisades, and taking every precaution to render a
landing of the enemy a perilous enterprise.[1]   In Essex
they anticipated the coming of the commissioners by
digging dykes and throwing up ramparts ; at Harwich
the Lord Chancellor saw " women and children working
with shovels at the trenches and bulw; rks ".   Whatever
we may think of the roughness and rigour of Henry's
rule, his methods were not resented by the mass of his
people.   He had not lost his hold on the nation ; whenever he appealed to his subjects in a time of national
danger, he met with an eager response ; and, had the
schemers abroad, who idly dreamt of his expulsion from
the throne, succeeded in composing their mutual quarrels
and launching their bolt against England, there is no
reason to suppose that its fate would have differed from
that of the Spanish Armada.

In spite of the fears of invasion which prevailed in the
spring of 1539, Pole's second mission had no more
success than the first ;[2] and the hostile fleet, for the
sight of which the Warden of the Cinque Ports was
straining his eyes from Dover Castle, never came from
the mouths of the Scheldt and the Rhine ; or rather, the
supposed Armada proved to be a harmless convoy of
traders.[3]   The Pope himself, on second thoughts, with-
held his promised bull.   He distrusted its reception at
the hands of his secular allies, and dreaded the contempt
and ridicule which would follow an open failure.[4]   Moreover, at the height of his fervour against Henry, he
could not refrain from attempts to extend his temporal
power, and his seizure of Urbino alienated Francis and
afforded Henry some prospect of creating an anti-papal
party in Italy.[5]   Francis would gladly join in a prohibition
of English commerce, if Charles would only begin ;
but without Charles he could do nothing, and even

[1] *L. and P.* XIV. i. 540, 564, 573, 615, 655, 682, 711, 712.
[2] *Ibid.* XIV. i. Introd. pp. xi.-xiii.
[3] *Ibid.* XIV. i. 714, 728, 741, 767.
[4] Cf. *ibid.* XIV. i. 1011, 1013 ; ii. 99.
[5] *Ibid.* XIV. i. 27, 37, 92, 98, 104, 114, 144, 188, 235, 884 ; ii. 357.

L

when his amity with the Emperor was closest, he was compelled, at Henry's demand, to punish the French priests who inveighed against English enormities.[1] To Charles, however, English trade was worth more than to Francis, and the Emperor's subjects would tolerate no interruption of their lucrative intercourse with England. With the consummate skill which he almost invariably displayed in political matters, Henry had, in 1539, when the danger seemed greatest, provided the Flemings with an additional motive for peace. He issued a proclamation that, for seven years, their goods should pay no more duty than those of the English themselves;[2] and the thrifty Dutch were little inclined to stop, by a war, the fresh stream of gold. The Emperor, too, had more urgent matters in hand. Henry might be more of a Turk than the Sultan himself, and the Pope might regard the sack of St. Thomas's shrine with more horror than the Turkish defeat of a Christian fleet; but Henry was not harrying the Emperor's coasts, nor threatening to deprive the Emperor's brother of his Hungarian kingdom; and Turkish victories on land and on sea gave the imperial family much more concern than all Henry's onslaughts on the saints and their relics. And besides the Ottoman peril, Charles had reason to fear the political effects of the union between England and the Protestant princes of Germany, for which the religious development in England was paving the way, and which an attack on Henry would at once have cemented.

The powers conferred upon Henry as Supreme Head of the Church were not long suffered to remain in abeyance. Whatever the theory may have been, in practice Henry's supremacy over the Church was very different from that which Kings of England had hitherto wielded; and from the moment he entered upon his new ecclesiastical kingdom, he set himself not merely to reform practical abuses, such as the excessive wealth of the clergy, but to define the standard of orthodox faith, and to force his subjects to embrace the royal theology. The Catholic faith was to

[1] *L. and P.* XIV. i. 37, 92, 371.   [2] *Ibid.* XIV. i. 373.

hold good only so far as the Supreme Head willed ; the " King's doctrine " became the rule to which " *our* Church of England," as Henry styled it, was henceforth to conform ; and " unity and concord in opinion " were to be established by royal decree.

The first royal definition of the faith was embodied in ten articles submitted to Convocation in 1536. The King was, he said, constrained by diversity of opinions " to put his own pen to the book and conceive certain articles . . . thinking that no person, having authority from him, would presume to say a word against their meaning, or be remiss in setting them forth ".[1] His people, he maintained, whether peer or prelate, had no right to resist his temporal or spiritual commands, whatever they might be. Episcopal authority had indeed sunk low. When Convocation was opened in 1536, a layman, Dr. William Petre, appeared, and demanded the place of honour above all bishops and archbishops in their assembly. Pre-eminence belonged, he said, to the King as Supreme Head of the Church ; the King had appointed Cromwell his Vicargeneral ; and Cromwell had named him, Petre, his proctor.[2] The claim was allowed, and the submissive clergy found little fault with the royal articles of faith, though they mentioned only three sacraments, baptism, penance and the sacrament of the altar, denounced the abuse of images, warned men against excessive devotion to the saints, and against believing that " ceremonies have power to remit sin," or that masses can deliver souls from purgatory. Finally, Convocation transferred from the Pope to the Christian princes the right to summon a General Council.[3]

With the *Institution of a Christian Man*, issued in the following year, and commonly called *The Bishops' Book*, Henry had little to do. The bishops debated the doctrinal questions from February to July, 1537, but the King wrote, in August, that he had had no time to examine

---

[1] *L. and P.* xi. 1110 ; cf. *ibid.* 59, 123, 377, 954.

[2] Wilkins, *Concilia* iii. 803.

[3] Fuller, *Church History*, ed. 1845 iii. 145-59 ; Burnet, *Reformation*, ed. Pocock iv. 272-90 ; Strype, *Cranmer* i. 58-62.

their conclusions.[1] He trusted, however, to their wisdom, and agreed that the book should be published and read to the people on Sundays and holy-days for three years to come. In the same year he permitted a change, which inevitably gave fresh impulse to the reforming movement in England and destroyed every prospect of that " union and concord in opinions," on which he set so much store. Miles Coverdale was licensed to print an edition of his Bible in England, with a dedication to Queen Jane Seymour; and in 1538 a second English version was prepared by John Rogers, under Cranmer's authority, and published as Matthew's Bible.[2] This was the Bible " of the largest volume " which Cromwell, as Henry's Vice-gerent, ordered to be set up in all churches. Every incumbent was to encourage his parishioners to read it; he was to recite the Paternoster, the Creed and the Ten Commandments in English, that his flock might learn them by degrees; he was to require some acquaintance with the rudiments of the faith as a necessary condition from all before they could receive the Sacrament of the Altar; he was to preach at least once a quarter; and to institute a register of births, marriages and deaths.[3]

Meanwhile, a vigorous assault was made on the strong-holds of superstition; pilgrimages were suppressed, and many wonder-working images were pulled down and destroyed. The famous Rood of Boxley, a figure whose contortions had once imposed on the people, was taken to the market-place at Maidstone,[4] and the ingenious mechanism, whereby the eyes and lips miraculously opened and shut, was exhibited to the vulgar gaze.[5] Probably these little devices had already sunk in popular esteem, for the Blood of St. Januarius could not be treated at Naples to-day in the same cavalier fashion as

[1] L. and P. XII. ii. 618; Cranmer, Works ii. 469; cf. Jenkyns, Cranmer, ii. 21; and Cranmer, Works ii. 83, 359, 360.

[2] See the present writer's Cranmer pp. 110-13; Dixon, Church History ii. 77-79.

[3] See these injunctions in Burnet iv. 341-46; Wilkins, Concilia iii. 815.

[4] L. and P. XIII. i. 231, 348.

[5] Father Bridgett in his Blunders and Forgeries repudiates the idea that these " innocent toys " had been put to any superstitious uses.

the Blood of Hailes was in England in 1538,[1] without a riot. But the exposure was a useful method of exciting popular indignation against the monks, and it filled reformers with a holy joy. " Dagon," wrote one to Bullinger, " is everywhere falling in England. Bel of Babylon has been broken to pieces."[2] The destruction of the images was a preliminary skirmish in the final campaign against the monks. The Act of 1536 had only granted to the King religious houses which possessed an endowment of less than two hundred pounds a year ; the dissolution of the greater monasteries was now gradually effected by a process of more or less voluntary surrender. In some cases the monks may have been willing enough to go ; they were loaded with debt, and harassed by rules imposed by Cromwell, which would have been difficult to keep in the palmiest days of monastic enthusiasm ; and they may well have thought that freedom from monastic restraint, coupled with a pension, was a welcome relief, especially when resistance involved the anger of the prince and liability to the penalties of elastic treasons and of a *præmunire* which no one could understand. So, one after another, the great abbeys yielded to the persuasions and threats of the royal commissioners. The dissolution of the Mendicant Orders and of the Knights of St. John dispersed the last remnants of the papal army as an organised force in England, though warfare of a kind continued for many years.

These proceedings created as much satisfaction among the Lutherans of Germany as they did disgust at Rome, and an alliance between Henry and the Protestant princes seemed to be dictated by a community of religious, as well as of political, interests. The friendship between Francis and Charles threatened both English and German liberties, and it behoved the two countries to combine against their common foe. Henry's manifesto against the authority of the Pope to summon a General Council had been received with rapture in Germany ; at least

[1] *L. and P.* XIII. i. 347, 564, 580 ; ii. 186, 409, 488, 709, 710, 856.
[2] John Hoker of Maidstone to Bullinger in Burnet (ed. Pocock vi. 194, 195).

three German editions were printed, and the Elector of
Saxony and the Landgrave of Hesse urged on him the
adoption of a common policy.[1] English envoys were
sent to Germany with this purpose in the spring of 1538,
and German divines journeyed to England to lay the
foundation of a theological union.[2] They remained five
months, but failed to effect an agreement.[3] To the three
points on which they desired further reform in England,
the Communion in both kinds, the abolition of private
masses and of the enforced celibacy of the clergy, Henry
himself wrote a long reply,[4] maintaining in each case the
Catholic faith. But the conference showed that Henry
was for the time anxious to be conciliatory in religious
matters, while from a political point of view the need for
an alliance grew more urgent than ever. All Henry's
efforts to break the amity between Francis and Charles
had failed; his proposals of marriage to imperial and
French princesses had come to nothing; and in the
spring of 1539 it was rumoured that the Emperor would
further demonstrate the indissolubility of his intimacy
with the French King by passing through France from
Spain to Germany, instead of going, as he had always
hitherto done, by sea, or through Italy and Austria.
Cromwell seized the opportunity and persuaded Henry
to strengthen his union with the Protestant princes by
seeking a wife from a German house.

This policy once adopted, the task of selecting a bride
was easy. As early as 1530[5] the old Duke of Cleves had
suggested some marriage alliance between his own and
the royal family of England. He was closely allied to
the Elector of Saxony, who had married Sibylla, the
Duke of Cleves' daughter; and the young Duke, who
was soon to succeed his father, had also claims to the
Duchy of Guelders. Guelders was a thorn in the side of

[1] Gairdner, *Church History* p. 195 ; *L. and P.* XII. i. 1310 ; ii. 1088-89.
[2] *L. and P.* XIII. i. 352, 353, 367, 645, 648-50, 1102, 1166, 1295, 1305,
1437.
[3] *Ibid.* XIII. ii. 741 ; Cranmer, *Works* ii. 397 ; Burnet i. 408 ; Strype,
Eccl. Mem. i. App. Nos. 94-102.
[4] Burnet iv. 373.   [5] *L. and P.* iv. 6364.

the Emperor; it stood to the Netherlands in much the same relation as Scotland stood to England, and when there was war between Charles and Francis Guelders had always been one of the·most useful pawns in the French King's hands. Hence an alliance between the German princes, the King of Denmark, who had joined their political and religious union, Guelders and England would have seriously threatened the Emperor's hold on his Dutch dominions.[1] This was the step which Henry was induced to take, when he realised that Charles's friendship with France remained unbroken, and that the Emperor had made up his mind to visit Paris. Hints of a marriage between Henry and Anne of Cleves[2] were thrown out early in 1539; the only difficulty, which subsequently proved very convenient, was that the lady had been promised to the son of the Duke of Lorraine. The objection was waived on the ground that Anne herself had not given her consent; in view of the advantages of the match and of the Duke's financial straits, Henry agreed to forgo a dowry; and, on the 6th of October, the treaty of marriage was signed.[3]

Anne of Cleves had already been described to Henry by his ambassador, Dr. Wotton, and Holbein had been sent to paint her portrait (now in the Louvre), which Wotton pronounced " a very lively image ".[4] She had

[1] See the present writer in *Cambridge Modern History* ii. 236, 237. The Duke of Cleves was not a Lutheran or a Protestant, as is generally assumed. He had established a curious Erasmian compromise between Protestantism and Roman Catholicism, which bears some resemblance to the ecclesiastical policy pursued by Henry VIII, and by the Elector Joachim II of Brandenburg; and the marriage of Anne with Henry did not imply so great a change in ecclesiastical policy as has usually been supposed. The objections to it were really more political than religious; the Schmalkaldic League was a feeble reed to lean upon, although its feebleness was not exposed until 1546-47.

[2] *L. and P.* XIV. i. 103; cf. Bouterwek, *Anna von Cleve*; Merriman, *Cromwell* chap. xiii.; and articles on the members of the Cleves family in the *Allgemeine Deutsche Biographie*.

[3] *L. and P.* XIV. ii. 285, 286.

[4] *Ibid.* XIV. ii. 33. Holbein did not paint a flattering portrait any more than Wotton told a flattering tale; if Henry was deceived in the matter it was by Cromwell's unfortunate assurances. As a matter of fact

an oval face, long nose, chestnut eyes, a light complexion, and very pale lips. She was thirty-four years old, and in France was reported to be ugly ; but Cromwell told the King that " every one praised her beauty, both of face and body, and one said she excelled the Duchess of Milan as the golden sun did the silver moon ".[1] Wotton's account of her accomplishments was pitched in a minor key. Her gentleness was universally commended but she spent her time chiefly in needlework. She knew no language but her own ; she could neither sing nor play upon any instrument, accomplishments which were then considered by Germans to be unbecoming in a lady.[2] On the 12th of December, 1539, she arrived at Calais ; but boisterous weather and bad tides delayed her there till the 27th. She landed at Deal and rode to Canterbury. On the 30th she proceeded to Sittingbourne, and thence, on the 31st, to Rochester, where the King met her in disguise.[3] If he was disappointed with her appearance, he concealed the fact from the public eye. Nothing marred her public reception at Greenwich on the 3rd or was suffered to hinder the wedding which was solemnised three days later.[4] Henry " lovingly embraced and kissed " his bride in public, and allowed no hint to reach the ears of any one but his most intimate counsellors of the fact that he had been led willingly or unwillingly into the most humiliating situation of his reign.

Such was, in reality, the result of his failure to act on the principle laid down by himself to the French ambassador two years before. He had then declared that the choice of a wife was too delicate a matter to be left to a deputy, and that he must see and know a lady some time before he made up his mind to marry her. Anne of Cleves had been selected by Cromwell, and the lady,

---

Anne was at least as good looking as Jane Seymour, and Henry's taste in the matter of feminine beauty was not of a very high order. Bishop Stubbs even suggests that the appearance of his wives was "if not a justification, at least a colourable reason for understanding the readiness with which he put them away " (*Lectures*, 1887, p. 284).

[1] *L. and P.* XIV. i. 552.   [2] *Ibid.* XIV. ii. 33.
[3] *Ibid.* XIV. ii. 664, 674, 677, 726, 732, 753, 754, 769.
[4] Hall, *Chronicle* p. 836.

whose beauty was, according to Cromwell, in every one's mouth, seemed to Henry no better than "a Flanders mare ".[1] The day after the interview at Rochester he told Cromwell that Anne was "nothing so well as she was spoken of," and that, "if he had known before as much as he knew then, she should not have come within his realm ". He demanded of his Vicegerent what remedy he had to suggest, and Cromwell had none. Next day Cranmer, Norfolk, Suffolk, Southampton and Tunstall were called in with no better result. "Is there none other remedy," repeated Henry, "but that I must needs, against my will, put my neck in the yoke ? "[2] Apparently there was none. The Emperor was being fêted in Paris ; to repudiate the marriage would throw the Duke of Cleves into the arms of the allied sovereigns, alienate the German princes, and leave Henry without a friend among the powers of Christendom. So he made up his mind to put his neck in the yoke and to marry "the Flanders mare ".

Henry, however, was never patient of matrimonial or other yokes, and it was quite certain that, as soon as he could do so without serious risk, he would repudiate his unattractive wife, and probably other things besides. For Anne's defects were only the last straw added to the burden which Henry bore. He had not only been forced by circumstances into marriage with a wife who was repugnant to him, but into a religious and secular policy which he and the mass of his subjects disliked. The alliance with the Protestant princes might be a useful weapon if things came to the worst, and if there were a joint attack on England by Francis and Charles ; but, on its merits, it was not to be compared to a good understanding with the Emperor ; and Henry would have no hesitation in throwing over the German princes when once he saw his way to a renewal of friendship with Charles.

[1] Burnet i. 434. The phrase appears to have no extant contemporary authority, but Burnet is not, as a rule, imaginative, and many records have been destroyed since he wrote.
[2] Cromwell to Henry VIII, in Merriman ii. 268-72.

He would welcome, even more, a relief from the necessity of paying attention to German divines. He had never wavered in his adhesion to the cardinal points of the Catholic faith. He had no enmity to Catholicism, provided it did not stand in his way. The spiritual jurisdiction of Rome had been abolished in England because it imposed limits on Henry's own authority. Some of the powers of the English clergy had been destroyed, partly for a similar reason, and partly as a concession to the laity. But the purely spiritual claims of the Church remained unimpaired ; the clergy were still a caste, separate from other men, and divinely endowed with the power of performing a daily miracle in the conversion of the bread and wine into the Body and Blood of Jesus Christ. Even when the Protestant alliance seemed most indispensable, Henry endeavoured to convince Lutherans of the truth of the Catholic doctrine of the mass, and could not refrain from persecuting heretics with a zeal that shook the confidence of his reforming allies. His honour, he thought, was involved in his success in proving that he, with his royal supremacy, could defend the faith more effectively than the Pope, with all his pretended powers ; and he took a personal interest in the conversion and burning of heretics. Several instances are recorded of his arguing a whole day with Sacramentaries,[1] exercises which exhibited to advantage at once the royal authority and the royal learning in spiritual matters. His beliefs were not due to caprice or to ignorance ; probably no bishop in his realm was more deeply read in heterodox theology.[2] He was constantly on the look-out for books

---

[1] E.g. *L. and P.* v. 285 ; XIII. ii. 849, Introd. p. xxviii. Sir John Wallop admired the " charitable dexterity " with which Henry treated them (*ibid*. xv. 429).

[2] When a book was presented to him which he had not the patience to read he handed it over to one of his lords-in-waiting to read ; he then took it back and gave it to be examined to some one of an entirely different way of thinking, and made the two discuss its merits, and upon that discussion formed his own opinion (Cranmer to Wolfgang Capito, *Works* ii. 341 ; the King, says Cranmer, " is a most acute and vigilant observer "). Henry was also, according to modern standards, extraordinarily patient of theological discourses ; when Cranmer obtained for

by Luther and other heresiarchs, and he kept quite a respectable theological library at hand for private use. The tenacity with which he clung to orthodox creeds and Catholic forms was not only strengthened by study but rooted in the depths of his character. To devout but fundamentally irreligious men like Henry VIII and Louis XIV, rites and ceremonies are a great consolation; and Henry seldom neglected to creep to the Cross on Good Friday, to serve the priest at mass, to receive holy bread and holy water every Sunday, and daily to use " all other laudable ceremonies ".[1]

With such feelings at heart, a union with Protestants could never for Henry be more than a *mariage de convenance*; and in this as in other things he carried with him the bulk of popular sympathy. In 1539 it was said that no man in London durst speak against Catholic usages, and in Lent of that year, a man was hanged apparently at the instance of the Recorder of London for eating flesh on a Friday.[2] The attack on the Church had been limited to its privileges and to its property; its doctrine had scarcely been touched. The upper classes among the laity had been gorged with monastic spoils; they were disposed to rest and be thankful. The middle classes had been satisfied to some extent by the restriction of clerical fees, and by the prohibition of the clergy from competing with laymen in profitable trades, such as brewing, tanning, and speculating in land and houses. There was also the general reaction which always follows a period of change. How far that reaction had gone, Henry first learnt from the Parliament which met on the 28th of April, 1539.

The elections were characterised by more court interference than is traceable at any other period during the

Latimer an appointment to preach at Court, he advised him not to preach more than an hour or an hour and a half lest the King and Queen should grow weary ! (*L. and P.* vii. 29).

[1] *L. and P.* XIV. i. 967, an interesting letter which also records how the King rowed up and down the Thames in his barge for an hour after evensong on Holy Thursday " with his drums and fifes playing ".

[2] *Ibid.* i. 967. This had been made a capital offence as early as the days of Charlemagne (Gibbon, ed. 1890 iii. 450 n.).

reign, though even on this occasion the evidence is fragmentary and affects comparatively few constituencies.[1] It was, moreover, Cromwell and not the King who sought to pack the House of Commons in favour of his own particular policy ; and the attempt produced discontent in various constituencies and a riot in one at least.[2] The Earl of Southampton was required to use his influence on behalf of Cromwell's nominees at Farnham, although that borough was within the Bishop of Winchester's preserves.[3] So, too, Cromwell's henchman, Wriothesley, was returned for the county of Southampton in spite of Gardiner's opposition. Never, till the days of the Stuarts, was there a more striking instance of the futility of these tactics ; for the House of Commons, which Cromwell took so much pains to secure, passed, without a dissentient, the Bill of Attainder against him ;

[1] In 1536 Henry had sent round a circular to the sheriffs ; but its main object was to show that another Parliament was indispensable, to persuade the people that " their charge and time, which will be very little and short, would be well spent," and to secure " that persons are elected who will serve, and for their worship and qualities be most meet for this purpose " (*L. and P.* x. 815). The sheriffs in fact were simply to see that the burden was placed on those able and willing to bear it. The best illustration of the methods adopted and of the amount of liberty of election exercised by the constituents may be found in Southampton's letter to Cromwell (*ibid*. XIV. i. 520). At Guildford he told the burgesses they must return two members, which would be a great charge to the town, " but that if they followed my advice it would cost little or nothing, for I would provide able men to supply the room ". They said that one Daniel Modge wanted one of the seats, but Southampton might arrange for the other. About the Sussex election he was doubtful, but various friends had promised to do their parts. Farnham, he said, returned burgesses (though it does not appear in the *Official Return*), but that was the bishop's town, " and my Lord Chamberlain is his steward there ; so I forbear to meddle ".

[2] *L. and P.* XIV. i. 662, 800, 808. By a singular fatality the returns for this Parliament have been lost, so there is no means of ascertaining how many of these nominees were actually elected.

[3] *Ibid.* XIV. i. 573," and " although he fears my lord of Winchester has already moved men after his own desires ". He also spoke with Lord St. John about knights of the shire for Hampshire, and St. John " promised to do his best ". Finally he enclosed a " schedule of the best men of the country picked out *by them*, that Cromwell may pick whom he would have chosen ".

and before it was dissolved, the bishop, against whose influence Cromwell had especially exerted himself, had taken Cromwell's place in the royal favour. There was, indeed, no possibility of stemming the tide which was flowing against the Vicegerent and in favour of the King; and Cromwell was forced to swim with the stream in the vain hope of saving himself from disaster.

The principal measure passed in this Parliament was the Act of Six Articles and it was designed to secure that unity and concord in opinions which had not been effected by the King's injunctions. The Act affirmed the doctrine of Transubstantiation, declared that the administration of the Sacrament in both kinds was not necessary, that priests might not marry, that vows of chastity were perpetual, that private masses were meet and necessary, and auricular confession was expedient and necessary. Burning was the penalty for once denying the first article, and a felon's death for twice denying any of the others. This was practically the first Act of Uniformity, the earliest definition by Parliament of the faith of the Church. It showed that the mass of the laity were still orthodox to the core, that they could persecute as ruthlessly as the Church itself, and that their only desire was to do the persecution themselves. The bill was carried through Parliament by means of a coalition of King and laity[1] against Cromwell and a minority of reforming bishops, who are said only to have relinquished their opposition at Henry's personal intervention;[2] and the royal wishes were communicated, when the King was not present in person, through Norfolk and not through the royal Vicegerent.

It was clear that Cromwell was trembling to his fall. The enmity shown in Parliament to his doctrinal tendencies was not the result of royal dictation; for even this

[1] "We of the temporality," writes a peer, "have been all of one mind" (*L. and P.* XIV. i. 1040; Burnet vi. 233; *Narratives of the Reformation* p. 248).

[2] See the present writer's *Cranmer* p. 129 n. Cranmer afterwards asserted (*Works* ii. 168) that the Act would never have passed unless the King had come personally into the Parliament house, but that is highly improbable.

Parliament, which gave royal proclamations the force of
law, could be independent when it chose. The draft of
the Act of Proclamations, as originally submitted to the
House of Commons, provoked a hot debate, was thrown
out, and another was submitted more in accord with the
sense of the House.[1] Parliament could have rejected
the second as easily as it did the first, had it wished.
Willingly and wittingly it placed this weapon in the royal
hands,[2] and the chief motive for its action was that overwhelming desire for " union and concord in opinion "
which lay at the root of the Six Articles. Only one class
of offences against royal proclamations could be punished
with death, and those were offences " against any proclamation to be made by the King's Highness, his heirs
or successors, for or concerning any kind of heresies
against Christian doctrine ". The King might define the
faith by proclamations, and the standard of orthodoxy
thus set up was to be enforced by the heaviest legal
penalties. England, thought Parliament, could only be
kept united against her foreign foes by a rigid uniformity
of opinion ; and that uniformity could only be enforced by
the royal authority based on lay support, for the Church
was now deeply divided in doctrine against itself.

Such was the temper of England at the end of 1539.
Cromwell and his policy, the union with the German
princes and the marriage with Anne of Cleves were
merely makeshifts. They stood on no surer foundation
than the passing political need of some counterpoise to
the alliance of Francis and Charles. So long as that
need remained, the marriage would hold good, and Henry

[1] Husee (*L. and P.* XIV. i. 1158) says the House had been fifteen days
over this bill ; cf. *Lords' Journals*, 1539.

[2] Parliament is sometimes represented as having almost committed
constitutional suicide by this Act ; but cf. Dicey, *Law and Custom of
the Constitution* p. 357, " Powers, however extraordinary, which are
conferred or sanctioned by statute, are never really unlimited, for they
are confined by the words of the Act itself, and what is more by the
interpretation put upon the statute by the judges ". There was a world
of difference between this and the prerogative independent of Parliament
claimed by the Stuarts. Parliament was the foundation, not the rival,
of Henry's authority.

would strive to dissemble ; but not a moment longer.
The revolution came with startling rapidity ; in April,
1540, Marillac, the French ambassador, reported that
Cromwell was tottering.[1] The reason was not far to
seek. No sooner had the Emperor passed out of France,
than he began to excuse himself from fulfilling his
engagements to Francis. He was resolute never to yield
Milan, for which Francis never ceased to yearn. Charles
would have found Francis a useful ally for the conquest
of England, but his own possessions were now threatened
in more than one quarter, and especially by the English
and German alliance. Henry skilfully widened the breach
between the two friends, and, while professing the utmost
regard for Francis, gave Charles to understand that he
vastly preferred the Emperor's alliance to that of the
Protestant princes. Before April he had convinced himself that Charles was more bent on reducing Germany and
the Netherlands to order than on any attempt against
England, and that the abandonment of the Lutheran
princes would not lead to their combination with the
Emperor and Francis. Accordingly he returned a very
cold answer when the Duke of Cleves's ambassadors
came, in May, to demand his assistance in securing for
the Duke the Duchy of Guelders.[2]

Cromwell's fall was not, however, effected without
some violent oscillations, strikingly like the quick changes
which preceded the ruin of Robespierre during the
Reign of Terror in France. The Vicegerent had filled
the Court and the Government with his own nominees ;
at least half a dozen bishops, with Cranmer at their head,
inclined to his theological and political views ; Lord
Chancellor Audley and the Earl of Southampton were
of the same persuasion ; and a small but zealous band of
reformers did their best, by ballads and sermons, to prove
that the people were thirsting for further religious
change. The Council, said Marillac, was divided, each
party seeking to destroy the other. Henry let the factions
fight till he thought the time was come for him to
intervene. In February, 1540, there was a theological

[1] *L. and P.* xv. 486.   [2] *Ibid.* xv. 735.

encounter between Gardiner and Barnes, the principal
agent in Henry's dealings with the Lutherans, and
Barnes was forced to recant ;[1] in April Gardiner and one
or two conservatives, who had long been excluded from
the Council, were believed to have been readmitted ;[2]
and it was reported that Tunstall would succeed Cromwell
as the King's Vicegerent.[3] But a few days later two of
Cromwell's satellites, Wriothesley and Sadleir, were made
Secretaries of State ; Cromwell himself was created Earl
of Essex ; and in May the Bishop of Chichester and two
other opponents of reform were sent to the Tower.[4] At
last Henry struck. On the 10th of June Cromwell was
arrested ; he had, wrote the Council, " not only been
counterworking the King's aims for the settlement of
religion, but had said that, if the King and the realm
varied from his opinions, he would withstand them, and
that he hoped in another year or two to bring things to
that frame that the King could not resist it ".[5] His cries
for mercy evoked no response in that hardened age.[6]
Parliament condemned him unheard, and on the 28th
of July he was beheaded.

Henry had in reality come to the conclusion that it
was safe to dispense with Anne of Cleves and her relatives ;
and with his will there was easily found a way. His case,
as stated by himself, was, as usual, a most ingenious
mixture of fact and fiction, reason and sophistry. His
" intention " had been defective, and therefore his
administration of the sacrament of marriage had been
invalid. He was not a free agent because fear of being
left defenceless against Francis and Charles had driven
him under the yoke. His marriage had only been a
conditional form. Anne had never received a release
from her contract with the son of the Duke of Lorraine ;
Henry had only gone through the ceremony on the
assumption that that release would be forthcoming ; and
actuated by this conscientious scruple, he had refrained

---

[1] L. and P. xv. 306, 312, 334.   [2] Ibid. xv. 486, 804.
[3] Ibid. XIV. ii. 141.   [4] Ibid. xv. 737.
[5] Burnet iv. 415-23 ; L. and P. xv. 765-67.
[6] Merriman, Cromwell ii. 268, 273.

from consummating the match. To give verisimilitude
to this last statement, he added the further detail that
he found his bride personally repugnant. He therefore
sought from " our " Church a declaration of nullity.
Anne was prudently ready to submit to its decision;
and, through Convocation, Henry's Church, which in
his view existed mainly to transact his ecclesiastical
business, declared, on the 7th of July, that the marriage
was null and void.[1] Anne received a handsome endowment of four thousand pounds a year in lands, was given
two country residences, and lived on amicable terms
with Henry[2] and his successors till 1558, when she died
and was buried in Westminster Abbey.

Henry's neck was freed from the matrimonial yoke
and the German entanglement. The news was promptly
sent to Charles, who remarked that Henry would always
find him his loving brother and most cordial friend.[3]
At Antwerp it was said that the King had alienated the
Germans, but gained the Emperor and France in their
stead.[4] Luther declared that " Junker Harry meant to be
God and to do as pleased himself ";[5] and Melancthon,
previously so ready to find excuses, now denounced the
English King as a Nero, and expressed a wish that God
would put it into the mind of some bold man to assassinate
him.[6] Francis sighed when he heard the news, foreseeing
a future alliance against him,[7] but the Emperor's secretary
believed that God was bringing good out of all these
things.[8]

[1] For the canonical reasons on which this decision was based, see the
present writer's *Cranmer* pp. 140, 141.
[2] " She is," writes Marillac in August, " as joyous as ever, and wears
new dresses every day " (xv. 976; cf. Wriothesley, *Chronicle* i. 120).
[3] *L. and P.* xv. 863.   [4] *Ibid.* xv. 932.
[5] *Ibid.* xvi. 106.   [6] *Ibid.* xvi. Introd. p. ii. n.
[7] *Ibid.* xv. 870.   [8] *Ibid.* xv. 951.

CHAPTER XV

THE FINAL STRUGGLE

THE first of the "good things" brought out of the divorce of Anne of Cleves was a fifth wife for the much-married monarch. Parliament, which had petitioned Henry to solve the doubts troubling his subjects as to the validity (that is to say, political advantages) of his union with Anne, now besought him, "for the good of his people," to enter once more the holy state of matrimony, in the hope of more numerous issue. The lady had been already selected by the predominant party, and used as an instrument in procuring the divorce of her predecessor and the fall of Cromwell; for, if her morals were something lax, Catherine Howard's orthodoxy was beyond dispute. She was niece of Cromwell's great enemy, the Duke of Norfolk; and it was at the house of Bishop Gardiner that she was first given the opportunity of subduing the King to her charms.[1] She was to play the part in the Catholic reaction that Anne Boleyn had done in the Protestant revolution. Both religious parties were unfortunate in the choice of their lady protagonists. Catherine Howard's father, in spite of his rank, was very penurious, and his daughter's education had been neglected, while her character had been left at the mercy of any chance tempter. She had already formed compromising relations with three successive suitors. Her music master, Mannock, boasted that she had promised to be his mistress; a kinsman, named Dereham, called her his wife; and she was reported to be engaged to her cousin, Culpepper.[2] Marillac thought her beauty was commonplace;[3] but that, to judge by her portraits,

[1] *Original Letters*, Parker Society i. 202; cf. *L. and P.* xv. 613 [12]. Winchester, says Marillac, "was one of the principal authors of this last marriage, which led to the ruin of Cromwell" (*ibid.* xvi. 269).

[2] *L. and P.* xvi. 1334.

[3] So says the *D.N.B.* ix. 308; but in *L. and P.* xv. 901, Marillac describes her as "a lady of great beauty," and in xvi. 1366 he speaks of her "beauty and sweetness".

seems a disparaging verdict. Her eyes were hazel, her
hair was auburn, and Nature had been at least as kind
to her as to any of Henry's wives. Even Marillac admitted
that she had a very winning countenance. Her age is
uncertain, but she had almost certainly seen more than
the twenty-one years politely put down to her account.
Her marriage, like that of Anne Boleyn, was private.
Marillac thought she was already wedded to Henry by the
21st of July, and the Venetian ambassador at the Court
of Charles V said that the ceremony took place two
days after the sentence of Convocation (7th July).[1] That
may be the date of the betrothal, but the marriage itself
was privately celebrated at Oatlands on the 28th of July,[2]
and Catherine was publicly recognised as Queen at
Hampton Court on the 8th of August, and prayed for as
such in the churches on the following Sunday.

The King was thoroughly satisfied with his new
marriage from every point of view. The reversal of the
policy of the last few years, which he had always disliked
and for which he avoided responsibility as well as he
could, relieved him at once from the necessity of playing
a part and from the pressing anxiety of foreign dangers.
These troubles had preyed upon his mind and impaired
his health ; but now, for a time, his spirits revived and his
health returned. He began to rise every morning, even
in the winter, between five and six, and rode for four or
five hours. He was enamoured of his bride ; her views
and those of her uncle, the Duke of Norfolk, and of her
patron, Bishop Gardiner, were in much closer accord with
his own than Anne Boleyn's or Cromwell's had been.
Until almost the close of his reign Norfolk was the
chief instrument of his secular policy, while Gardiner

[1] *Venetian Cal.* v. 222.

[2] This is the date given by Dr. Gairdner in *D.N.B.* ix. 304, and is
probably correct, though Dr. Gairdner himself gives 8th August in his
Church History, 1902, p. 218. Wriothesley (*Chron.* i. 121) also says
8th August, but Hall (*Chron.* p. 840) is nearer the truth when he says :
" The eight day of August was the Lady Katherine Howard . . . *shewed
openly as Queen* at Hampton court ". The original authority for the
28th July is the 3rd Rep. of the Deputy Keeper of Records, App. ii. 264,
viz. the official record of her trial.

represented his ecclesiastical views;[1] but neither succeeded to the place which Wolsey had held and Cromwell
had tried to secure. Henceforth the King had no Prime
Minister; there was no second Vicegerent, and the
praise or the blame for his policy can be given to no one
but Henry.

That policy was, in foreign affairs, a close adherence
to the Emperor, partly because it was almost universally
held to be the safest course for England to pursue, and
partly because it gave Henry a free hand for the development of his imperialist designs on Scotland. In domestic
affairs the predominant note was the extreme rigour with
which the King's secular autocracy, his supremacy over
the Church, and the Church's orthodox doctrine were
imposed on his subjects. Although the Act of Six Articles
had been passed in 1539, Cromwell appears to have prevented the issue of commissions for its execution. This
culpable negligence did not please Parliament, and, just
before his fall, another Act was passed for the more
effective enforcement of the Six Articles. One relaxation
was found necessary; it was impossible to inflict the
death penalty on "incontinent"[2] priests, because there
were so many. But that was the only indulgence granted.
Two days after Cromwell's death, a vivid illustration was
given of the spirit which was henceforth to dominate the
Government. Six men were executed at the same time;
three were priests, condemned to be hanged as traitors for
denying the royal supremacy; three were heretics, condemned to be burnt for impugning the Catholic faith.[3]

And yet there was no peace. Henry, who had succeeded
in so much, had, with the full concurrence of the majority
of his people, entered upon a task in which he was foredoomed to failure. Not all the whips with six strings,
not all the fires at Smithfield, could compel that unity
and concord in opinion which Henry so much desired,

---

[1] It was popularly thought that Henry called Gardiner "his own bishop" (L. and P. XIV. i. 662).

[2] 32 Henry VIII, c. 10. Married priests of course would come under this opprobrious title.

[3] Wriothesley, Chron. i. 120 121.

but which he had unwittingly done so much to destroy. He might denounce the diversities of belief to which his opening of the Bible in English churches had given rise ; but men, who had caught a glimpse of hidden verities, could not all be forced to deny the things which they had seen. The most lasting result of Henry's repressive tyranny was the stimulus it gave to reform in the reign of his son, even as the persecutions of Mary finally ruined in England the cause of the Roman Church. Henry's bishops themselves could scarcely be brought to agreement. Latimer and Shaxton lost their sees ; but the submission of the rest did not extend to complete recantation, and the endeavour to stretch all his subjects on the Procrustean bed of Six Articles was one of Henry's least successful enterprises.[1] It was easier to sacrifice a portion of his monastic spoils to found new bishoprics. This had been a project of Wolsey's, interrupted by the Cardinal's fall. Parliament subsequently authorised Henry to erect twenty-six sees ; he actually established six, the Bishoprics of Peterborough, Oxford, Chester, Gloucester, Bristol and Westminster. Funds were also provided for the endowment, in both universities, of Regius professorships of Divinity, Hebrew, Greek, Civil Law and Medicine ; and the royal interest in the advancement of science was further evinced by the grant of a charter to the College of Surgeons, similar to that accorded early in the reign to the Physicians.[2]

---

[1] Henry soon recognised this himself, and a year after the Act was passed he ordered that " no further persecution should take place for religion, and that those in prison should be set at liberty on finding security for their appearance when called for " (*L. and P.* xvi. 271). Cranmer himself wrote that " within a year or a little more " Henry " was fain to temper his said laws, and moderate them in divers points ; so that the Statute of Six Articles continued in force little above the space of one year " (*Works* ii. 168). The idea that from 1539 to 1547 there was a continuous and rigorous persecution is a legend derived from Foxe ; there were outbursts of rigour in 1540, 1543, and 1546, but except for these the Six Articles remained almost a dead letter (see *L. and P.* XVIII. i. Introd. p. xlix. ; pt. ii. Introd. p xxxiv. ; *Original Letters*, Parker Society ii. 614, 627 ; Dixon, *Church Hist.* vol. ii. chaps. x., xi.).

[2] In 1518 (*L. and P.* ii. 4450).

Disloyalty, meanwhile, was no more extinct than diversity in religious opinion. Early in 1541 there was a conspiracy under Sir John Neville, in Lincolnshire, and about the same time there were signs that the Council itself could not be immediately steadied after the violent disturbances of the previous year. Pate, the ambassador at the Emperor's Court, absconded to Rome in fear of arrest, and his uncle, Longland, Bishop of Lincoln, was for a time in confinement ; Sir John Wallop, Sir Thomas Wyatt, diplomatist and poet, and his secretary, the witty and cautious Sir John Mason, were sent to the Tower ; both Cromwell's henchmen, Wriothesley and Sadleir, seem to have incurred suspicion.[1] Wyatt, Wallop and Mason were soon released, while Wriothesley and Sadleir regained favour by abjuring their former opinions ; but it was evident that the realisation of arbitrary power was gradually destroying Henry's better nature. His suspicion was aroused on the slightest pretext, and his temper was getting worse. Ill-health contributed not a little to this frame of mind. The ulcer on his leg caused him such agony that he sometimes went almost black in the face and speechless from pain.[2] He was beginning to look grey and old, and was growing daily more corpulent and unwieldy. He had, he said, on hearing of Neville's rebellion, an evil people to rule ; he would, he vowed, make them so poor that it would be out of their power to rebel ; and before he set out for the North to extinguish the discontent and to arrange a meeting with James V, he cleared the Tower by sending all its prisoners, including the aged Countess of Salisbury, to the block.

A greater trial than the failure of James to accept his invitation to York awaited Henry on his return from the North. Rumours of Catherine Howard's past indiscretions had at length reached the ears of the Privy Council. On All Saints' Day, 1541, Henry directed his confessor, the Bishop of Lincoln, to give thanks to God with him

---

[1] L. and P. xvi. 449, 461, 466, 467, 469, 470, 474, 482, 488, 506, 523, 534, 611, 640, 641 ; cf. the present writer in D.N.B., on Mason and Wriothesley.

[2] Ibid. XIV. ii. 142 ; xvi. 121, 311, 558, 589, 590 ; D.N.B. xxvi. 89.

for the good life he was leading and hoped to lead with his present Queen,[1] " after sundry troubles of mind which had happened to him by marriages ".[2] At last he thought he had reached the haven of domestic peace, whence no roving fancy should tempt him to stray. Twenty-four hours later Cranmer put in his hand proofs of the Queen's misconduct. Henry refused to believe in this rude awakening from his dreams ; he ordered a strict investigation into the charges. Its results left no room for doubt. Dereham confessed his intercourse ; Mannock admitted that he had taken liberties ; and, presently, the Queen herself acknowledged her guilt. The King was overwhelmed with shame and vexation ; he shed bitter tears, a thing, said the Council, " strange in his courage ". He " has wonderfully felt the case of the Queen," wrote Chapuys ;[3] " he took such grief," added Marillac, " that of late it was thought he had gone mad ".[4] He seems to have promised his wife a pardon, and she might have escaped with nothing worse than a divorce, had not proofs come to light of her misconduct with Culpepper after her marriage with Henry, and even during their recent progress in the North. This offence was high treason, and could not be covered by the King's pardon for Catherine's pre-nuptial immorality. Henry, however, was not at ease until Parliament, in January, 1542, considerately relieved him of all responsibility. The faithful Lords and Commons begged him not to take the matter too heavily, but to permit them freely to proceed with an Act of Attainder, and to give his assent thereto by commission under the great seal without any words or ceremony, which might cause him pain. Thus originated the practice of giving the royal assent to Acts of Parliament by commission.[5] Another innovation was introduced into the Act of Attainder, whereby it was declared treason for any woman to marry the King if her previous life had been unchaste ; " few, if any, ladies

[1] L. and P. xvi. 1334.
[2] Herbert, Life and Reign, ed. 1672, p. 534.
[3] Ibid. xvi. 1403.   [4] Ibid. xvi. 1426.
[5] Lords' Journals pp. 171, 176.

now at Court," commented the cynical Chapuys, " would henceforth aspire to such an honour ".[1] The bill received the royal assent on the 11th of February, Catherine having declined Henry's permission to go down to Parliament and defend herself in person. On the 10th she was removed to the Tower, being dressed in black velvet and treated with " as much honour as when she was reigning ".[2] Three days later she was beheaded on the same spot where the sword had severed the fair neck of Anne Boleyn.

Thus ended one of the " good things " which had come out of the repudiation of Anne of Cleves. Other advantages were more permanent. The breach between Francis and Charles grew ever wider. In 1541 the French King's ambassadors to the Turk were seized and executed by the order of the imperial governor of Milan.[3] The outrage brought Francis's irritation to a head. He was still pursuing the shadow of a departed glory and the vain hope of dominion beyond the Alps. He had secured none of the benefits he anticipated from the imperial alliance ; his interviews with Charles and professions of friendship were lost on that heartless schemer, and he realised the force of Henry's gibe at his expectations from Charles. " I have myself," said Henry, " held interviews for three weeks together with the Emperor." Both sovereigns began to compete for England's favour. The French, said Chapuys, " now almost offer the English *carte blanche* for an alliance " ;[4] and he told Charles that England must, at any price, be secured in the imperial interest. In June, 1542, Francis declared war on the Emperor, and, by the end of July, four French armies were invading or threatening Charles's dominions. Henry, in spite of all temptations, was not to be the tool of either ; he had designs of his own ; and the breach between Francis and Charles gave him a unique opportunity for completing his imperialist projects, by extending his sway over the one portion of the British Isles which yet remained independent.

[1] *L. and P.* xvii. 124.   [2] *Ibid.*
[3] *Ibid.* xvi. 984, 991, 1042.   [4] *Ibid.* xvii. 124.

As in the case of similar enterprises, Henry could easily find colourable pretexts for his attack on Scots independence.[1] Beton had been made cardinal with the express objects of publishing in Scotland the Pope's Bull against Henry, and of instigating James V to undertake its execution ; and the Cardinal held a high place in the Scots King's confidence. James had intrigued against England with both Charles V and Francis I, and hopes had been instilled into his mind that he had only to cross the Border to be welcomed, at least in the North, as a deliverer from Henry's oppression. Refugees from the Pilgrimage of Grace found shelter in Scotland, and the ceaseless Border warfare might, at any time, have provided either King with a case for war, if war he desired. The desire varied, of course, with the prospects of success. James V would, without doubt, have invaded England if Francis and Charles had begun an attack, and if a general crusade had been proclaimed against Henry. So, too, war between the two European rivals afforded Henry some chance of success, and placed in his way an irresistible temptation to settle his account with Scotland. He revived the obsolete claim to suzerainty, and pretended that the Scots were rebels.[2] Had not James V, moreover, refused to meet him at York to discuss the questions at issue between them ? Henry might well have maintained that he sought no extension of territory, but was actuated solely by the desire to remove the perpetual menace to

[1] For relations with Scotland see the *Hamilton Papers*, 2 vols., 1890-92 ; Thorp's *Scottish Calendar*, vol. i., 1858, and the much more satisfactory *Calendar* edited by Bain, 1898. A few errors in the *Hamilton Papers* are pointed out in *L. and P.* vols. xvi.-xix.

[2] This had been asserted by Henry as early as 1524 ; Scotland was only to be included in the peace negotiations of that year as " a fief of the King of England " ; it was to be recognised that *supremum ejus dominium* belonged to Henry, as did the guardianship of James and government of the kingdom during his minority (*Sp. Cal.* ii. 680). For the assertion of supremacy in 1543 see the present writer's *England under Somerset* p. 173 ; *L. and P.* xvii. 1033. In 1527 Mendoza declared that all wise people in England preferred a project for marrying the Princess Mary to James V to her betrothal to Francis I or the Dauphin (*Sp. Cal.* iii. 156) and that the Scots match was the one really intended by Henry (*ibid.* p. 192 ; cf. *L. and P.* v. 1078, 1286).

England involved in the presence of a foe on his northern
Borders, in close alliance with his inveterate enemy across
the Channel. He seems, indeed, to have been willing
to conclude peace, if the Scots would repudiate their
ancient connection with France ; but this they considered
the sheet-anchor of their safety, and they declined to
destroy it. They gave Henry greater offence by defeating
an English raid at Halidon Rig, and the desire to avenge
a trifling reverse became a point of honour in the English
mind and a powerful factor in English policy.

The negotiations lasted throughout the summer of
1542. In October Norfolk crossed the Borders. The
transport broke down ; the commissariat was most
imperfect ; and Sir George Lawson of Cumberland was
unable to supply the army with sufficient beer.[1] Norfolk
had to turn back at Kelso, having accomplished nothing
beyond devastation.[2] James now sought his revenge. He
replied to Norfolk's invasion on the East by throwing the
Scots across the Borders on the West. The Warden was
warned by his spies, but he had only a few hundreds to
meet the thousands of Scots. But, if Norfolk's invasion
was an empty parade, the Scots attempt was a fearful
rout. Under their incompetent leader, Oliver Sinclair,
they got entangled in Solway Moss ; enormous numbers
were slain or taken prisoners, and among them were
some of the greatest men in Scotland. James died
broken-hearted at the news, leaving his kingdom to the
week-old infant, Mary, Queen of Scots.[3] The triumph of
Flodden Field was repeated ; a second Scots King had
fallen ; and, for a second time in Henry's reign, Scotland
was a prey to the woes of a royal minority.

Within a few days of the Scots disaster, Lord Lisle
(afterwards Duke of Northumberland) expressed a wish
that the infant Queen were in Henry's hands and betrothed to Prince Edward, and a fear that the French
would seek to remove her beyond the seas.[4] To realise

[1] *L. and P.* xvii. 731, 754, 771.
[2] *Ibid.* xvii. 996-98, 1000-1, 1037.
[3] See *Hamilton Papers* vol. i. pp. lxxxiii-vi. ; and the present writer
in *D.N.B.*, *s.v.* " Wharton, Thomas," who commanded the English.
[4] *L. and P.* xvii. 1221, 1233.

the hope and to prevent the fear were the main objects of Henry's foreign policy for the rest of his reign. Could he but have secured the marriage of Mary to Edward, he would have carried both England and Scotland many a weary stage along the path to Union and to Empire. But, unfortunately, he was not content with this brilliant prospect for his son. He grasped himself at the Scottish crown ; he must be not merely a suzerain shadow, but a real sovereign. The Scottish peers who had been taken at Solway Moss, were sworn to Henry VIII, " to set forth his Majesty's title that he had to the realm of Scotland ".[1] Early in 1543 an official declaration was issued, " containing the just causes and considerations of this present war with the Scots, wherein also appeareth the true and right title that the King's most royal Majesty hath to the sovereignty of Scotland " ; while Parliament affirmed that " the late pretensed King of Scots was but an usurper of the crown and realm of Scotland," and that Henry had " now at this present (by the infinite goodness of God), a time apt and propice for the recovery of his said right and title to the said crown and realm of Scotland ".[2] The promulgation of these high-sounding pretensions was fatal to the cause which Henry had at heart. Henry VII had pursued the earlier and wiser part of the Scottish policy of Edward I, namely, union by marriage ; Henry VIII resorted to his later policy and strove to change a vague suzerainty into a defined and galling sovereignty. Seeing no means of resisting the victorious English arms the Scots in March 1543, agreed to the marriage between Henry's son and their infant Queen. But to admit Henry's extravagant claims to Scottish sovereignty was quite a different matter. The mere mention of them was sufficient to excite distrust and patriotic resentment. The French Catholic party led by Cardinal Beton was strengthened, and, when Francis declared that he would never desert his ancient ally, and gave an earnest of his intentions by sending ships and money and men to their aid, the Scots repudiated their compact with England,

---

[1] Wriothesley, *Chron.* i. 140.
[2] 35 Hen. VIII, c. 27.

and entered into negotiations for marrying their Queen to a prince in France.[1]

Such a danger to England must at all costs be averted. Marriages between Scots kings and French princesses had never boded good to England; but the marriage of the Queen of Scotland to a French prince, and possibly to one who might succeed to the French throne, transcended all the other perils with which England could be threatened. The union of the Scots and French crowns would have destroyed the possibility of a British Empire. Henry had sadly mismanaged the business through vaulting ambition, but there was little fault to be found with his efforts to prevent the union of France and Scotland; and that was the real objective of his last war with France. His aim was not mere military glory or the conquest of France, as it had been in his earlier years under the guidance of Wolsey; it was to weaken or destroy a support which enabled Scotland to resist the union with England, and portended a union between Scotland and France. The Emperor's efforts to draw England into his war with France thus met with a comparatively ready response. In May, 1543, a secret treaty between Henry and Charles was ratified; on the 22nd of June a joint intimation of war was notified to the French ambassador; and a detachment of English troops, under Sir John Wallop and Sir Thomas Seymour, was sent to aid the imperialists in their campaign in the north of France.

Before hostilities actually broke out, Henry wedded his sixth and last wife. Catherine Parr was almost as much married as Henry himself. Thirty-one years of age in 1543, she had already been twice made a widow; her first husband was one Edward Borough, her second, Lord Latimer. Latimer had died at the end of 1542, and Catherine's hand was immediately sought by Sir Thomas Seymour, Henry's younger brother-in-law. Seymour was handsome and won her heart, but he was to be her fourth, and not her third, husband; her will " was over-

---

[1] *L. and P.* vol. xviii. *passim.*

ruled by a higher power," and, on the 12th of July, she was married to Henry at Hampton Court.[1] Catherine was small in stature, and appears to have made little impression by her beauty ; but her character was beyond reproach, and she exercised a wholesome influence on Henry during his closing years. Her task can have been no light one, but her tact overcame all difficulties. She nursed the King with great devotion, and succeeded to some extent in mitigating the violence of his temper. She intervened to save victims from the penalties of the Act of Six Articles ; reconciled Elizabeth with her father ; and was regarded with affection by both Henry's daughters. Suspicions of her orthodoxy and a theological dispute she once had with the King are said to have given rise to a reactionary plot against her.[2] "A good hearing it is," Henry is reported as saying, "when women become such clerks ; and a thing much to my comfort to come in mine old days to be taught by my wife ! " Catherine explained that her remarks were only intended to "minister talk," and that it would be unbecoming in her to assert opinions contrary to those of her lord. "Is it so, sweetheart ? " said Henry ; "then are we perfect friends ; " and when Lord Chancellor Wriothesley came to arrest her, he was, we are told, abused by the King as a knave, a beast and a fool.

The winter of 1543-44 and the following spring were spent in preparations for war on two fronts.[3] The punishment of the Scots for repudiating their engagements to England was entrusted to the skilful hands of Henry's brother-in-law, the Earl of Hertford ; while the King himself was to renew the martial exploits of his youth by crossing the Channel and leading an army in person against the French King. The Emperor was to invade France from the north-east ; the two monarchs were then to effect a junction and march on Paris.

[1] D.N.B. ix. 309.   [2] Foxe, ed. Townsend v. 553-61.
[3] See for the Scottish war the *Hamilton Papers*, and for the war in France *Spanish Cal.* vol. vii. and *L. and P.* vol. xix. pt. ii. (to December, 1544).

There is, however, no instance in the first half of the
sixteenth century of two sovereigns heartily combining
to secure any one object whatever. Charles and Henry
both wanted to extract concessions from Francis, but the
concessions were very different, and neither monarch
cared much for those which the other demanded. Henry's
ultimate end related to Scotland, Charles's to Milan and
the Lutherans. The Emperor sought to make Francis
relinquish his claim to Milan and his support of the
German princes; Henry was bent on compelling him
to abandon the cause of Scottish independence. If
Charles could secure his own terms, he would, without
the least hesitation, leave Henry to get what he could
by himself; and Henry was equally ready to do Charles
a similar turn. His suspicions of the Emperor determined
his course; he was resolved to obtain some tangible
result; and, before he would advance any farther, he
sat down to besiege Boulogne. Its capture had been one
of the objects of Suffolk's invasion of 1523, when Wolsey
and his imperialist allies had induced Henry to forgo
the design. The result of that folly was not forgotten.
Suffolk, his ablest general, now well stricken in years,
was there to recall it; and, under Suffolk's directions,
the siege of Boulogne was vigorously pressed. It fell
on the 14th of September. Charles, meanwhile, was
convinced that Boulogne was all Henry wanted, and that
the English would never advance to support him. So,
five days after the fall of Boulogne, he made his peace
with Francis.[1] Henry, of course, was loud in his indignation; the Emperor had made no effort to include him
in the settlement, and repeated embassies were sent in
the autumn to keep Charles to the terms of his treaty
with England, and to persuade him to renew the war in
the following spring.

His labours were all in vain, and Henry, for the first
time in his life was left to face an actual French invasion
of England. The horizon seemed clouded at every
point. Hertford, indeed, had carried out his instructions

[1] For Charles's motives see the present writer in *Cambridge Modern
History* ii. 245, 246.

in Scotland with signal success. Leith had been burnt and Edinburgh sacked. But, as soon as he left for Boulogne, things went wrong in the North, and in February, 1545, Evers suffered defeat from the Scots at Ancrum Moor. Now, when Henry was left without an ally, when the Scots were victorious in the North, when France was ready to launch an Armada against the southern coasts of England, now, surely, was the time for a national uprising to depose the bloodthirsty tyrant, the enemy of the Church, the persecutor of his people. Strangely enough his people did, and even desired, nothing of the sort. Popular discontent existed only in the imagination of his enemies ; Henry retained to the last his hold over the mind of his people. Never had they been called to pay such a series of loans, subsidies and benevolences ; never did they pay them so cheerfully. The King set a royal example by coining his plate and mortgaging his estates at the call of national defence ; and in the summer he went down in person to Portsmouth to meet the threatened invasion. The French attack had begun on Boulogne, where Norfolk's carelessness had put into their hands some initial advantages. But before dawn on the 6th of February, Hertford sallied out of Boulogne with four thousand foot and seven hundred horse. The French commander, Maréchal du Biez, and his fourteen thousand men were surprised, and they left their stores, their ammunition and their artillery in the hands of their English foes.[1]

Boulogne was safe for the time, but a French fleet entered the Solent, and effected a landing at Bembridge. Skirmishing took place in the wooded, undulating country between the shore and the slopes of Bembridge Down ; the English retreated and broke the bridge over the Yar. This checked the French advance, though a force which was stopped by that puny stream could not have been very determined. A day or two later the French sent round a party to fill their water-casks at the brook which trickles down Shanklin Chine ; it was attacked and cut to

[1] Herbert, ed. 1672, p. 589 ; Hall p. 862.

pieces.[1] They then proposed forcing their way into Portsmouth Harbour, but the mill-race of the tide at its mouth, and the mysteries of the sandbanks of Spithead deterred them ; and as a westerly breeze sprang up, they dropped down before it along the Sussex coast. The English had suffered a disaster by the sinking of the *Mary Rose* with all hands on board, an accident repeated on the same spot two centuries later, in the loss of the *Royal George*. But the Admiral, Lisle, followed the French, and a slight action was fought off Shoreham ; the fleets anchored for the night almost within gunshot, but, when dawn broke, the last French ship was hull-down on the horizon. Disease had done more than the English arms, and the French troops landed at the mouth of the Seine were the pitiful wreck of an army.[2]

France could hope for little profit from a continuance of the war, and England had everything to gain by its conclusion. The terms of peace were finally settled in June, 1546.[3] Boulogne was to remain eight years in English hands, and France was then to pay heavily for its restitution. Scotland was not included in the peace. In September, 1545, Hertford had revenged the English defeat at Ancrum Moor by a desolating raid on the Borders ;[4] early in 1546 Cardinal Beton, the soul of the French party, was assassinated, not without Henry's connivance ; and St. Andrews was seized by a body of Scots Protestants in alliance with England. Throughout the autumn preparation was being made for a fresh attempt to enforce the marriage between Edward and Mary ;[5] but the further prosecution of that enterprise was reserved for other hands than those of Henry VIII. He left the relations between England and Scotland in no better state than he found them. His aggressive imperialism paid little heed to the susceptibilities of a stubborn, if weaker, foe ; and he did not, like Cromwell,

[1] Du Bellay, *Memoirs* pp. 785-9.
[2] *State Papers*, ed. 1830-51 i. 794, 816.
[3] *Ibid.* ed. 1830-51 i. 877, 879 ; Odet de Selve pp. 31, 34.
[4] *State Papers*, v. 448-52 ; *Harleian MS.* 284 ; *Original Letters* i. 37.
[5] Odet de Selve, *Corresp. Politique* 1886 pp. 50-120 *passim*.

possess the military force to crush out resistance. He would not conciliate and he could not coerce.

Meanwhile, amid the distractions of his Scottish intrigues, of his campaign in France, and of his defence of England, the King was engaged in his last hopeless endeavour to secure unity and concord in religious opinion. The ferocious Act of Six Articles had never been more than fitfully executed ; and Henry refrained from using to the full the powers with which he had been entrusted by Parliament. The fall of Catherine Howard may have impaired the influence of her uncle, the Duke of Norfolk, who had always expressed his zeal for the burning of heretics ; and the reforming party was rapidly growing in the nation at large, and even within the guarded precincts of the King's Privy Council. Cranmer retained his curious hold over Henry's mind ; Hertford was steadily rising in favour ; Queen Catherine Parr, so far as she dared, supported the New Learning ; the majority of the Council were prepared to accept the authorised form of religion, whatever it might happen to be, and, besides the Howards, Gardiner was the only convinced and determined champion of the Catholic faith. Even at the moment of Cromwell's fall, there was no intention of undoing anything that had already been done ; Henry only determined that things should not go so fast, especially in the way of doctrinal change, as the Vicegerent wished, for he knew that unity was not to be sought or found in that direction. But, between the extremes of Lutheranism and the *status quo* in the Church, there was a good deal to be done, in the way of reform, which was still consistent with the maintenance of the Catholic faith. In May, 1541, a fresh proclamation was issued for the use of the Bible.[1] He had, said the King, intended his subjects to read the Bible humbly and reverently for their instruction, not reading aloud in time of Holy Mass or other divine service, nor, being laymen, arguing thereon ; but, at the same time, he ordered all curates and parishioners who had failed to obey his former

[1] *L. and P.* xvi. 819 ; Burnet iv. 509.

M

injunctions to provide an English Bible for their Church
without delay. Two months later another proclamation
followed, regulating the number of saints' days ; it was
characteristic of the age that various saints' days were
abolished, not so much for the purpose of checking
superstition, as because they interfered with the harvest
and other secular business.[1] Other proclamations came
forth in the same year for the destruction of shrines
and the removal of relics. In 1543 a general revision
of service-books was ordered, with a view to eradicating
" false legends " and references to saints not mentioned
in the Bible, or in the " authentical doctors ".[2] The
Sarum Use was adopted as the standard for the clergy
of the province of Canterbury, and things were steadily
tending towards that ideal uniformity of service as well
as of doctrine, which was ultimately embodied in various
Acts of Uniformity. Homilies, " made by certain
prelates," were submitted to Convocation, but the
publication of them, and of the rationale of rites and
ceremonies, was deferred to the reign of Edward VI.[3]
The greatest of all these compositions, the Litany, was,
however, sanctioned in 1545.[4]

The King had more to do with the *Necessary Doctrine*,
commonly called the " King's Book " to distinguish it
from the Bishops' Book of 1537, for which Henry had
declined all responsibility. Henry, indeed, had urged on
its revision, he had fully discussed with Cranmer the
amendments he thought the book needed, and he had
brought the bishops to an agreement, which they had
vainly sought for three years by themselves. It was the
King who now " set forth a true and perfect doctrine for
all his people ".[5] So it was fondly styled by his Council.
A modern high-churchman[6] asserts that the King's Book
taught higher doctrine than the book which the bishops
had drafted six years before, but that " it was far more
liberal and better composed ". Whether its excellences
amounted to " a true and perfect doctrine " or not, it

[1] *L. and P.* xvi. 978, 1022, 1027.   [2] *Ibid.* xvi. 1262 ; xvii. 176.
[3] See the present writer's *Cranmer* pp. 166-72.
[4] *Ibid.* pp. 172-75.   [5] *L. and P.* XVIII. i. 534.   [6] Canon Dixon.

failed of its purpose. The efforts of the old and the new
parties were perpetually driving the Church from the
Via Media, which Henry marked out. On the one hand,
we have an act limiting the use of the Bible to gentlemen
and their families, and plots to catch Cranmer in the
meshes of the Six Articles.[1] On the other, there were
schemes on the part of some of the Council to entrap
Gardiner, and we have Cranmer's assertion[2] that, in the
last months of his reign, the King commanded him to
pen a form for the alteration of the Mass into a Communion, a design obviously to be connected with the
fact that, in his irritation at Charles's desertion in 1544,
and fear that his neutrality might become active hostility,
Henry had once more entered into communication with
the Lutheran princes of Germany.[3]

The only ecclesiastical change that went on without
shadow of turning was the seizure of Church property
by the King ; and it is a matter of curious speculation
as to where he would have stayed his hand had he lived
much longer. The debasement of the coinage had proceeded apace during his later years to supply the King's
necessities, and for the same purpose, Parliament, in
1545, granted him all chantries, hospitals and free
chapels. That session ended with Henry's last appearance
before his faithful Lords and Commons, and the speech
he then delivered may be regarded as his last political
will and testament.[4] He spoke, he said, instead of the
Lord Chancellor, " because he is not so able to open
and set forth my mind and meaning, and the secrets of
my heart, in so plain and ample manner, as I myself
am and can do ". He thanked his subjects for their
commendation, protested that he was " both bare and
barren " of the virtues a prince ought to have, but

[1] See the present writer's *Cranmer* pp. 144-60.

[2] Foxe, on the authority of Cranmer's secretary, Morice, in *Acts and
Monuments* v. 563, 564 ; it receives some corroboration from Hooper's
letter to Bullinger in *Original Letters* i. 41.

[3] See Hasenclever, *Die Politik der Schmalkaldener vor Ausbruch des
Schmalkaldischen Krieges*, 1901.

[4] Hall, *Chron.* pp. 864-66 ; Foxe, ed. Townsend v. 534-36 ; Herbert,
ed. 1672 pp. 598-601.

rendered to God " most humble thanks " for " such small
qualities as He hath indued me withal. . . . Now, since
I find such kindness in your part towards me, I cannot
choose but love and favour you ; affirming that no prince
in the world more favoureth his subjects than I do you,
nor no subjects or Commons more love and obey their
Sovereign Lord, than I perceive you do ; for whose
defence my treasure shall not be hidden, nor my person
shall not be unadventured. Yet, although I wish you,
and you wish me, to be in this perfect love and concord,
this friendly amity cannot continue, except both you, my
Lords Temporal and my Lords Spiritual, and you, my
loving subjects, study and take pains to amend one thing,
which surely is amiss and far our of order ; to the which
I most heartily require you. Which is, that Charity and
Concord is not amongst you, but Discord and Dissension
beareth rule in every place. Saint Paul saith to the
Corinthians, the thirteenth chapter, *Charity is gentle*,
Charity is not envious, Charity is not proud, and so forth.
Behold then, what love and charity is amongst you, when
one calleth another heretic and anabaptist, and he
calleth him again papist, hypocrite and Pharisee ? Be
these tokens of Charity amongst you ? Are these signs of
fraternal love amongst you ? No, no, I assure you that
this lack of charity among yourselves will be the hindrance
and assuaging of the perfect love betwixt us, except this
wound be salved and clearly made whole. . . . I hear
daily that you of the Clergy preach one against another,
without charity or discretion ; some be too stiff in their
old *Mumpsimus*, others be too busy and curious in their
new *Sumpsimus*. Thus all men almost be in variety and
discord, and few or none preach truly and sincerely the
Word of God. . . . Yet the Temporalty be not clear
and unspotted of malice and envy. For you rail on
Bishops, speak slanderously of Priests, and rebuke and
taunt preachers, both contrary to good order and
Christian fraternity. If you know surely that a Bishop or
Preacher erreth, or teacheth perverse doctrine, come and
declare it to some of our Council, or to us, to whom is
committed by God the high authority to reform such

causes and behaviours. And be not judges of yourselves of your fantastical opinions and vain expositions. . . . I am very sorry to know and to hear how unreverently that most precious jewel, the Word of God, is disputed, rhymed, sung, and jangled in every Ale-house and Tavern. . . . And yet I am even as much sorry that the readers of the same follow it in doing so faintly and so coldly. For of this I am sure, that charity was never so faint amongst you, and virtuous and godly living was never less used, nor God Himself among Christians was never less reverenced, honoured, or served. Therefore, as I said before, be in charity one with another like brother and brother; love, dread, and serve God; to which I, as your Supreme Head and Sovereign Lord, exhort and require you; and then I doubt not but that love and league, that I spake of in the beginning, shall never be dissolved or broke betwixt us."

The bond betwixt Henry and his subjects, which had lasted thirty-eight years, and had survived such strain as has rarely been put on the loyalty of any people, was now to be broken by death. The King was able to make his usual progress in August and September, 1546; from Westminster he went to Hampton Court, thence to Oatlands, Woking and Guildford, and from Guildford to Chobham and Windsor, where he spent the month of October. Early in November he came up to London, staying first at Whitehall and then at Ely Place. From Ely Place he returned, on the 3rd of January, 1547, to Whitehall, which he was never to leave alive.[1] He is said to have become so unwieldy that he could neither walk nor stand, and mechanical contrivances were used at Windsor and his other palaces for moving the royal person from room to room. His days were numbered and finished, and every one thought of the morrow. A child of nine would reign, but who should rule? Hertford or Norfolk? The party of reform or that of reaction? Henry had apparently decided that neither should

[1] This itinerary is worked out from the *Acts of the Privy Council*, ed. Dasent, vol. I.

dominate the other, and designed a balance of parties in the council he named for his child-successor.[1]

Suddenly the balance upset. On the 12th of December, 1546, Norfolk and his son, the Earl of Surrey, were arrested for treason and sent to the Tower. Endowed with great poetic gifts, Surrey had even greater defects of character. Nine years before he had been known as " the most foolish proud boy in England ".[2] Twice he had been committed to prison by the Council for roaming the streets of the city at night and breaking the citizens' windows,[3] offences venial in the exuberance of youth, but highly unbecoming in a man who was nearly thirty who aspired to high place in the councils of the realm, and who despised most of his colleagues as upstarts. His enmity was specially directed against the Prince's uncles, the Seymours. Hertford had twice been called in to retrieve Surrey's military blunders. Surrey made improper advances to Hertford's wife, but repudiated with scorn his father's suggestion for a marriage alliance between the two families.[4] His sister testified that he had advised her to become the King's mistress, with a view to advancing the Howard interests. Who, he asked, should be Protector, in case the King died, but his father ? He quartered the royal arms with his own, in spite of the heralds' prohibition. This at once roused Henry's suspicions ; he knew that, years before, Norfolk

[1] This is the usual view, but it is a somewhat doubtful inference. Henry's one object was the maintenance of order and his own power ; he would never have set himself against the nation as a whole, and there are indications that at the end of his reign he was preparing to accept the necessity of further changes. The fall of the Howards was due to the fear that they would cause trouble in the coming minority of Edward VI. Few details are known of the party struggle in the Council in the autumn of 1546, and they come from Selve's *Correspondance* and the new volume (1904) of the *Spanish Calendar* (1545-47). These should be compared with Foxe, vol. v.

[2] *L. and P.* XIV. ii. 141.

[3] *Acts of the Privy Council* i. 104 ; Bapst, *Deux Gentilshommes poètes à la cour d' Henri* VIII p. 269.

[4] See the present writer in *D.N.B.*, *s.v.* " Seymour, Edward " ; cf. Herbert pp. 625-33. G. F. Nott in his life of Surrey prefixed to his edition of the poet's works takes too favourable a view of his conduct.

had been suggested as a possible claimant to the throne, and that a marriage had been proposed between Surrey and the Princess Mary.

The original charge against Surrey was prompted by personal and local jealousy, not on the part of the Seymours, but on that of a member of Surrey's own party. It came from Sir Richard Southwell, a Catholic and a man of weight and leading in Norfolk, like the Howards themselves; he even appears to have been brought up with Surrey, and for many years had been intimate with the Howard family. When Surrey was called before the Council to answer Southwell's charges, he wished to fight his accuser, but both were committed to custody. The case was investigated by the King himself, with the help of another Catholic, Lord Chancellor Wriothesley. The Duke of Norfolk confessed to technical treason in concealing his son's offences, and was sent to the Tower. On the 13th of January, 1547, Surrey was found guilty by a special commission sitting at the Guildhall;[1] a week later he was beheaded.[2] On the 18th Parliament met to deal with the Duke; by the 24th a bill of attainder had passed all its stages and awaited only the King's assent. On Thursday, the 27th, that assent was given by royal commission.[3] Orders are said to have been issued for the Duke's execution the following morning.

That night Norfolk lay doomed in his cell in the Tower, and Henry VIII in his palace at Westminster. The Angel of Death hovered over the twain, doubting which to take. Eighteen years before, the King had said that, were his will opposed, there was never so noble a head in his kingdom but he would make it fly.[4] Now his own hour was come, and he was loth to hear of death. His physicians dared not breathe the word, for to prophesy the King's decease was treason by Act of Parliament. As that long Thursday evening wore on,

[1] See an account of his trial in *Stowe MS.* 396.
[2] Wriothesley, *Chron.* i. 177, says 19th January; other authorities give the 21st.
[3] *Lords' Journals* p. 289.   [4] *L. and P.* iv. 4942.

Sir Anthony Denny, chief gentleman of the chamber,
" boldly coming to the King, told him what case he was
in, to man's judgment not like to live ; and therefore
exhorted him to prepare himself to death ".[1] Sensible of
his weakness, Henry " disposed himself more quietly to
hearken to the words of his exhortation, and to consider
his life past ; which although he much abused, ' yet,' said
he, ' is the mercy of Christ able to pardon me all my sins,
though they were greater than they be ' ". Denny then
asked if he should send for " any learned man to confer
withal and to open his mind unto ". The King replied
that if he had any one, it should be Cranmer ; but first
he would " take a little sleep ; and then, as I feel myself,
I will advise upon the matter ". And while he slept,
Hertford and Paget paced the gallery outside, contriving
to grasp the reins of power as they fell from their master's
hands.[2] When the King woke he felt his feebleness
growing upon him, and told Denny to send for Cranmer.
The Archbishop came about midnight : Henry was
speechless, and almost unconscious. He stretched out
his hand to Cranmer, and held him fast, while the
Archbishop exhorted him to give some token that he put
his trust in Christ. The King wrung Cranmer's hand
with his fast-ebbing strength, and so passed away about
two in the morning, on Friday, the 28th of January, 1547.
He was exactly fifty-five years and seven months old,
and his reign had lasted for thirty-seven years and three-
quarters.

" And for my body," wrote Henry in his will,[3] " which
when the soul is departed, shall then remain but as a
cadaver, and so return to the vile matter it was made of,
were it not for the crown and dignity which God hath
called us unto, and that We would not be counted an
infringer of honest worldly policies and customs, when

---

[1] Foxe, ed. Townsend v. 692 ; Fuller, *Church History*, 1656 pp.
252-55.

[2] *Cotton MS.*, Titus, F. iii. ; Strype, *Eccl. Mem*. II. ii. 430.

[3] The original is in the Record Office ; a copy of it was made for each
executor, and it has been often printed ; see *England under Protector
Somerset* p. 5 n.

they be not contrary to God's laws, We would be content to have it buried in any place accustomed to Christian folks, were it never so vile, for it is but ashes, and to ashes it shall return. Nevertheless, because We would be loth, in the reputation of the people, to do injury to the Dignity, which We are unworthily called unto, We are content to will and order that Our body be buried and interred in the choir of Our college of Windsor." On the 8th of February, in every parish church in the realm, there was sung a solemn dirge by night, with all the bells ringing, and on the morrow a Requiem mass for the soul of the King.[1] Six days later his body " was solemnly with great honour conveyed in a chariot towards Windsor," and the funeral procession stretched four miles along the roads. That night the body lay at Sion under a hearse, nine storeys high. On the 15th it was taken to Windsor, where it was met by the Dean and choristers of the Chapel Royal, and by the members of Eton College. There in the castle it rested under a hearse of thirteen storeys ; and on the morrow it was buried, after mass, in the choir of St. George's Chapel.

Midway between the stalls and the Altar the tomb of Queen Jane Seymour was opened to receive the bones of her lord. Hard by stood that mausoleum " more costly than any royal or papal monument in the world,"[2] which Henry VII had commenced as a last resting-place for himself and his successors, but had abandoned for his chapel in Westminster Abbey. His son bestowed the building on Wolsey, who prepared for his own remains a splendid cenotaph of black and white marble. On the Cardinal's fall Henry VIII designed both tomb and chapel for himself *post multos et felices annos*.[3] But King and Cardinal reaped little honour by these strivings after posthumous glory. The dying commands of the monarch, whose will had been omnipotent during his life, remained unfulfilled ; the memorial chapel was left

[1] Wriothesley, *Chron.* i. 181.
[2] *L. and P.* iv. Introd. p. dcxviii.
[3] *Ibid.* ; cf. Pote, *Hist. of Windsor Castle* 1749.

incomplete; and the monument of marble was taken down, despoiled of its ornaments and sold in the Great Rebellion. At length, in a happier age, after more than three centuries of neglect, the magnificent building was finished, but not in Henry's honour; it was adorned and dedicated to the memory of a prince in whose veins there flowed not a drop of Henry's blood.

CHAPTER XVI

CONCLUSION

So died and so was buried the most remarkable man who ever sat on the English throne. His reign, like his character, seems to be divided into two inconsistent halves. In 1519 his rule is pronounced more suave and gentle than the greatest liberty anywhere else ; twenty years later terror is said to reign supreme. It is tempting to sum up his life in one sweeping generalisation, and to say that it exhibits a continuous development of Henry's intellect and deterioration of his character. Yet it is difficult to read the King's speech in Parliament at the close of 1545 without crediting him with some sort of ethical ideas and aims ; his life was at least as free from vice during the last, as during the first, seven years of his reign ; in seriousness of purpose and steadfastness of aim it was immeasurably superior ; and at no time did Henry's moral standard vary greatly from that of many whom the world is content to regard as its heroes. His besetting sin was egotism, a sin which princes can hardly, and Tudors could nowise, avoid. Of egotism Henry had his full share from the beginning ; at first it moved in a limited, personal sphere, but gradually it extended its scope till it comprised the whole realm of national religion and policy. The obstacles which he encountered in prosecuting his suit for a divorce from Catherine of Aragon were the first check he experienced in the gratification of a personal whim, and the effort to remove those impediments drew him on to the world-wide stage of the conflict with Rome. He was ever proceeding from the particular to the general, from an attack on a special dispensation to an attack on the dispensing power of the Pope, and thence to an assault on the whole edifice of papal claims. He started with no desire to separate England from Rome, or to reform the Anglican Church ; those aims he adopted, little by little, as subsidiary to

the attainment of his one great personal purpose. He
arrived at his principles by a process of deduction from
his own particular case.

As Henry went on, his " quick and penetrable eyes,"
as More described them, were more and more opened to
the extent of what he could do ; and he realised, as he
said, how small was the power of the Pope. Papal
authority had always depended on moral influence and
not on material resources. That moral influence had long
been impaired ; the sack of Rome in 1527 afforded further
demonstration of its impotence ; and when Clement
condoned that outrage, and formed a close alliance with
the chief offender, the Papacy suffered a blow from which
it never recovered. Temporal princes might continue to
recognise the Pope's authority, but it was only because
they chose, and not because they were compelled so to
do ; they supported him, not as the divinely commissioned Vicar of Christ, but as a useful instrument in the
prosecution of their own and their people's desires. It
is called a theological age, but it was also irreligious,
and its principal feature was secularisation. National
interests had already become the dominant factor in
European politics ; they were no longer to be made
subservient to the behests of the universal Church. The
change was tacitly or explicitly recognised everywhere ;
and *cujus regio, ejus religio* was the principle upon which
German ecclesiastical politics were based at the Peace
of Augsburg. It was assumed that each prince could do
what he liked in his own country ; they might combine
to make war on an excommunicate king, but only if
war suited their secular policy ; and the rivalry between
Francis and Charles was so keen that each set greater
store upon Henry's help than upon his destruction.

Thus the breach with Rome was made a possible,
though not an easy, task ; and Henry was left to settle
the matter at home with little to fear from abroad, except
threats which he knew to be empty. England was the
key of the situation, and in England must be sought
the chief causes of Henry's success. If we are to believe
that Henry's policy was at variance with the national

will, his reign must remain a political mystery, and we can offer no explanation of the facts that Henry was permitted to do his work at all, and that it has stood so long the test of time. He had, no doubt, exceptional facilities for getting his way. His dictatorship was the child of the Wars of the Roses, and his people, conscious of the fact that Henry was their only bulwark against the recurrence of civil strife, and bound up as they were in commercial and industrial pursuits, were willing to bear with a much more arbitrary government than they would have been in less perilous times. The alternatives may have been evil, but the choice was freely made. No government, whatever its form, whatever its resources, can permanently resist the national will; every nation has, roughly speaking, the government it deserves and desires, and a popular vote would never in Henry's reign have decreed his deposition. The popular mind may be ill-informed, distorted by passion and prejudice, and formed on selfish motives. Temporarily, too, the popular will may be neutralised by skilful management on the part of the government, by dividing its enemies and counterworking their plans; and of all those arts Henry was a past master. But such expedients cannot prevail in the end; in 1553 the Duke of Northumberland had a subtle intellect and all the machinery of Tudor government at his disposal; Queen Mary had not a man, nor a shilling. Yet Mary, by popular favour, prevailed without shedding a drop of blood. Henry himself was often compelled to yield to his people. Abject self-abasement on their part and stupendous power of will on Henry's, together provide no adequate solution for the history of his reign.

With all his self-will, Henry was never blind to the distinction between what he could and what he could not do. Strictly speaking, he was a constitutional king; he neither attempted to break up Parliament, nor to evade the law. He combined in his royal person the parts of despot and demagogue, and both he clothed in Tudor grace and majesty. He led his people in the way they wanted to go, he tempted them with the baits they

coveted most, he humoured their prejudices against the
clergy and against the pretensions of Rome, and he used
every concession to extract some fresh material for
building up his own authority. He owed his strength
to the skill with which he appealed to the weaknesses of
a people whose prevailing characteristics were a passion
for material prosperity and an absolute indifference to
human suffering. " We," wrote one of Henry's Secretaries
of State, " we, which talk much of Christ and His Holy
Word, have, I fear me, used a much contrary way ; for
we leave fishing of men, and fish again in the tempestuous
seas of this world for gain ,and wicked Mammon."[1] A
few noble examples, Catholic and Protestant, redeemed,
by their blood, the age from complete condemnation,
but, in the mass of his subjects, the finer feelings seem to
have been lost in the pursuit of wealth. There is no sign
that the hideous tortures inflicted on men condemned
for treason, or the equally horrible sufferings of heretics
burnt at the stake, excited the least qualm of compassion
in the breast of the multitude ; the Act of Six Articles
seems to have been rather a popular measure, and the
multiplication of treasons evoked no national protest.

Henry, indeed, was the typical embodiment of an age
that was at once callous and full of national vigour, and
his failings were as much a source of strength as his
virtues. His defiance of the conscience of Europe did
him no harm in England, where the splendid isolation of
Athanasius contra mundum is always a popular attitude ;
and even his bitterest foes could scarce forbear to admire
the dauntless front he presented to every peril. National
pride was the highest motive to which he appealed. For
the rest, he based his power on his people's material
interests, and not on their moral instincts. He took no
such hold of the ethical nature of men as did Oliver
Cromwell, but he was liked none the less for that ; for
the nation regarded Cromwell, the man of God, with
much less favour than Charles II, the man of sin ; and
statesmen who try to rule on exclusively moral principles

[1] Sir William Petre in Tytler's *Edward VI and Mary* i. 427.

are seldom successful and seldom beloved. Henry's successor, Protector Somerset, made a fine effort to introduce some elements of humanity into the spirit of government ; but he perished on the scaffold, while his colleagues denounced his gentleness and love of liberty, and declared that his repeal of Henry's savage treason-laws was the worst deed done in their generation.[1]

The King avoided the error of the Protector ; he was neither behind nor before the average man of the time ; he appealed to the mob, and the mob applauded. *Salus populi*, he said in effect, *suprema lex*, and the people agreed ; for that is a principle which suits demagogues no less than despots, though they rarely possess Henry's skill in working it out. Henry, it is true, modified the maxim slightly by substituting prince for people, and by practising, before it was preached, Louis XIV's doctrine that *L'État, c'est moi*. But the assumption that the welfare of the people was bound up with that of their King was no idle pretence ; it was based on solid facts, the force of which the people themselves admitted. They endorsed the tyrant's plea of necessity. The pressure of foreign rivalries, and the fear of domestic disruption, convinced Englishmen of the need for despotic rule, and no consideration whatever was allowed to interfere with the stability of government ; individual rights and even the laws themselves must be overridden, if they conflicted with the interests of the State. Torture was illegal in England, and men were proud of the fact, yet, in cases of treason, when the national security was thought to be involved, torture was freely used, and it was used by the very men who boasted of England's immunity. They were conscious of no inconsistency ; the common law was very well as a general rule, but the highest law of all was the welfare of the State.

This was the real tyranny of Tudor times ; men were dominated by the idea that the State was the be-all and end-all of human existence. In its early days the State is a child ; it has no will and no ideas of its own, and its

---

[1] Sir John Mason, quoted in Froude iv. 306 n.

first utterances are merely imitation and repetition. But by Henry VIII's reign the State in England had grown to lusty manhood ; it dismissed its governess, the Church, and laid claim to that omnipotence and absolute sovereignty which Hobbes regretfully expounded in his *Leviathan*.[1] The idea supplied an excuse to despots and an inspiration to noble minds. " Surely," wrote a genuine patriot in 1548,[2] " every honest man ought to refuse no pains, no travail, no study, he ought to care for no reports, no slanders, no displeasure, no envy, no malice, so that he might profit the commonwealth of his country, for whom next after God he is created." The service of the State tended, indeed, to encroach on the service of God, and to obliterate altogether respect for individual liberty. Wolsey on his deathbed was visited by qualms of conscience, but, as a rule, victims to the principle afford, by their dying words, the most striking illustrations of the omnipotence of the idea. Condemned traitors are concerned on the scaffold, not to assert their innocence, but to proclaim their readiness to die as an example of obedience to the law. However unfair the judicial methods of Tudor times may seem to us, the sufferers always thank the King for granting them free trial. Their guilt or innocence is a matter of little moment ; the one thing needful is that no doubt should be thrown on the inviolability of the will of the State ; and the audience commend them. They are not expected to confess or to express contrition, but merely to submit to the decrees of the nation ; if they do that, they are said to make a charitable and godly end, and they deserve the respect and sympathy of men ; if not, they die uncharitably, and are held up to reprobation.[3] To an age

[1] The *Leviathan* is the best philosophical commentary on the Tudor system ; Hobbes was Tudor and not Stuart in all his ideas, and his assertion of the Tudor *de facto* theory of monarchy as against the Stuart *de jure* theory brought him into disfavour with Cavaliers.

[2] John Hales in *Lansdowne MS.* 238 ; *England under Protector Somerset* p. 216.

[3] *L. and P.* x. 920; " all which died charitably," writes Husee of Anne Boleyn and her fellow-victims ; Rochford " made a very catholic address to the people saying he had not come there to preach but to

like that there was nothing strange in the union of
State and Church and the supremacy of the King over
both ; men professed Christianity in various forms, but
to all men alike the State was their real religion, and the
King was their great High Priest. The sixteenth century,
and especially the reign of Henry VIII, supplies the most
vivid illustration of the working, both for good and for
evil, of the theory that the individual should be subordinate in goods, in life and in conscience to the supreme
dictates of the national will. This theory was put into
practice by Henry VIII long before it was made the
basis of any political philosophy, just as he practised
Erastianism before Erastus gave it a name.

The devotion paid to the State in Tudor times inevitably made expediency, and not justice or morality, the
supreme test of public acts. The dictates of expediency
were, indeed, clothed in legal forms, but laws are primarily
intended to secure neither justice nor morality, but the
interests of the State ; and the highest penalty known to
the law is inflicted for high treason, a legal and political
crime which does not necessarily involve any breach
whatever of the code of morals. Traitors are not executed
because they are immoral, but because they are dangerous.
Never did a more innocent head fall on the scaffold than
that of Lady Jane Grey ; never was an execution more
fully justified by the law. The contrast was almost as
flagrant in many a State trial in the reign of Henry VIII ;

serve as a mirror and example, acknowledging his sins against God and
the King " (*ibid*. x. 911 ; cf. xvii. 124). Cromwell and Somerset had more
cause to complain of their fate than other statesmen of the time, yet
Cromwell on the scaffold says : " I am by the law condemned to die,
and thank my Lord God that hath appointed me this death for mine
offence. . . . I have offended my prince, for the which I ask him heartily
forgiveness " (Foxe v. 402). And Somerset says : " I am condemned by
a law whereunto I am subject, as we all ; and therefore to show obedience
I am content to die " (Ellis, *Orig. Letters* II. ii. 215 ; *England under
Somerset* p. 308). Compare Buckingham in Shakespeare, *Henry VIII*,
Act II, Sc. i. :—

> " I bear the law no malice for my death
> . . . my vows and prayers
> Yet are the King's ; and till my soul forsake
> Shall cry for blessings on him."

no king was so careful of law,[1] but he was not so careful of justice. Therein lay his safety, for the law takes no cognisance of injustice, unless the injustice is also a breach of the law, and Henry rarely, if ever, broke the law. Not only did he keep the law, but he contrived that the nation should always proclaim the legality of his conduct. Acts of attainder, his favourite weapon, are erroneously supposed to have been the method to which he resorted for removing opponents whose conviction he could not obtain by a legal trial. But acts of attainder were, as a rule, supplements to, not substitutes for, trials by jury;[2] many were passed against the dead, whose goods had already been forfeited to the King as the result of judicial verdicts. Moreover, convictions were always easier to obtain from juries than acts of attainder from Parliament. It was simplicity itself to pack a jury of twelve, and even a jury of peers; but it was a much more serious matter to pack both Houses of Parliament. What then was the meaning and use of acts of attainder? They were acts of indemnity for the King. People might cavil at the verdict of juries; for they were only the decisions of a handful of men; but who should impugn the voice of the whole body politic expressed in its most solemn, complete and legal form? There is no way, said Francis to Henry in 1532, so safe as by Parliament,[3] and one of Henry's invariable methods was to make the whole nation, so far as he could, his accomplice. For pardons and acts of grace the King was ready to assume the responsibility;

[1] " I never knew," writes Bishop Gardiner a few months after Henry's death, " man committed to prison for disagreeing to any doctrine unless the same doctrine were established by a law of the realm before " (Foxe, ed. Townsend vi. 141).

[2] The Countess of Salisbury and Cromwell are the two great exceptions.

[3] L. and P. vi. 954. It may be reading too much into Francis I's words, but it is tempting to connect them with Machiavelli's opinion that the French *parlement* was devised to relieve the Crown of the hostility aroused by curbing the power of the nobles (*Il Principe* c. 19). A closer parallel to the policy of Henry VIII may be found in that which Tacitus attributes to Tiberius with regard to the Senate; " he must devolve on the Senate the odious duty of trial and condemnation and reserve only the credit of clemency for himself " (Furneaux, *Tacitus* Introd.).

but the nation itself must answer for rigorous deeds. And acts of attainder were neither more nor less than deliberate pronouncements, on the part of the people, that it was expedient that one man should die rather than that the whole nation should perish or run any risk of danger.

History, in a democratic age, tends to become a series of popular apologies, and is inclined to assume that the people can do no wrong; some one must be the scapegoat for the people's sins, and the national sins of Henry's reign are all laid on Henry's shoulders. But the nation in the sixteenth century deliberately condoned injustice, when injustice made for its peace. It has done so before and after, and may possibly do so again. It is easy in England to-day to denounce the cruel sacrifices imposed on individuals in the time of Henry VIII by their sub-ordination in everything to the interests of the State; but, whenever and wherever like dangers have threatened, recourse has been had to similar methods, to government by proclamation, to martial law, and to verdicts based on political expediency.

The contrast between morals and politics, which comes out in Henry's reign as a terrible contradiction, is inherent in all forms of human society. Politics, the action of men in the mass, are akin to the operation of natural forces; and, as such, they are neither moral nor immoral; they are simply non-moral. Political movements are often as resistless as the tides of the ocean; they carry to fortune, and they bear to ruin, the just and the unjust with heedless impartiality. Cato and Brutus striving against the torrent of Roman imperialism, Fisher and More seeking to stem the secularisation of the Church, are like those who would save men's lives from the avalanche by preaching to the mountain on the text of the sixth commandment. The efforts of good men to avert a sure but cruel fate are the truest theme of the Tragic Muse; and it is possible to represent Henry's reign as one long nightmare of " truth for ever on the scaffold, wrong for ever on the throne "; for Henry VIII embodied an inevitable movement of politics, while Fisher and More stood only for individual conscience.

That is the secret of Henry's success. He directed the storm of a revolution which was doomed to come, which was certain to break those who refused to bend, and which may be explained by natural causes, but cannot be judged by moral considerations. The storm cleared the air and dissipated many a pestilent vapour, but it left a trail of wreck and ruin over the land. The nation purchased political salvation at the price of moral debasement; the individual was sacrificed on the altar of the State; and popular subservience proved the impossibility of saving a people from itself. Constitutional guarantees are worthless without the national will to maintain them; men lightly abandon what they lightly hold; and in Henry's reign, the English spirit of independence burned low in its socket, and love of freedom grew cold. The indifference of his subjects to political issues tempted Henry along the path to tyranny, and despotic power developed in him features, the repulsiveness of which cannot be concealed by the most exquisite art, appealing to the most deep-rooted prejudice. He turned to his own profit the needs and the faults of his people, as well as their national spirit. He sought the greatness of England, and he spared no toil in the quest; but his labours were spent for no ethical purpose. His aims were selfish; his realm must be strong, because he must be great. He had the strength of a lion, and like a lion he used it.

Yet it is probable that Henry's personal influence and personal action averted greater evils than those they provoked. Without him, the storm of the Reformation would still have burst over England; without him, it might have been far more terrible. Every drop of blood shed under Henry VIII might have been a river under a feebler king. Instead of a stray execution here and there, conducted always with a scrupulous regard for legal forms, wars of religion might have desolated the land and swept away thousands of lives. London saw many a hideous sight in Henry's reign, but it had no cause to envy the Catholic capitals which witnessed the sack of Rome and the massacre of St. Bartholomew; for all Henry's iniquities, multiplied manifold, would not equal the volume of murder and sacrilege wrought at Rome in May, 1527, or at Paris in August, 1572.[1] From such orgies of violence and crime England was saved by the strong right arm and the iron will of her Tudor king. "He is," said Wolsey after his fall,[2] "a prince of royal courage, and he hath a princely heart; and rather than he will miss or want part of his appetite he will hazard the loss of one-half of his kingdom." But Henry discerned more clearly than Wolsey the nature of the ground on which he stood; by accident, or by design, his appetite conformed to potent and permanent forces; and wherein it did not, he was, in spite of Wolsey's remark, content to forgo its gratification. It was not he, but the Reformation, which put the kingdoms of Europe to the hazard. The Sphinx propounded her riddle to all nations alike, and all were required to answer. Should they cleave to the old, or should they embrace the new? Some pressed forward, others held back, and some, to their own confusion, replied in dubious tones. Surrounded by faint hearts and fearful minds, Henry VIII neither faltered nor failed. He ruled in a ruthless age with a ruthless hand, he dealt with a violent crisis by methods of blood and iron, and his measures were crowned with whatever sanction worldly success can give. He is Machiavelli's *Prince* in action. He took his stand on efficiency rather than principle, and symbolised the prevailing of the gates of Hell. The spiritual welfare of England entered into his thoughts, if at all, as a minor consideration; but for her peace and material comfort it was well that she had as her King, in her hour of need, a man, and a man who counted the cost, who faced the risk, and who did with his might whatsoever his hand found to do.

[1] In three months of " peace " in 1568 over ten thousand persons are said to have been slain in France (*Cambr. Mod. Hist.* ii. 347). At least a hundred thousand were butchered in the Peasants' War in Germany in 1525-6, and thirty thousand Anabaptists are said to have suffered in Holland and Friesland alone between 1523 and 1546. Henry VIII's policy was *parcere subjectis et debellare superbos*, to protect the many humble and destroy the mighty few.

[2] *L. and P.* iv. Introd. p. dcxvi.

INDEX

A

Abbeville, 114.

Abergavenny, Baron. *See* Neville, George.

Abingdon, 102.

Acts of Succession. *See* Succession.

Adrian VI., Pope, 124, 125 *n*, 129, 130.

Agnadello, battle of, 41, 42.

Agostini, Augustine, 198, 199 *n*.

Albany, Duke of. *See* Stewart, John.

Albret, Jean d', 68, 74, 109, 115.

Aless, Alexander, 278.

Alexander VI., Pope, 170, 184.

Amicable Loan, 132, 195.

Ampthill, 283.

Ancona, Peter, Cardinal of, 171 *n*.

Ancrum Moor, battle of, 331, 332.

André, Bernard, 16 and *note*.

Angus, Earl of. *See* Douglas, Archibald.

Annates, 232 and *note*, 238, 242, 256. *See also* First-fruits.

Anne Boleyn. *See* Boleyn.

—— of Brittany, wife of Louis XII., 59, 170, 174.

—— of Cleves, suggested marriage of, 307; arrival in England and marriage, 308; repudiation of, 169, 314, 316, 318, 324.

—— of Hungary, 41.

Antigone, 267.

Antwerp, 317.

Apparel, Act of, 102.

Appeals, Acts of, 239, 240, 256.

Aquinas, St. Thomas, 98, 268.

Aragon, 20, 22, 25, 40, 73, 84, 250.

—— Catherine of. *See* Catherine.

—— Ferdinand of. *See* Ferdinand.

Arc, Jeanne d', 51.

Ardres, 51, 113, 114.

Armada, Spanish, 200, 246, 301.

Army, Henry VIII.'s, 2, 87, 251, 252, 284; wages of, 45, 46; commissariat difficulties, 54; invasions of France, 51, 63, 128, 129.

Arthur, King, 11.

—— Prince of Wales, 9, 11, 30, 38, 227.

Artois, 74, 126.

Ashton, Christopher, 9 *n*.

Aske, Robert, 284, 285, 286.

76 ; his love of pleasure in the beginning of his reign, 36-37 ;
his morality, 148-150 ; his love of gambling, 194 ; his hasty
temper, 106, 107 ; his hardening of character, 193, 259, 322 ; his
affection for Mary, 243 ; his egotism, 343 ; his imperial ideas, 290-
291 ; his piety, 84, 85, 219 ; his illnesses, 193 and *note*, 322, 339.

Henry VIII., gradual evolution of his character, 343 ; causes of his dictatorship, 345 ; a constitutional king, 345 ; the typical embodiment of his age, 346 ; careful of law, but careless of justice, 350 ;
use of Acts of Attainder, 350 ; imitates Tiberius, 350 *n* ; illustrates
the contrast between morals and politics, 351, 352 ; character
of his aims, 352 ; comparison of the good and evil that he did,
352, 353.

" Henry VIII." by Shakespeare, 88 and *note*, 92 *n*, 159 *n*, 349 *n*.

Henry of Navarre, 149.

Herbert, Lord, of Cherbury, 13.

Hereford, Bishops of. *See* Foxe, Edward, and Bonner, Edmund.

Hertford, Earl of. *See* Seymour, Edward.

Hildebrand, 187.

Hobbes, Thomas, 348 and *note*.

Holbein, Hans, 112, 297, 307 and *note*.

Holy League (of 1511), 42, 44, 71, 85.

—— —— (of 1526), 135, 136, 181.

—— Roman Empire. *See* Empire.

Horsey, Dr. William, Chancellor of London, 189 and *note*.

Houghton, John, 265.

Howard, Admiral Sir Edmund, 50.

—— Catherine. *See* Catherine.

—— Henry, Earl of Surrey, poet, 16, 338, 339.

—— Thomas I., Earl of Surrey, afterwards second Duke of Norfolk,
one of the four dukes in Henry VIII.'s reign, 2 *n* ; Lord High
Treasurer, 39 ; wins Flodden and is made Duke of Norfolk,
54, 64 ; his opinions on the imperial election, 81 ; his pensions, 92.

—— Thomas II., Earl of Surrey, afterwards third Duke of Norfolk,
was one of the four dukes in Henry VIII.'s reign, 2 *n* ; his
military campaigns, 126, 331, 338 ; his relationship to Anne
Boleyn, 163, 275 *n* ; takes the seal from Wolsey, 198 ; his
pocket-boroughs, 203 ; speaks of the " infinite clamours "
against the Church, 218, 233 ; sent to the papal nuncio,
226 ; talks to Sir Thomas More of the fickleness of princes,
199 ; presides at Anne Boleyn's trial, 275 ; is sent to the
North, 284, 286 and *note*, 326 ; mouthpiece of the King in
Parliament, 313 ; his relationship to Catherine Howard, 318,
319, 333 ; possibility of ruling during Edward VI.'s minority,
337 ; is attainted, 338, 339.

Hull, 286.

Hungary, 41, 181 *n*.

Hunne, Richard, 189 *n*.

Hurst Castle, 300.

T

U

V

JONATHAN CAPE PAPERBACKS